Arthur Schwartz's
NEW YORK CITY FOOD

For Bob Harned, My Rock

Published in 2008 by Stewart, Tabori & Chang
An imprint of Harry N. Abrams, Inc.

Originally published in hardcover in 2004 by
Stewart, Tabori & Chang

Library of Congress Cataloging-in-Publication Data
Schwartz, Arthur (Arthur R.)
Arthur Schwartz's New York City food : an opinionated history and more than 100 legendary recipes /
Arthur Schwartz ; photographs by Chris Callis.
p. cm.
Includes bibliographical references and index.
ISBN-13: 978-1-58479-677-0
ISBN-10: 1-58479-677-4
1. Cookery, American. 2. Cookery—New York (State)—New York.
I. Title: New York City food. II. Title.
TX715.S1457 2004   641.59747'1—dc22
2004016068

Editor: Beth Huseman
Additional Editorial: Liana Fredley and Katherine Epstein
Design: Eric Baker & Jason Vogel / Eric Baker Design Associates
Production Manager: Kim Tyner

The text of this book was composed in Trade Gothic and Tribute.
Printed in China
10 9 8 7 6 5 4 3 2 1

HNA
harry n. abrams, inc.
a subsidiary of La Martinière Groupe

115 West 18th Street
New York, NY 10011
www.hnabooks.com

Arthur Schwartz's
NEW YORK CITY FOOD

AN OPINIONATED HISTORY AND MORE THAN
100 LEGENDARY RECIPES

ARTHUR SCHWARTZ
PHOTOGRAPHS BY CHRIS CALLIS

STEWART, TABORI & CHANG

NEW YORK

CONTENTS

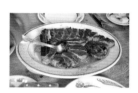

INTRODUCTION

I WAS BORN IN BROOKLYN IN 1947. My parents, Sydell Bedona Sonkin and Lawrence Schwartz, were born in Brooklyn, too. And three of my four grandparents were native New Yorkers. The fourth, my maternal grandfather, Louis Sonkin, was born in one of the many shtetls around Minsk, in Russia, but he came to New York City in 1917 when he was only thirteen.

I am not the first in my family to be obsessed with food. I like to say I was born with a wooden spoon in my mouth because there was always cooking going on, and I was always asked to taste and offer my comments. Enough salt? Enough pepper? Does it have the right taam? That's the Yiddish word for deep, soul-satisfying flavor. That's how I became a food critic. They trained me young.

We are a Jewish family, but my maternal grandmother, Elsie Binder Sonkin, who was the daughter of a rabbi and grocer, had abandoned the Jewish dietary laws (kashruth) by the time I was born. Her Russian-Jewish cooking, strictly traditional but not strictly kosher, was the envy of the neighborhood. My mother's friends always turned to my grandmother for advice, knowing that her versions of the traditional dishes were invariably more refined than their own mother's, and that she knew how to communicate her recipes so they came out well. We lived in the same house as my maternal grandparents, so she communicated to me, as well, and always enlisted me to do the cooking chores a child is good for—peeling potatoes and onions, snapping string beans, shelling nuts, cranking the meat grinder, chopping various foods—such as liver, gefilte fish, herring, eggs, chicken for salad—in her big wooden bowl with the moon-bladed chopper.

My paternal grandmother, Rose Cohen Schwartz, was also a good cook, but she had an American repertoire, accented with a few of the Hungarian specialties of her childhood, and some of the southern Italian dishes she'd learned from her downstairs neighbors, a large Neapolitan family that grew many of its vegetables on a lot on Fountain Avenue, behind their house on Logan Street in the East New York section of the borough. Jerry Nicotra, or Genarro, from downstairs made his own wine in the basement. So I was exposed to winemaking at a very young age, too. However, Rose always admitted, in her thick New York City accent, that she "didn't even know how to burl an egg" until my grandfather taught her.

That would be my paternal grandfather, Bernard Schwartz (called Barney by his friends), who ran away from home when he was nine years old and, by the time he was a teenager, was a professional cook and boxer in San Francisco. He remained feisty until he died at the age of ninety-three. Having made his small fortune on the West Coast, he returned to New York City in about 1920 and worked in various businesses that involved food, including opening a restaurant on 24 Fifth Avenue, which to this day is a restaurant space. When the stock market crashed in 1929, he lost everything and supported his young family by making coleslaw, potato salad, and pickles at home and selling them to bars and grills off a pushcart. In the late 1930s, he manufactured bar mixers in a factory on Carmine Street in Greenwich Village. By the time I came along in 1947, he was a curmudgeonly waiter in a Roumanian-Jewish steak house, the Little Oriental on Pitkin Avenue in the Brownsville section of Brooklyn. When the Little Oriental closed, he waited tables at the Famous, a Jewish dairy restaurant on Eastern Parkway and Utica Avenue (now a McDonald's).

His grandfather's interest in food made my father into a food adventurer. Larry didn't cook, but he could assemble great meals. He knew where to find the best this, that, and the other thing. He befriended chefs in Chinatown, Italian bakers in Bensonhurst, fish smokers in Williamsburg, and waiters everywhere. He loved going to new restaurants with my mother, and telling me about the experience in detail the next day. My mother appreciated the dining out, although she didn't love to cook. She did it well, but, except when she went all out for holidays and company, we ate very simply and healthfully. She did not embrace the frozen dinners and convenience products that were so popular in the 1950s. We never ate a casserole that started out with a can of soup. We ate mostly fresh vegetables (canned peas were an exception) and always had fresh fruit for dessert instead of cakes or sweets. Those were reserved for those special occasions and company.

Is it any wonder that I became a food writer? I graduated from the University of Maryland in 1968 with a degree in journalism and had an education in cooking from my grandparents, Italian neighbors, and the cookbooks of Julia Child and Fanny Farmer. Within a year of graduation, I was the assistant food editor of *Newsday*, the Long Island newspaper. Craig Claiborne was the first male food editor in the country (see page 305).

I believe I was the third, although, despite my love of food, I had no intentions of becoming a food writer. I actually fell into it. After failing to find a reporting or editing job that would pay me enough to afford my rent and support a wife who was in school, a friend of my mother suggested I market myself as a specialist. My knowledge of food and wine was the only marketable specialty I had, so instead of looking under "R" for reporter, or "E" for editor in the *New York Times* Sunday want ads, I looked under "F" for food. Miraculously, the first week I looked an ad said, "Assistant Food Editor, Large Suburban Daily, Up to $10,000." I immediately wrote a letter that said:

This is a dream job but as you can see by my resume (attached) I have no proven qualifications. I have gathered instead three personal endorsements.

> *Arthur's oysters Rockefeller saved our marriage. —Elaine Schwartz, wife*
> *Arthur's pot roast is even better than my mother's. —Sydell Schwartz, mother*
> *Arthur's chocolate soufflé aggravates my diabetes. —Eva Rothseid, mother-in-law."*

I got the job on Friday.

I worked at *Newsday* for nine years, cooking with as many good home cooks as I could, writing about them, writing the question and answer column (called "Feedback"), writing a wine column, at one point writing a healthy cooking column that was rather pretentiously called "The Sane Kitchen" and, finally, reviewing restaurants in Queens on top of everything. I used my vacation time to travel in Europe and North Africa but mainly in Italy. Eventually, I taught Tuscan cooking in Florence with Giuliano Bugialli.

In 1979, I left Newsday to become the executive food editor of the *New York Daily News*. It was the heyday of newspaper food sections, when national advertisers were doing all their print pitches in the daily food sections. With a staff of three, a test kitchen with a prep and clean-up helper, a few freelance columnists, and the wire services, I put out what amounted to a thirty-six- to forty-two-page weekly food magazine. I made myself the restaurant critic. These were the days when no one took you seriously as a food writer unless you reviewed restaurants. So I had my hands full.

This is how my radio program happened: In 1978, the year before I started working in New York City—although I lived in the city even while working on Long Island—all the newspapers were on strike. To keep up their beats, many reporters and editors from all three city newspapers—the *New York Times*, *Daily News*, *Post*— came together for a radio program. It was so successful that when the strike ended, WOR radio picked up the show, installed the legendary broadcaster Barry Gray as its host, and enlisted *Daily News* staff to report on what was in the paper the next day. We did the show in front of a live audience. I was called upon on Tuesdays to plug the food section and on Thursdays to discuss my restaurant review. Before long, and to my great surprise since I always hated my voice, I was in demand as a guest on other radio programs, including Joan Hamburg's on WOR. In 1992, the station finally found a slot for me.

Meanwhile, I decided I'd had enough of editing the food section. The advertisers were putting their money in the Sunday papers, not the weekday, and consequently not just the *Daily News*, but all the New York City newspapers (except to its credit, *Newsday*) lost interest in their weekday food sections. My staff dwindled. It was no fun anymore. I negotiated a deal where I worked from home, remained the restaurant critic, and wrote a weekly column called "The Schwartz Who Ate New York." The center of the page was a supposedly humorous (and thoughtful) essay. It was surrounded by short where-to-buy and what-to-eat items, and a recipe or two. After four years of doing both the newspaper work and the radio program, I was burned out and left the newspaper.

I was still thinking of myself as a writer, however, and my passion was southern Italian culture and food. Since no one had yet written a book on Neapolitan food, which is the mother cuisine of Italian-American, I decided to do it myself. *Naples At Table: Cooking in Campania* was published by Harper Collins in 1998. I've also written three other cookbooks, *Cooking in a Small Kitchen* was published in 1979, *What to Cook When You Think There's Nothing in the House to Eat* was published in 1992, and *Soup Suppers* was published in 1994.

However, all along what I really wanted to write was this New York City book. Given my background as a life-long New Yorker as well as a devoted and critical eater, I thought I was a natural for the subject. Publishers had other ideas. At the time I was passing my proposal around, one publisher hired a woman from Ohio to write a New York City cookbook, another hired a woman from Pittsburgh to write a Brooklyn cookbook. It took fifteen years before I found someone with enough sense to let a New Yorker write a New York cookbook.

CHAPTER 1

IN THE BEGINNING

WHAT THE INDIANS ATE

PICTURE MANHATTAN PRIMEVAL: LARGE SWATHS OF THE ISLAND WERE covered by towering forests of hickory, walnut, chestnut, maple, and oak. There were vast meadows where the first Europeans were stunned to find grass "as high as a man's middle." There were tidal marshes and rushing streams that fed ponds and lakes. The island was hillier. (It's been flattened.) It was narrower. (It's been broadened with landfill.) Native roses bloomed all over—some Europeans claimed they could smell them as they approached the land from the ocean. Wild strawberries, nuts, and other fruits provided a feast for the birds and small mammals that the native people, the Lenape tribe, hunted for food and furs to cover their bodies. Their territory extended from just north of what is now New York City to what is now Central New Jersey. They called their land Lenapehoking, after themselves, yet, historians say they did not consider themselves landowners. They were merely users of the land.

OPPOSITE: New Amsterdam, 1624 to 1669, at the tip of Manhattan island

When the Europeans arrived in what is now New York City, the Lenape numbered about fifteen thousand, according to *Gotham*, Edwin G. Burrows's and Mike Wallace's massive history of the city to 1898. About sixty-five hundred years ago, when the Lenape first arrived in this paradise of diverse environments, temperate climate, and "sweet air," as the first Europeans called it, they were small game hunters and foragers who "subsisted on a diet of deer, wild turkey, fish, shellfish, nuts, and berries....Roughly twenty-five hundred years ago, they discovered the use of the bow and arrow, learned to make pottery, and started to cultivate squash, sunflowers, and possibly tobacco. Later, about a thousand years ago, they may have also begun to plant beans and maize."

The diversity of their environments, each offering foods of the season, encouraged movement from one camp to another. In the summer they would be at the shore, fishing and clamming. In the fall, they would turn their attention to harvesting crops they'd planted at other locations. In the winter, they might be hunting deer and other game. Even though they planted crops, their diet is thought to have been protein-heavy. There were simply so many animals to eat.

Because the Lenape moved constantly, cooking utensils were kept light, a fact the first European traders discovered when they offered iron pots and the natives rejected them. The regular movement of camps also had beneficial ecological effects: land was not depleted by continuous cultivation, neither were animal populations depleted by overhunting, and waste was distributed over a large area. On the other hand the Lenape did leave their mark in some places. Pearl Street in lower Manhattan gets its name, given by the Dutch, from the piles of oyster shells deposited there by the Lenape.

The Lenape system of agriculture also contributed to the diversity of environments that the Europeans found. It was not nature alone that created this paradise, say the authors of *Gotham*: *Consciously or not, [the Lenape] used it in ways that extended the diversity of plant and animal life on which their survival depended. The heavy use of firewood around their principal habitation sites, combined with the annual spring burn off of active planting fields, left vast, open, park-like forests where deer, rabbits, birds, and other game flourished. Their abandoned planting fields became the meadows and prairies that were home to a tangle of flowers and edible berries. And because Lenape spiritual beliefs emphasized the interdependence of all life, hunting was an enterprise loaded with such supernatural significance that excessive killing was avoided. The abundance that so amazed early European visitors was thus no mere accident of nature, for "nature" was an artifact of culture as well as geology.*

THE DUTCH

The amazing thing about the Dutch rule of New York City is that it was so short—really only forty-five years—and its cultural influence so long—until this day.

Contrary to popular belief, New Amsterdam was never truly a colony of the Netherlands. Historians used to argue this point, but it now seems clear that most, if not all, of the people who arrived in 1624 (and for years after) under the auspices of the West India Company came to make money, not to create a permanent settlement. Even though they may have wanted their life in the New World to be nearly as comfortable as it was at home, this wild place was to be no more—and definitely no less—than a place to do business, a trading post.

Fur, particularly luxurious beaver fur, was how the Dutch hoped to get rich. It was in demand in Europe as the fashionable way to keep warm for both men and women. The natives the Dutch encountered here, the Lenape, were eager to supply the Europeans with pelts in exchange for beads, tools, and other trade goods, not to mention, in short time, drinking alcohol and firearms.

With all its promise, New Amsterdam turned out to be a bad investment. It had a forty-five-year run with marginal returns and a lot of bother, corruption, and deceit—all very distasteful and embarrassing back in the old country to the proper burgher shareholders of the West India Company.

The settlement was, however, blessed with many natural advantages. The climate was mild. The land was fertile. The waters teemed with fish and shellfish. It was at the head of a large but easily secured bay and harbor with coastal undulations perfect for moorings. (The water's depth

Homes, genuine, happy Dutch Homes, in abundance were found within and without the city, where uncultured minds and affectionate hearts enjoyed life in dreamy, quiet blissfulness unknown in these bustling times. The city people then rose at dawn, dined at eleven, and went to bed at sunset, except on extraordinary occasions, such as Christmas Eve, a tea party, or a wedding. Then those who attended the fashionable soirées of the "upperden" assembled at three o'clock in the afternoon and went away at six, so that daughter Maritchie might have the pewter plates and delf teapot cleaned and cupboarded in time for evening prayer at seven. Knitting and spinning held the places of whists and flirting in these "degenerate days;" and utility was as plainly stamped on all their pleasures as the maker's name on our silver spoons.

FROM JAMES D. MCCABE, JR.'S
Lights and Shadows of New York Life

was another advantage, but not of great consequence until the twentieth century, when huge, deep-hulled ships plied the seas.) Crowning it all was the wide and majestic river leading to the wild and fur-rich interior. And even if it was not what the Dutch intended, their little, unsuccessful business post made the land an even more desirable place to colonize.

The desirability of this place, now called New York City, was immediately evident to Europeans. There was also early European contact with the native North Americans. It is speculated that cod fishermen who never recorded their travels must have previously found their way this far south from the New England coast and traded with the natives. Proof of this can be traced to European trade goods from the era that have been found at inland Indian sites. Another piece of evidence is that, when Europeans who did report their experiences arrived, they said the locals already knew exactly what they wanted: beaver skins.

Discovering New Netherland

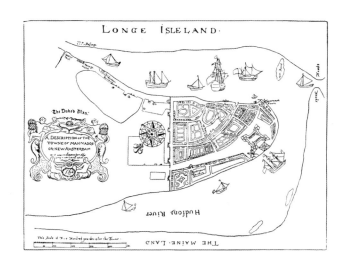

New Amsterdam took up only a small fraction of what we know as Manhattan today.

In 1524 Giovanni da Verrazzano, a Florentine working for the French, sailed into the area. Looking for a passage to "the Indies," he found the entrance to what is now New York Harbor. He sailed through the Lower Bay, as far as the Narrows, where the sleek bridge named for him now connects Staten Island and Brooklyn. (The Port Authority of New York and New Jersey changed the spelling to Verrazano, with one "z.") Beyond that narrowing portion of the Bay, he saw the Upper Bay, but called it a great lake. A storm prevented him from exploring any further. Verrazzano turned around and sailed back to France without knowing that his great lake was really the mouth of a great river.

It took Henry Hudson, an Englishman in service to the Dutch, in 1609, to go further up the river, and he was impressed with what he encountered. One of Hudson's men, Robert Juet, reported that the Lenape were "loving people" and many of them brought beaver and otter skins, which they were willing to exchange for beads, knives, and hatchets.

On his ship the Half Moon, Hudson went all the way to what is now Albany. At the end of the wide river, a quick left turn would have taken him into the Mohawk River, but it was apparently unnavigable even then. When he realized that this was not the passage to the Orient that he hoped it was, he declared everything in his path, from Albany down to the Atlantic, New Netherland. He bought a lot of furs and went home.

When word of Hudson's fur purchases got around Amsterdam it created a stir. Over the next fifteen years, many Dutch captains made the voyage, and most of them traded successfully with the natives. But it wasn't until early summer of 1624 that thirty Dutch adventurers and families came to make their fortune, under contract with the West India Company on board a ship with Captain Cornelius May, for whom Cape May, New Jersey is named. It seems strange now, but most of them went up the river to a west bank site they called Fort Orange (now in Rockland County).

Some settled in the Delaware and Connecticut River valleys. No one had yet settled on Manhattan itself, which was already relatively densely inhabited by the Lenape, whose camps dotted the island and trails crisscrossed it. The Lenape moved seasonally from one area to another, instinctively saving their environment from overuse. A few of May's passengers cleared land on what is now Governor's Island, in the Upper Bay, and not long after that they crossed the channel and started cultivating the tip of Manhattan.

The Dutch Move In

By the end of 1624, Dutch West India Company ships had returned to their homeland bearing pelts worth fifty thousand guilders and with the news that both the new land and its native people were most welcoming. According to one report, the earth was so fertile, the food so plentiful that "had we cows, hogs, and other cattle fit for food (which we daily expect in the first ships) we would not wish to return to Holland, for whatever we desire in the paradise of Holland, is here to be found." On the other hand, there were complaints. Dominie Johannes Michaelius, New Amsterdam's first minister, wrote to his friends in the homeland that fresh food was scarce and overpriced, and the company supplied "hard, stale food, such as men are used to on board ship."

A second wave of Dutch arrived in the spring of 1625, and they must have relieved the situation. There may have been more than a hundred people this time, mainly from Leyden in the Walloon region (now in Flemish-speaking Belgium), as were most of May's passengers. The new group brought with them more than one hundred head of livestock—cows, goats, sheep, pigs, and horses—as well as many kinds of supplies. There were wagons, plows, tools, and seeds for farming. There was food and clothing for immediate needs. There were firearms. And there were cheap goods to trade for lavish furs. Food and drinkable water are always the first needs of any settlement, and it didn't take long for fields of wheat, rye, and buckwheat to be planted on

Manhattan, or for the Dutch cows to graze on its abundant pastureland. At first fresh water was not a problem. The island and area had many streams and ponds.

Those who sailed to New Netherland came under the strict rules of the West India Company. The company could tell you where to live and plant, order you to construct fortifications and other public works, and enlist you as military for the protection of the settlement. It, or more specifically its director and council, on which there was settler representation, was to mete out justice, too. However, those who intended to stay were promised certain things in return: cheap livestock, easy credit, and freedom of worship. This last guarantee was to prove most important to New Amsterdam, and it helped set the tone for modern New York City, a place where people from all over the globe can find a place to worship.

Before the end of 1625, Willem Verhulst, who had been appointed director of New Netherland by the home office of the West India Company, and Cryn Fredericks, an engineer, decided that the tip of Manhattan was the best place to build a fortification. They were not building Fort Amsterdam to protect themselves from the Lenape, as some old histories say. The Dutch built a fort to secure themselves and their land up river from the Spanish, with whom they were still warring over rights in the New World. Indeed, the West India Company was chartered, in part, to vex the Spanish.

Verhulst turned out to be an embezzler and was replaced in 1626, only about six months after he was appointed. Peter Minuit, a Walloon, like most of the residents of the post, was selected as the new director by the council. By now it was three decades after contact with New York, but only two years after the Dutch arrived in numbers. In that time, the European presence, and their demand for animal pelts, had warped the delicate balance of nature, tribal life, and relations between tribes. So as not to have settlers caught in the crossfire of warring natives, those who settled at Fort Orange and in the Connecticut and Delaware River valleys were called back to the tip of Manhattan. Meanwhile, the Lenape population was beginning to be decimated by European disease.

It is in front of this backdrop that Minuit offered some trinkets for the purchase of Manhattan. Were they worth twenty-four dollars as the legend says? They were probably worth very little, but the amount would have been immaterial to the natives. They had no concept of land and resource ownership, only of land use. One has to suppose that they took the Dutch offerings as a gift of friendship, perhaps even a mere symbolic offering from the new neighbors who would be sharing the land—not their land, *the* land.

Hudson had said that the soil was the finest for cultivation he had ever set foot on, and he was soon proved right. Rye grew "so tall that a man could bind the ears together above his head." The barley stems were reportedly seven feet high. The soil seemed inexhaustible. The climate allowed two crops a year of peas and buckwheat, as well as, according to one source, good crops of cabbage, carrots, beets, parsnips, radishes, artichokes, and chicory between the woods, meadows, and swamps, and "every environment offered abundant wildlife."

Although the Lenape were mainly hunters and gatherers, they had learned to cultivate squash, corn, beans, sunflowers, and tobacco. Indeed, they had cleared whole tracts of land in what is now Greenwich Village, and in Brooklyn, in what are now the neighborhoods of Redhook and Gowanus. The Canarsee Indians had cleared land and planted in what is now the area called Canarsie, also in Brooklyn. It was these tracts of cleared land and cultivation that soon led the Dutch to spread out to areas away from the tip of Manhattan. In 1636 and 1638, in "purchases" that were every bit as dramatic as the supposed sale of Manhattan for twenty-four dollars, Wouter van Twiller bought all these cleared properties from the Indians and planted them mainly with tobacco, a cash crop.

Van Twiller had succeeded Minuit as director of New Amsterdam in 1633. He arrived with more than one hundred soldiers and orders from his uncle, company home-office kingpin Kiliaen van Rensselaer, to depose Minuit. Minuit was being blamed for the high costs and low return on New Netherland, and in fact he was probably not very honest. The minister Michaelius called him "a slippery man."

What the Dutch Ate and Ate and Ate

Among the various foods the Lenape cultivated, the Dutch adopted two immediately. Already dedicated cereal eaters, the Dutch loved the porridge they could make from ground corn. *Turkie-wheat* is what they called the grain itself. *Samp* is what they called that grain when it was pounded into a meal, and also after it was boiled with water. (The word *samp* is still used in English to mean exactly those two things.)

Samp fused with the traditional Dutch *hutespot*, or hodgepot (where we get the word "hodge-podge"), to create a sort of soup-stew (see page 25). The result was a polenta-like dish flavored with bits of meat (salt beef or pork, or perhaps even salt-cured and smoked ham, which Dutch farmers processed in their chimneys) and vegetables, especially root vegetables. *Samp* could be eaten in its creamy state, or cooked until it turned into a dense mass that then could be unmolded, sliced, and reheated over a fire, much like polenta.

The Lenape turned their corn into meal by pounding the grain in a mortar fashioned out of a block of wood. They apparently performed this task for the Dutch, who also used the meal to make another kind of porridge, *suppawm,* which was prepared with milk as the Dutch might make barley porridge at home. The Dutch were known as dairymen—"milk and cheese men." Eaten for breakfast, snacks, and supper, cheese was an important part of their daily diet. While the midday meal would be the heavily meat-based meal, cheese with bread was a mainstay. Toward the end of Dutch rule there seems to have been some cheese made, but it was an easy food to ship from the Netherlands.

The Dutch also had a reputation as people who enjoyed food, and they did in large quantities. Seventeenth-century Dutch painting is full of lovingly executed food-based still lifes. Fruits,

Seventeenth-century Dutch still-life painting expresses the Dutch love of food as shown here in Floris van Schooten's *Still Life with Ham*. Oil on wood, 24¹/₂ x 32⁵/₈ in. (62 x 83 cm). Louvre, Paris. Reunion des Musees Nationaux/ Art Resource, NY. Photo: Jean Schormans

vegetables, cheese, bread, meat, fish and especially shellfish, and the material things of the table—tankards, glasses, decorated and utilitarian pottery—are glorified. Sometimes the food is shown in almost divine lighting. Paintings of a single food— chestnuts, raspberries, oysters, fish, melons, bread, pretzels—give the foods meaning beyond their necessity as sustenance, their beauty as objects, even their succulence or deliciousness. In genre scenes, the people are plump and comfortable, and domestic bliss and affluence are evidenced not only in the rich cloth that dresses people but in the well-clothed and well-set table, or well-equipped hearth. "There is no doubt that the Dutch colonists were very valiant trenchermen," wrote Alice Morse Earle in 1896 in *Colonial Days in Old New York*.

Oranges, lemons, and pomegranates were particularly exalted in seventeenth-century Dutch art, most certainly because these fruits were exotica from the Orient. Still, humble apples got their due, too, and apple trees were one of the first plants brought to New Netherland from Europe. Hudson had noted that in the valley he dubbed New Netherland, there grew many kinds of trees. He couldn't have known, however, that what we now call the Hudson Valley turned out to be climatically and agronomically perfect for growing apples. The English also loved apples, and between the Dutch and the English, the Hudson Valley became an Eden of apples.

The Dutch love of the cake–bread–sweets axis of cookery has left an indelible legacy on contemporary New York. Crullers mean "twists" in Dutch, and they were ribbons or ropes of egg-rich dough twisted, knotted or crimped, then deep fried. Even without leavening, they puff up, much as Italian *struffoli* and Jewish *tayglach* do. All three of these light, crispy twists are made from essentially the same dough. Crullers continue to be a specialty of New York City, and we now have several kinds, including one that is really a kind of doughnut. You might say the Dutch invented doughnuts, too. They had another kind of fried dough that they called *oeli-koeken*, which we believe evolved into the fried ring with the hole. The word, which can be spelled several ways, translates to "oily cakes."

Waffles and pancakes were made for both daily meals and celebrations. There were flat waffles, what we would call wafers, and puffy waffles, reasonably like the waffles of today, and many kinds of pancakes made from different grains and seasonings, including pancakes flavored with pumpkin.

Kool Slaa is another Dutch legacy. We know it as coleslaw, cole being the Dutch word for cabbage and its cruciferous cousins (think kohlrabi and cauliflower); slaw meaning "shreds." The original salad was dressed with oil and vinegar, or butter and vinegar, the Dutch being such great dairymen. The mayonnaise-dressed, shredded cabbage version was probably introduced by German immigrants in the mid-nineteenth century. And, as in the case of pancakes, other salads of shredded cabbage have found broad acceptance in New York City, including the late Second Avenue Delicatessen's Health Salad (see page 140), Sardi's Katherine Cornell Salad (see page 263), and Mrs. Fan's Cabbage (see page 196).

Governing the Land

Wouter van Twiller turned out to be no better and no more honest a governor of New Amsterdam than his predecessors. Meanwhile, back in the Netherlands, there was an economic crisis created by speculation on tulip bulbs. Called Tulip Mania, it left many people jobless and made rich men go broke. Because these unlucky Dutchmen were being encouraged to seek their fortunes in the New World, the West India Company decided it had better replace the corrupt Twiller. Unfortunately, their choice of Willem Kieft was disastrous. His stewardship did result in growth in the hinterlands of Long Island (mainly Brooklyn) and Staten Island, but the Lenape were also tortured and persecuted under his watch.

When Kieft arrived in New Amsterdam in 1638, the settlement had eighty to ninety dilapidated structures and about four hundred and forty citizens of many nationalities. It is said eighteen different languages were spoken, with only a slight majority of the mostly male residents being Dutch. There were also some French, Irish, Swedes, Danes, and Germans, among others. (New Amsterdam's most respected Dane was Jonas Bronck, who eventually bought a tract of land north of Manhattan—hence, the Bronx.) There was a Muslim mulatto, a man of mixed Dutch and Moroccan ancestry who was called "The Turk." There were also a few free black men and a handful of slaves owned by the West India Company. They were not privately owned at this point, although the women slaves did do domestic service. The male slaves helped maintain and build the infrastructure of the settlement, and some were taught skills, such as carpentry or blacksmithing.

Like any frontier town, New Amsterdam was a rough place. The Dutch loved their drink so much that Kieft reported to the home office that nearly a quarter of the town's buildings were "grog shops or houses where nothing is to be got but tobacco and beer." The West India Company had built a brewery on Staten Island almost as soon as their fort was built, and the company also imported wine and brandy. Kieft also opened a tavern in 1642, which he called Staat's Herberg, although he soon leased it stipulating, however, that it serve only spirits distilled by the Dutch West India Company. The taverns also served food, however rudimentary. They were the only places new immigrants or visitors could sleep, eat, drink—and arrange for sex. Drinking and public rowdiness were a huge problem. Indeed, the first laws enacted in New Amsterdam were to control drinking. It was forbidden to sell alcohol on the Sabbath—Sunday—and no alcohol was to be sold to the Indians or slaves. Apparently the enforcement of these laws was lax because the problems continued to the end of the next century.

ENGLISH TAVERNS

"New York [City] was pretty much alone in establishing taverns in the seventeenth century. The Puritans of New England were too tight-laced, the Quakers of Pennsylvania were homebodies and models of sobriety, and the colonists in the South were widely dispersed on isolated plantations, with no cities large enough to make the exploitation of restaurants profitable."

— WAVERLY ROOT AND RICHARD DE ROCHEMONT, *Eating in America*

Dutch New Amsterdam was a rowdy town until the English arrived in 1664. Then it got rowdier. Compared to uptight Boston and refined and cultured Philadelphia, New York was a rough and tumble town, a backwater interested only in making money. Most meals were still cooked and eaten at home through the eighteenth century, but there were taverns to provide food, beds, and sex to visitors. More importantly the taverns became the social centers of the city.

In the Dutch days, all classes met and mingled in the same taverns, but soon after the English arrived, each tavern started finding its own particular clientele. There are some records of these. Farmers from outside the city, traveling to sell their crops or do other business, congregated at a tavern called Sergeant Litschoe's. The White Horse Tavern (not related to the current but antique one in Greenwich Village) opened in 1641, eventually attracting servants and soldiers. The Blue Dove attracted soldiers, too, but also sailors and tradesmen apprentices. Montayne's was known as "the house where all the Riotous Liberty Boys met in 1765 and 1766," according to Sharon V. Salinger's *Taverns and Drinking in Early America*.

Political tensions in New York were very high in the mid-eighteenth century because British troops were quartered in the city, and revolutionary fever started to build as the century went on. The mix of alcohol and political opinion caused many riots. Apparently, no amount of food could serve as ballast against the vast amounts of alcohol, although the English taverns did turn roasts on their spits and grilled meats on grills in the open hearth. By the end of the century, a fashion for more respectable establishments flourished, and the English chop house emerged. Although beef was prized, pork ruled the day. Hogs wandered the streets, scavenging a city not yet organized enough to properly dispose of its garbage. Although fresh pork was available during late fall and early winter, the slaughter season, and innards had to be consumed immediately, hams and other smoked or cured parts of the pig were available through to spring. There were even imported meats: Most notably, from about 1720, when the English started trading with the Irish, mainly for flax that was spun into linen in New York, Irish bacon was imported.

Coffeehouses, which were becoming fashionable in Europe in the seventeenth century, started opening during the Dutch period, but they didn't really flourish until the end of the eighteenth century. At these cafes, businessmen could share market information and make deals over coffee, but they also served alcoholic beverages and were the prototypes for the men's cafes of the nineteenth century, which eventually evolved into what we now call bars. The most important of these cafes was Tontine's Coffee House, built in 1794 on the corner of Wall and Water Streets. Tontine's not only had a

Clay pipes on the ceiling and a mutton chop at Keens, in the English chop house tradition.

dining room, a tearoom, mahogany furniture, chandeliers, and bathrooms, it served as the first stock exchange. The arrivals and departures of ships were recorded here, and all these things attracted the middle class and upper crust.

Just in time for the civilizing influence of Tontine's, the French philosopher of the table, Jean Anthelme Brillat-Savarin, author of *The Physiology of Taste*, which is still read and revered today, arrived for a two-year stay in New York. He recorded a dinner at Little's Tavern, where he approvingly ate roast beef, turkey, vegetables, salad, fruit tart, cheese, and nuts, accompanied by large quantities of claret (Bordeaux), Port, and Madeira, followed by rum, brandy, and whiskey.

One of the most famous English taverns of the eighteenth century was the Mason's Arms, opened sometime before 1763 by Sam Francis, a dapper and cosmopolitan man of half black, half white ancestry born in the French West Indies. As Michael and Ariane Batterberry say in *On the Town in New York*, "He was, like most noted professional hosts, a connoisseur, an extrovert, and an autocrat. Above all, he was a sworn revolutionary." It was at a later tavern of his, the Queen's Head in the former DeLancey mansion on the corner of Broad and Pearl Streets, that the Sons of Liberty and the Vigilance Committee met in 1774 to protest the landing of British tea and lay plans for dumping it.

Francis changed his name to Fraunces after the revolution and it was at his tavern, which is today in a reconstructed building known as Fraunces Tavern, where George Washington said farewell to his officers. Fraunces staged a dinner for the occasion, but the menu has not passed down to us; only the alcoholic details. One hundred and twenty guests consumed one hundred and thirty-five bottles of Madeira, thirty-six bottles of Port, sixty bottles of English beer, and thirty bowls of punch.

New York City, with about ten thousand residents, became the capital of the new country in 1784. Fires, riots, and war left the city in shambles, but it was quickly rebuilt, and by the turn of the century the population, boosted by immigration from Europe and migration from the hinterlands, had soared to sixty thousand. New York was still a rough place, although it was, as it would be throughout its history, a city of contrasts. The poor were very poor. The rich wallowed in luxury. New Yorkers of all classes, however, still ate a high-protein diet. Game of all kinds remained abundant; domestic meats, too. The waters were still bursting with fish and shellfish. It would take another twenty-five years, though, until the opening of the Erie Canal in 1825 made the city a commercial boomtown, for the city's tables to gain sophistication.

CRULLERS

I include this recipe more for historical interest than deliciousness, although these simple fried doughnut twists do have their appeal when fresh out of the oil and sprinkled with granulated sugar, dusted with confectioners' sugar, or glazed with sugar as their contemporary equivalents sometimes are. Crullers are a prime example of the enduring influence of the Dutch on New York City. Look at any coffee cart in town and you'll still see twisted lengths of dough being sold as crullers, the direct descendent of the Dutch *crulla* meaning "twist."

Of course, chemical leavening (baking powder) was not invented until the mid-nineteenth century, after the following cruller formula was outlined in the handwritten cookbook of Magdalena Douw (1750–1817) and her daughter, Ann Stevenson (1774–1821), wife of Dutch descendent Pierre van Cortlandt II. Contemporary crullers made with baking powder are, therefore, lighter and have a cake-like crumb, while these are sturdier, though surprisingly light. The dough is similar to one that would be used for Italian *struffoli* or Jewish Eastern European *tayglach*. It is raised only by eggs and the moisture of the dough vaporizing.

Note that New York coffee carts and bakeries also offer another pastry called crullers. These are scalloped rings with a circular doughnut shape, deep-fried cream-puff pastry dough that we call French crullers. The French call them beignets. These are also exactly what Neapolitans call *Zeppole di San Giuseppe*, and Sicilians call *sfingi* or *sfinci*. New York's French crullers have no filling and are hollow inside. The Italian versions, made widely in New York, too, are a delicacy for Saint Joseph's Day, which falls on March 19. They are split and filled with a dab of preserved sour cherries and either thick pastry cream or ricotta cream. Most New York City Italian bakeries and cafes sell them from the week before to the week after Saint Joseph's feast day.

Makes about 20 doughnuts

In her book, *The Sensible Cook: Dutch Foodways in the Old and New World*, Peter G. Rose quotes Stevenson's recipe: "3 lbs. flour, 12 Eggs, 1 lb. sugar, a little butter & some nutmeg." This version for the modern kitchen was freely adapted from one developed by Rose.

The crullers will puff up nicely enough if fried immediately after they are shaped. But if you let the dough rest for at least eight hours, they will expand even more, becoming lighter and much more appealing to contemporary tastes.

5 tablespoons unsalted butter

¼ cup granulated sugar

2 eggs

2 cups all-purpose flour

⅛ teaspoon freshly grated nutmeg

Oil for deep-frying (preferably peanut)

Confectioners' sugar or cinnamon-sugar (optional)

In a medium bowl, cream the butter and granulated sugar.

Add the eggs one at a time, beating well after each.

Add the flour and nutmeg, then mix well to make a smooth dough. Turn the dough out onto a board and cut into 20 even pieces.

Roll each piece of dough into a 6-inch rope. Fold each rope in half and twist the halves together. An alternate method for shaping the crullers is to roll out the dough ¼ inch thick. With a pie jagger, cut into strips ½ inch wide and 3 inches long. Twist two strips together. For optimum expansion, arrange the shaped crullers on a platter, cover with plastic, and let rest in the refrigerator for at least 8 hours.

Heat the oil to 375 degrees and deep-fry the crullers until deep golden, less than 1 minute.

Remove from the oil and sprinkle with confectioners' sugar or cinnamon-sugar, if desired. Serve immediately.

BRABANT HUTSPOT

The *hutspot* was the main, daily fare of the Dutch, as well as, in its more elaborate forms, a dish for feasts. It is nothing more than beef, veal, mutton, venison, or game of some other kind, cooked in water with seasonings and sometimes vegetables. We might call the "hot pot" a stew, but the ample broth was as important as the solids. Then again, it has more substance than soup.

Given that it is three hundred and fifty years old, the following recipe, adapted from *The Sensible Cook: Dutch Foodways in the Old and the New World*, is amazingly contemporary tasting. It is also very easy to make, and delicious.

At first, fresh ginger may seem like an ingredient that would be impossible to obtain in New Amsterdam, or even in old Amsterdam. But, at the same time they were settling New Amsterdam, the Dutch were trading on the tropical islands of the Caribbean, where ginger does grow. Keep in mind that the entity that settled New Amsterdam was the far reaching Dutch West India Company.

Serves 4 to 6

The Brabant is one of the Netherlands' seven provinces. The stew is brothy, so I love to dunk bread into it. You can also serve it with boiled potatoes or rice for sopping up the delicious juices. Or drink the juices with a soup spoon.

6 tablespoons unsalted butter
2 pounds stew beef (such as chuck), cut into
    1-inch cubes
2 tablespoons finely chopped, peeled
    fresh ginger

¼ teaspoon ground mace, or freshly
    grated nutmeg
1 teaspoon salt, or more to taste
½ cup coarsely chopped parsley

In a 3-quart saucepan, melt 3 tablespoons of the butter over medium heat. Add a few of the meat cubes and brown on all sides; remove the meat to a plate while you brown the remaining cubes a few at a time.

Add the ginger, mace, and salt just before you are finished browning the meat and return the cooked meat to the pan. When the meat is brown, add enough water to almost cover.

Bring to a boil, then reduce the heat. Simmer gently for about 1 hour, or until the meat is fork tender. Add water by the tablespoon, as needed, to keep the water level about the same.

Just before serving, stir in the remaining 3 tablespoons butter and the parsley. Serve immediately.

NEW YEAR'S COOKIES

By the late 1970s, when I got this recipe from an elderly reader of the *New York Daily News* (I was then the food editor), New Year's cookies or cakes had not been sold in local bakeries for some time. It was at least long ago enough that those who remembered them fondly would wax nostalgic about them and seek a recipe. On the other hand, it couldn't have been longer than twenty-five years ago, because they were still sold in bakeries from Christmas to New Year's Day when I was a child in Brooklyn in the 1950s.

Some of the last vestiges of Dutch culture were still around in the Flatlands section of the borough, where the First Dutch Reform Church of Brooklyn is situated on East Thirty-ninth Street and Kings Highway. My elementary school friends and I would bike over to the church graveyard looking for arrowheads after our teacher told us that Indians were buried there. There still is a Dutch homestead on East Thirty-eighth Street and another on the corner of East Fortieth Street and Kings Highway.

As was the case then and still is now, Brooklynites often sit on the "stoop," the Dutch word for the stairs leading up to a house's front door. In the Netherlands, they built high entrances to their houses because of the frequent flooding. The architectural tradition continues to this day in New York City, even without the floods. The existence of stoops in New York's boroughs inspired a game called stoop ball, wherein you bounce the ball off different steps and earn points depending on which step it hits.

As with the churches and stoops these cookies are clearly of Dutch origin. There is a similar recipe for a caraway-scented cookie in *The Sensible Cook* by Peter G. Rose. That means that caraway New Year's cakes were popular for about three hundred years, and deservedly so. They are simple and plain, but if you like the taste of caraway, they are exemplary. In many cultures, seeds are often symbolic of plenty and fertility (for all too obvious reasons), which explains these cookies' appearance for the New Year.

Makes about 30 (3-inch) round cookies

Store these in a tin or other air-tight container for at least 24 hours before serving. It takes at least one day for the caraway flavor to permeate the cookies. They are even better when several days old.

3 cups sifted all-purpose flour
2 tablespoons baking powder
1 cup sugar
⅛ teaspoon salt

¾ cup (1½ sticks) cold unsalted butter, cut
   into pieces
1 tablespoon caraway seeds, crushed lightly in
   a mortar with a pestle
½ cup milk

Preheat the oven to 375 degrees. Grease a baking sheet or line it with parchment.

In a large mixing bowl, combine the flour, baking powder, sugar, and salt. Mix well.

With a pastry blender, two knives, or your fingertips, cut the butter into the dry ingredients until the mixture resembles coarse meal.

Stir in the caraway seeds, then the milk. Gather the dough into a ball, adding a few more drops of milk if necessary to make the dough come together.

On a lightly floured surface, roll out the dough ⅛ inch thick. Cut into 2-by-3-inch rectangles or cut with any shape cookie cutters. Arrange ½ inch apart on the prepared baking sheet.

Bake on the middle rack of the oven for 12 to 15 minutes, until very light brown.

Cool thoroughly on a wire rack.

CHAPTER 2
SEAFOOD CITY

WATER, WATER EVERYWHERE

I WAS ONCE ASKED TO GIVE A FOOD TOUR OF BROOKLYN TO A GROUP OF journalists from around the country. When we got to the Brighton Beach boardwalk, the theoretically intelligent editor from Chicago, looking out over the beautiful white sand beach, the water, and the waves, asked: "What lake is this?"

It's the ocean honey, it's the Atlantic Ocean. ("If you look hard you can see Portugal," teased one of the other journalists.)

That New York City is on the ocean and surrounded by water is, indeed, sometimes hard to imagine while walking around the skyscraper canyons of Manhattan. The East River, which runs between Manhattan on the west and Brooklyn and Queens on the east, is actually an estuary connecting Long Island Sound and the Atlantic Ocean. The Hudson, a true river, which flows between Manhattan on the east and New Jersey on the west, lets out into New York Harbor and then the ocean. When you ride the Staten Island ferry from Staten Island to the tip of Manhattan you get the whole watery picture. You might think you were in Venice. Indeed, the only borough of the city that is on the mainland is the Bronx, and it, too, has a shoreline—Long Island Sound on the east, the Hudson on the west.

And where there is water there are fish and shellfish.

In the beginning, our waters were teeming with oysters, scallops, and clams. The oysters were particularly abundant around Staten Island. Mussels attached themselves to rocks everywhere. The scallops liked Jamaica Bay, at the south end of Brooklyn and Queens. Shad and sturgeon spawned in the Hudson. Yes, at one time there was such a thing as New York City caviar. The Lenape were known for their planked shad roasts during the April season. Eels squirmed in our huge harbor. Schools of bluefish, flounder, fluke, striped bass, and mackerel surrounded the city. There were whales; perhaps not as abundant as in New England, but enough for there to be a whaling industry.

Fish were so plentiful, it is said, that all the Lenape people had to do when they wanted fish to eat was stick their hands in the water. The Dutch and other early Europeans all commented on the amazing amount of seafood and fish, and the huge size of some of them. There were twelve-inch oysters and lobsters so ancient that they ran to an astounding six feet. A few observers of the Dutch and the English warned that if the people of New Amsterdam, then New York, continued to eat seafood at the rate they did, there would be none left eventually. How prescient they were!

The abundance didn't last long. By the beginning of the nineteenth century, Staten Island's natural oyster beds were depleted, and seed oysters had to be brought from Virginia. By the 1830s,

OPPOSITE:
Shelly Fireman with his seafood display at Shelly's New York on Fifty-seventh Street.

oysters were mainly farmed, though the waters were receptive enough for oyster farming to become a major industry, and for oyster bars to become a popular form of eatery. The Canal Street oyster bars, many of them operated by African-Americans after slavery was abolished in New York State in 1827, were for the lower classes. The so-called Canal Street Plan offered customers as many oysters as they could eat for six cents. At the higher class oyster bars, the price was much higher. Most everyone—high class and low—preferred them raw, with perhaps a dash of vinegar and a sprinkle of pepper, or a squeeze of lemon at the more expensive bars. Oysters were also cooked in many ways: baked with crumbled crackers and cream for scalloped oysters, fried with a coating of breadcrumbs, stewed with butter and cream, and much later, in the early twentieth century, and as still served at the Oyster Bar in Grand Central Terminal, pan-roasted, which means cooked in a sauce of cream with a dash of Worcestershire sauce and Heinz tomato-based chile sauce (see page 42). Heinz ketchup and chile sauce were invented in about 1914, just after the Oyster Bar opened.

According to the *Encyclopedia of New York City,* in 1850, New Yorkers consumed six million dollars' worth of oysters, and the merits of different types were hotly debated. Old menus list kinds of oysters we know nothing about these days—Rockaways, for instance. By the 1870s, most of the local oyster beds were dredged, oysters needed to be brought in from the Chesapeake Bay, and prices rose. Still, oysters were such an accepted part of New York gastronomy that until the end of the nineteenth century every formal dinner started with oysters. Charles Ranhofer, the great chef of Delmonico's, always started his menus with oysters. Diamond Jim Brady was said to eat a few dozen even before considering what he might eat as an appetizer.

Clams were not and still are not considered as elegant as oysters, but the local Cherrystones and Littlenecks were also offered on both high-brow and low class menus. At one time, local waters must have supported the soft-shelled clams that they still farm in Ipswich, Massachusetts. At least they appear on old menus. Until it closed in February 2004, one of the chief specialties of Gage & Tollner in Brooklyn, which opened in 1879, was what they called broiled clam bellies, which were actually soft-shell clams (see page 44).

Crabmeat was a popular seafood, too, although I find no records that crabs were found in New York waters in any great number. Most likely, they were brought in from the Chesapeake Bay. New Yorkers are still fond of crabmeat, and Maryland-style crab cakes are enormously popular, as are fish and shrimp stuffed with crabmeat. In the Italian-American kitchen, tomato sauce cooked with crabs is still considered a delicacy.

Bluefish are New York City's game fish. The small ones don't put up much of a fight, but a large blue can wear a fisherman out. During summer evenings, charter boats still leave from the Sheepshead Bay Marina, taking fishermen to the deep ocean where the blues run in the dark. The boats also take groups out for daylight fishing of flounder and flukes, striped bass, and porgies, a small boney but very tasty fish that is a favorite of both Greek-American and African-American New Yorkers.

The Fulton Fish Market started as a market for all kinds of food in 1822, on the opposite side of the street from where it developed as strictly a fish market. It moved to the East River side of the street in 1831, where it remained until 2001. The permanent building went up in 1869 and it became the largest fish market on the East Coast of North America, supplying fish not only to New York City, but as far north as Boston and equally as far south and west. The fishing boats came directly to the market until the mid-1970s and almost until its last days it was the best show in town from four o'clock in the morning until daybreak. Across the street from the market were two of the city's best, if least refined seafood restaurants—Sweets (see page 32) and Sloppy Louie's. The South Street Seaport project, which created a shopping mall atmosphere on Fulton Street and Pier 17, put the restaurants out of business. The tourists didn't understand the restaurants' rough seaport ways, and New Yorkers, after more than a century of coming from all over to enjoy this ultimate New York seafood experience, rejected the South Street Seaport as being too Disney.

New Yorkers have always loved seafood restaurants, however. Even our restaurants that don't specialize in seafood offer more fish dishes than do restaurants in other parts of the country, with the exception of the Northwest. At least half and often more than half of the menu offerings in an upscale New York City restaurant will be fish dishes. And there are many specialty fish and seafood houses. In the last few years, Greek-owned fish restaurants that serve Greek appetizers and plainly broiled fresh fish have become popular. Eating through a huge French-style seafood platter, mainly composed of raw shellfish, has become a stylish way to spend an evening with friends. And need I mention that New York spearheaded the national— and now international—craze for sushi when huge numbers of Japanese businessmen temporarily moved to New York in the 1970s. Indeed, raw is the way many New Yorkers prefer their fish today—whether eaten as Japanese sashimi and sushi, as Italian-style *crudo* (actually a word that simply means "raw") dressed with extra-virgin olive oil, as tartars of chopped or minced and seasoned fish, or as South American ceviche, which is actually not raw fish, but fish marinated in citrus juices.

SWEETS

Sweets opened in 1845 at 2 Fulton Street, on the second floor of a wooden building across the street from the Fulton Fish Market. In its heyday, which lasted into the late 1980s, the line to get a table could extend down the stairs and into the street because no reservations were ever taken. The line was especially long on Fridays, when the city's Catholic population eschewed meat. Sweets was frequented by both Wall Street financiers and their clerks—it was great, but not expensive, and the portions were large—but fish lovers from all over the city would travel to it, knowing that its position across from the fish market gave it special access to the best seafood the fishmongers offered that day.

Always a hard-core plain seafood house, with a hard-core bar that offered Manhattans three ways (with blended rye whiskey, with Seagram's V.O., and with Canadian Club), but never with bourbon (see page 86), Sweets was always known for the freshest possible, plainest possible fish. In 1957, in a story in *Coronet* magazine, Peter Cheuces, the chef, was quoted as saying that "the only secrets of successful seafood cookery are really fresh fish, butter, and just enough cooking." The man said he cooked about a ton of fish a week, using around three hundred pounds of butter.

RIGHT:
The simplicity of Sweets was typical of all seafood houses until the last half of the twentieth century.
OPPOSITE:
Facts about Paddy's are from its 1951 menu.

MAIN DINING ROOM
Sweets Restaurant
NEW YORK'S OLDEST SEAFOOD RESTAURANT

PADDY'S CLAM HOUSE

Paddy's Clam House was my grandfather Barney Schwartz's favorite seafood restaurant, and, as he was the chef in the family, who was I to question his taste? I liked it mainly because he and my grandmother liked it, because it was inexpensive enough that they let me order anything I wanted—even a lobster—and because the restaurant served my absolute favorite desserts, the pies Nesselrode (page 100), Coconut Custard, and Banana Cream.

Paddy's opened in about 1900 and was at 215 West Thirty-fourth Street, which eventually was the hub of the city's main shopping area—Herald Square. It was a plain restaurant, frequented in the 1940s through the 1960s mainly by shoppers who came from all over the metro area.

Hart's 1961 *Guide to New York City* goes as far as to describe it as "drab," saying that "the service offers no niceties." My grandfather had friends among the waitstaff—he was a union waiter himself—so I remember everyone being nice and friendly. And the restaurant's scrubbed wooden tables and floors, and the coat hooks at the end of every pale green painted wooden booth, didn't seem drab at all. I thought that was the way a seafood house should look.

Special 5 Course Lobster Dinner — Sundays

PADDY'S CLAM HOUSE

COMPLETE LUNCHEON DAILY $1.29

215 W. 34th Street
Bet. 7th & 8th Aves.
New York City

Facts About Paddy's

We serve between 2,000 to 3,000 people daily with an all time high of 6,928.

We average about 5,000 Lobsters a week with an all time high of 6,928 in a day.

We use approximately 35 bushels of shell fish daily.

We use approximately 1,700 pounds of fish daily.

We have used over a ton of French Fried potatoes in one day.

We serve about a million customers a year.

Mr. J. P. White who is Mr. Paddy is in business 51 years. "Paddy" has served more than 10,000,000 Lobsters in his career.

GRAND CENTRAL OYSTER BAR

What could Commodore Cornelius Vanderbilt have been thinking when, in 1913, he installed an oyster bar in the bowels of his new, sensationally grand Beaux Arts train terminal at the epicenter of Manhattan? Was it his fascination with the sea? Was it his nostalgia for the long-gone oyster bars of old New York City, usually basement eateries? Was it a personal love of oysters?

He was criticized for the idea when the terminal opened, but the Grand Central Oyster Bar is a natural in a city that loves seafood, and a logical concept for a train station. People are coming and going in a hurry. A dozen oysters or clams on the half shell, or a bowl of chowder or seafood stew, is an appropriate snack for the passing crowds. Maybe that's what Vanderbilt had in mind.

The Grand Central Oyster Bar has had its ups and downs. Its lowest point was in 1972, when, after nearly sixty years in business, it went bankrupt and its doors were chained closed. Its demise might be blamed on the decline in long-distance passenger train service, making Grand Central Terminal more a commuter station than a national railroad hub. But, by most accounts, the food had not been good for a long time. In 1964, Craig Claiborne in the *New York Times* dismissed all but the "rich and buttery seafood stews and pan roasts." In fact, it was always these dishes that the critics raved about and still do. In 1955, Harry Botsford included it among "New York's 100 Best Restaurants" and wondered what the "top secret" ingredient in the pan roasts might be (diced scallops, clam juice?), "in spite of the fact that you watch it being done." He also noted that 10 million oysters, 1.6 million clams, and about 23,000 pounds of lobster were consumed there each year.

From 1972 to 1974 that number was zero. Then Jerome Brody of Restaurant Associates was approached by the New York Metropolitan Transit Authority. "The marble columns in the restaurant today were then painted aquamarine over wallpaper. The wall covering was yellow Cello-tex. The furniture was upholstered yellow, in unsettling contrast with the red tablecloths. The famous Guastavino tiles were black with grime," he told his biographer, Lawrence S. Freundlich, author of *A Time Well Spent*.

Those vaulted tile ceilings of the Oyster Bar are one of the city's most distinctive architectural motifs. They appear in other locations—most notably underneath the Queensboro Bridge (also called the Fifty-ninth Street Bridge), where a restaurant called Guastavino is now; inside Brooklyn's Prospect Park boathouse; in the great hall of Ellis Island; and at the Cloisters and Grant's Tomb. A Spanish émigré and architect-engineer, Raphael Guastavino patented a fireproof system of ceramic coursing that he used to create the dramatic vaults and domes in New York City and elsewhere. One of Brody's decorative innovations was to emphasize the vaulted

OPPOSITE:
Executive chef
Sandy Ingber and
me at the Grand
Central Oyster Bar.

ceiling by outlining it in tiny light bulbs. But the feature that fascinated me as a child and that I delight in introducing to others when visiting the Oyster Bar is that if two people stand outside the doors of the restaurant, each person facing the wall in a diagonally opposite corner of the Guastavino vault, they can whisper and still be heard by each other loud and clear.

With the advice of fish expert A. J. McClane, author of *The Encyclopedia of Fish*, Brody turned the Oyster Bar's largely Continental menu into a true seafood house, accessing the best local and national species and suppliers, serving fish that were rare in New York City restaurants, if they existed at all. With the help of Harold Bearak, a Queens wine merchant, he developed an all-American white wine list, which brought him even more press than the new all-fish menu did. Mario Staub managed the restaurant through this period and into the 1990s. He upgraded the dessert menu, started the annual Dutch herring festival, and wooed the press as the city's resident seafood expert.

Today, the Grand Central Oyster Bar is being franchised by Brody's widow, Marlene, and there are two other Grand Central Oyster Bars, one in Kansas City and one in Tokyo.

LUNDY'S

If the Dodgers leaving for Los Angeles in 1957 was the beginning of the end of Brooklyn's heyday—a time when Brooklyn was the world, as a book title put it—then Lundy's closing in 1979 was the end of the end. Lundy's wasn't just a seafood restaurant. It was a source of Brooklyn pride—perhaps the best seafood restaurant in New York City, maybe on the East Coast, maybe in the country, maybe in the world, maybe in the century or in the history of mankind—a place that every Brooklynite owned. And its final days were so sordid.

Like many a great seafood restaurant, Lundy's started as a fish market. The patriarch of the Lundy family, Frederick, an orphan, arrived in Brooklyn from Bremenhaven, in Germany, in 1838, although late-twentieth-century family members believe the Lundys were originally Dutch with a bit of English, much like Brooklyn itself.

Lundy went into the fish business, supplying products to the grand Brighton Beach and Manhattan Beach hotels of the day, where society went for its weekend getaways—sort of the Hamptons of the mid-nineteenth century. Lundy had several sons, including Frederick, Junior, who was born in 1862. By the 1880s, the Lundys had made their fortune. Besides the wholesale fish business, they now had three retail fish markets, their own clam beds, and they rented boats for sailing, rowing, and fishing. Eventually, they would open a seafood restaurant, really just a shack, on a pier of the Sheepshead Bay Marina, across the street from where the restaurant's landmark building would be erected in 1934 and still is now.

In a history of the city of Brooklyn published in 1884 (fourteen years before it became part of Greater New York City), the Lundy family is cited as leading citizens, famous citywide as one of the largest seafood purveyors. Then, adding to the family's fortunes just as it was coming into social prominence, the Sheepshead Bay Racetrack was built by August Belmont, William K. Vanderbilt, Leonard Jerome (the grandfather of Winston Churchill), H. P. Whitney, and other high-rolling, high-society investors of the Coney Island Jockey Club. Then the Brighton Beach Race Course was built, then the Gravesend Racetrack. The area became the horse-racing capital of the country, and Lundy sold fish to all the hotels that catered to the gilded racing set.

The third generation to run the Lundy fish empire was Frederick, Junior's son, Frederick William Irving Lundy, who was born in 1895 and was to become the last and by far most notorious member of the family. He had three brothers and three sisters, but only his younger brother, quiet Allen, who many of us remember as the man in charge, actively worked with him in the final Lundy business, the famous restaurant on Emmons Avenue. Irving, as F.W.I.L. liked to be called, may have been born rich and privileged, but by 1907, the Sheepshead Bay racing era was over. Attendance at the race tracks was declining, blamed on the advent of the automobile.

Eventually, some of the Sheepshead Bay horse tracks were converted to auto tracks, but the car crowd was not as classy as the horsey set; they didn't spend in the same way. The hotels closed, the tracks were abandoned, and Sheepshead Bay's and the Lundy's family fortunes declined. The neighborhood was no more than a collection of shanties by the end of World War I.

Then, in the early 1920s, Brooklyn hit a new stride. It had more housing starts of any municipality in the country. The new residents were mostly Italians, Irish, and Jews, with a good sprinkling of Germans, Chinese, and Scandinavians. Most of them were coming out of the dark and overcrowded tenements of the Lower East Side, or the first-generation communities of Williamsburg and Brownsville, into the relatively bucolic daylight of neighborhoods like Flatbush, Flatlands, Bensonhurst, and Bay Ridge. (Almost equally vigorous development was going on in the Bronx at this time.)

Lundy's Spanish Mission building in Brooklyn is a designated New York City landmark.

Prohibition also started in 1920 and the Lundys owned clam beds as well as prime property on the ocean waterfront, all of which were perfect for receiving bootleg alcohol, which the family did for a decade. They were well set to make their next move when Sheepshead Bay redevelopment began. The summer bungalows of Manhattan Beach, on the other side of the marina from the old Lundy's restaurant, were torn down to make way for grand houses. In order to widen Emmons Avenue, the old Bayside Hotel and Casino was demolished and Lundy bought that property across from their restaurant on the water. It took years to work out the deal, demolish the old and build the new. But, finally, on October 15, 1934, the famous, block-long, two-story Spanish Mission–style building opened. It was 28,000 square feet. It seated 2,200 people. On a busy day, it employed two hundred waiters, all of them black, none of them unionized. Its stucco walls were mixed with broken seashells, windows were stained glass, railings were custom-made wrought iron. The long clam bar had a wide window on the street (it still does), so you could down a couple dozen clams or oysters without even stepping into the place.

Lundy's upwardly mobile customers easily bought into Irving Lundy's dream of Brooklyn having the biggest, best, and most beautiful seafood restaurant in the city. For the poorer people of Brooklyn going to Lundy's was something to aspire to. For the rest it was where you went to appreciate your good fortune at having made it. Lundy's represented the good life in Brooklyn.

The Shore Dinner was the big-deal, expensive, show-off dinner, although your appetite had to be even bigger than your wallet to manage it all. It started with your choice of clam, oyster, shrimp, or crabmeat cocktail, then moved on to a bucket of steamers—with broth to rinse them in and melted butter to dip them in—before getting to the main event, half a broiled lobster and half a broiled chicken. These came with fried potatoes (called julienne on the menu) and a vegetable, and either ice cream or pie for dessert, a hard decision as the ice cream came in huge round balls and the huckleberry pie was sensational.

> *The service at Lundy's was terrible. The saving grace was that the waiters used to bring plate after plate of hot biscuits. I used to split the biscuit, then split a pat of butter. I'd put half of the butter pat on the top half of the biscuit, and half the butter on the bottom, then wolf them down.*
> —LEONARD MARCUS, *who was born in Brooklyn three years before the restaurant opened*

My family always ordered a la carte—fried shrimp, fried oysters, broiled whatever, the humongous chopped steak, Lyonnaise potatoes, and, my favorite, the thick and creamy Clam Bisque, which was Lundy's sly name for New England clam chowder. At Lundy's, the red chowder, our local, Manhattan Clam Chowder, was simply called chowder.

And then there were the biscuits. It's what everyone remembers most about Lundy's. First thing, the waiters brought you tiny biscuits piled on a white plate. The butter was in hard pats on waxed white cardboard squares. It melted quickly enough, since the biscuits were hot. It was a divine combination.

Tragic is the only word to describe what became of the Lundy family, however. In the early 1970s, the restaurant was plagued with robberies. During one, Irving's nephew George Higgins was badly injured, and George's son, Bruce, was grazed by a bullet. In 1974, during another robbery, George had Irving lock himself into his apartment above the restaurant—with his fourteen Irish setters—while he started shooting at the supposed burglars. Unfortunately, George was shooting at the police. A year later, George's parents—Irving's sister and brother-in-law—were murdered in their home in Forest Hills in Queens. Irving died a year later at the age of eighty-two. He was found slumped over in his office by his long-time chauffeur and companion, Ciro Autorino, who later was found to have staged all those robberies and to have embezzled and defrauded Irving Lundy to the tune of eleven million dollars.

The Lundy's that is open now in Sheepshead Bay is a faint shadow of its former self, but at least the last time I tried them, the biscuits were awfully good.

MANHATTAN CLAM CHOWDER

No one really knows who made the first clam chowder with tomatoes, the chowder known as Manhattan. New Englanders, mainly those from Massachusetts and Maine, whose chowder is enriched with cream (or evaporated milk in more modern recipes), laugh at the folly of a tomato-flavored chowder. Neighboring Connecticut and Rhode Island, however, states with New England coast credentials as valid as Cape Cod, make chowder without either cream or tomatoes. The traditional Rhode Island chowder is a gray clam broth with nothing more than salt pork, potato, and, interestingly, thyme as the seasoning, the same as New York City's. Indeed, some Rhode Island chowderheads speculate that Manhattan chowder is really a variant of Rhode Island chowder, the chopped tomatoes a contribution of Rhode Island's large Italian-American community, most of whom hail from the tomato-rich Italian south. But, there are other theories, too.

Whatever the origin, clam chowder made with tomatoes and thyme was popular in the Coney Island, Brighton Beach, and Manhattan Beach hotel restaurants of the 1880s to the turn of the century. When Coney Island became the beach resort of the people streaming off the new subway lines in 1921, Manhattan Clam Chowder really took off. (I have also read a few references to caraway being the seasoning in Coney Island Chowder.)

My grandfather, Bernard (Barney) Schwartz was a professional Manhattan Clam Chowder chef. During the Depression, after he had lost his restaurant business, he sold chowder, along with some other bar foods of the day, off a pushcart to bars and grills. I watched him make chowder many times, along with his other specialties—pickles, coleslaw, and potato salad. He always insisted on using really big chowder clams, never Littlenecks or Cherrystones, which he put through the meat grinder. I have tried making chowder with the smaller clams, but Barney was right. The result tastes more like vegetable soup than clam chowder. You need the strong flavor of big clams to make this work.

Serves about 8

2 dozen large chowder clams, well-washed
4 ounces bacon or salt pork, cut into
 ½-inch pieces
2 tablespoons vegetable oil
2 medium onions, cut into ¼-inch dice
1 medium carrot, cut into ¼-inch dice
1 large rib celery, cut into ¼-inch dice
1 large green pepper, cut into ¼-inch dice

1½ pounds potatoes, cut into ½-inch
 cubes (about 3 cups)
1 (28-ounce) can peeled plum tomatoes, with
 their juice, the tomatoes coarsely chopped
1 teaspoon dried thyme
1 large bay leaf
Freshly ground black pepper
Salt to taste

In a 5-quart pot, combine the clams and 6 cups of cold water. Cover and place over high heat. When the water begins to boil, uncover the pot and boil the clams until they open, 2 to 3 minutes.

Remove the clams from their shells. Set aside in a large bowl.

Strain the broth through a sieve lined with a few layers of cheesecloth or a tightly woven cloth napkin. Leave behind any sand that may have settled in the pot. You should have slightly less than 8 cups of liquid. Set aside.

Rinse out the 5-quart pot and dry it.

Put the bacon or salt pork in the pot and cook over medium-low heat until some of the fat has rendered and the meat has lost its raw color.

Add the diced onion, carrot, celery, and green pepper. Toss well, then cook over medium heat until the vegetables are well wilted, 10 to 12 minutes.

Add the potatoes and the reserved and strained clam broth. Bring to a boil, then adjust heat so broth just simmers. Cook until the potatoes are tender, about 15 minutes.

Add the chopped tomatoes, the thyme, and the bay leaf. Continue to simmer another 30 minutes or so, until the vegetables are very tender.

Meanwhile, push the clams through the medium blade of a meat grinder, or finely chop them in a food processor.

When the chowder has cooked for half an hour, add the clams, then shut off the heat.

Add freshly ground pepper to taste. Correct the salt—the chowder may not need any because clams are salty, and the tomatoes have salt, but usually it does.

The chowder is much better when it is allowed to stand for several hours, or refrigerated overnight, then gently reheated just to the simmering point.

Serve very hot.

davy jones **SEA FOOD** house   1279 SIXTH AVENUE, AT 51st STREET / RADIO CITY 19, NEW YORK

OYSTER PAN ROAST

One of New York City's greatest gastronomic attractions, and one of its greatest indoor sights of any kind, is "the bar" at the Grand Central Oyster Bar, where watching the cooks prepare the pan roasts and seafood stews is as beautiful and engrossing as sitting in the audience of the New York City Ballet. The cooks work as gracefully as dancers, using the antique steam-sleeved swivel pots as their partners, to make old dishes as delicious as any new dishes in town. The silvery pots are stationary, but they can be tipped, so their contents can be poured into big white bowls lined with toast. The pan roasts of oysters and clams is among the oldest dishes still served in New York City, dating from the second decade of the twentieth century, when Heinz ketchup and chili sauce were still new, cutting-edge ingredients. The shrimp, scallop, and mixed seafood versions they now serve at the Oyster Bar are newer, but no less wonderful.

Serves 1

2 tablespoons unsalted butter

2 tablespoons to ¼ cup oyster or clam juices

8 to 10 Bluepoint oysters or small clams
    (Littlenecks or Cherrystones), shucked

1 generous tablespoon Heinz chili sauce

1 teaspoon Worcestershire sauce

Dash of celery salt

½ cup heavy cream

4 toast points: 2 slices firm white bread,
    toasted, cut diagonally to form triangles

1 teaspoon butter, in a pat (optional)

Sweet paprika

In a 1-quart saucepan, or in the top of a double boiler over boiling water, combine the 2 tablespoons butter, the oyster or clam juices, the oysters or clams, chili sauce, Worcestershire sauce, and celery salt.

Stir briskly and heat until the mixture simmers around the edge of the pan and the oysters or clams begin to curl around the edges. Add the cream and return to a simmer.

Pour the mixture into a bowl lined with the toast points. Top with a pat of butter, if using, and a liberal sprinkling of paprika.

Eat immediately.

CLAMS CASINO

Clams Casino is one of the most enduring dishes in New York City culinary history, at least in name. All kinds of baked clam dishes are now passed off as Clams Casino but it's a very specific baked clam dish—Littlenecks baked with shallot and bell pepper butter, topped with a piece of bacon. Recipes vary, with some adding a touch of anchovy to the butter, some lemon juice, some both. Some recipes call for fresh green pepper, some only jarred (or canned) red pimiento, which is probably the ingredient that was used when the dish was created for a society ladies' luncheon. Or so the story goes.

It was 1917, and Mrs. Paran Stevens was planning her party at the Casino Club on Narragansett Pier, with its views of the Palisades of New Jersey. She asked Julius Keller, the maître d', to create something special, something her jaded friends had never eaten before. As restaurateurs often did then to flatter important customers, she expected him to name it after her—Clams Stevens, one must suppose. Obviously, Keller named it after his club instead.

Serves 4

Placing the clams on a bed of salt looks polished and professional, suitable for a fancy meal. It also keeps the clams steady, preventing tip-overs and the loss of precious butter. But the clams cook just as well if placed directly on a metal pan. Just be careful as you carry them from oven to table.

The recipe was originally made with pimiento, the canned product. Today's tastes demand fresher flavor. Cooked with fresh ingredients, the green and red peppers will still have crunch. You can also use all red pepper and no green, or any color combo you like.

3 tablespoons finely minced shallots
¼ cup finely minced raw green bell pepper
¼ cup finely minced raw or roasted red bell pepper
Coarse salt

2 dozen raw Littleneck clams on the half shell
Juice of ½ lemon
½ cup (1 stick) unsalted butter
2 slices bacon, each cut into 12 pieces

Preheat the oven to 450 degrees.

In a small bowl, combine the shallots and the green and red peppers. Toss to combine well.

Spread a thick bed of salt in a baking pan large enough to accommodate all the clams, or in 4 individual pans, such as small pie plates or gratin dishes.

Arrange the clams in the dish(es). Put a couple of drops of lemon juice on each clam.

Cut off 1 teaspoon of butter at a time and dredge it very well in the shallot-pepper mixture, pressing the vegetables into the butter. Put the butter under a clam.

Place a piece of bacon on top of each clam. Bake until the bacon has crisped, 8 to 10 minutes. Serve immediately.

BROILED CLAM BELLIES

These were a specialty of Gage & Tollner until its very last day of operation on February 15, 2004. At one time, soft-bellied clams were available in local waters. After they were depleted, clams from Ipswich, Massachusetts, were used. The restaurant also fried these clams, as they do in New England, but a generous drizzling of butter makes these broiled clams almost as crisp as the fried version (though broiling doesn't decrease the fat at all). The original presentation is as below, on toast points. For its last few years in business, however, the restaurant served the clams on a bed of julienned vegetables drenched in beurre blanc and placed in a small hard-shell clam shell.

Serve 2 to 4

2 dozen Ipswich clams, shucked
Unseasoned breadcrumbs
½ cup melted butter

Toast points: 3 slices white bread, toasted, cut diagonally to form triangles
Lemon wedges

Preheat the broiler to high.

Dredge the clams in the breadcrumbs to coat well.

Arrange the clams in pie plates (you will need two), keeping them well separated.

Drizzle the butter over the clams.

Place the clams under the broiler, about 5 inches from the heat source. Broil for 2 minutes.

Serve on toast points with lemon wedges on the side.

Gage & Tollner opened in Brooklyn in 1879. The gas-lit interior is a designated landmark.

LUNDY'S BISCUITS

These have been taste-tested by a number of people with strong memories of Lundy's, including me. Are they the same as our old beloved Brooklyn biscuits? Does it matter when they are so delicious they have the same effect? You can't stop eating them.

The recipe was developed by food writer and radio broadcaster Kathy Gunst, who lives in Maine but has Brooklyn roots. It is in the cookbook called *Lundy's* that she wrote with Robert Cornfield, a native of Sheepshead Bay. They are, as Kathy says, a fluffy biscuit with an almost crunchy exterior.

Makes about 14

To get the full effect, these must be served the second they come out of the oven, and with chilled pats of butter. You might say these were almost an *amuse gueule* at Lundy's. You ate them before anything else, while you were waiting for everything else. As with all baked goods that you want to be tender, handle the dough lightly and as little as possible.

1½ cups plus 3 tablespoons all-purpose flour
1 tablespoon baking powder
1 tablespoon sugar
½ teaspoon salt

¼ cup unsalted butter (½ stick)
¼ cup shortening
½ cup milk

Preheat the oven to 375 degrees.

Sift the flour, baking powder, sugar, and salt into a large bowl. Stir well.

Cut the butter and shortening into small pieces and add to the flour mixture. Using your hands or, better, a pastry blender, crumble the fat into the flour mixture until the butter and shortening are pea-sized pieces and the rest of the mixture resembles coarse cornmeal.

Add the milk and mix the dough just until it comes together. Be careful not to over-mix.

Knead the dough gently on a lightly floured work surface.

Roll out the dough ½ inch thick. This is a crucial step in making successful biscuits. If you roll the dough out too thin, the biscuits will be dry and over-cooked. If you roll the dough out too thick, they will not cook properly.

Using a 2-inch biscuit cutter, or a sharp-edged, 2-inch-wide glass, cut out the biscuits.

Place the biscuits on an ungreased baking sheet. Knead the scraps together, roll the dough out to a ½-inch thickness, and cut any additional biscuits. (Position them so you can identify them later: they will be less tender than the main batch.)

Bake in the preheated oven for 14 to 15 minutes, or until the biscuits are golden brown.

Serve hot.

CHAPTER 3
DELMONICO'S

A GROWING CITY

DELMONICO'S WAS FRENCH, HAUGHTY, PRETENTIOUS, AND EXPENSIVE. And, for nearly one hundred years, by dint of Delmonico's existence, New York could claim it was a civilized city.

When the Erie Canal opened in 1825, it rapidly changed New York City from a rough backwater town into an international center of commerce and wealth. John Delmonico, born Giovanni Del Monico in the canton of Ticino, near the Italian border of Switzerland, saw it coming. In 1824, at the age of thirty-six, he had accumulated enough wealth as a sea captain to retire, settle in New York City, and start a wine importing business near the Battery. He bought bulk wines in Spain and France, then bottled and sold it in New York. Seeing the growth of the city around him, he soon returned to Switzerland to get his brother Peter (or Pietro) to emigrate, too. Peter was a pastry chef, and also being a prudent man Peter had saved some money. Together, with Peter's wife, the brothers returned to New York City to establish a fine pastry and confectionery shop and cafe. Of course they sold John's imported wines as well.

That first Delmonico's opened on December 13, 1827, at 23 William Street, then expanded next door into 25 William Street. In 1830 it became a full-fledged "Restaurant Français," modeled on those that were becoming popular in Europe. The last Delmonico's closed in 1923, a few years after Prohibition began. The restaurant said it couldn't possibly continue to serve fine French cuisine without wines to accompany it. At least that was the public statement. Business had already been declining for years.

From the day it opened to the day it closed it was the highest level and most influential restaurant in New York City. It spawned legends, myths, and recipes, not to mention waiters, maître d's, and chefs who opened their own restaurants or carried the Delmonico standards on to other establishments. Every time the restaurant moved to a new location, which was frequent, its management, with the best architects, decorators, and chefs of their day, made innovations that we now take for granted, think of as clichés, or still find startlingly fresh. Whatever the case, Delmonico's is still very much with us.

It is hard to imagine that one family and one establishment could have had such an immense impact, and for such a long time, but the Delmonico family was very unusual. It was creative yet conservative, obsessed with quality and proper service, incredibly hard working, and, perhaps its greatest asset, it was always very well capitalized. The Delmonico family understood money, people, and food—all you need to know as a New York City restaurateur.

Delmonico's created the standard for civilized restaurant behavior in a city of rushed eaters. By the end of the 1820s, Europeans, mainly import-export traders, came in droves to New York City, the new economic center of the United States, and they flocked to Delmonico & Brother (as the cafe was then called). Peter Delmonico's pastries were apparently superior to anything in the city, but another attraction was the presence of Peter's wife, who acted as cashier. A woman working in a restaurant was then unheard of in New York City and could have perhaps been considered risqué. To the Europeans who were accustomed to such family enterprises, however, it was reassuring. John managed the business and, in white apron and cap, worked out front as the counterman, apparently charming the guests as well. Behind the scenes Peter made his French pastry.

The cafe and pastry shop started with six small pine tables and chairs to match. On one side of the room was a counter covered in white table linen. The day's cakes and pastries were arranged there. Aside from the pastries that Peter confected, the shop sold coffee, chocolate, bonbons, orgeats (almond milk drinks), bavaroises (gelled custards), wines, liquors, and "fancy ices."

By the summer of 1831, the two brothers needed more help to run the business. Luckily John and Peter had another brother, Francesco (or François), whom they had left in Switzerland. Francesco agreed to send his nineteen-year-old son, Lorenzo, to help work in the family business. Lorenzo Delmonico arrived on September 1, 1831, and began work immediately. For the next forty years, Lorenzo guided the restaurant to international status and a reputation for excellence that was not matched by a New York City restaurant until the late twentieth century. In Lorenzo's day, Delmonico's was compared favorably, even by Frenchmen, to the best restaurants in Paris.

Delmonico's was also the first successful a la carte restaurant in the country, as opposed to the taverns, inns, or hotels where the dining room was an adjunct to some other operation, and the customer ate what was served by the host or proprietor. In these dining rooms there were no choices except among those plates put on the table, meals were at set times, and customers were charged a flat rate. On the other hand, customers could go to Delmonico's at any time and order from a list of dishes, a menu. And they could order as few or as many dishes as they wanted. Moreover, with the a la carte restaurant model the price of each dish was indicated separately, so you could also spend as little or as much as you wanted.

The convenience of these innovations was an immediate hit with the merchants who lunched and dined at Delmonico's in the early years. Meals could be taken at convenient times during the day, and the choices were not merely a few daily "specials," but an immense menu. Before long, the Delmonico system was copied by others in New York City, and in other

American cities. Restaurants run on the a la carte plan became fixtures in American life, the grand life at any rate.

Neither of the Delmonico brothers was trained as a chef, but that didn't matter because the prosperity in New York City, and the much heralded opportunities available here, were attracting Europeans of all trades, including French chefs. The Delmonicos must have paid well because they attracted the best cooking talent. New Yorkers were astonished by the kitchen's finesse and "subtle sauces."

Good French cooking wasn't the only appeal of the restaurant. The Delmonicos introduced New York City to vegetables then unknown, such as eggplant, endive, artichokes, and tomatoes. They were fanatics about quality and as early as 1834 they were finding fault with the produce they could buy at the Washington Market and other public markets, which each year was coming from farmlands further and further from Manhattan. They decided to grow their own. They bought two hundred and twenty acres in Williamsburg, which was then still a town unto itself on Long Island. (Williamsburg did not become part of Brooklyn until 1855.) They built a large stone house, stables, and other outbuildings—it was their country seat. And they grew vegetables for the restaurant.

Also in 1834, the brothers purchased a lodging house at 76 Broad Street. A lodging house in those days was not a hotel in the modern sense, since most of the house guests were long-term residents. These included foreign businessmen who remained in America for a year or more. As was the custom with lodging houses of the day, all guests were provided regular meals in the "ordinary" form. The word "ordinary" was an alternate for "tavern" in the seventeenth and eighteenth centuries, and the lodging house continued the habits of the "ordinary" meals—all guests were given the same meal, served at set times, whether it be breakfast, lunch, or dinner. This lodging house was soon to prove more important than the Delmonico's realized. Disaster was about to strike. On December 16, 1835, a devastating fire swept across New York City. The fire destroyed much of lower Manhattan, including all of the old Dutch buildings (what was left) and the William Street Delmonicos. The 76 Broad Street house was not damaged, however, and the Delmonicos were able to continue operating from that address while they rebuilt.

By that point, Lorenzo was actively managing the business with his uncles, and he viewed the fire more as an opportunity than a disaster. The William

This image from Delmonico's last restaurant has become highly collectible.

Street addresses were rentals, and it was time, he thought, for the family to own property. So, in August of 1836 he bought a parcel on the oddly angled corner of Beaver Street and South William Street and began the construction of a new Delmonico's, specifically built as a very grand restaurant. The building went up quickly by today's standards, and in August of the following year, Delmonico's reopened at 2 South William Street, in a building that has since been rebuilt (but still houses a restaurant called Delmonico's, although it has no relation whatsoever to the original). The building was three and a half stories high, and the entrance was flanked by marble columns supposedly from ancient Pompeii. These columns are still there. They were salvaged from the original building and incorporated into the newer one.

The first and second floors featured large dining rooms decorated with inlaid floors and, of course, opulent furnishings and decorations. The third floor held several private dining rooms, as well as the kitchen. The cellar included wine vaults stocked with sixteen thousand bottles of French wine. For the first time, the brothers gave it the name Delmonico's Restaurant, while the public soon called it the Citadel.

Celebrities from around the world were drawn to the Citadel to enjoy Delmonico's famous elegance, service, and cuisine. The brothers hired John Lux as chef de cuisine. For fifteen years, he provided culinary excellence while Lorenzo himself always tried to learn about the most fashionable trends in Parisian dining.

"Gallic inventions, when transferred to Delmonico's kitchens, often proved superior to their prototypes at Paris, because Delmonico's cooks considered themselves ambassadors charged with upholding the honor of their national cuisine; and in fulfilling this mission they were able to draw upon the greater abundance of fine foodstuffs available in America. Finally, their very nostalgia for France spurred them to intenser efforts," wrote Lately Thomas, in his book *Delmonico's*.

For five years, the restaurant's fame and fortune grew. Then, on November 10, 1842, John died suddenly. After being closed four days, the following notice was printed in the newspapers:

The establishment will be reopened today under the same firm of Delmonico Brothers, and no pains of the bereft family will be spared to give general satisfaction. Restaurant, bar-room [cafe] and private dinners. No. 2 South William Street, furnished rooms No. 76 Broad Street, as usual.

There were some eyebrows raised by that notice. It seemed as if the family was more interested in money and business than in mourning the loss of the dynasty's founder. But this was New York City. Sentiment was and still is superceded by business.

In any case, Lorenzo was twenty-nine years old and had pretty much been managing the restaurant and lodging house himself. Lorenzo kept a consistent schedule. Today we might say he was obsessive-compulsive, although that is a virtuous neurosis for a restaurateur. Every morning he would arrive at the market at four o'clock to supervise the purchase of meat, game, vegetables, and other necessities for the restaurant. At exactly eight, he would return to the restaurant with his purchases. There he would smoke a cigar and, at precisely nine in the morning, he walked home and slept. At six o'clock in the evening he returned to the restaurant to greet guests and supervise the dining room until midnight.

On July 19, 1845, another great fire swept through the city. The Citadel survived, but this time the lodging house did not. Lorenzo, ever the optimist and opportunist, reacted to the destruction of the building by opening a new hotel. On June 1, 1846, the Delmonico Hotel opened at Broadway and Morris Street, just north of Bowling Green. This was the only hotel that was ever operated by the Delmonicos. (The Delmonico Hotel that opened on Park Avenue and Fifty-ninth Street in 1929 was not run by the family.) And it was the first major hotel in the United States to be operated on the European rather than the American plan. Under the American system, guests paid one price for room and board, while under the European system, the room and meals were priced separately, and meals were a la carte rather than "ordinary."

Around this time Lorenzo's uncle Peter was losing interest in the business. In 1848, Peter retired and sold his half interest to Lorenzo. Without the conservative encumbrances of his uncle to deal with, Lorenzo spread his flamboyant wings and the truly grand era of Delmonico's began. The hotel was a huge success. One of its innovations was a true bar, as we know it today. Although the French-style cafe that the Delmonicos had become famous for served wine and liquor, as well as coffee and pastries, American men preferred a room where only alcohol was consumed.

BELOW: Delmonico's made it acceptable for women to dine out; even without men.

Eventually, the Delmonico's bar overshadowed its cafe.

As prescient as his uncle John, who saw in 1824 that New York City was becoming an international metropolis, Lorenzo noted that the city center was continuing to move north, and he decided to follow. In 1856, he opened a new restaurant on the corner of Broadway and Chambers Street, across from City Hall. At the same time, he changed the Citadel at South William Street, gearing it up for more lunch business in what had become New York City's financial district—Wall Street.

The Chambers Street restaurant was an immediate success with several segments of New Yorkers: the politicians, the lawyers, stockbrokers, and bankers at dinner, and the social set—the "select crowd"—for late dining and private parties. The "select crowd" were those who "keep carriages, live above Bleecker, are subscribers to the opera, go to Grace Church, have a town house and country house, give balls and parties," according to Nathaniel P. Willis, editor of *The Home Journal* at the time.

Many other restaurants were now providing good French cuisine, but Delmonico's had a cachet of its own. It wasn't about food. Delmonico's knew how to serve rich people, and they made a point of having the highest prices in town. Having the highest prices around not only kept out the people you did not want, but it became a marketing ploy that has been used effectively ever since in New York City.

Following his clientele even further north, Lorenzo opened another Delmonico's on April 9, 1862, in a converted mansion at 1 East Fourteenth Street, on the corner of Fifth Avenue, one block from Union Square. A *Tribune* reporter wrote (as quoted by Lately Thomas), "As New York spreads herself, so must the House of Delmonico dilate." The new place housed a cafe, as well as a restaurant. The cafe was called "the best club in town." *The New York World* described it as:

the resort of more native and foreign notabilities than perhaps any other place in the city. There distinguished literary and political persons stop daily to sip the matutinal cocktail, the anti-prandial sherry-and-bitters, and the evening 'pony.' There the Wall Street magnates drop in on their way uptown to sip the insidious mint-julep, or quaff the foaming champagne cocktail. There the Frenchman, Spaniard, and Italian may have their absinthe, the American his Bourbon straight, the Englishman his half-and-half. Morning, noon, and evening the place is alive with a chattering, good-natured, oft-imbibing throng of domestic and imported celebrities.

By the late 1860s, one conspicuous change at Delmonico's was the presence of women in the restaurant, although never in the cafe and never without an escort in the restaurant. Until then, respectable women would not be seen in a public eating room.

In May of 1862, one month after the Fourteenth Street Delmonico's opened, Lorenzo Delmonico hired Charles Ranhofer (see page 56) as the chef de cuisine. Ranhofer followed

Alessandro Filippini, an Italian-born chef, who had been Delmonico's top chef through the 1850s. Apparently Filippini had had enough of the kitchen, but not the Delmonico family or the restaurant business. He remained in the Delmonico's employ as the manager. Ranhofer turned out to be the greatest French chef America ever knew until, some might argue, very recently.

Lorenzo opened yet another restaurant in 1865, at 22 Broad Street, so there were four Delmonico's. This time Lorenzo selected a cousin, John Longhi, to manage the new restaurant. Each restaurant had a distinct clientele. The Fourteenth Street and Fifth Avenue restaurants drew society types. Chambers Street drew politicians, merchants, lawyers, and brokers. The Citadel at South William and Beaver Street drew bankers and shipping magnates, while the new Broad Street restaurant drew stockbrokers and other financial operators.

Following the growth of the city, and the ever-more northern edge that the rich called home, Delmonico's moved again in 1876, to Madison Square. Other hotels and some theaters had opened there already. Lorenzo closed the Fourteenth Street restaurant and opened on Twenty-sixth Street, but still on fashionable Fifth Avenue. The building took up the south side of Twenty-sixth Street between Fifth and Broadway. Big windows in the first floor restaurant famously faced Fifth Avenue and the little park of Madison Square. In the 1932 Edna Ferber and George Kaufman play, *Dinner at Eight*, Carlotta Vance, a faded grand dame of the theater played by Marie Dressler in the hit 1933 movie version, wistfully reminisces about lunching at Delmonico's with that very view.

About the same time that Delmonico's opened on Madison Square, Lorenzo closed Chambers Street's and opened a much larger and vastly grander multi-story restaurant complex at 112 and 114 Broadway, near Pine Street. He apparently knew what he was doing since the new restaurant prospered from the moment it opened. A tribute to Lorenzo's public relations abilities and to the newsworthiness of anything he did, descriptions of the new Delmonico's filled the newspapers. In fact, there were numerous innovations worth reporting. A sub-cellar was built for storage, and the basement was taken by the bakery. "Open, airy, pleasant" kitchens were placed on the top floors, and a system of dumbwaiters carried the food to the dining rooms below. On the ground floor was a quick service counter. The proper dining room was a few steps up from the ground floor with lace curtained windows facing Broadway. On the floor above the grand public dining room were private dining rooms. On the fourth floor, there was a dining hall for workers in the Equitable Building. They went back and forth through doorways that were cut into their adjoining walls. It is said that more than a thousand people a day ate there.

On September 3, 1881, Lorenzo Delmonico died at the age of sixty-eight. The newspapers ran laudatory obituaries. *The Sun* said that he "raised the standards of hotel and restaurant kitchens" and it credited him with a "general improvement in our cookery." The *New York Times* said,

"For many years the name of Delmonico had been everywhere received as the synonym for perfection in gastronomy. Delmonico dinners are famous the world over."

By 1890, all that was left was Twenty-sixth Street and the Citadel. But in 1896, following Delmonico tradition, the family announced that it was moving Delmonico's uptown again, this time to Fifth Avenue and Forty-fourth Street. As the city center continued to move north, the rich people continued to move even further north. Where the rich went, the Delmonicos followed. They were one of them by now.

And the Delmonicos also continued to innovate on Forty-fourth Street. When it opened on November 15 of the following year, smoking was permitted in the dining room. Previously, smoking had been permitted only in the men's cafe and various retiring rooms. The change was supposedly encouraged by Delmonico's women customers. Many resented the fact that the men would leave them at the table after dinner to smoke in other rooms. With smoking allowed in the dining room, they felt the men wouldn't abandon them after dessert. It was the height of the woman's suffrage movement.

In 1917, the South William Street restaurant was closed and the property was sold. Long "obituaries" for the restaurant appeared in the newspapers. In 1919, a continuing battle between the siblings and owners flared anew and a bankruptcy was filed in U.S. District Court. That year the last remaining Delmonico's Restaurant was sold to a restaurateur named Edward L.C. Robins. Unfortunately, the transfer took place on the very day that Prohibition went into effect.

Prohibition brought an immediate and vast change in the eating habits of the wealthy. Long and elaborately prepared meals were not possible at restaurants, so the wealthy no longer ate at Delmonico's or other restaurants. Instead, they enlarged their kitchens at home and entertained there with the help of private cooks. At home, the wealthy had their own wine cellars—as often as not stocked from the cellars of their favorite restaurants, which had been forced to dispose of their holdings. The emerging middle class dealt with the war and Prohibition by changing their entertainment habits away from restaurants and toward private clubs, dance halls, burlesque houses, and (soon) the movies. As they say, jazz and gin ruled the age.

In April of 1921, Delmonico's Restaurant was raided by "Dry Agents," who arrested a waiter and manager for serving vodka and gin. On May 21, 1923, a final dinner was held at Delmonico's Restaurant. The new owner realized the impossibility of continuing the business. The last banquet at the Forty-fourth Street restaurant featured mineral water with dinner.

> *The two most remarkable bits of scenery in the States are undoubtedly Delmonico's and the Yosemite Valley, and the former place has done more to promote a good feeling between England and America than anything else in [that] country.*
> —PALL MALL GAZETTE

Chef Charles Ranhofer's monumental cookbook (opposite) and his vast Forty-fourth Street kitchen, 1902.

CHARLES RANHOFER

Charles Ranhofer was the chef at Delmonico's from 1862 to 1896, with a break of three years, and during those thirty-four years he set the standards for classic French cuisine in New York City. Those standards were maintained until Prohibition began in 1920 and not regained until fairly recently. The Ranhofer years were during the Gilded Age in America, with its incomparable wealth and ostentation, and they were the Golden Age of French cuisine in New York City. It was said, even by French visitors, that you could eat at least as well at Delmonico's as in Paris.

During the Ranhofer years, Delmonico's had a seven-page menu, written in French and English, and a wine cellar that stocked the best Bordeaux and Burgundy of France. Ranhofer was responsible for many recipes which continue to be famous, such as Baked Alaska (see page 64), which he created in 1867 to celebrate the purchase of Alaska from Russia; Eggs Benedict (see page 62), which, as the legend goes, he created to please a customer, and Lobster Newberg (see page 58), which also has an amusing story attached to its creation.

In 1894, Ranhofer published *The Epicurean*, a treatise on food with 1,183 pages and more than 3,500 recipes. American food historians note with glee that it was not until 1903, almost a decade after Ranhofer's book, that Auguste Escoffier, perhaps the most famous French chef and food author in history, working for Caesar Ritz at his many European hotels, published his *Le Guide Culinaire*.

Ranhofer was born in 1836 in Saint-Denis, France. He was the son and grandson of chefs, and at age twelve, he was sent to Paris to apprentice. By the time he was sixteen, he was chef to an Alsatian prince.

He moved to New York in 1856 and immediately began trying to convert the American dining public, declaring, "It is a wonder that you have not ruined the nation's digestion with your careless cooking and hasty eating!" Ranhofer is also reported to have said in one contemporary article, "I must teach you something."

His first job was with the Russian consul, with whom he went to Washington, D.C., then New Orleans. After returning briefly to France in 1860, he came back to New York City as the chef at Delmonico's chief competition, Maison Doree. It wasn't just on the gastronomic level that they competed. The Civil War was raging and those most supportive of the Union ate at Maison Dorée while those with less political conviction ate at the more elitist Delmonico's. Lorenzo Delmonico saw the public relations advantage of hiring Ranhofer away when he opened his new location on Fourteenth Street and Fifth Avenue. Lorenzo, a man who was not easily intimidated, said of Ranhofer, as quoted by Lately Thomas in his book *Delmonico's*, "He was perfect in dress and manner, and his attitude was such as to make me feel that he was doing me a great favor by coming into my employment."

Ranhofer was a true man of the world and besides laying down some rules of menu design that are accepted as basic today—sauces and meats should not be repeated within a menu, foods should be eaten in their respective seasons, preserved foods should be used only when you have preserved them yourself and no others can be obtained—he was open to new ingredients. Game played a big part on his menus, because there was so much of it still available in local habitats. *The Epicurean* contains recipes for canvasback, redhead, mallard, and teal ducks along with prairie hen. Bear steaks are recommended, with the note, "bear's meat when young can be broiled and after it is cooked has much the same flavor as beef." He included recipes for strictly American dishes, such as jambalaya and gumbo. He has non-French foreign dishes, such as blinis, *kugelhopfen*, risotto, and borscht. He knew enough about Chinese bird's nest soup to distinguish between nests from the Philippines and those from China. A recipe also appears that puts soy sauce in a red wine and stock reduction.

A formal dinner, as Ranhofer laid it out, always started with oysters. Then there were two soups, a clear one and a thick one. Next came a fish course, then "removes," which were elaborately presented meat courses accompanied by vegetables that people ate at their discretion before they were removed from the table. Then came entrees of plated meats accompanied by a vegetable followed by punch or sherbets as an intermezzo course. Then roasts, although they were often not roasts at all but novelty items, served just in case you were still hungry. Also there were cold dishes, such as terrines and salads. Finally, there were sweets: hot desserts, cold desserts, fresh fruit, candies, and "fancy cakes," what we call petit fours.

LOBSTER NEWBERG

Lobster Newberg leads the pantheon of classic New York City dishes. For about a hundred years, from its creation at Delmonico's in the mid-1870s until the coming of nouvelle cuisine in the 1970s, you could always find a form of Newberg on New York City menus. The spelling might have been Newburg or Newburgh, and instead of lobster, the seafood could have been shrimp, crab, a seafood mixture, a lobster cake, or a seafood or fish cake. The sauce could be flavored with either Madeira or Sherry. It started as an elegant restaurant dish and ended up in cookbooks for homemakers, sometimes with a béchamel-based sauce—eventually with one made from a can of soup. For the record, this is Charles Ranhofer's version, exactly as written in his monumental work, *The Epicurean*. He also called the dish Lobster Delmonico.

Cook six lobsters each weighing about two pounds in boiling salted water for twenty-five minutes. Twelve pounds of live lobster when cooked yields from two to two and a half pounds of meat with three to four ounces of coral. When cold detach the bodies from the tails and cut the latter into slices, put them into a sautoir, each piece lying flat, and add hot clarified butter; season with salt and fry lightly on both sides without coloring; moisten to their height with good raw cream; reduce quickly to half; and then add two or three spoonfuls of Madeira wine; boil the liquid once more only, then remove and thicken with a thickening of egg yolks and raw cream. Cook without boiling, incorporating a little cayenne and butter; then arrange the pieces in a vegetable dish and pour the sauce over.

The story of Lobster Newberg is possibly even more delicious than the dish itself, which is saying something. It all started on an evening in 1876. Ben Wenberg, a wealthy sea captain who plied the fruit trade between New York City and Cuba, was also a regular at Delmonico's on Fourteenth Street and later at Twenty-sixth Street. One time he came in for dinner and told Charles Ranhofer about a new way he had learned to cook lobster. The captain showed Delmonico's staff how to do it. He ordered from the kitchen a freshly boiled lobster, sweet cream, clarified sweet butter, cognac, and sherry. Then he provided, from a silver snuff box, the secret ingredient. The procedure must have been pretty much the way Ranhofer outlines it above. Naturally, as soon as the great chef tasted the dish, he pronounced positively that the secret ingredient was cayenne pepper. The dish was added to the menu as Lobster à la Wenberg, and it was a hit.

Some months later, however, Wenberg had an argument with Charles Delmonico, and the restaurateur decided to remove the dish from his menu. If Wenberg was banished, so should be his namesake dish. Patrons, however, continued to demand it. (Today we would call it a signature dish.) Somehow though, it wasn't selling under its new name, Lobster Delmonico. Since no Delmonico would ever turn down a dollar for the sake of something as trivial as a personal grudge, Charles cleverly changed the spelling of the dish, simply reversing the *W* and the *N* in Wenberg's name—and plenty of Lobster Newberg was sold.

Serves 4 to 6 as a first course, 2 to 4 as a main course

This is one of those dishes that can be prepared in a chafing dish at the table. It was not done so originally, but it lends itself to drama. Although it requires good timing so as not to curdle the egg once it is added, the recipe is very simple, uses few ingredients, and the result is as rich and glamorous as can be.

Ranhofer makes no mention of serving the dish on toast points, but that would have been typical of the day, and a delicious way to serve it. The toast sops up the sauce and to some this is even better than the seafood

itself. White rice makes a good bed for Newberg, too. The ultimate presentation, however, and befitting such a grand dish, would be in puff pastry *vol-au-vents*, or, in a more modern mode, with a garnish of puff pastry shapes placed around the seafood and on the sauce.

To make the measuring and mixing a little easier, pour the full amount of cream in the recipe—1 cup—into a mixing cup. Pour out the first addition into the pan, then beat the egg yolks into the remaining cream right in the measuring cup.

2 tablespoons unsalted butter
3 to 3 ½ cups cooked lobster (from 2-pound lobsters; see Note), body meat cut into ½ -inch-thick crosswise slices (or medallions), claw meat cut into chunks

1 cup heavy cream
½ teaspoon salt, or to taste
2 egg yolks
3 tablespoons Madeira
⅛ teaspoon ground cayenne pepper, or to taste

In an 8- to 10-inch skillet, over medium-high heat, heat the butter until the foam begins to subside. Immediately add the lobster and sauté, turning all the pieces, for about 2 minutes.

Add ¾ cup of the cream and the salt. Stir and simmer for 2 minutes.

Meanwhile, beat the remaining ¼ cup cream together with the egg yolks.

Add the Madeira and cayenne pepper to the lobster and cream in the pan. Continue to simmer for another minute.

Stir a few tablespoons of the simmering cream mixture into the egg yolk and raw cream mixture.

Remove the lobster from the heat and, when the simmering subsides, stir in the egg yolk and cream mixture. Return the pan to low heat and stir until thickened, but not boiling.

Serve immediately.

Note: To cook lobster, bring a large pot of lightly salted water to a rolling boil. Add the lobster(s), head first, pushing the entire lobster under water if possible. Otherwise, wait until the lobster stops moving and then arrange it so it will be entirely under water. Cook for 12 minutes from the time the lobster is fully in the water. (Cook for about 15 minutes if you are eating the lobsters immediately, instead of cooking them further, as in this recipe.) Remove from the boiling water and let cool. The lobster can be refrigerated for up to 1 day.

Variation: For shrimp à la Newberg, substitute 1 pound jumbo shrimp (16 to 18 shrimp), shelled, for the lobster. Follow the directions exactly, sautéing the shrimp until they turn pink on both sides. For large, not jumbo, shrimp, this should take only about 1 minute, instead of 2.

DELMONICO POTATOES

There must be dozens of recipes published in books and on the internet that purport to be Delmonico Potatoes. At one time, the name Delmonico was such a seller in restaurants that chefs all over the country put Delmonico Potatoes (and Delmonico Steak) on their menus, simply creating a potato dish to go with the name. Some of these recipes list ingredients that have no business in a potato dish, such as rice; and some recipes include ingredients that didn't even exist when the dish was named, such as American cheese. To set the record straight, the following is the only recipe for Delmonico Potatoes that was ever set down by a chef from Delmonico's. It is in *The International Cook Book*, which was written by Alessandro Filippini, the great restaurant's second chef:

Place four good-sized boiled and finely handshed potatoes in a frying pan with one and a half gills cold milk, half gill cream, two saltspoons salt, one saltspoon white pepper, and a saltspoon grated nutmeg; mix well and cook on the range for ten minutes, lightly mixing occasionally. Then add one tablespoon grated Parmesan cheese, lightly mix again. Transfer the potatoes into a gratin dish, sprinkle another light tablespoon grated Parmesan cheese over and set in the oven to bake for six minutes, or until they have obtained a good golden color. Remove and serve.

So, in essence, Delmonico Potatoes is a gratin of potatoes seasoned lightly with Parmesan. Still, there is a mystery. We know how much was in a "saltspoon" and a "gill," but "handshed" poses questions when translating the original recipe into contemporary terms. Were the potatoes shredded? Were they cut into julienne? Were they sliced, say, on a mandolin? Were they cubed? I have tried all these methods, and followed the other directions exactly, and I think there is good reason for today's gratins always to be made with sliced potatoes. Slices layer neatly, they offer plenty of surface to absorb the milk and cream, they retain their shape, and they bake nicely into a unit, where the other shapes do not.

Serves 6 to 8

In the following recipe, I take some liberties with Filippini's published version. Perhaps potatoes were harder in those days, but the initial boiling is not necessary. Instead, I precook the peeled and sliced potatoes directly in milk. A mandolin or food processor makes slicing easy. I also use slightly more Parmesan, because today's palates demand more pronounced flavor. You can even add a few tablespoons more if you like.

8 medium Russet potatoes (about 3 pounds)	¼ teaspoon freshly grated nutmeg
3 cups whole milk	¼ cup freshly grated Parmesan cheese
2 teaspoons salt	½ cup heavy cream
Freshly ground black pepper to taste	2 tablespoons unsalted butter

Preheat the oven to 325 degrees. Generously butter a shallow 3-quart baking dish or gratin pan. I use an oval Pyrex that is 14 by 9 inches.

Peel the potatoes and place them in a big bowl of cold water as you do. Slice the potatoes into rounds about ⅛ inch thick. Spread on a towel. Do not put them back in the water.

In a large saucepan, combine the potatoes and the milk. Toss the potatoes in the milk. Add the salt, pepper, and nutmeg. Toss again. Cover and, over medium-low heat, bring slowly to a simmer; adjust the heat so the milk simmers very gently, then uncover the pot and cook for 10 minutes.

Sprinkle 1 tablespoon of the cheese evenly over the bottom of the prepared baking dish. Transfer half of the potatoes and milk to the baking dish, spreading them into an even layer. Sprinkle 1 tablespoon of the cheese over the potatoes in the dish and cover with the remaining potatoes and milk.

Pour the cream over the potatoes. The liquid in the dish should barely cover the top layer of potatoes. Add a tiny bit more cream, as necessary.

Sprinkle the remaining 2 tablespoons cheese evenly over the top and dot with the butter all over.

Bake on the middle rack of the oven for 1 to 1 ½ hours. The top should be nicely golden when done. The potatoes should offer no resistance when you push a fork into them. The liquid should be mostly absorbed, but there will be some looseness around the edges.

Remove from the oven and let rest for 10 minutes before serving, to allow the gratin to set and to continue absorbing liquid. The potatoes can be served very hot or warm. They can be reheated, covered with tinfoil, in a 325-degree oven, but they will not be as creamy as when freshly made.

(If you want to prepare the gratin somewhat ahead of time, it can be completely assembled, covered with plastic, then refrigerated for up to 1 day before it is baked.)

EGGS BENEDICT

There are two stories, or I should say two myths, about the origin of Eggs Benedict. In one, the dish was created at Delmonico's in 1892 or 1893 for a Mrs. LeGrand Benedict, an apocryphal name if there ever was one. In the other, this iconic dish of the American brunch was invented at the Waldorf-Astoria in 1894 for a Mr. Lemuel Benedict.

Both stories are pretty simple. In one, Mrs. Benedict wanted to eat something new and different at Delmonico's (as if the laundry list menu didn't provide enough variety) and with the help of the maître d'hotel, they came up with ham and poached eggs on an English muffin topped with Hollandaise. In the other story, equally apocryphal, Mr. Benedict, presumably not the husband of Mrs. Benedict, seeking a hangover cure, ordered toast, bacon, poached eggs and, on the side, a pitcher of hollandaise. The rich sauce was supposedly the active ingredient in this cure.

There may be a grain of truth in both stories, but the cold fact is that the great chef of Delmonico's, Charles Ranhofer, published the recipe in his magnum opus cookbook, *The Epicurean*, in 1893, casting doubt on the 1894 Waldorf story. He doesn't even call it Benedict. It's Eggs à la Benedick. There is even a small illustration of the dish inserted into the text of the recipe.

In Ranhofer's words:

Cut some muffins in halves crosswise, toast them without allowing to brown, then place a round of cooked ham an eighth of an inch thick and the same diameter as the muffins on each half. Heat in a moderate oven and put a poached egg on each toast. Cover the whole with hollandaise sauce.

Serves 2

Make the hollandaise sauce before starting the rest of the recipe. The sauce can be kept warm over hot water, either in a bowl over a pot or in a double boiler.

Warm hollandaise (recipe follows)
4 eggs
2 English muffins

4 (¼-inch-thick) slices ham, cut to the size of
    the muffin; or slices of Canadian bacon
    (cured pork loin)

Poach the eggs. Meanwhile, toast the muffins and gently heat the ham in a skillet. Do not let the ham dry out or brown.

When the eggs are cooked, place a slice of ham on each muffin half, then set a poached egg on top. Spoon the Hollandaise over the egg.

Serve immediately.

Variations: These days, instead of ham, other items are used as a base for the eggs, such as smoked salmon (very New York), sautéed or creamed spinach, prosciutto, lobster medallions, salt cod (baccalà), and so on.

HOLLANDAISE
(Makes about 1 cup)

This easily prepared and ever-reliable hollandaise recipe is from *Joy of Cooking*.

3 egg yolks
2 teaspoons fresh lemon juice, or to taste
Ground white pepper or hot red pepper sauce
    to taste

Salt to taste
½ cup unsalted butter, melted, kept very
    warm or hot

Place the egg yolks, lemon juice, white pepper, and salt in the jar of a blender. Blend on high speed for 1 minute.

With the machine running, add the butter in a slow, steady stream. By the time all of the butter has been added—about 1 minute—the sauce should be thick. If not, process on high speed for about 20 seconds more. Taste and adjust the seasonings.

Serve immediately or keep warm by submerging the blender jar in warm (not hot) water. Serve warm.

BAKED ALASKA

As they say on Madison Avenue, it's all about marketing. Here's another case in point, where a great dish went nowhere until it got the right name and the right spin.

In eighteenth-century France, long before it was dubbed Baked Alaska in New York City, there was *omelette à la norvégienne* meaning "Norwegian omelet," and *glace au four*, translating loosely as "ice in the oven." Both were desserts of sponge cake topped with ice cream, encased in meringue, and browned in the oven so the meringue was magically warm over the frozen cream. It was called Omelette Surprise, too, in 1804, by a Benjamin Thompson, an American physicist who invented a firegrate, double boiler, oil lamp, coffee percolator, and a kitchen range. He obviously had an interest in cooking technology, and his Omelette Surprise was the tour de force at demonstrations of his new home ovens.

It wasn't until 1867, however, that the dessert got the name and the pedigree by which it became an international classic. The celebrated chef Charles Ranhofer of Delmonico's served his version of the dessert to celebrate the U.S. purchase of Alaska from the Russians. At first, it was called Alaska-Florida Cake and nobody ordered it, but when it was renamed Baked Alaska it flew out of the kitchen.

Since then the dessert has always been associated with glamour, especially as Flaming Baked Alaska. In 1987, when the Joe Baum-Michael Whiteman Company reopened the Rainbow Room, Baked Alaska, brought to the table in full conflagration, was one of the retro attractions.

4 Individual Baked Alaskas

1 loaf-style pound cake
4 single-serving vanilla ice cream cups
4 egg whites, at room temperature
¼ teaspoon cream of tartar

½ cup superfine sugar
½ teaspoon vanilla extract
Confectioners' sugar

Cut the cake into ½-inch-thick slices so that you will have enough cake surface to cut out rounds the size of the ice cream cup lids.

Using a lid as a guide, cut out 4 cake rounds.

Using a sharp scissors or a knife, cut the cups away from the ice cream. Turn the ice cream onto the cake rounds. Place on a parchment-lined baking sheet and place in the freezer for at least 20 minutes, or, covered with plastic, for several days.

Preheat the oven to 500 degrees.

In a large bowl, with an electric hand mixer, or in a standing mixer using the wire whisk, beat the egg whites until frothy. Add the cream of tartar and continue beating until the whites hold peaks.

Beat in the superfine sugar 1 tablespoon or so at a time. The meringue should be firm and glossy.

Using a spatula, or a pastry bag, cover the ice cream and cake with the meringue. Be very sure to completely cover the bottom, where the ice cream meets the cake. Use all of the meringue.

Through a fine strainer, sprinkle the tops with confectioners' sugar.

Bake for 3 minutes, until the meringues are browned.

Serve immediately.

Variations: Spread each cake round with strawberry preserves or other fruit spread before topping with the ice cream, and/or douse the cake with a light sprinkling of rum, brandy, or a liqueur. The dessert is delicious served with either Strawberry Sauce (page 360), caramel sauce, or chocolate sauce.

DELMONICO STEAK

There are many possible definitions of Delmonico Steak. It has, in essence, become a fanciful name for the best steak money can buy, no matter where the steak is cut from. This could be a full rib steak, on or off the bone, or just the rib eye, which is the central, round muscle (also called Club Steak). Others sell other cuts under the name: for instance the chuck eye, which is also called a mock tender. There is only one true Delmonico, however. After more than one hundred and fifty years, it is still the steak that New Yorkers most desire and most frequently order. Technically it is top loin from the short loin, but we often call it a sirloin strip today, and it's also known as a shell steak. Outside New York City, it is known as a New York Strip, or simply as a New York Steak. A Kansas City Strip is the same thing.

The Delmonico Steak is obviously named after the great restaurant. The steak first appeared on its menu sometime between 1840 and 1850. Delmonico's may have been a fancy French restaurant, but New York City was—and still is—very much a meat and potatoes town. By all accounts, it was an exceptionally popular item from the time it was introduced.

Charles Ranhofer himself describes the steak in his massive cookbook, *The Epicurean*, so there is no confusion here. To make a Delmonico, he cut the long muscle of the short loin (the top loin, the opposite side of the bone having the fillet) two inches thick, then pounded them out to one and a half inches thick. After the pounding, the top loin could well look like the rounder rib eye, which is perhaps where the idea that a Delmonico Steak is a rib steak came from. Ranhofer liked to serve his with Béarnaise.

CHILDS

THE IDEA BEHIND WILLIAM AND SAMUEL CHILDS' FIRST RESTAURANT, WHICH WAS situated on Cortlandt Street and opened in 1889, was to feed the downtown working masses well and wholesomely in hygienic surroundings. Germs had only recently come into the popular consciousness, and cleanliness had just become next to Godliness. The *New York Times* called it "a lust for sanitation." To assure their customers, at least visually, that their restaurant met modern standards of hygiene, the Childs brothers covered the floors and walls with white tile and topped the tables with white marble. The waitresses looked more like nurses in their starched white uniforms. To counter all that reassuring pristine whiteness, the brothers knowingly installed stylish chandeliers. So much did the chandeliers stand out from the surrounding simplicity that they eventually became a trademark.

What is most remembered about Childs, however, is that its Wheat Cakes and Butter Cakes were griddled in the window of the restaurant. Oriented toward the street, the cooks attracted crowds and became a beloved feature of New York City street life, for locals as well as tourists.

By the end of the nineteenth century, there were nine Childs restaurants in New York, serving up to twenty thousand people a day. In 1898, they revolutionized the restaurant business by turning their 130 Broadway location into a cafeteria. It wasn't New York City's first self-service restaurant though. The Exchange Buffet (as in Stock Exchange), which opened in 1885, gets credit for that, but the Exchange, as it was known, was exclusively for men. Childs provided an air of respectability that women needed to eat there on their own.

In 1900, the Childs restaurants were still "Childs Lunchrooms" serving a menu of their pancakes, a variety of eggs and omelets, and some other breakfast items, such as soda crackers with milk, hominy, and cream; dipped toast (French toast); and graham crackers and milk. For larger lunch appetites there was a small steak, hamburger steak, cold ham with beans, ham cakes, both creamed chicken and creamed oysters on toast, and roast beef hash with mashed potatoes, although it was Childs's corned beef hash that later became famous. A stack of wheats cost ten cents, coffee was a nickel as were the famous Butter Cakes.

The brothers divided responsibilities. William was head of operations while Samuel searched for real estate. Apparently both William and Samuel did their jobs well. By the mid-1920s, there were more than one hundred Childs restaurants, more than half of them in New York City, and the chain grossed twenty-five million dollars. Throughout the 1920s, Childs diversified the design of its restaurants and was serving a full dinner menu, which attracted a broader cross-section of the city, not just the working masses of the downtown financial district. The list of Childs specialties expanded to include breaded veal cutlet with tomato sauce, chicken and mushroom croquettes, and chicken salad with bacon and a side of cranberry jelly.

One of the most important Childs buildings, and the only freestanding one to survive, is at the intersection of the Boardwalk and West Twenty-first Street in Coney Island, in Brooklyn. It was built in 1924 and designed by an elite architecture firm, Ethan Allen Dennison and Fredric C. Hirons. Its gray stucco façade is punctuated by a series of arches, which contained windows to the restaurant (now boarded up) that make it look vaguely Spanish Colonial. The stucco is embellished with exuberantly colorful and well-crafted terracotta ornaments depicting marine life—fish, clams, oysters, crabs, seaweed, and snails. The only reason it is not an official city landmark is that it has been owned by the same family since 1947 and has been well-cared for without landmark designation. (For a long while, it was the Tell Chocolate Company.)

Samuel died in 1925 and William, a vegetarian and teetotaler, took the opportunity to remove meat from his restaurants' menus, which proved disastrous. Profits plummeted, and in 1928, the company passed out of Childs family hands.

Still, the chain endured, and once again thrived. A 1931 restaurant guide, *New York After Dark,* by Charles G. Shaw, describes, in a section called "Late Night Chow," the Childs restaurants that were open all night:

Childs Spanish Garden, at 8 East Fifty-ninth Street, which boasts a patio, stucco walls, and a tony clientele.

10 Columbus Circle, where the brand of customer is, to say the least, mixed.

The Paramount Childs, in the Paramount Building, which caters to a Broadway trade and features a dash of lavender. [By "lavender," Shaw probably meant homosexuals.]

The Grand Central Childs, on Forty-second Street, between Madison and Vanderbilt Avenues, a favorite with commuters.

Lexington Avenue and Forty-fourth Street, which is done a l'art moderne.

724 Fifth Avenue, where you will find evening togs by the cab-load.

In 1939, another guidebook, *Dining Out in New York,* by G. Selmer Fougwer, said, "No gastronomical tour of New York would be complete without a visit to one of the Childs restaurants, were it only to sample the Butter Cakes, Buckwheat Cakes, and excellent coffee which the chain has been serving in New York for over a quarter a century [actually a lot longer]." Childs held on to its last outlet, in Times Square, until the late 1950s.

In the 1940s Childs hired illustrators, photographers, and other artists to design menu covers.

HORN & HARDART

Horn & Hardart is a New York City institution that began in Philadelphia. From its roots as a modest lunchroom opposite Wanamaker's Department Store at 39 South Thirteenth Street in Philly, it grew to a chain with more than one hundred and sixty-five locations, including Automats, or waiterless restaurants as they were first called; cafeterias; and retail food shops that were among the first, if not the very first, to provide prepared foods for home consumption.

Joe Horn and Frank Hardart couldn't have come from more different backgrounds. Horn was born into a comfortable Philadelphia family, while Hardart, who emigrated from Bavaria with his family in 1858, was a poor boy from New Orleans. Both men, however, had a love of food and a fascination with restaurants.

To prevent Horn from going into the restaurant business, which two of his siblings had already done, his mother sent him on a cross-country trip in the hopes he would forget that dream and find another business venture. When he returned to Philadelphia, at twenty-seven years old, he was more determined than ever to become a restaurateur in his beloved city.

Meanwhile, Hardart, ten years Horn's senior, was working in restaurants in New Orleans when he had a revelation about coffee, one of the Crescent City's most notable gastronomic specialties. One of his tasks was to roast and grind the coffee, and brew it according to the French

HOW AN AUTOMAT WORKS

FIRST DROP YOUR NICKELS IN THE SLOT

THEN TURN THE KNOB. THE GLASS DOOR CLICKS OPEN

LIFT THE DOOR AND HELP YOURSELF

HORN & HARDART

Interior of One of the Fifty Automat-Cafeterias in Philadelphia and New York drip method. Knowing that New Orleans coffee was superior to the percolated or boiled coffee most of the rest of the country was drinking, Frank traveled to Philadelphia for the 1876 Centennial Exhibition. He'd heard that the exhibition's restaurant business was booming.

Frank Hardart had no luck selling his New Orleans brew in Philadelphia, but he was a determined man. Figuring his refined coffee was ahead of its time in 1876, he returned to Philadelphia in 1888 to again seek his fortune.

Meanwhile Horn had just returned from his cross-country excursion and convinced his mother to give him one thousand dollars to get started on his restaurant. He had learned a lot traveling, but he didn't know enough to run a restaurant by himself. Horn put an ad in the newspaper soliciting an experienced partner.

Legend has it that Hardart used a torn-off piece of a sugar bag to write Horn this note: "I'm your man."

The first Horn & Hardart opened in Philadelphia on December 22, 1888. Although one thousand dollars was a decent investment at the end of the nineteenth century, the original restaurant was just a long counter with fifteen stools. Horn took care of the customers while Hardart cooked. His French drip coffee was an immediate success. Indeed, throughout its nearly hundred-year history, Horn & Hardart was always known for its superior coffee. Horn & Hardart called it their gilt-edge brew. Later, the coffee became famous not just because of its high quality, but also because, in the self-service Automats, it was dispensed from spouts shaped like dolphins, just like fountain figures Horn had seen in Italy.

The luncheonette near Wanamaker's was such a success that Horn & Hardart opened others. The company also opened a central commissary where the food for all the restaurants could be prepared under their eagle eyes.

This was all before the first Automat appeared. Then along came an unknown salesman with a new Swiss invention being manufactured in Germany. It was an automatic food dispenser; you might say an early vending machine. With some modification and new design ideas by John Fritsche, an engineer who continued to work for Horn & Hardart until his death in 1947, it became the walls of windowed food-filled compartments that fascinated—nay, transfixed—the public.

One of the last moderne Horn & Hardart buildings, on Fifty-seventh Street near Sixth Avenue, now houses another restaurant.

The first Automat opened in Philadelphia in 1902. A second opened in 1905, a third in 1907, a fourth in 1912. By then, Horn & Hardart thought it was time to tackle New York City. After testing the waters with two small coffee shops—serving only coffee and baked goods—they opened the first New York City Automat on Broadway and Forty-sixth Street later in 1912.

It wasn't really Horn & Hardart's food—as wholesome, fresh, and even as delicious as that might be—that made Horn & Hardart the huge success it became. And it wasn't only the revolutionary and amusing way the food was dispensed, as decisive as that was. Horn and Hardart's goal was not only to feed the masses, but to uplift their customers at the same time, to give them a feeling of grandeur, a glimpse of art and beauty that they certainly could not have in their private lives. To that end, they hired the best architects and designers. When the first New York City Automat opened on July 2, 1912, customers entered through a façade of stained glass windows designed by Nicola D'Ascenzo, who had designed windows for the city's Cathedral of Saint John the Divine. The window walls were thirty feet wide and two stories high. Inside, the tables were topped with Carrara marble, the floors were constructed with inlaid marble. Another part of D'Ascenzo's design was the richly carved and colored ceiling.

Then there were the nickels. The windowed doors, behind which were plates of sandwiches, slices of cake, wedges of pie, cups of custard, crocks of beans, casseroles of baked macaroni and cheese, and so forth, required one to several nickels to open them. On opening day in 1912, it is said 8,693 nickels were pushed into the Automat's slots. Marble booths were built on the dining room floor. Here cashiers changed quarters into nickels, and later, as prices rose, dollars into nickels. They worked so fast, it was almost magic.

By 1920, there were fifteen Automats in New York City. In September of 1922, the first combination Automat and cafeteria opened, "heralded in newspaper ads as the largest restaurant in New York City, with a capacity to feed ten thousand customers per day," according to *The Automat*, a history of the chain by Lorraine B. Diehl and Frank Hardart's great granddaughter, Marianne Hardart. Also in 1922, in Philadelphia, Horn & Hardart opened its first retail store, selling its restaurant specialties for home consumption. It was an advertising man named Ike Clements who came up with the slogan "Less Work for Mother" in order to sell the concept of take-home food. Was it Horn or Hardart who had the brilliant idea of positioning the stores near or in railroad, elevated, and subway stations? Eventually, there were eighty-four retail shops in

New York City and Philadelphia, including one at either end of what is now the Amtrak line connecting the two cities.

From the beginning, the chain was known for its attention to design. But until Ralph B. Bencker, a forward-thinking Philadelphia architect, was hired, the restaurants did not have a cohesive look. It was 1929—the Chrysler Building had just opened and the Empire State Building was just about to. Bencker had introduced Philadelphia to the moderne style, or the skyscraper style, the successor to Art Deco, and his vision matched Horn's and Hardart's. The new architecture symbolized energy, speed, and efficiency. It was as glamorous as Fred Astaire and Ginger Rogers, and as technological as, well, the Automat. Bencker's first building for Horn & Hardart was in Philadelphia, on Sixteenth Street and Chestnut Street. It was the company's headquarters, with a restaurant on the first floor. Touted as "Philadelphia's Most Beautiful Restaurant," it became the prototype for thirty-nine more restaurants in New York City and Philadelphia.

The first New York City Automat that was outside Manhattan opened in the Bronx in September of 1932, a Bencker building on 170th Street. In June of 1936, a Bencker Automat in bronze-framed terracotta opened in Downtown Brooklyn, on Willoughby Street, near the then genteel Fulton Street and its white glove department stores.

CHOCK FULL O' NUTS

Chock Full o' Nuts is that heavenly coffee,
Heavenly coffee, heavenly coffee.
Chock Full o' Nuts is that heavenly coffee,
Better coffee a millionaire's money can't buy.

Those of us with good memories may remember when the last line of that jingle, which, from 1953 through the late 1960s was heard day and night on New York City radio, was "Better coffee a Rockefeller's money can't buy." When Nelson Rockefeller, who was governor of New York from 1958 to 1970, and more pertinently owned coffee companies in Latin America, heard the advertising song, he sued. No problem. Chock Full o' Nuts owner William Black just changed the word. His products were already known for their high quality.

Black, who was born William Schwartz, liked to tell everyone he was a poor boy from Brooklyn. But he was actually born in Russia and came to New York when he was four years old, according to his three daughters. His family legend has it that after getting an engineering degree from Columbia University, Black couldn't find work. More likely, given his personality,

For a short time in the 1950s, Chock Full o' Nuts put mobile restaurants on the street.

he was too restless and ambitious to wait for a job to turn up. Walking through Times Square one day he noticed the long lines at a discount theater ticket outlet. He decided to be an entrepreneur instead of an engineer and he opened a nut stand, to sell snacks to the people on line. That was the first Chock Full o' Nuts. It was in a below-grade space on the corner of Broadway and Forty-third Street, and it had nothing to do with coffee.

The opening is variously reported as both 1922 and 1926, but the latter is more likely if you consider that Black would have been only nineteen in 1922 and probably had not yet graduated from Columbia. On the other hand, the later date makes Black's success seem even more astounding since it is said he had eighteen nut stands by 1932. He became the nut king of Times Square.

Then the Depression hit badly and Black's nut business declined. A very determined and strong-willed man until his death in 1979, he simply decided to sell something more necessary than nuts—breakfast and lunch. But he already had the well-known brand name, Chock Full o' Nuts. Using that name, in 1933, he opened what may have been the first fast food chain in the city, well known for its short and simple menu, good quality, low prices, immaculate housekeeping, takeout counters, and mostly African-American staff. Black, a Jew, who is said to have deeply felt the anti-Semitism of New York City in his youth, was an early activist for racial equality. He focused public attention on this in 1957 when, with a great deal of bally-hoo publicity, he hired retiring Brooklyn Dodgers star, Jackie Robinson, who had broken the color barrier in baseball. As head of personal and community relations, Robinson became vice president of the company.

The famous Chock Full o' Nuts cafe policy of no tipping is related to Black's views on equality. He thought tipping was degrading. He preferred to pay a fair wage, and he gave his employees a health plan, which was revolutionary for restaurant workers.

Gastronomically, it was Chock Full o' Nuts' practical simplicity that was revolutionary. The most memorable item on the menu—and also the least expensive—was the cream cheese with walnuts on whole-wheat raisin bread. This was no mere schmeer between two slices of bread, but a thick layer of cheese with big pieces of nuts on moist but dense bread. The city adored Chock's cakey whole-wheat donuts, too. And if you could splurge a little, the lobster salad sandwiches were slim but divine.

By 1953 the firm owned twenty-five restaurants in Manhattan and two in Brooklyn, and had expanded into selling its prepackaged coffee in cans in supermarkets. According to Mark Pendergrast, author of *Uncommon Grounds*, a history of coffee, Black "astonished the coffee trade by coming out with his own brand in the midst of a price crisis brought on by the great Brazilian frost. Everyone thought it would flop, particularly with such a stupid name."

Black was a big believer in advertising, however, and his catchy Chock Full o' Nuts jingle was, in part, responsible for the brand's success. Incidentally, the Chock jingle was not written for the company. It was a song called "That Heavenly Feeling," written by Wayne and Bruce Silbert. Black's third wife, Page Black, is remembered as the singer of the tune, probably because she sang it in the television ads, but it was actually Black's second wife, Jean Martin, who introduced it.

Black put the coffee in a black and yellow can designed after the New York City Checker taxi cabs, giving it what was then an upscale look (who could afford cabs at that time?), and he marketed it as high-priced coffee that was worth the money. That strategy was ironic since the restaurants were always marketed for every man. The tactic worked—within a year, Chock was the third most popular canned coffee in New York. Soon distribution expanded to southern New England, Canada, and the Middle Atlantic states. After being bought by the Sara Lee Corporation in 1999, and having lost a good share of its supermarket coffee market, Chock introduced a new New York blend in 2003 and launched a nostalgia-laden advertising campaign to back it.

At the company's height, in the 1960s and early 1970s, Black owned as many as one hundred and fifty restaurants. In time, the company concentrated its attention more on the more lucrative coffee business than the restaurants. The very last Chock Full o' Nuts cafe was on Forty-first Street and Madison Avenue, and it closed in 1992.

SCHRAFFT'S

With a few notable exceptions, until the end of the nineteenth century, most eating establishments were created for men, not for women. Schrafft's was the opposite—serving women without men. At the turn of the twentieth century, the women's suffrage movement was making headway. Women would not get the vote until 1920, but the pressures to that end were there many years before. As places where people of like mind, like wallet, or like class, occupation, or business gather, restaurants can be, if not a force for social change, an accomplice in change—or at least a symbol of those efforts.

Schrafft's was designed explicitly for women.

Frank Garrett Shattuck, a hard-driving candy salesman, certainly had no intentions of abetting social change when, in 1898, he opened his first shop, where Macy's now stands on Herald Square. It was a candy and ice cream shop, with confections and ice cream supplied by William Schrafft and Sons of Boston, for whom Shattuck was a traveling salesman. Schrafft's, as Shattuck called the store, evolved quickly. To get the buyers into the store to purchase candy and ice cream, he added a modest menu of soda fountain treats, sandwiches, and simple dishes, as well as samples from the candy and cookie cases. The concept was a huge success, and by 1910 Shattuck had several stores. In 1915, the company had nine stores in Manhattan, one in Brooklyn, and one in Syracuse. By 1925, the chain had grown to twenty-one stores. By 1950, there were more than fifty Schrafft's in New York City alone.

The chain's development was heavily influenced by Frank Shattuck's sister Jane, who joined the company early on and whose idea it was to serve sandwiches and cakes that she made herself at the second Schrafft's location, 54 West Twenty-third Street. Most tea rooms then were owned and managed by men, but because of Jane's influence Schrafft's was one of the first to be managed by women. Also, said the trade journal *The Restaurateur* in the mid 1920s, "Miss Shattuck's thorough understanding of the value of absolute cleanliness, daintiness, supreme food and cooking" was the secret to Schrafft's success.

"Ask any woman . . . where she is going to lunch and the nearest Schrafft's is an odds-on favorite," reported a restaurant reviewer in 1925. At that time, Schrafft's was being managed entirely by women, many of whom were college students in domestic science, working under Jane's supervision. Schrafft's became a training ground for many women who would go on to open their own tea rooms.

"Many of our customers are secretaries and stenographers...who must watch their pocketbooks," Frank Shattuck reported to an industry trade journal.

Although the restaurants were originally exclusively for women, many a son was taken there by his mother. Schrafft's remained primarily a women's restaurant, right up until its last outlet opened, in the 1960s, but many old men now remember it fondly, too.

In the 1920s, the trade journal *The Soda Fountain* found the Schrafft's stores "equipped with fine fixtures and decorated with dignity and taste. In most of the stores, fine selected walnut has been used for wood work [sic] and the decorative scheme carried out in early American period furniture."

As noted by Jan Whitaker in her book *Tea at the Blue Lantern Inn*, Schrafft's "offered its patrons restful, but rather stuffy, club-like interiors in which to consume their tea and light repasts. The 383 Fifth Avenue Schrafft's was done in Colonial style, as was the mezzanine at 13 West Forty-second Street, while the small tea room at 2 West Thirty-ninth Street was Italianate. Many of Schrafft's stores had classically styled large rooms with high ceilings, huge windows with shirred-silk, Roman shades, chandeliers, and molded plaster pilasters and ceiling medallions."

Schrafft's architecture and design did, however, keep up with the times. The last freestanding Schrafft's building in Manhattan still exists on the corner of Fifth Avenue and Twelfth Street in Greenwich Village. It was built in the 1930s in the moderne style, and although it had a famous second life in the 1970s and early 1980s as a country-western music cafe, the Lone Star Cafe, which had a giant iguana sculpture on its roof, it now suffers the ignominy of being an ordinary grocery and food bar.

CHILDS' WHEAT CAKES

I got this recipe from an elderly woman who worked as a home economist for Childs. It came to me as a carbon copy of a typed recipe on brittle and yellowing onion skin paper. It looked like the real thing, and I believe it is. It would justify Childs's reputation for superior pancakes. These "wheats" are simply sensational—thick, fluffy, and flavorful, and the batter makes fabulous waffles, too. The batter has a slightly higher proportion of fat and baking powder than is typical of a contemporary recipe, which is what makes the pancakes particularly high and light and the waffles very crisp and airy. The original recipe calls for melted solid white shortening. I have tried substituting butter and substituting vegetable oil, but the shortening version is the fluffiest. Butter gets points for flavor, while vegetable oil would be my last choice of fat.

Makes 12 (4 ½-inch) pancakes

There's no reason you must make Childs-size pancakes, but it is interesting to note that pancakes were only 4½ inches in the early twentieth century. Now, pancakes are 6 or 7 inches across. This batter recipe makes a little less than 3 cups: Use about ⅓ cup batter for a modern-size pancake. (You'll need a generous ½ cup to ⅔ cup batter for most waffle irons. Waffles take about 5 minutes, depending on the waffle iron.)

1 egg

1½ cups whole milk

1½ cups all-purpose flour

2 tablespoons sugar

¾ teaspoon salt

1 tablespoon plus ¾ teaspoon baking powder

¼ cup melted then cooled vegetable shortening, melted unsalted butter, or vegetable oil

In a mixing bowl, beat the egg slightly and mix in the milk.

In another bowl, sift together the flour, sugar, salt, and baking powder.

Using a whisk, blend the dry ingredients into the wet.

Stir in the shortening until well blended. (The mixture can stand for several hours. Keep refrigerated until 30 minutes before baking, then return to room temperature.)

Lightly grease a griddle or a large skillet over medium heat. (The griddle needs to be greased only for the first batch.) Take care not to overheat the pan. A drop of water should sizzle on the surface, but not dance across it. Try out one pancake before proceeding with all the batter.

Pour the batter into a measuring cup. (You should have 3 cups.) Use a scant ¼ cup batter for each pancake. If the griddle is too hot, the pancakes will develop ray-like marks on their first side; if too hot, turn down the heat. The perfect cakes are high and fluffy and dry.

As soon as the tops of the pancakes are covered with bubbles that are bursting, flip them over. Bake until the second side is lightly browned.

Serve immediately. (If necessary, keep the baked cakes hot in a 200-degree oven while baking the remainder.)

CHILDS' BUTTER CAKES

Childs' Butter Cakes are similar to English muffins, both being thick, griddled yeast breads related to crumpets. It is probably no coincidence that they were introduced in New York City at about the same time, in the late nineteenth century.

I don't know why the Childs brothers called them Butter Cakes since there is only a small measure of butter in the dough. Perhaps it is because they really only come alive when slathered with butter, and some jam or preserves. They are hard to resist hot off the griddle when they are soft, fragrant, white-bready buns. But they are much better when allowed to cool thoroughly, and to compose themselves for a day. Just like an English muffin, they are best split and toasted.

I found this recipe in the 1908 *New York Evening Telegram Cookbook*.

Makes about 24

The recipe is easily divided in half, but since the griddle-baked cakes store so well in the freezer, there's reason to make the full amount of dough.

1 (7-gram) package active dry yeast
3 cups warm water (about 100 degrees)
2 teaspoons salt

2 tablespoons unsalted butter
8½ cups all-purpose flour, plus more for rolling

Dissolve the yeast in 2 cups warm water (100 degrees). Add the salt and butter and stir until the butter is melted.

Gradually add 2 cups of the flour, stirring with a fork or whisk to blend the flour into the liquid. When you have a thin batter, cover the bowl with a clean kitchen towel and set aside in a draft-free place until the mixture is light and seething, bubbles bursting regularly on the top—30 to 45 minutes.

Add 1 cup more warm water and stir it in.

Gradually add the remaining flour, stirring it in with a wooden spoon, until a cohesive dough forms.

Turn the dough out onto a well-floured board and knead for 5 minutes. You should have a soft and silky dough. Return the dough to the bowl. Cover with a towel and let it rise again, this time until doubled in bulk, about 30 minutes.

Turn the dough out onto the well-floured board.

Using about a quarter of the dough at a time, roll out the dough ¾ inch thick. Using a 3-inch round cookie cutter, cut out circles of the dough.

Let the rounds of dough rise for about 15 minutes.

With a spatula, transfer the rounds to a well-seasoned griddle preheated over medium-low heat. As soon as the first side of a cake is lightly browned, turn it over. Repeat this turning several times to ensure even cooking. When finished, both sides will be nicely browned, and the muffin will be puffy but firm to the touch. Continue with the remaining dough.

Cool on wire racks. Store in the refrigerator wrapped in tinfoil. Or split the cakes and store them in plastic bags in the freezer. (Presplit, they are ready to be toasted without thawing.)

To serve, split the cakes with a serrated knife and toast on the cut side. Serve with butter, jam, jelly, or preserves.

HORN & HARDART'S MACARONI AND CHEESE

The Automat's macaroni and cheese was at one time the whole city's soul food, a comfort to us all. This recipe comes from the files of the *New York Daily News* where I was the food editor. It was one of several Automat recipes published in a pamphlet by the *News* sometime in the 1950s. There are several other versions, but this fits my taste memory, too. The last Automat was only feet away from the landmark News Building where I worked, and, in emotionally weak moments, I would run downstairs for a plate of the fortifying mac and cheese.

Serves 2 or 3

1½ tablespoons unsalted butter

2 tablespoons flour

1½ cups milk

2 tablespoons light cream (see Note)

1 packed cup shredded cheddar cheese

¼ cup crushed tomatoes

½ teaspoon sugar

Dash of ground cayenne pepper, or more to taste

Dash of ground white pepper, or more to taste

½ teaspoon salt, or to taste

½ pound small elbow macaroni, cooked until barely done

Preheat the oven to 400 degrees. Butter a shallow baking dish.

In a small saucepan, over low heat, melt the butter, then blend in the flour and cook for about 2 minutes.

Beat in the milk, then the cream, and cook over medium heat, stirring constantly, until the mixture comes to a boil and thickens. Remove from the heat.

Stir in the cheese and cook until melted, then add the tomatoes, sugar, cayenne, and white pepper. Taste for salt, and add to taste, starting with about ½ teaspoon.

Stir in the macaroni.

Pour into the prepared baking dish. Bake until the surface browns, 25 to 30 minutes.

Serve hot.

Note: This recipe must have been broken down from one that made an enormous quantity, which explains the small amount of light cream. If you don't want to purchase a half-pint container of light cream just for 2 tablespoons, simply add 2 tablespoons more milk. You'll never know the difference.

HORN & HARDART'S BAKED BEANS

If ever you ate the baked beans at the Automat, you will be surprised at how saucy and creamy these are. If you want the beans to really taste as they did out of the Automat's wall of food, then put the beans in small ramekins or custard cups (the Automat had brown ceramic ones) and let them stand in a low oven for several hours. They'll get dried out and crusted over just like in the old days.

Makes about 7 cups

1 pound great Northern or navy beans, soaked for at least 8 hours

1 cup finely minced onion (1 medium onion)

4 slices bacon, diced

2 tablespoons sugar

1 tablespoon dry mustard

¼ teaspoon ground cayenne pepper

⅔ cup molasses

2 tablespoons cider vinegar

1½ cups tomato juice

1 teaspoon salt

Drain the beans and place them in a large saucepan. Add fresh water to cover the beans by about 1 inch. Bring to a boil, then adjust the heat so the beans simmer gently, uncovered. Making sure they are always covered with water, cook them until they're very tender but not falling apart, about 1 hour. (When you add the acidic ingredients the beans will firm up again.) Drain.

Preheat the oven to 300 degrees.

Place the beans in a 3-quart bean pot or casserole. Add the remaining ingredients and stir well.

Bake, covered, for about 6 hours, or until the beans are tender again and colored as brown as the sauce around them. Stir the beans at least once an hour while they cook.

Serve hot.

SCHRAFFT'S CHEESE BREAD

It was not easy getting this recipe, one of the items that people remember most fondly from Schrafft's. Although Frank Shattuck, a Schrafft's descendant, lent me a box of more than 2,500 Schrafft's recipes, the Cheese Bread was not among them. It was, however, among the papers of his father, George Shattuck, although the recipe was written without instructions and it made 100 pounds of dough. George Greenstein to the rescue! George is a retired professional baker, and he was able, with educated guesses, to come up with this excellent recipe.

Schrafft's offered the Cheese Bread as one of its sandwich bread options. It would be great with ham and mustard, or egg salad or chicken salad, or for a BLT. It is so rich, however, that you may want to enjoy it for its own sake, with a cup of tea. It doesn't even need butter, especially when it is toasted.

Makes 2 loaves

¼ cup warm water
2 (7-gram) packages active dry yeast
   (2 scant tablespoons)
1¾ cups milk, at room temperature
5 to 5½ cups unbleached all-purpose flour
2 tablespoons sugar

2 teaspoons salt
2 tablespoons unsalted butter, softened
8 ounces sharp cheddar cheese, shredded
   (about 2 cups)
Vegetable oil, for the bowl

Mix the water and yeast and let stand for 5 minutes.

Add the milk, flour, sugar, salt, butter, and 1½ cups of the cheese. Mix at slow speed until the ingredients are combined.

Using a dough hook, mix for 8 to 10 minutes, until the dough is well developed. The dough will be softer than usual for a bread dough, but it should not feel sticky. If necessary, add more flour.

Remove the dough from the bowl. Add a tiny bit of oil to the bowl. Return the ball of dough to the bowl, and turn to coat it lightly with oil. Cover and let stand in a warm place until doubled in bulk. This will take 30 to 60 minutes.

Punch the dough down. Sprinkle on the remaining ½ cup cheese and knead the cheese in only enough to incorporate it. Do not knead the dough too much while doing this.

Divide the dough in half. Shape each piece into a loaf shape and place in 2 greased loaf pans, each about 8 by 5 by 3 inches.

Cover the pans with a clean dish towel, and let the loaves rise again, this time until well above the rim of the pans, about 30 minutes.

Preheat the oven to 375 degrees.

Brush the tops of the loaves with water.

Place in the oven; for the optimum crust, place a pan of water under the loaf pans and, after the loaf pans are in place on the shelf above, put a heated brick or piece of metal in the water to create steam. Bake with steam for about 15 minutes, then remove the pan of water and place a piece of tinfoil in a tent shape over each loaf. Bake for an additional 35 min-utes, or until the tops are nicely browned and the bottoms, when the breads are removed from their pans, make a hollow thump when tapped.

Remove the loaves from the pans immediately, and let them cool thoroughly, either on a rack or by leaning the loaves against a bowl or backsplash.

To store the bread, wrap tightly in foil.

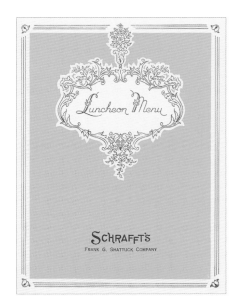

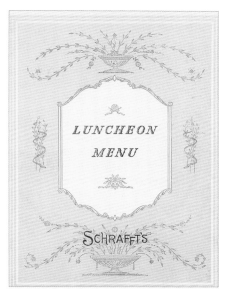

CHAPTER 5

THE GOLDEN AGE OF COCKTAILS

A STORY FOR EVERY DRINK

IN THE LAST FEW YEARS, WHOLE VOLUMES HAVE BEEN WRITTEN ABOUT THE history of cocktails. I highly recommend William Grimes's *Straight Up or On the Rocks: The Story of the American Cocktail*, David Wondrich's *Esquire Drinks: An Opinionated & Irreverent Guide to Drinking*, Dale Degroff's *The Craft of the Cocktail*, and Gary Regan's *The Joy of Mixology*. Although I am no slouch at the bar, I couldn't begin to compete with these authors' erudition and research.

Suffice to say, much important cocktail history happened in New York City, and some of the most famous bartenders plied their trade in the city's hotels and respectable bars. The heyday of the cocktail was the post–Civil War period, the Gilded Age, and through to the end of the nineteenth century, the Gay '90s. Then, men's cafes or bars opened in the elegant hotels, and a man's masculinity was no longer questioned if he didn't order his whiskey straight and his beer in copious quantity. The city was full of saloons and beer halls for that. There were the workingman's bars that offered free lunch. The "groceries" that sold more alcoholic drink than household goods and food. There were the Irish pubs where men gathered to have a social life apart from their families, and the German beer gardens and halls where families could gather on Sundays. The cocktail, a genteel drink, was part of the city's upper-crust life.

The earliest concoctions, all outlined in the 1862 edition of *How to Mix Drinks* by Jerry Thomas, the most famous bartender in history, were punches, flips, toddies, crustas, slings, and sangarees (yes, like sangria). Some of these date back to colonial days. Only ten out of 236 beverages could be rightly considered "cocktails," according to William Grimes.

It should go without saying that the Volstead Act, what we know as Prohibition, which began in January 1920 and wasn't repealed until November 1933, put an abrupt stop to creative cocktail making. Prohibition had an effect that was opposite to its intention, however. It encouraged drinking. The Twenties roared because they were fueled by bathtub gin and bootleg whiskey, not to mention an awful lot of Champagne. The cocktail didn't go away, but it was not a genteel drink that the masses were after. When the saloons closed, the speakeasies opened. By the end of the era, there were twice as many of the illegal later as the legit former.

As soon as the Repeal bells rang, however, Hollywood glamorized the cocktail again. The Thin Man drank Martinis; Fred Astaire, too. By the 1950s, New York City's businessmen were famous for indulging in the two (or three) Martini lunch. Then, in the late 1960s/early 1970s, alcohol became less attractive than drugs. It all reversed again in the 1990s when the Baby Boomer's children came of drinking age and rejected their parent's "weed" in favor of brightly colored cocktails with enough sweetness to remind them of the soda pop they drank as children. That brings us to a current national favorite, the Cosmopolitan (page 91).

OPPOSITE: The legendary Bull & Bear Bar in the current Waldorf-Astoria Hotel.

THE MANHATTAN

The Manhattan is making a comeback on the tail of the Martini. The younger drinking generation's love affair with that glamorous v-shaped cocktail glass, and their taste for sweetened cocktails, has brought them back to the quintessential New York City cocktail, a very old drink, a classic from the golden age of cocktails, the late nineteenth century.

Before Prohibition, New York City was a rye whiskey town. (Next in popularity was Scotch. Last came bourbon; which my New York City-centric, Scotch-drinking grandfather called "country club whiskey.") The original Manhattan was a rye drink, sweetened with Italian vermouth, sharpened with orange bitters, and garnished with a maraschino cherry.

Today, if you order a Manhattan in Manhattan you will invariably be served a bourbon cocktail. The fashion now, in fact, is to specify which single-cask, or otherwise super-premium bourbon you prefer.

There is a creation story attached to the Manhattan, although it is unlikely. Legend has it that the cocktail was created in 1874 at the Manhattan Club, at a dinner given by Lady Jenny Jerome Churchill, the daughter of the notoriously ruthless and powerful Brooklyn financier Leonard Walter Jerome, wife of Lord Randolph, and mother of Winston—in honor of the newly elected governor of New York State, Samuel J. Tilden, a Democratic reformer and, until Al Gore, the only presidential candidate to lose the election (two years later) while winning the popular vote.

The story is unlikely because it would have been nearly impossible for Jenny Jerome to be in Manhattan at the end of 1874. On November 30, she was in England, giving birth to Winston. Besides, records from the exclusive Manhattan Club neither give a year for the creation of the Manhattan nor confirm any details of the preceding story, while they do offer a recipe. It calls for "whiskey," not mentioning which kind, although, as already pointed out, it was most likely rye, and for orange bitters, not Angostura.

Furthermore, the late Carol Truax, who wrote twenty-four cookbooks before she passed on well into her eighties sometime in the 1980s, always claimed that her father created the cocktail. He was New York Supreme Court Judge Charles Henry Truax and he was president of the Manhattan Club in 1890. "It's true that the old Manhattan Club on lower Fifth Avenue was originally the home of Jenny Jerome," Carol told our mutual friend, the food writer James Villas, "but she had nothing to do with the creation of the cocktail. What really happened was that my father, who was very fat, would stop his carriage at the club every day on his way home from court and drink a few Martinis—two at a time, since they were two for a quarter! When the doctor told him he absolutely had to cut out the Martinis if he hoped to lose weight, he swiftly dropped by the club, told the bartender they had to come up with a new cocktail, and the Manhattan was born— named after the club. Of course, when he later returned to his physician, heavier than ever, and told him about the delicious substitution for Martinis he'd come up with, the doctor roared, 'But that's even worse!'"

If this story is true, than Carol Truax must have had her dates confused, because William Grimes reports in his book that the legendary bartender, Jerry Thomas, includes "in recognizable form" a recipe for the Manhattan in the 1876 and 1887 editions of his book *How to Mix Drinks*.

Makes 1

2 ounces rye or blended whiskey (such as
Jim Beam or Old Overholt)
¾ to 1 ounce sweet vermouth (depending
on taste)

2 or 3 dashes Angostura bitters (or orange
bitters, if you can find them)
1 maraschino cherry, preferably on its stem

In a mixing glass half-filled with ice cubes, combine all the ingredients except the cherry. Stir about
20 times.

Strain into a cocktail (Martini) glass. Let the
cherry drop to the bottom of the glass.

BLOODY MARY

New York City–based drink historian Gary Regan, whose syndicated newspaper column is called "The Cocktailian," has done more research on the Bloody Mary than anyone could dream there is research to do. In his recently published book, *The Joy of Mixology*, he writes:

One story about the birth of the Bloody Mary has it that the owner of a New York speakeasy created it during Prohibition, and it was originally known as the Bloody Meyer. But the more popular and almost certainly true tale about the creation of this drink is that it was first concocted at Harry's New York Bar in Paris, circa 1924, by bartender Fernand "Pete" Petiot.

In 1934, Petiot was hired by Vincent Astor, then owner of the St. Regis Hotel, and there he presided over the King Cole Bar, introducing New Yorkers to his creation. At some point, the Bloody Mary was known as the red snapper, and one story has it that it was Astor who objected to the Bloody Mary name and insisted it be changed. A recipe for the red snapper is detailed in the 1945 book, Crosby Gaige's Cocktail Guide and Ladies' Companion. *. . . It's a far cry from the drink we know today as the Bloody Mary. The main differences between today's and yesteryear's versions is that the latter contained as much vodka as tomato juice, and it was served straight up as a cocktail as opposed to being presented on the rocks in a highball glass.*

When did the red snapper regain its original name? Probably sometime during the late 1940s. The first printed recipe for a Bloody Mary I can find is in 1951's The Bartender's Book, *and the authors, Jack Townsend and Tom Moore McBride, didn't much care for the drink, calling it "a savage combination of tomato juice and vodka." The following year, David Embury, in the second edition of* The Fine Art of Mixing Drinks, *described the Bloody Mary as being "strictly vile."*

In the mid-1950s, comedian George Jessel was featured in a Smirnoff vodka advertising campaign for the Bloody Mary, in which he claimed to have invented the drink at "five in the morning" when the bartender was asleep. The tale, of course, isn't true, but the campaign served to popularize the drink throughout the U.S.A.

RIGHT: Maxfield Parrish's mural, *Old King Cole*, is the backdrop at the St. Regis Hotel bar.

Makes 1

Horseradish is apparently a New York touch. In the rest of the country "out of town," as New Yorkers say—the drink is mostly made without horseradish and with less piquancy in general than the following formula provides.

1½ ounces vodka
2 or 3 dashes Worcestershire sauce
4 or more dashes hot pepper sauce
2 teaspoons white (prepared) horseradish
Juice of ¼ lemon

⅛ teaspoon celery salt
4 ounces tomato juice
1 small, inside rib celery (celery heart), with leaves if possible (optional)
Lemon or lime wedge (optional)

Combine the vodka, Worcestershire, hot pepper sauce, horseradish, lemon juice, celery salt, and tomato juice in a mixing glass. Either stir or rock back and forth to mix well.

Pour into a large tumbler three-quarters filled with ice.

Garnish as desired, with a celery stick and/or a lemon or lime wedge.

ROB ROY

The Rob Roy is basically a Manhattan mixed with Scotch rather than rye or blended whiskey. It was supposedly created at the Bull & Bear Bar in the old Waldorf Hotel on Thirty-fourth Street and Fifth Avenue, where the Empire State Building is today.

Makes 1

2½ ounces Scotch

1 ounce sweet vermouth

Dash of Angostura bitters

Lemon peel, for garnish

Pour the Scotch, vermouth, and bitters over ice into a mixing glass and stir as you would a Martini.

Strain into a chilled cocktail (Martini) glass, and garnish with the lemon peel.

THE GIBSON

This variant on the Martini was created at the Waldorf Hotel, before it moved to its current location in 1932. Bartender Albert Stevens Crockett outlines the recipe in his 1931 book, *Old Waldorf Bar Days* and says it was named after Billie Gibson, a fight promoter.

Makes 1

Make a Martini to taste (I like 3 ounces of gin to ½ ounce dry vermouth)

Garnish it with pickled pearl onions instead of olives.

THE BRONX

The Bronx cocktail was created by bartender Johnnie Solon at the old Waldorf before Prohibition. The story goes that he concocted the drink the night after he'd visited the Bronx Zoo. Every chronicler seems to agree with that. How exactly the zoo inspired the name is less certain. Because the animals he saw at the zoo reminded him of people who drank too much? Because drunks claim to see such beasts? Apparently, Solon wanted to be subtle, or perhaps just vague.

Makes 1

1½ ounces gin

¼ ounce sweet vermouth

¼ ounce dry vermouth

1½ ounces fresh orange juice

Orange peel, for garnish

Shake or stir the gin, vermouth, and orange juice together in a mixing glass half full of ice cubes. Strain into a cocktail (Martini) glass.

Garnish with the orange peel: Twist it over the glass to release its oil, and put it in the drink.

THE COSMOPOLITAN

Dale Degroff was the chief bartender at the Rainbow Room for twelve years, from 1987 to 1999 (when it changed management). He started many drink-making trends during his tenure, including the Cosmopolitan. He humbly denies having invented it, although numerous publications have said he did. All he takes credit for is popularizing it.

The Cosmo, as it is affectionately called since it became a household name through the television program *Sex and the City*, first appeared in New York City sometime in the early 1980s. It was first served at the Odeon, a French brasserie-style restaurant initially frequented by the downtown art community and now by a great cross-section of downtown habitués. There are some who claim the Cosmo was actually invented at the Odeon, but the drink began being served almost simultaneously at the Fog City Diner in San Francisco. So who knows? It could have been, as many gastronomic things are, created spontaneously and simultaneously in more than one place, a variant, a mutant that goes on to greater popularity than the thing that spawned it. The parent of the Cosmopolitan is probably the Harpoon, a drink that was created by the Ocean Spray Cranberry cooperative to promote cranberry juice in the 1970s. The Harpoon is an ounce of vodka, an ounce of cranberry juice, and a squeeze of lime juice. The Cosmo is only a little orange liqueur away.

The Cosmopolitan was redesigned in the early 1990s, says Degroff, to support the introduction of Absolut Citron Vodka. That makes sense, as so many classic cocktails have been created specifically to sell the spirits in them. Degroff didn't actually put his version on the menu at the Rainbow Room until 1996. Shortly thereafter, Madonna was seen sipping one at his bar. It is a very obvious, red drink in a Martini glass. And that's when the drink skyrocketed to fame and popularity.

"Overnight I was getting calls from as far away as Germany and Australia for the recipe," Degroff says in his book *The Craft of the Cocktail*. "I added the additional touches of Cointreau and a flamed orange peel for garnish and presented it several times on television around the country." (He was hired by Cointreau to do these demonstrations.) This is how, he thinks, it came to be that *New York* magazine incorrectly credited him with its invention, and other publications just repeated the false credit.

Makes 1

1½ ounces citron vodka
½ ounce Cointreau
¼ ounce fresh lime juice

1 ounce cranberry juice
Flamed orange peel for garnish

Shake the vodka, Cointreau, lime juice, and cranberry juice with ice. Pour into a chilled cocktail glass. Garnish with the flamed orange peel.

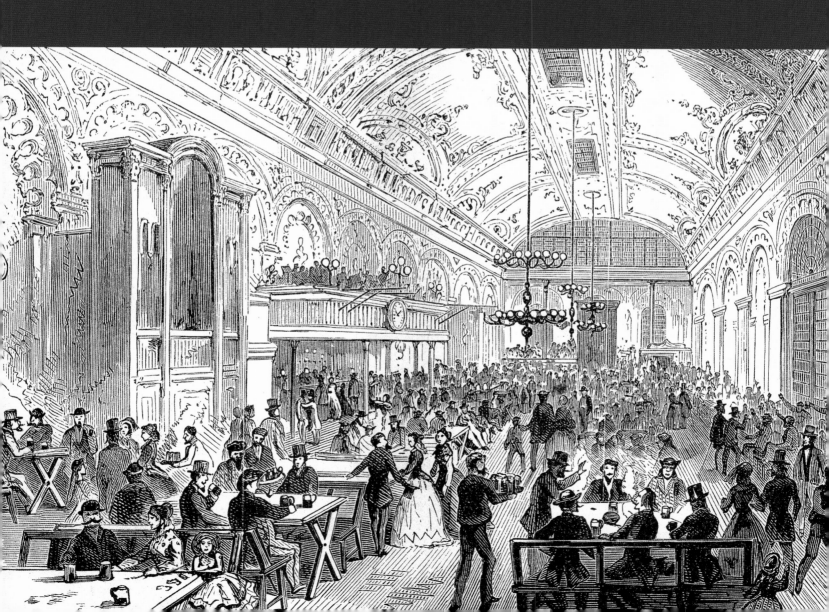

AN UNDERRATED CULINARY INFLUENCE

THERE HAVE BEEN GERMANS IN NEW YORK CITY FROM THE VERY EARLIEST days of New Amsterdam, and they continued to settle here in small numbers through the eighteenth and into the early nineteenth century. They clustered mainly on lower Greenwich Avenue, near the former site of the World Trade Center, and in greater numbers around Tompkins Square Park, west to the Bowery, and north to Houston Street—the Lower East Side. By the 1840s, this area was overwhelmingly German and called "Little Germany," Kleindeutschland to its inhabitants.

Then, starting in 1846 and peaking in 1853 and 1854, a flood of Germans arrived. With nearly every country in Europe having some kind of revolution, and after a succession of bad harvests throughout the continent, large numbers of German peasants, as well as artisans, teachers, lawyers, doctors, poets, and musicians left to find their fortune in America. In 1854 alone, about three hundred thousand came. All told, more than a million Germans arrived at East Coast ports of entry during the period. Many moved on to the West, but hundreds of thousands stayed in New York City, becoming the first ethnic group to make a gastronomic contribution to the city. They often came with liberal political beliefs, some money in their pockets, and food ways that they continued.

The Germans brought their baking tradition, perhaps their most enduring but unrecognized contribution to New York City food culture. They brought the hot dog and other delicatessen items, perhaps their most obvious contribution. And they introduced light, low-alcohol lager beer to a nation weaned on the heavy and strong English style of beer. They opened breweries and beer gardens and eventually made New York City the beer capital of the country and one of the most lubricated cities on earth.

Because some of the German immigrants were Jews, and prepared their breads, cakes, and processed meats according to the Jewish dietary laws, and because later waves of Jews from Eastern Europe adopted German foods and popularized them, and because some food became so quickly and fully assimilated into the general culture, the Germans don't get their due for certain iconic New York City foods—rye bread, "corn" bread (a sour rye), pumpernickel, hard rolls (they are after all called Kaiser rolls for a reason), and crumb cake (see page 295). Corned beef and sour dill pickles were German introductions, and one can argue whether the New York City soft pretzel is Dutch or German. On the other hand, every American enjoys the Germans' light amber, easily quaffed lager. It's our national beverage.

Beer halls and gardens opened by the dozens. Unlike the old-time rowdy taverns of the English, the male-bastion bars of the Irish further downtown, the low-class Bowery saloons and dives, the free lunch saloons, and the back rooms of "groceries" where whiskey was sold by the glass, the German beer halls and gardens were respectable places. Whole families would go to the halls and gardens, which scandalized non-Germans. Sundays, after church, the Germans would sit and listen to music, full orchestras with pianos, harps, violins, drums, and plenty of brass. The adults would play cards or dominoes or dice. Occasionally everyone would burst into song together, usually pieces that expressed nostalgia for the old country. The Volksgarten was a famous Bowery beer hall, and it survived until Prohibition. The largest was the Atlantic Garden, also on the Bowery, next to the still existing Old Bowery Theater. It seated more than one thousand people on two floors. The beer "consumption by its patrons was such," says Luc Sante in his 1991 book *Low Life*, "that two four-horse drays were kept in constant rotation to the brewery and back for ten hours a day." Many of the beer halls and gardens were extensions of the breweries, but not all. In any case, they always offered food, too. A journalist of the 1850s described "a large low ceiling, square room with a bar on either hand, groaning with the weight of dripping kegs, piles of crystal glasses of all dimensions and variety; loaded with sausages, those famous snake-looking, American 'Bolognas,' with cakes and bread, brown and shiny, contorted and twisted, patted and moulded [sic] as only the German brain could devise; green, fresh-looking salads dripping with oil, dimpled with red beets and scarlet turnips, salads of fish, salads of meat, salads of herring."

Meanwhile, further uptown, two other German enclaves were emerging. There was one in the East Fifties—Saint Peter's Lutheran Church in the Citicorp Center is a vestige of that community—and another between East Eighty-third and Eighty-ninth Streets. The area furthest uptown was first settled in the 1790s and was called Yorkville to emphasize its connection to the city downtown. It was an isolated community surrounded by wealthy country estates until 1834 when the New York and Harlem Railroad extended its line through the area. With the rail link, new housing was constructed, attracting some of the better-off Germans. The Rupperts, Ringlings, and Rhinelanders, all names that would now be considered New York City society, built houses there. The Ruppert Brewery was there, too.

"Little Germany" on the Lower East Side thrived until June 15, 1904, when the horrific, so-called "Slocum Disaster" decimated it. Fifteen hundred members of the Saint Mark's Lutheran Church, mostly women and children, took an East River excursion on the General Slocum, a pleasure boat, and it went up in flames. More than one thousand people died. The community couldn't bear the loss, and the tragedy encouraged a great number to move away from the memories and uptown to the already established, but small German enclave of Yorkville.

The survivors transformed the area around East Eighty-sixth Street into another Kleindeutschland. German became the dominant language, and the street became an avenue of

German pastry shops (*Konditereien*), butchers, grocers, restaurants, and beer halls. There was even a German language entertainment hall, the Yorkville Casino, which showed German movies.

Restaurateur George Lang, who came from Hungary after World War II, knew to go to Yorkville, where there was, by then, also a well-established community of other Central and Eastern Europeans. While East Eighty-sixth Street was mainly the German enclave, Second Avenue had become home to Hungarians, Poles, Czechs, Slavs, and, as always and everywhere in New York City, a sprinkling of Irish.

Until the early 1990s there were still many restaurants, bakeries, butchers, and specialty food shops of old European Yorkville. Now there is one German food purveyor, Schaller and Weber, the pork store and specialty grocery, still just off the corner of Second Avenue and Eighty-sixth Street and one German restaurant—Heidelberg—around the corner.

The bar in the Hans Jaeger restaurant, circa 1890.

GERMAN DELICATESSENS

The first delicatessens in New York City were owned and run by Germans, both Christian and Jewish. The word delicatessen is German—*essen* means "to eat," the word *deli* comes from the same root as delicacy—and the shops carried various sausages and cured meats, salads and condiments, much of it later co-opted by Eastern European Jews who transformed them into the Jewish deli, what some might consider quintessential New York City foods.

When New Yorkers of a certain age talk about the German deli, however, they mean a genre of neighborhood grocery. Exactly when these evolved is anyone's guess, but I'll take a stab at the turn of the century, with a heyday beginning in the 1920s and lasting well into the 1960s. At these stores one could count on finding Düsseldorf mustard, preserves imported from Europe, packaged German cookies and crackers, a huge array of cold cuts, cheeses, salads, and prepared foods, plus a line or two of specialty canned goods that were too fine and expensive to be carried in the supermarket—S&W, Haddon House, Cross and Blackwell. The German deli also sold essentials like milk, bread, eggs, and toilet paper.

> *I remember running from store to store, grabbing as many ballots as I could. In the neighborhood there sure wasn't talk about the election for mayor or governor...but when it came to the Miss Rheingold Contest, everybody was involved. The talk was all about it. Everybody talked about it...and everybody voted.*
> —JOHN CORRADO, *resident of East Harlem during the 1940s and 1950s*

You didn't have to live in a German neighborhood to have a delicatessen—they served every part of the city. They were called German because they were owned by Germans and followed a particular format. Because of a quirk in the Sunday blue laws that prevented supermarkets from being open on the Christian Sabbath but not small specialty stores, the German delicatessens were, from the 1920s through the 1960s, the only place you could fill in with basic grocery items on Sunday. It is from these German delicatessens, not the Jewish ones, that today's so-called "gourmet" deli is descended.

There are almost no German delis left in New York City. Korean immigrants, who started coming in the 1970s, have taken over the corner grocery business in the city, turning former fruit stands (and building many new ones) into markets that are open twenty-four hours a day. Instead

of strong mustard and fruit preserves, they carry kimchee and pickled ginger.

The German delis also served as
an early take-out shop with a small
list of prepared foods. The better
delis roasted a turkey every day
and glazed a ham. They roasted
"steamer rounds" of beef, which
was sliced and sold by the pound.
They made baked beans and baked
macaroni that were often sold in
small, single-portion foil cups. You
could also find fried meat cakes
during the week, and salmon croquettes and fish cakes on Friday, all
of which were displayed in neat
stacks on the high glass counter.

In Brooklyn,
one of the last of
the city's German
delicatessens.

They baked spaghetti in a very un-Italian tomato sauce, and sold this as a casserole dish cut into
squares. They offered an array of mayonnaise-bound salads—tuna, egg, chicken, salmon, and
ham—plus coleslaw, macaroni salad, and two versions of potato salad, with mayo and also sweet
and sour with oil and vinegar, and crumbled bacon. With all their salads and cold cuts, they made
sandwiches for lunch. And New Yorkers still talk about the creamy rice pudding (page 101) and
tapioca pudding.

The German delicatessens also had a certain look. They were, above all, immaculate. Their
storefront windows often had black mirrored panels advertising the brand of cold cuts they carried, and a neon Rheingold or other beer sign. It was at the German deli in the 1950s that you
went to vote for Miss Rheingold, a very popular, city-wide beauty contest conducted by the
brewery. The floors were mosaic tile, sometimes covered with sawdust. The refrigerated case,
which was the most important piece of equipment in the store, as it housed all the hams, sausage,
and cheeses, was along one long wall. The opposite wall was floor to ceiling canned and jarred
goods. Behind the store proper was usually a small kitchen where all the prepared foods were
made. A very few German delicatessen storefronts still exist around the city, but they've been
taken over by other ethnic groups.

LÜCHOW'S

To conjure an image of the great Lüchow's in its heyday, picture the Harmonia Gardens, the restaurant in *Hello Dolly* where Dolly Levi (a part originated by Carol Channing on Broadway and played by Barbra Streisand in the movie) makes her grand entrance to the musical's showstopping title song. No one like Louis Armstrong would have been there leading the orchestra in 1882, when Lüchow's opened, but, as a sign in the entrance was eventually able to boast: "Through the doors of Lüchow's pass all the famous people of the world." For a good part of its one hundred years in business it was true.

Lüchow's opened during the era of German beer halls and gardens, but with a location at the hub of the city's artistic, literary, political, and musical life—Union Square—Lüchow's was so much more than the others. Proof that it had attractions other than alcohol is that it survived Prohibition, while all the German places where beer was king were forced to close.

August Guido Lüchow was, by all accounts, a gregarious and generous man, an immigrant who worked as a bartender and waiter for three years before he bought out his employer and opened his restaurant. It was a smart move. Tammany Hall (it's a theater now), home to the city's all-powerful Democratic machine, was on the northeast corner of Union Square. On the west side of the square were some of the most fashionable stores in the city. Tiffany, Macy's, and Brentano's are the names still recognized today. Steinway Hall (as in the famous piano company) was nearby, as was the Academy of Music, Tony Pastor's Theater, and an array of German and Hungarian bars and eateries, ranging from the venerable Lienau's German beer hall, Brubacher's Wine Garden, the Cafe Hungaria, the Alhambra Gardens, and down to a group of more plebeian places where, for the price of a nickel beer, you got a free lunch of pretzels, cheese, sausage, and pickles.

As the sign in the entrance to Lüchow's said, the names that passed through it were staggeringly famous, although many would be unrecognizable now. Those who are remembered include Andrew Carnegie, J.P. Morgan, O. Henry, H.L. Mencken, George Jean Nathan, Anna Held, Al Smith, Theodore Dreiser, Mack Sennett (who supposedly came up with the idea for the Keystone Cops while lunching there one summer day in 1912), and Gus Kahn, the songwriter who claimed he wrote "Yes, Sir, That's My Baby" on a tablecloth at Lüchow's. Among the politicians, Theodore Roosevelt was a regular customer, from the time he was New York City's police commissioner and whenever he could come while President. Victor Herbert conducted an eight-piece Viennese orchestra every Sunday night for four years.

Diamond Jim Brady and Lillian Russell seemed to have been regulars at every important restaurant of their day ("Diamond Jim Ate Here" used to be a sign almost as ubiquitous as

"Washington Slept Here"), but they definitely came frequently to Lüchow's. Like many high-rollers of his day, Diamond Jim would give parties there, and it is said that if a woman was in favor with him he might even tuck an important piece of jewelry under her napkin. I personally remember this huge scale that was part of the entry's furniture. Diamond Jim supposedly weighed himself on it before and after his meals, and didn't think the dinner was a success unless he gained a certain number of pounds while at table. As we left the restaurant, my father would always warn me that if I wasn't careful, I would end up as big as Diamond Jim. I haven't been careful.

Jan Mitchell, who bought Lüchow's in 1950, called William Steinway "the restaurant's patron saint" in *Lüchow's German Cookbook,* which he penned in 1952. Steinway "and his noted family entertained the great musicians of the world there, both in the downstairs room and in the private rooms upstairs." Steinway also lunched at Lüchow's every day, usually with his senior executives. The room where they ate was named for him, "The Steinway Room," and was immortalized in a drawing by Ludwig Bemelmans, the illustrator and writer who also executed sketches for Lüchow's cookbook. Bemelmans is most famous for his creation of the "Madeline" stories about a little French girl who has adventures with her Catholic schoolmates, and Bemelmans Bar in the Carlyle Hotel is named for him because he drew the delightful decorations on the walls.

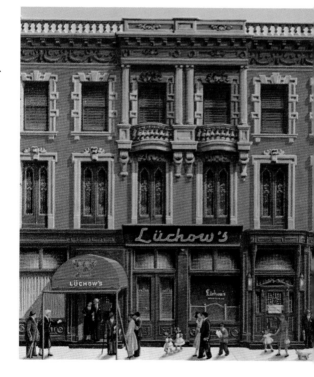

Lüchow's did not survive the decline of both Union Square and the city's recession of the 1970s. Before he closed the restaurant permanently, Peter Ashkenazy, its last owner, moved some of the famous German, Dutch, and Austrian oil paintings to an otherwise spare and modern Times Square location, hoping to cash in on the restaurant's fame where the tourists gathered. Without the authentic old German atmosphere of the original building, however, he did not succeed.

Some preservationists tried to get the Fourteenth Street building landmark status, but for some reason the city's landmark commission didn't understand its importance. It closed permanently in 1982, then briefly became a gay disco, then a private party space before the building was boarded up. After a suspicious fire in 1995, Lüchow's was torn down and replaced by a New York University dormitory.

LÜCHOW'S HERRING IN MUSTARD-DILL SAUCE

This was the favorite appetizer of Frederick Augustus III, the last King of Saxony. Oscar Hofmann was his chef. August Lüchow, on a trip to Germany, was entertained at the royal household. He liked the cooking so much that, with the king's consent, he persuaded Hofmann to come to America with him and made him the chef at his restaurant. The Herring in Dill Sauce is one of the recipes he brought with him.
—from *Lüchow's German Cookbook*, 1952

Serves 10

1 cup Düsseldorf (or strong imported Dijon)
    mustard (or other mustard)
1 cup peanut oil
¼ cup white wine vinegar
2 tablespoons lemon juice (juice of 1 lemon)
1 cup finely chopped fresh dill
½ tablespoon freshly ground black pepper
½ tablespoon whole allspice
2 tablespoons sugar
10 pickled herring fillets (about 1½ pounds)

In a mixing bowl, whisk together the mustard and oil. It should be the consistency of mayonnaise.

Add the vinegar in a thin stream, beating constantly.

Beat in the lemon juice, dill, pepper, allspice, and sugar.

In a deep dish or bowl, arrange the herring fillets, pouring sauce between the layers. Top with more sauce. Marinate in the refrigerator for 2 to 3 days before serving.

Serve one fillet per person with a garnish of radish roses, plus thin slices of buttered pumpernickel.

RICE PUDDING

I had no idea that New York City was somewhat unusual in being a rice pudding town until I was asked by Riviana Foods (Carolina and Mahatma brands) to propose a rice recipe category for a promotional contest. When I said rice pudding they were stunned. Apparently, no one in Texas, where much of our rice is grown and the company is based, cares about rice pudding. I had to tell them that everyone in New York City cares about rice pudding, even passionately cares, and that we love several kinds. I don't think the city has ever met a rice pudding it didn't like.

The following is the old-time favorite that was sold out of big stainless steel trays at the German delis. It is usually heavily (too heavily for me) sprinkled with cinnamon and sometimes contains raisins. The supposedly hard to reproduce creaminess is what everyone remembers and even waxes nostalgic about.

It's amazing how long New Yorkers have been loving rice pudding, and at every level of society. It has been on menus as high-flown as Delmonico's in the nineteenth century (there are two recipes in chef Charles Ranhofer's *The Epicurean*), and as pedestrian as Dinty Moore's in the 1950s. My paternal grandmother made a type of rice pudding that has since disappeared but that used to be popular in the Jewish dairy restaurants. It was started as the recipe below, but then egg yolks were stirred in, it was poured into a baking pan, topped with a meringue made from the egg whites, and baked. It was stiff enough that you could cut it into neat blocks for serving. In the dairy restaurants they often served this with warm, cornstarch-thickened canned fruit cocktail as a sauce, which is how they also sauced Jewish noodle pudding. Interestingly, one of the Ranhofer recipes is similar, except that candied fruits are mixed into the rice before it is baked in a decorative mold.

Makes 7 cups

At the Milleridge Inn on Long Island, a direct descendent of the Patricia and Lorraine Murphy restaurants (see page 248), they make their rice pudding extra creamy by stirring melted ice cream into it after it has cooled.

2 cups water	2 quarts whole milk
1 cup long-grain rice	¾ cup sugar
¼ teaspoon salt	1 tablespoon vanilla extract

Bring the water to a boil then add the rice and salt. Stir, then cover tightly and adjust the heat to the lowest possible. Cook 12 to 15 minutes, until all the water has been absorbed by the rice.

Transfer the rice to a 4- to 5-quart pot. Add the milk. Stir well and let simmer gently, uncovered, for about an hour. After 45 minutes, stir in the sugar.

When done, the rice should be fully puffed out, but the mixture will seem a little soupy.

Stir in the vanilla, and allow to cool. The pudding will thicken as it cools.

Chill well before serving.

The pudding will hold well for about two days in the refrigerator, but it may separate slightly. As long as the rice is still soft, stir any liquid back into the pudding, and enjoy.

A HERITAGE OF HOSPITALITY

YOU'VE PROBABLY HEARD THE JOKE. WHAT'S THE SHORTEST BOOK EVER written? *Irish Cooking.* It's a one-ingredient cookbook: Potatoes.

Only it's no joke. Food and communal eating are not part of Irish culture. The Irish identity is tied to drink and communal drinking. And potatoes were, astoundingly, the only food a majority of Irish ate throughout the eighteenth century and until the catastrophic potato famine of 1845. Then, suddenly, because a virus killed their only crop, there was literally nothing to eat, and all, not just most of their calories came from alcohol. It was time to leave Ireland.

Way before the starving Irish arrived here in the 1840s, however, there were plenty of Irish in New York City. They came during the English period, starting in about 1720, when trade with Ireland increased. They came in larger numbers after the American Revolution. In the 1830s, in the notorious Five Points section of the city, there were Irish gangs, Irish bars, and Irish groceries, which were as much vendors of alcoholic beverage as sellers of food.

I have another joke: The Irish are very good cooks . . . of other people's food. In the nineteenth century, the opposite was thought to be true. The inept Irish cook was the subject of jokes and cartoons. She was ubiquitous, that Irish cook, as most young Irish immigrants went into domestic service. In 1855, something like seventy-four percent of all domestics in New York City were Irish; more than one in four citizens of Manhattan and Brooklyn said they were born in Ireland, and that doesn't count the second and third generation Irish Americans.

In my lifetime, the joke works better: When an Irish girl marries a Sicilian boy she cooks Sicilian food good enough to please his grandmother. When an Irish lassie marries a Polish laddie she can do pierogis and kielbasi as well as his bubbie. Even when an Irish woman intermarries with a Jewish man, she learns to make chicken soup and matzoh balls like his mamma. Again, the Irish are cooking other people's food.

Both these jokes reveal truths about the Irish because, as Hasia R. Diner argues so persuasively in *Hungering for America*, "the Irish relate to hunger, not to food." As one proof, she notes that the architectural plans for two major Irish-American community centers (that were never built) account for every conceivable activity except cooking and eating. The buildings were being planned with no kitchens or dining rooms. Yet another example of how little the Irish consider food: at Irish-American festivals, there is Irish art, craft, song, and poetry, but no food stalls selling a national dish, as there would be at other ethnic gatherings. The Irish have literature. They have theater. They have music. They don't have cuisine.

Still, the Irish in New York City have always been associated with food. As just cited, the earliest arrivals often ended up in the grocery business, although the grocery stores (groceries) of the early nineteenth century mainly sold alcoholic beverages. Food, except for the barrels of pickled herring that people ate with their alcohol, was decidedly secondary.

The Irish were big in the boardinghouse business, too. Irish women—women in dire financial straits, widows and wives who may have been abandoned by men whose alcoholism prevented them from supporting their families—took in guests to make ends meet, and that meant feeding the guests, too. From the boardinghouse business to the restaurant business was not such a far cry, and restaurants did become an avenue that the Irish followed toward the American Dream. Not only did they dominate the police department, the fire department and, by 1880, the city's political system, but chances were your waiter, waitress, and bartender had an Irish brogue—well into the twentieth century.

Even if food meant little to the Irish, their unrivaled sociability made them great restaurateurs. Many an Irish bar became an Irish bar and grill, then a full-scale restaurant.

DINTY MOORE'S

If it wasn't for that infamous canned stew on every convenience store shelf, hardly anyone would remember the name Dinty Moore. Well, that's an exaggeration, as there are several Dinty Moore restaurants in the United States, and one in Canada.

During the first half of the twentieth century, however, the original New York Dinty Moore's at 216-220 West Forty-sixth Street was among the most famous restaurants in the country. Both the restaurant, which attracted the Broadway crowd in its heyday, and its owner, a rough, rather foul-mouthed man according to firsthand accounts, figured in a very popular comic strip, *Bringing Up Father*, created by cartoonist George McManus in 1913. It ran in William Randolph Hearst's newspaper, *New York American*, and eventually Hearst's papers across the country. In 1946, it even was made into a feature film by the same name.

Bringing Up Father was the story of an Irish American named Jiggs, a former bricklayer, and his wife Maggie, a former laundress, who achieved sudden wealth. Snobby Maggie and their beautiful daughter Nora constantly tried to raise Jiggs to a new social status. Jiggs, on the other hand, liked nothing better than sitting down at Dinty Moore's to finish off several dishes of corned beef and cabbage, as well as considerable drink, with the boys from the old neighborhood. The clash of wills between Jiggs and Maggie often ended up in Jiggs fending off a rolling pin, frying pan, or flying dishes.

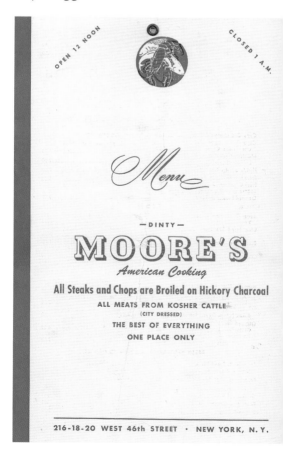

One running gag of *Bringing Up Father* was Jiggs's obsession with corned beef and cabbage, a dish that didn't originate in Ireland, but that Irish Americans had adopted as their Sunday and important occasion dish. According to McManus, himself an Irish American from St. Louis, Jiggs's deep interest in the dish was meant to represent his connection with his poor Irish past, while Maggie's detestation of the dish represented her American desire to move up and on.

Dinty Moore's apparently started in business as an Irish bar, then got through Prohibition as a speakeasy and hangout for Broadway types, then became a tourist restaurant specializing not in the traditional Irish stew—none of the old guide books mention stew—but in corned beef and cabbage. According to a 1940s menu, the corned beef (listed in red type to indicate it was a signature dish) was "cured with sugar and honey" and it was served with New Florida Cabbage. Other red letter specialties included Sugar Cured Ham, cured on the premises, Moore's Hamburger Steak (with Onions), and Moore's Homemade Rice Pudding with Cream, but the stew was in the ordinary green type: Special Irish Stew made with Kosher Lamb and Prime Ribs of Beef.

It may seem strange today for a non-kosher restaurant menu to note that the meat is kosher, but this was the norm on post–World War II menus in New York City. Mainstream restaurants were attracting recently assimilated and newly affluent Jews who were willing to eat in non-kosher restaurants but not eat non-kosher meat. Underscoring the point, Dinty Moore's 1940s menu cover boasted "All Meats From Kosher Cattle." So even though it was served with bacon, the menu lists Kosher Fresh Killed Calf Liver. And, like many other New York City menus of the 1940s, it lists a gefilte fish next to sautéed jumbo shrimp.

During Prohibition, according to Ruth Gordon, the actress and screenwriter, Dinty Moore's "was like the end of paradise." Gordon goes on to note:

Now, Jim Moore, who owned it—they called him Dinty—was a very tough character right out of the funny papers. George S. Kaufman came in once and asked for a hamburger and could they please leave out the onions. He said that to the waiter who went over and told Mr. Moore, who marched over to George's table. "Which one's the bastard who ordered the hamburger without the onions?" Kaufman said, "I did." Mr. Moore took him by the lapel and said, "Out. . . . Get out of here!" George asked him, "What's the idea?" Moore said, "I don't tell you how to write your goddamned plays and you don't tell me how to cook my hamburgers!"

Nobody ever saw Mrs. Moore. She was in a wheelchair and lived upstairs in their residence. But every day, about noon, down the elevator would come a waiter carrying this great huge pan, and in it was homemade rice pudding that she had made. You never tasted anything like it!

Fanny Brice used to take the corner table and Mr. Moore would bring over this big yellow bowl with boiled potatoes in it and cream and butter on the side. She and Mr. Moore would sit there talking while she stirred it all up. Fanny made the world's greatest mashed potatoes. And he'd ask her how the show was going and she'd ask about business.

Just to show you the atmosphere at Dinty Moore's, they had Sapolito to wash your hands with in the ladies room. They used to use Sapolito to scrub the floors. Your hands used to come apart after you used it.

CAVANAGH'S

Cavanagh's opened at 260 West Twenty-third Street around 1880 and for nearly eighty-five years remained one of New York City's favorite restaurants, ending up as part of the Longchamp's chain.

"Here is a great restaurant of Little Old New York which has maintained the same high standard of American cooking for close to half a century," wrote G. Selmer Fougher in his 1931 guide, *Dining Out in New York*. "Although many of the important persons in political and social life who made the restaurant famous have moved away from the Chelsea area, Cavanagh's seems to have increased in popularity and its patrons visit it at regular intervals whatever may be their present home." Fougher goes on to rave about the Club Steak and English South-down Chop (a mutton chop).

CAVANAGH'S Restaurant - 260 W. 23rd St. New York

It was still a great place to eat meat in 1955 when Harry Botsford wrote in *New York's 100 Best Restaurants* that "for nearly eight decades carnivores and solvent man has wended his way to [its] portals and eventually departed full of fine victuals." He touted the steak, the roast beef, the "lordly" baked potato, "the best Manhattan clam chowder in town," and the waiters, whom he called "elderly and knowing."

Cavanagh's closed sometime in the early 1960s. The menu in the late 1950s was notable for the great number of classic New York City dishes it offered. Among them: Oyster Stew and Oysters Casino, Eggs Benedict, Chicken à la King, Broiled Shad Roe (with bacon), Veal Cutlet à la Parmigiana, Curry of Shrimp Madras, Lobster à la Newburg, Crab Dewey, Nesselrode Pie, Cheese Cake, and Rice Pudding. A note about "Cavanagh's Famous Old-Fashioned Beefsteak Parties: A New York Tradition for Over 70 Years" (see page 223) is set off in a box.

CORNED BEEF AND CABBAGE

First came Irish bacon. It probably appeared sometime in the mid-eighteenth century, probably as a bonus of the increasing flax trade between several Irish ports and New York City. Certainly, in the 1830s, when the Irish first arrived in numbers, Irish bacon was already a staple of the city's chop houses. But the Irish immigrants couldn't afford to eat Irish bacon—it was a luxury product. It probably wasn't until the late nineteenth century, when the Irish in Ireland had advanced enough economically to treat themselves to a festive dish of bacon and greens, that any Irish American considered the possibility.

How bacon and greens evolved into Corned Beef and Cabbage is anybody's guess. Some surmise that the Irish adopted the meat of their German, Jewish, or even German-Jewish neighbors or WASP employers and turned it into a dish to help celebrate their Saint Patrick's Day, an essentially New York City–Irish holiday that is now part of all Irish American culture.

It's said that "everyone in New York City is Irish on Saint Patrick's Day." The beer is green, the bagels are green, Italian pastries are filled with green cream, Latinos eat green rice, and everyone enjoys Corned Beef and Cabbage.

Serves 6 to 8

The hardest thing about cooking corned beef is finding a good piece of meat. "Corned" refers only to the brining/pickling process that the meat has been through, not the cut, which is brisket. There are two muscles to the whole brisket, and their grains run diagonally to each other. The bottom, leaner muscle, which today often has too little integral fat to cook up juicy and tender, is usually called "first cut," "thin cut," or "flat cut." The so-called second cut, or point, the top and smaller piece, has more fat and is more succulent. Between the two muscles is a layer of fat.

Ideally, you want to cook a whole brisket (both sections together) with all its fat. You can trim off the fat after the meat is cooked. Unfortunately, whole corned briskets (even fresh briskets) are difficult to find, and second-cut corned beef brisket is even more difficult to find. What most supermarkets carry is first-cut corned beef vacuum-packed in plastic. Look for the fattiest piece in the case, then be sure to treat it gently.

Many people cook the cabbage and potatoes in the same water as the corned beef. Because the vegetables need to be cooked in water that simmers more violently than the meat, I prefer to scoop out water from the corned beef pot and cook the vegetables in a separate pot or pots.

1 (4- to 5-pound) corned beef brisket
1 teaspoon pickling spices
1 head cabbage
2 pounds boiling potatoes

6 to 8 small carrots (optional)
Parsnips (optional)
Turnips (optional)

Place the corned beef in a pot that holds at least 5 quarts. Cover completely with cold water. Place over high heat and bring to a simmer.

As soon as bubbles start to break on the surface of the water, adjust the heat so the water simmers very, very gently. With a slotted spoon, skim off the scum as it accumulates on the surface. When the scum stops coming to the surface, add the pickling spices.

Continue to cook, with bubbles just gently breaking on the surface, for 3 to 4 hours, until fork tender.

The meat can be safely held in its water for about 2 hours; reheat gently.

Cook the vegetables until fork tender in separate pots of boiling fresh water, or, especially for the cabbage, use some of the water in which the corned beef was cooked.

Serve the corned beef sliced, on a platter, surrounded with some of the vegetables or with vegetables in a separate bowl. Serve with mustard and/or horseradish.

IRISH SODA BREAD

This recipe was first published in the *New York Daily News* in the 1950s, and is by now many families' "family recipe."

Makes 1 loaf, serving 6 to 8

2 cups bleached all-purpose flour
1½ teaspoons baking powder
¾ teaspoon baking soda
1 teaspoon salt
¼ cup sugar
1½ teaspoons caraway seeds

3 tablespoons unsalted butter or vegetable shortening
1 cup buttermilk or sour milk
⅔ cup raisins, dark or golden, coarsely chopped
1 tablespoon unsalted butter, melted
¼ teaspoon ground cinnamon

Preheat the oven to 375 degrees. Grease an 8- or 9-inch round cake pan.

In a medium bowl, combine the flour, baking powder, baking soda, salt, 3 tablespoons of the sugar, and the caraway seeds. Stir to combine.

Add the 3 tablespoons butter and cut it into the flour mixture with a pastry blender, two knives, or your fingertips until the fat is in tiny pieces.

Make a well in center of the flour mixture. Pour in the buttermilk and add the raisins. Mix lightly.

Turn out onto a lightly floured board and knead

gently a few times to form a cohesive dough. Do not overwork. Shape into a 5-inch round loaf and place in the prepared pan.

Using a sharp knife or scissors, cut an X in the dough about one third of the way through. Brush the top surface with the melted butter and sprinkle with the remaining 1 tablespoon sugar mixed with the cinnamon.

Bake for 35 to 45 minutes, until golden brown. Cool. Eat at room temperature.

BEYOND THE PALE

THE INFLUENCE OF JEWS ON NEW YORK CITY'S FOOD CULTURE CANNOT BE overestimated. One can safely say that some of the most quintessential New York City foods are of Central and Eastern European Jewish origin: bagels (and lox), pastrami on rye, corned beef, pickles, cheesecake, matzoh balls, knishes, and egg creams. The hot dog is not a Jewish concept. It's German. But one can argue it was Jewish entrepreneurs who made it the food of the people.

OPPOSITE: Orchard Street, looking south from Hester Street, was a veritable outdoor mall in 1898.

During the last quarter of the nineteenth century and until 1924, when the immigration laws were changed, two million Jews migrated to America. Most of them remained in New York City, the main port of entry, if only temporarily, changing many of the city's cultural aspects forever. Unlike some other ethnic groups—particularly the southern Italians, whose culinary and cultural contributions to New York City and the country are also legion—the Jews came to America with the intention of staying. Most Italians, at least when they arrived, thought of themselves as temporary residents, here to earn money before going back to the Italian good life that they actually never knew in Italy. For the Jews, who were escaping racial persecution as well as poverty, America was to be their new permanent home, their country. Consequently, they learned English quickly, encouraged their children to become educated Americans, and immediately set up institutions that would foster their assimilation and their attainment of the American Dream.

By 1910, there were about one million Jews in New York City. In 1957, the city's Jewish population was more than two million. One in four New Yorkers was a Jew. Even today, nearly three generations after the post–World War II exodus to the suburbs, Jews still account for thirty-four percent of the non-Hispanic white population of the city. In 2003, there were nearly a million Jews in the five boroughs—one in eight New Yorkers—and almost half a million more in the commutable suburbs.

Not least of the Jewish influences on New York City's food culture is the peculiar Jewish openness and taste for the exotic. Peculiar because, after generations of living in small villages in Russia, Poland, Romania, and other nearby countries, about the most exotic food Jews might have eaten was the occasional orange. But, forced to wander the world, Jews have become famous for adjusting their ways to new circumstances and adopting new cultures. Although the Jewish religious dietary laws were almost always followed in Europe before the twentieth century, creating a closed system of food production and distribution that held the Jews together as a community and set them apart from their neighbors, within those parameters Jews are usually willing to adopt and adapt the cuisine of their host culture. That's why Moroccan Jews cook Moroccan food, Spanish Jews cook Spanish food, and Italian Jews cook Italian food. In

One of the first things Jews did when they arrived on the Lower East Side was establish food stores that adhered to Jewish dietary laws, including closing on the Sabbath.

55
סטריק טלי
כשר
טשיקען מארקעט
פריש געשחטען ירע שטונע
CHICKEN MARKET

Israel, it took only one generation for the children of World War II's European refugees to make falafel and hummus—Middle Eastern foods (Arab foods!)—the most popular dishes of the Jewish state.

In any case, in Judaism, food is sacred. Eating at the Sabbath table is said to be akin to partaking of the sacrificial lamb at the inner sanctum altar in the ancient Temple in Jerusalem. There is symbolism, ritual, and many regulations built around food's production, purchase, preparation, and consumption. That New York City is a food-obsessed city is in part due to the Jewish obsession with food, and in eating well, which is a sign that you are blessed.

In New York City, in America, kosher Jewish foodways continued for a time, but not for long. At first, "Jews lived primarily where they could buy Jewish food," says Hasia R. Diner in *Hungering for America*, which is one good reason why so many stayed in New York City, and not many became pioneer farmers in Minnesota. Even in urban areas it was often difficult, if not impossible, to obtain kosher meats and poultry. New York City, however, had such a concentration of Jews that kosher butchers, fish markets, bakeries, and groceries soon supported the community. If you spoke only Yiddish when you arrived, opening a store in the Jewish enclave was a good way to earn a living.

In 1899, a survey of the Lower East Side counted 631 Jewish food purveyors. Among them were 140 groceries, 131 butchers, 36 bakeries, 14 butter and egg stores, 62 candy stores, 21 fruit and vegetable stands, and 10 delicatessens. In 1910, there were 60 delicatessens. During the early years of the century, the streets became congested with peddlers and carts. Even as late as the 1950s, Orchard Street and Essex Street, as well as other streets in that old immigrant neighborhood of Manhattan, still sported both stores and street carts bursting with Jewish foods. And it was the same in the newer Jewish commercial centers of Blake and Belmont Avenues in Brooklyn's Brownsville and East New York sections. They were veritable food festivals. The few remnants of this world include Guss' Pickles on Orchard Street (see page 123), Gertel's Bakery on Hester Street, Economy Candy on Orchard Street, Yonah Shimmel's knishes on Houston Street (see page 142), Katz's delicatessen on the corner of Ludlow and Houston Streets, and Russ & Daughters' "appetizing" store on the next block of Houston, between Orchard and Allen Streets.

In New York City Jews could also eat away from home and keep their dietary laws. In 1903, the word *oyesessen*, meaning "eating out," first appeared in the *Forverts*, the *Jewish Daily Forward*, the Yiddish language newspaper. "The newspaper considered the growing interest in eating outside the home a positive step in immigrants' education and part of a larger process of social evolution," according to Diner.

But eating out was hardly a new concept for Jews in New York City. By the time that Russians, Poles, and Romanians began arriving at the end of the nineteenth century, German and Austrian Jews had already established themselves in New York City. Many of them had reached the pinnacles of economic success. They had their own coffee houses and delicatessens. Indeed, Diner credits a Berlin-born Jew, Isaac Gellis, a sausage manufacturer on Essex Street, for popularizing the typical German-Jewish delicatessen meats. Already in 1872, she says, he was producing "mountains of kosher sausages, frankfurters and other cold cuts" that, along with the pastrami of Eastern Europe (namely Romania), became the hallmarks of the New York Jewish delicatessen.

Although Eastern European Jews "had not eaten these foods before migration, as American Jews they learned to think of them as traditional," says Diner. This would explain the popular belief among New York City Jews that the first Jewish delicatessens were opened by and for immigrant

men who came to America without women (much like the Chinese did a half century before them), calling for their wives and young children only after they had found work and a place to live. But this would not fit the pattern of German-Jewish immigration. It fits only the later Eastern European immigration, which came after Jewish delicatessens already existed. What is true is that the delicatessen became a home away from home for many new immigrant men. The deli was a simple, non-intimidating restaurant that provided familiar foods, as well as the kosher but unfamiliar foods of Jews from other European Jewish communities.

When Jews started doing business away from the immigrant ghettos, they faced the enticement and convenience of non-Jewish food stores and restaurants. Upwardly mobile Jews found it difficult to keep the kosher laws. This, as well as a whole spectrum of food-related problems, became a subject of much contention in the Jewish community. It wasn't just the divisive question of whether to keep kosher or not, but also the politics of supervision, of regulating food production, of the observance of Sabbath by some stores and not others. The end result was that most New York City Jews gradually started abandoning their religious foodways.

In America, the individual Jew's acceptance of non-kosher foods and foodways came to symbolize—even measure—his climb up the socioeconomic ladder, the distance he had traveled on the road to assimilation, and his attainment of the American Dream. This is one of several reasons that New

York City's Jews are famously in love with Chinese food (see page 133), and perhaps why, to this day, they are often the backers of fancy French or fusion restaurants.

At the same time that Jews were moving away from their dietary laws, mainstream America started catering to them. In New York City, the Maxwell House coffee company courted Jewish customers by publishing a Passover Haggadah, the book that outlines the order of the seder and is read at the ritual table of the holiday. A big move on a national level was Proctor and Gamble's introduction of Crisco in 1925. The vegetable fat was neither dairy nor meat and so foods made with it, particularly baked goods, could be *pareve*, a word that means suitable for meals of either kind. Crisco allowed Jews to eat some all-American dishes with their traditional foods.

After the delicatessens, Jews opened full-service restaurants to feed each other. By the 1920s, the area between Delancey Street and Houston Street was filled with Jewish eateries that catered to the better-off area residents, but even more to the Jews who had moved out, mainly to the Bronx and Brooklyn, but came back to eat their soul food. The era of the Romanian Steakhouse began (see page 127). The flip side of the steakhouses were restaurants that served only dairy and vegetarian dishes—from blintzes to fish entrees—among them the only recently demised Ratner's, and the long-gone Rappaport's. Then, as their clientele continued to move uptown and to the boroughs, and eventually to the suburbs, mingling with the city's non-Jewish citizens, mainly the Italians and Irish, so did the restaurants. Now they were not necessarily kosher.

By the 1940s and 1950s, mainstream menus, such as those at Solowey's across the street from Penn Station, and hot, late-night spots, such as Leon and Eddie's (a former speakeasy), listed blintzes and chicken soup with matzoh balls alongside such blatantly non-kosher food as grilled ham steak. These restaurants, although Jewish owned, and giving a culinary nod to their nouveau riche Jewish customers, were meant for all New Yorkers, and appealed to all New Yorkers. They offered the newly assimilated Jew his first taste of ham or Lobster Newberg, and also provided the non-Jew with his first taste of gefilte fish.

FROM UPPER-LEFT CORNER, CLOCKWISE:
Scallion cream cheese for bagels;
Barney Greengrass, the Sturgeon King;
chubs on the smoking rack;
bagels baking;
a kosher bagel bakery in Brooklyn;
herrings galore at Russ & Daughters on
Houston Street;
Acme, in Williamsburg, Brooklyn,
is the city's largest smokehouse;
smoked salmon.

JEWISH APPETIZING

In the world of kosher foods, appetizing is the opposite of delicatessen. Jewish delicatessens specialize in meats—most notably pastrami, corned beef, and salami—and the foods that are allowed to be eaten at kosher meat meals. Appetizing stores specialize in dairy products—cheese and other milk- and cream-based foods—and the foods that are allowed and that are traditional at the same meal with them. That would be pickled and smoked fish, which is even more important than the dairy itself.

Although in the Orthodox Jewish neighborhoods of Brooklyn—and in Jewish areas in the suburbs—the word "appetizing" may still be printed on a store awning, it is not a word uttered as much today as it used to be. Even in the observant sections of the city, where family incomes are high enough to afford many luxuries, the array of appetizing is more limited than it used to be. Often the edited line of appetizing products has been folded into the bagel bakery. In other parts of the city, ask a resident what "appetizing" means and, even if he is Jewish from St. Louis, he is likely to draw a blank. However, the now internationally famous Zabar's, on the Upper West Side, started out as a simple appetizing store and still prides itself on the high standards of its appetizing department. Barney Greengrass, the Sturgeon King, also on the Upper West Side, is one of just a few small, family-owned appetizing stores left. The most notable survivor is Russ & Daughters on Houston Street on the Lower East Side, now managed by a fourth generation of the Russ family. Its quality and variety is the best in town, which means the world.

Just as the word "delicatessen" refers to the store and the products it sells, the word "appetizing" refers to both the merchandise and to the store that sells it. You can say, for instance, "I'm going to the appetizing store to get a quarter-pound of lox." Or you can say, "We ate appetizing for dinner."

Appetizing even includes salty, black lumpfish caviar, a standard at bar mitzvahs and Jewish weddings for generations, but the mainstays are bright orange lox and paler, less salty smoked salmon, so-called Nova, although not all of it comes from Nova Scotia anymore; pickled cubes of lox floating in brine with spices, and thick slices of kippered (hot-smoked) salmon, which is also called "baked" salmon. Large, golden, smoked whitefish and tiny chubs looking like miniature white fish glisten in the glass-fronted cases. Smoked sturgeon and sable, a fatty, white-fleshed fish treated with a paprika coating, are always carved as carefully as the precious smoked salmon and lox. Last, but hardly least, there are numerous stainless steel trays of herring—from purple, salty *matjes* to blue-grey, pickled whole herrings and fillets in "wine" sauce, or in sour cream sauce, both with sliced pickled onions.

BAGELS

Bagels were called cement doughnuts years ago. Given today's huge, puffy rings, that sobriquet may be hard to understand. The original article was small, dense, and chewy. It had a chewy crust, but was soft and fragrant for about an hour after it came from the oven. Give it two hours and it needed to be reheated, revived. Give it a day and you had to split it and toast it to make it edible, by which process it also gained an entirely new character. A toasted bagel is a very different thing from a fresh bagel, and if you had one that was fresh it would have been weird to toast it. Those were the days when the sign "Hot Bagels" had real meaning and importance.

Bagels are to New York City what croissants are to France, even to the point that they have been debased by commercialization. Just like the flaky French crescent breakfast bread, bagels are everywhere today, though hardly a one is worth the name if you are an old-timer with a taste memory. Even in New York City. There was a time, in fact, more or less the 1960s and 1970s, when New York City's bagel bakers—along with many other New Yorkers escaping the city's changing ethnic character—"emigrated" to other American cities. They went to Baltimore, Philadelphia, Toledo, and wherever they went those cities got the benefit of their skills, while in New York City a Jewish bagel baker became a rare bird.

Bagels are originally Polish. They are still sold on the streets of Krakow. According to one legend, in 1683, a Jewish baker in Vienna, Austria, wanted to thank King John III Sobieski of Poland for protecting his country from a Turkish invasion. So he made a roll in the shape of a riding stirrup—*bugel* in Austrian means "bracelet" or "ring"—commemorating the king's skill as a horseman. Wouldn't that make bagels Austrian?

Contradicting that story is the fact that bagels are mentioned in Krakow municipal records of 1610. They traveled east. My maternal grandfather, who was born near Minsk, not far from Poland, in 1904 and came to New York City in 1917, remembered them being sold by peddlers who carried them on strings. Or so he told me.

Bagels must have arrived in New York City fairly early in the Eastern European migration because in 1910 a bagel bakers union was founded. There were thirty-six bagel bakeries in New York City at the time, and a few more than three hundred bagel bakers. It was a "closed shop," as they say in labor union circles. Only the sons or nephews of bakers were allowed in the union and given jobs.

Making bagels is a two-step process. The flour from very high-gluten wheat is made into a dough with yeast and a bit of malt. The dough is shaped into a ring, then boiled. The boiling gives the bagels their dense texture, their distinctive chewy crust, and it gives the bagel's surface its shine. Traditional bagels are baked only after they have been boiled.

This was all done by hand until the early 1960s, when Dan Thompson, a Canadian bagel baker, introduced the Thompson Bagel Machine, which both shapes and boils the bagels. The technology allowed a dramatic increase in production, with the machines capable of turning out as much as four times the capacity of a human bagel baker. This set the stage for the Americanization of the bagel.

When Did Bagels Meet Lox?

According to most sources, salted salmon—lox—became popular on the East Coast after the transcontinental railroad connected the coasts in 1869. The Pacific waters were teeming with salmon and the fish was sent to the East in barrels, layered with salt, which drew out their moisture, forming a brine that could keep them edible for the duration of the trip—and longer. Lox probably caught on with the poor Jews of the Lower East Side significantly before they had cream cheese, since preserved fish had been a mainstay in the old country. In New York City, the Jews lived in tenements with minimal cooking facilities. An already "cooked" product like lox was akin to a convenience food.

Questioning numerous members of my parents' generation, who are now in their late seventies and older (I even scouted Florida retirement communities), I found no one who remembers eating bagels with lox and cream cheese in their youth, but a few people remembered an Al Jolson song from the 1920s called "Bagels and Yox." This supports the theory of Joan Nathan, author of *Jewish Cooking in America,* that it was Al Jolson and other entertainers, in about 1933, on a two-hour radio show sponsored by James Lewis Kraft that put the cream cheese on the bagel. "Mr. Kraft's instructions were to include the word cream cheese as often as the comedians could in as many jokes about the product and the sponsor as possible," Nathan writes.

Bagels are boiled before they are baked.

"It would have just been like Jolson to use the words cream cheese as a springboard into some quick joke about lox and bagels," Nathan quotes Jolson's biographer, Herbert Goldman. "That may have been the start of the new Jewish trilogy of bagels, lox, and cream cheese, sort of a Jewish answer to the old Sunday triumvirate of bacon, eggs, and pancakes."

JEWISH DELICATESSENS

It is deeply offensive to real New Yorkers—or at least, old-time New Yorkers, like me—that today any neighborhood grocery, indeed any convenience store, calls itself a deli or a gourmet deli, no less. The New York City deli—or more properly the New York City delicatessen—is a venerable institution that dates back to the mid-nineteenth century. And, by definition, it is a store that sells delicacies, not Cheez Doodles. The word is German, not strictly Yiddish. *Delikat* means, according to my German dictionary, "delicate, delicious, exquisite." *Essen* means "to eat." In English, or I should say in Old New Yorkese, the word applies both to the store and to the products it sells.

The products of the true delis are mostly of German origin and mostly meats—sausages, cured and smoked meats, plus the salads and condiments that are served with them. The first delicatessens in New York City were, in fact, German not Jewish, and their cured, smoked, and otherwise processed meats were mainly, if not entirely, fabricated with pork. But as Jews generally adopt the foods of their homeland, German Jews had developed kosher versions of these and when they began arriving in New York City, they quickly brought their kosher laws to bear on the production of Jewish-German style delicatessen, and opened their own stores, serving beef-based products. It was all just as it was in the old country.

Katz's Deli on Houston Street is the oldest in the city.

Jewish delicatessens gained their particularly New York City Yiddish character in the 1880s, with the increase in Jewish migration from Eastern Europe. Most of the Jewish-German delicatessen meats, including frankfurters and corned beef, were foreign to the Russian, Polish, Hungarian, Czech, Romanian, and other Eastern European Jews. But delis were the only kosher public eating places, so they went. Eventually they became not only a place you could take the family, but a store where they sold prepared foods to take home. Even as full-fledged kosher restaurants opened, the deli remained the most popular type of restaurant.

Jews who left New York City to settle in smaller cities around the country took the delicatessen with them and the restaurants became, and still are, a meeting place for the Jewish community. As a college student, I worked at Hoffberg's, on the border of Washington, D.C., and Silver Spring, Maryland. There, on a weekend, the deli was jammed with people who came from all over the area, as much to see their friends as to eat. In Detroit, the deli meeting place was Boesky's. St. Louis has Protzel's. In Memphis, it was Goldstein's. In Los Angeles, there was the famous Cantor's.

Romanian pastrami, a European version of the Middle Eastern/Turkish *basturma*, which is spice-cured and air-dried beef, was added to the delicatessen menu sometime in the late 1880s. Patricia Volk, a New York City writer and the daughter of a famous New York City restaurateur, claims her paternal great-grandfather, Sussman Volk, was the first person to bring pastrami to the city. Pastrami would have been foreign to this Austrian immigrant. But it may well be true that Volk, in 1888, as his descendent says, introduced pastrami into the already established German-style delicatessen he owned.

Eventually, other foods that had a more Eastern European, not German, flavor were incorporated into the delicatessen's repertoire. It was at the delicatessen that you could get hearty Polish, Lithuanian, or Russian soups, such as barley with wild mushrooms, rib-sticking split pea, or sweet and sour cabbage borscht. The supreme soup at the deli—in fact, the supreme soup of the Jewish kitchen—is chicken soup. Once the delis left the Lower East Side and moved to the boroughs, serving an audience that had already climbed the socio-economic ladder a little, they even branched out into steaks and chops. Skirt steak, known as "Romanian tenderloin," was a favorite.

Cucumber pickles, some half-sour and still bright green, others full sours and a drab green, got plunked down, along with a cabbage slaw and pickled green tomatoes. These were put on the table even before the waiter—notoriously a sarcastic or grumpy older man—could say, "What'll you have?"

Added to the frankfurters, well-spiced salami, boiled tongue, corned beef, rolled beef, and pastrami, were roasted chickens to eat in or take out; sliced, freshly roasted turkey; knishes filled with kasha or mashed potatoes (see page 142); a garlicky sausage called *knublewurst* (the "k" is pronounced; *knuble* is garlic); and specials, a sausage as fat as knockwurst and spicier than a frank.

Hot dogs and knishes heat on a grill behind the front window of a deli.

Frankfurters were a big item at the delicatessen. You could get them grilled, served on a plate with Heinz vegetarian baked beans, or on a toasted hot dog bun topped with spicy brown mustard and sauerkraut. (Jewish delicatessens never used to have onions in tomato sauce, as the hot dog street carts do.) Every delicatessen grilled their hot dogs all neatly lined up on a griddle in the window, an enticement as you walked by. It's one I could never resist, so perhaps it is just as well that that custom is dying.

The Jewish delicatessen is not extinct, but it is sadly in decline. There are several in Manhattan and more in Brooklyn, a few in Queens, and one in the Bronx. The suburbs of New Jersey and Long Island, where many New York City Jews moved late in the twentieth century, have restaurants that serve the classic old deli foods. Only a handful are kosher. The rest serve shrimp salad and other *treyf,* forbidden foods, along with the chopped liver. Only in New York, folks, only in New York.

JEWISH CHAMPAGNE

Dr. Brown's Celery Tonic was developed in 1869 by a physician who treated immigrant children on the Lower East Side. It is carbonated water—seltzer—flavored with celery seeds and sweetened with sugar. It used to be considered a real tonic, a health drink. But the U.S. government decided otherwise and made the company change the name to Cel-Ray Soda. On the order of ginger ale, it really isn't as bizarre as it sounds. It's incredibly refreshing and thirst quenching and became the perfect foil to Jewish delicatessen, which tends to be salty. In fact, the soda was sold only in delis until the 1980s. Now, you can buy Cel-Ray in most New York City supermarkets and some other cities' stores, but the diet version is sold only in delis. Well, that's some kind of exclusivity. Dr. Brown's also makes a popular vanilla-flavored soda, called cream soda, and black cherry. Both have been distributed nationally since the late 1970s.

PICKLES

Sol Kaplan was the original owner of Guss and Hollander Pickles, now called Guss' Pickles. (It used to be on Essex Street. Now it is on Orchard Street.) He was born in 1911. Here he is speaking in *You Must Remember This*, an oral history of Manhattan :

There was business for everybody. They did it the same way they're doin' it now. You pickle 'em, you sell 'em right away green, or if you want for the winter to age 'em, you put them in storage in refrigeration.

Cucumbers used to come from Long Island—all the pickles. There's no Long Island no more. There's no farms. From Jersey they used to come. Now it comes from the South—North Carolina, South Carolina, Virginia.

When you're buying wholesale, you look for the quality. If it's a fresh pickle, that's good. It's gotta be hard, nice, crisp. If it's soft or wrinkled, it means it was travelin' long. Years ago you didn't have to watch, it was all near farms, but now it's a problem. It travels six or seven days on the train. What do you know if the guy doesn't put ice on the way?

After he buys 'em, then he'd throw 'em into barrels, make brine up, put in garlic and spice, water 'em and cover 'em up , press 'em down, that's all. The brine is made from salt and water. Then you put the spices in.

Rothman used to mix their spices specially. They didn't use mixed spices like we do now. They used to buy mostly cloves, the nagelach, and they bought hot peppers, and they used all kinds of coriander. It takes longer, but if you wanna make something good, you gotta do a lot of work. That's what the people came for.

Then you gotta age 'em. You age 'em as much as you want. Some people like 'em green, some like 'em a few weeks old. Some like 'em old like a few months old, so you gotta age it for them. Then they get brown. They get half sour, then sour, and then even more sour.

I also made my own sauerkraut during the war.

REUBEN'S

Reuben's Restaurant started as an ordinary Jewish delicatessen, maybe even a less-than-ordinary Jewish delicatessen. But it quickly went, as its own slogan boasted, "From a Sandwich Shop to a National Institution."

Arnold Reuben, a German immigrant, opened his first deli sometime between 1906 and 1908 at 802 Park Avenue. Only several years later, he relocated to Broadway and Eighty-second Street, which at the time would have been a more receptive neighborhood for his strictly Jewish operation. The Upper West Side, particularly West End Avenue, was then the part of Manhattan to which German Jews and other European Jews of substance were moving. German Jews were at the forefront of the Reform Jewish movement and most of them did not follow the Jewish dietary laws, known as the *kashruth*. It's not clear if the first Reuben's was kosher, but later incarnations definitely were not.

In 1916, Reuben's moved again, this time to the Ansonia Hotel (now one of New York City's most prestigious Upper West Side cooperative apartment buildings) at Broadway and Seventy-third Street. Everything changed at this location. One night, Reuben got an order to deliver pastrami sandwiches to an after-theater party. That gave him an idea. Instead of merely selling sandwiches to go, he'd set up a couple of tables and put out a sign telling the city that Reuben's was a good place to go for an after-theater sandwich.

The new Reuben's was such a success that he soon, in 1918, opened a second restaurant, at 622 Madison Avenue. It was here that Reuben made his fame, staying open seven days a week, twenty-four hours a day (see Ruth Gordon's reminiscence of eating out in the 1920s, page 234), and catering to, as one chronicler put it, "the bluebloods of Park Avenue and the hot-bloods of Broadway."

Using a marketing strategy that would eventually be used in every restaurant generation of New York City, Reuben tripled his prices to make sure he had the highest prices in town. It first worked for Delmonico's in the nineteenth century. During Prohibition, it would work for Jack and Charlie's '21.' In the 1970s it worked for the Palace. In the 1980s, the Quilted Giraffe made a point of "being the most expensive restaurant outside of Tokyo," chef-owner Barry Wine once said. In New York City, whether you have quality or not, when you raise prices you become more desirable; people think you must be better, the thing to strive for. Obviously, you then attract a crowd that spends more, and you make more money. This elevates you to the status of your customers.

The new Reuben's was more a restaurant than a deli, although it continued to serve Jewish deli foods. It was a lot like Lindy's, which was its main competitor for many years. It was an after theater, late night, early morning hangout, a magnet for celebrities and socialites, as well as a tourist destination.

The fame and importance of Reuben's was such that in 1935, when it again relocated, this time to 6 East Fifty-eight Street, just off fashionable Fifth Avenue, Mayor Fiorello LaGuardia attended the opening. Reuben's remained at that location until it closed in 1966, two years after it had been sold to Harry L. Gilman. Marion Burros, the *New York Times* food writer, who went to Reuben's as a child, remembers a beautiful Art Deco facade and that the interior had "Italian marble, a gold leaf ceiling, and lots of walnut paneling and dark red leather seats. To a small town girl it was the quintessential New York restaurant."

It has been said that you could get anything you wanted to eat at Reuben's, from chopped liver to a broiled lobster or the best caviar. The menu included chicken soup with matzoh balls, borscht, scrambled eggs with Irish bacon, and, most notably a list of sandwiches named for famous regulars.

The Jack Benny was sliced tongue, turkey, Swiss cheese, coleslaw, and Russing dressing on rye. The Walter Winchell was sturgeon, Swiss cheese, and sliced dill pickles on rye. The Ed Sullivan was chopped chicken liver, turkey, coleslaw, and Russian dressing on rye. The Barbara Stanwyck sandwich was sliced corned beef, bacon, and melted Swiss cheese on toasted rye. The list got longer and longer, the stars more notable with every new printing of the menu.

Reuben's Famous Sandwiches

1—REUBEN'S SPECIAL 2.35
  Turkey, Roast Virginia Ham, Swiss Cheese, Cole Slaw, Russian Dressing
2—REUBEN'S STEAK SANDWICH ..4.75
3—REUBEN'S HAMBURGER SANDWICH ON ROLL 2.65
4—REUBEN'S SUPERIOR 2.35
  Turkey, Roast Virginia Ham, Hard Boiled Egg, Tomato, Onion, Russian Dressing, Rye Bread
5—REUBEN'S PARADISE 2.20
  Turkey, Tongue, Tomato, India Relish, Rye Bread
6—HILDEGARDE 2.00
  Tongue, Swiss Cheese, Tomato, Russian Dressing, Rye Bread
7—ARNOLD REUBEN, 3rd 2.35
  Turkey, Tomato, Bacon, Melted Cheese on Toasted White
8—CLUB A LA REUBEN 2.85
  First Layer: Dark Meat of Turkey, Lettuce, Bacon and Toast
  Second Layer: White Meat of Turkey, Lettuce, Tomato and Bacon
9—PHIL BAKER 2.00
  Turkey, Hard Boiled Egg, Onions and Russian Dressing
10—DOROTHY SARNOFF 2.15
  Tongue, Turkey, Tomato and Sliced Dill Pickle
11—ELAINE MALBIN 2.95
  Raw Meat, Raw Egg, Chopped Onion
12—HARRY HERSHFIELD 2.15
  "CAN YOU TOP THIS"
  Tongue, Turkey, Tomato, Russian Dressing
13—JACK BENNY —
  MARY LIVINGSTON 2.35
  Tongue, Turkey, Swiss Cheese, Cole Slaw, Russian Dressing, Rye Bread
14—WALTER WINCHELL 2.20
  Sturgeon, Swiss Cheese and Sliced Dill Pickle
15—FRANK SINATRA 2.00
  Cream Cheese, Bar-le-Duc, Tongue, Sweet Pickle, Whole Wheat Bread
16—MARY MARTIN 2.00
  Virginia Ham, Swiss Cheese, Sliced Dill Pickle, Rye Bread
17—LUBA MALINA 5.50
  Imported Beluga Caviar and Cream Cheese on Rye or White Toast
18—ORSON WELLS 2.00
  Turkey, India Relish, Lettuce, Russian Dressing
19—JUDY GARLAND 2.20
  Nova Scotia Salmon and Swiss Cheese
20—GEORGIA GIBBS 2.20
  Nova Scotia Salmon and Cream Cheese

21—VIC DAMONE 2.15
  Turkey, Tongue, Cole Slaw, Whole Wheat Toast (No Butter)
22—JOE E. LEWIS 2.00
  Tongue, Mustard, Melted Swiss Cheese on Toasted Rye
23—MILTON BERLE 2.10
  Cream Cheese, Bar-le-Duc, Turkey, Whole Wheat Bread
24—MARK GOODSON-BILL TODMAN 2.60
  "I've Got a Secret"
  Turkey, Tongue, Cranberry Sauce, Broiled French Toast, Maple Syrup
25—HY GARDNER 2.35
  Corned Beef, Turkey, Bologna and Cole Slaw, Russian Dressing
26—JACKIE GLEASON 2.15
  Turkey, Bacon, Onion, Tomato, Russian Dressing
27—VIRGINIA GRAHAM 2.10
  Corned Beef, Melted Swiss Cheese on Toasted Rye Bread
28—JOEY ADAMS 2.10
  Tongue, Turkey and Mayonnaise
29—LOUIS SOBOL 1.90
  Cream Cheese and Bar-le-Duc, Chopped Pecans
30—DEAN MARTIN 2.10
  Turkey, Holland Ham, Rye Bread
31—CELESTE HOLM 2.20
  Sturgeon, Swiss Cheese, Rye Bread
32—ED SULLIVAN 2.15
  Chopped Chicken Liver, Turkey, Cole Slaw, Rye Toast
33—BETTY HUTTON 2.10
  Chicken Liver and Corned Beef on Rye Bread
34—MAGGI McNELLIS 2.35
  Turkey, Roast Beef, Cole Slaw, Russian Dressing
35—JERRY LEWIS 2.15
  Turkey, Tomato and Crisp Bacon
36—DOROTHY KILGALLEN 2.45
  Tongue, Turkey, Broiled French Toast
37—GINGER ROGER'S SPECIAL ..2.20
  Nova Scotia Salmon, Cream Cheese, French Fried Onions
38—THE 52 ASSOCIATION 2.15
  Tongue, Holland Ham, Tomato, Cole Slaw
39—ETHEL MERMAN 2.00
  Turkey, Tomato, Hard Boiled Egg, Russian Dressing
40—DANNY KAYE 2.35
  Turkey, Ham, Tongue, Cole Slaw
41—MIMI BENZELL 2.15
  Turkey, Tongue, Cole Slaw, Russian Dressing
42—JANE POWELL 1.95
  Grilled Cheese, Bacon, Tomatoes
43—SOPHIE TUCKER 2.25
  Turkey, Swiss Cheese and Salami
44—LILLIAN ROTH SPECIAL 2.25
  ("I'll Cry Tomorrow)
  Corned Beef, Melted Swiss Cheese, Bacon

(All Sandwiches Served with Pickle)

Turkey 1.90
Chopped Chicken Liver with Onions 1.45
Roast Virginia Ham and
  Imported Swiss Cheese 1.90
Turkey and Virginia Ham 2.10
Chicken Salad and Russian Dressing 1.85
Lake Sturgeon 2.10
Nova Scotia Salmon 2.10
Roast Virginia Ham and Egg Sandwich 1.90
Sturgeon and Nova Scotia Salmon 2.75

Fresh Imported Beluga Caviar 5.50
Roast Virginia Ham 1.70
Home Boiled Tongue 1.70
Brisket of Corned Beef 1.70
Imported Sardine 1.55
Salami 1.25
Liverwurst and Bermuda Onions 1.25
Swiss Cheese 1.30
Cream Cheese and Bar-le-Duc 1.10
Western Sandwich 1.90

REUBEN'S *Special Brand Coffee By The Pound*

Naming sandwiches after the famous not only attracted the non-famous, especially rubber-necking tourists from the hinterlands, but assured Reuben return visits from those for whom the sandwiches were named, as well as visits from those who hoped to have a sandwich named for them. In later days, competitors like the Stage Deli on Seventh Avenue and Fifty-fourth Street, and the Star Deli on Third Avenue in the Fifties, used the same tactic.

I remember eating a classic Reuben Sandwich at Reuben's in the 1960s—corned beef, sauerkraut, Swiss cheese, and Russian dressing on buttered grilled rye—but nowhere on earlier menus

is the famous sandwich listed. You would think that showman Arnold Reuben would have made the most of his namesake sandwich had he actually created it. He didn't because he probably never heard of it until 1956, when Fern Snider, a waitress at the Blackstone Hotel in Omaha, Nebraska, entered the recipe in a contest and won a national sandwich competition sponsored by the Wheat Council, whose agenda was promoting bread. She knew about the Reuben because it was on the menu at her hotel. It had been created there somewhere between 1922 and 1925 by a wholesale grocer named Reuben Kulakofsky. One night at the hotel, a local gathering place, Kulakofsky, also called Reuben K (or Kay), made up the sandwich for his buddies at a late-night poker game. Everyone liked it so much, the hotel owner put it on his menu, and named it for his friend Reuben.

The Reuben sandwich on the Reuben's Restaurant menu was a sandwich called the Reuben Special. It is nothing like the famous and classic Reuben from Omaha. In 1976, Craig Claiborne of the *New York Times* received this explanation of the Reuben Special and its name from Patricia R. Taylor of Manhattan, the daughter of Arnold Reuben, Senior. She said, in part:

I would like to share with you the story of the first Reuben's Special and what went into it. The year was 1914. Late one evening a leading lady of Charlie Chaplin's came into the restaurant and said, "Reuben, make me a sandwich, make it a combination. I'm so hungry I could eat a brick." He took a loaf of rye bread, cut two slices on the bias and stacked one piece with sliced baked Virginia ham, sliced roast turkey, sliced imported Swiss cheese, topped it off with cole slaw and lots of Reuben's special Russian dressing and the second slice of bread. He served it to the lady who said, "Gee, Reuben, this is the best sandwich I ever ate. You ought to call it an Annette Seelos Special." To which he replied, "Like hell I will. I'll call it a Reuben's Special."

After sandwiches named for celebrities, cheesecake was another famous specialty of Reuben's, as it was of Lindy's and many other restaurants of the same Jewish-edged, eclectic ilk. Even after the last Reuben's location was closed, Arnold Reuben, Junior, who had joined his father in business in 1930, continued to make cheesecake and sell it by mail order until the early 1990s. What distinguished this cake no one will ever know. It was always a secret.

JEWISH DAIRY

Because Jewish dietary laws require the separation of meat and dairy (any milk-based product), a genre of restaurant developed that was called the Jewish dairy restaurant. There are almost none left in the old sense, restaurants that served cheese-filled blintzes, vegetarian "cutlets" and "roasts," soups without a chicken or meat broth base, noodle puddings with cheese, some fish dishes, and desserts with real whipped cream. Today, the dairy restaurant serves pizza, falafel, some of the mayonnaise-based salads that mainstream restaurants serve, and innovations such as vegetable lasagna and other pastas with meatless sauces.

The three old, great dairy restaurants of the Lower East Side were Ratner's, which closed only a few years ago, the Garden Cafeteria, which closed about ten years ago, and Rappaport's, which was on Second Avenue, near the Yiddish theaters, and closed when the theaters closed or changed to off-Broadway houses or movie houses. There were plenty of dairy restaurants uptown, too. The garment center sported several. The Upper West Side, where many refugees from World War II settled, had several. Steinberg's, on Broadway and Eighty-first Street, was one of the classiest of these. Its 1961 menu can be considered a catalog of Jewish dairy dishes. It featured, for instance, the freshwater fish—pike, carp, and whitefish—favored by Eastern and Central Europeans, fish that you would not find in a non-kosher restaurant. It lists fried herring, served with a boiled potato and fried onions, a dish that is too salty for most contemporary tastes, but manna from heaven for those of us who recall it from our youths. Here, "cutlets" made with mushrooms, "steak" with eggplant, and vegetable chow mein "en casserole" gave the menu urbanity.

JEWISH ROUMANIAN

There aren't many people who remember the things that Seymour Kaye does. "The Russians use pepper, the Romanians use garlic, the Galitzianer (those from the Galitzia region of Poland) use sugar, and the Hungarians use paprika," says Kaye, explaining the seasoning differences between the various branches of Jewish cookery. Actually, they are sub-branches of what might more accurately be called Yiddish cooking. The Sephardim, those with Iberian heritage, may have been the first Jews to arrive in New York City in 1644. The German Jews may have come next, starting in the mid-nineteenth century. But none of them made an impact on New York City's public food until the Yiddim arrived from Central and Eastern Europe in the late nineteenth and well into the twentieth century.

No one knows, not even Kaye, how it was that the Roumanian [sic] Steakhouse emerged, sometime around World War I, as the dominant form of Jewish meat restaurant, after the corner

deli. We're talking about restaurants that have tables with linen, and waiters in bow ties—places like Phil Gluckstern's and Pollok's, which both first opened on Delancey Street, the grand boulevard of the Lower East Side.

Kaye worked at several other Roumanian places, and then owned three legendary Roumanian Steakhouses. He started, a man in his early twenties, as a waiter at Pollok's in the early 1950s, then he moved briefly to Gluckstern's before he bought his own place, the Parkway, on Chrystie Street, in 1957. The Parkway was above where Sammy's, the last of the breed, is now.

The Parkway became the Parkway East when Kaye was forced to move to Allen Street, around the corner. His final restaurant was Seymour Kaye's in Forest Hills. By that time, in 1971, he had a big name and a following. "I moved to Forest Hills because I thought it was a good Jewish neighborhood. But by then that generation, the younger generation, didn't want to eat their grandparents' food except on holidays." People were nostalgic for that food, already in the 1970s. Walter Matthau loved my place."

All the Roumanian Steakhouses had pretty much the same menu. Chopped liver was the almost obligatory appetizer, although the menus also listed such first course delicacies as sliced brains, *pitcha* (calf's feet pickled with a lot of garlic and served with its gelatin), chopped eggs and onions (a kind of egg salad), gefilte fish, and Romanian-style eggplant salad. Most groups would order many or all of these, maybe with a side of unborn eggs, which were (and still are) merely the yolks of an egg caught in the chicken's birth canal before the white and shells are formed. To this day, the mention of unborn eggs elicits great nostalgia, but really they taste just like egg yolks.

Among the so-called broilings was the famous Roumanian tenderloin, which in most restaurants was a skirt steak but in others was the shorter of the two diaphragm muscles, what we now call a hanger steak. Until the mid-1980s, this was an inexpensive cut of meat. When fajitas, the Tex-Mex specialty that is made from the same cut as Roumanian tenderloin, became nationally popular, the price of the meat soared.

The cooking at these Jewish restaurants was done by women. Kaye says:

You would have a first cook. She would be in charge of everyone. But then you would have a kreplach *lady, and a gefilte fish lady, a lady who made chicken, one who made the flanken, one the brisket. Like that. Each woman had her specialty. Maybe the kreplach lady and the gefilte fish lady were the same person. Maybe she did two things very well. Then you had a* bruta, *a bruta is a broiler. He was proficient and able to broil anything by eye. He could broil rare, medium rare, whatever you want. And we used to broil on charcoal. One of my favorite things was broiled sweetbreads. We used to weight them down and after they were cooked they'd be thin like a piece of matzoh. Delicious. In the 1930s, 1940s, even 1950s, everyone ate at the Jewish restaurants. The politicians would come, and the late-night crowd. The wise guys loved the Jewish restaurants. They called them "Jew Joints." But a place like Moskowitz and Lupowitz would have been called a "Carpet Joint" by the wise guys, a place with a carpet, a fancy restaurant.*

By the time Seymour Kaye's opened in Forest Hills in Queens in 1971, there were few women in the kitchens of Jewish restaurants. Kaye said, "The women sent their kids to college. The kids graduated and they took Mom out of the restaurant. Mom's Puerto Rican and Chinese assistants took over."

THE EGG CREAM

I don't think anybody has ever been shot by someone who had an egg cream in his hand.
—STANLEY AUSTER, GRANDSON OF LOUIS AUSTER, *who may have invented the egg cream, in* You Must Remember This

For at least sixty or so years, until the late 1960s, the corner candy store was the focal point of neighborhood life in New York City. The sign outside may have said Luncheonette, but lunch was the least of it. It was where you bought the newspaper and cigarettes. It was where they hand-packed Breyer's ice cream into white containers like the ones they used to use in Chinese restaurants. It was where you could get a grilled cheese or tuna sandwich and where children bought penny candy like sugar buttons on paper, malted milk balls, chocolate nonpareils, and wax bottles filled with brightly colored syrup, and wax lips. And it is where everyone of every age stopped to gossip over a soda at the fountain, like a Coke or a cherry lime rickey (cherry and lime syrups mixed with seltzer), or an egg cream, often with a well-salted, crisp pretzel rod or soft pretzel to munch on.

It just happened that Louis Auster's candy store, where the egg cream was supposedly born around 1910, was in a neighborhood filled with gangsters.

Stanley Auster, the grandson of Louis, the man whose family says they invented the egg cream, says he is the last living person privy to his grandfather's original formula. So, naturally, I called him. (It was more than a decade ago.) I wanted him to talk about egg creams on my radio program.

"I can't talk about egg creams," Stanley insisted, "I'm having heart problems."

"Stanley," a woman's voice, presumably Mrs. Auster's, yelled in the background. "Talk on the radio about egg creams. Give yourself a break from talking about yourself."

Auster says that his grandfather created a special chocolate syrup, made his own carbon-dioxide charged seltzer with a particularly vigorous bubble, and merchandised the egg cream into a local sensation. What it has since become is a symbol of the good old days in New York City. Still, Stanley says he won't even share the secret recipe with his daughter, "who couldn't care less." He will go to his grave with it. But Auster did tell me this:

My grandfather died around 1955. He was ninety-seven. Very few people came to the funeral. He left the store when he was eighty-five. He became quite feeble in his early nineties. A lot of people had moved away. The Jewish theaters started closing down. People weren't so interested in egg creams anymore. The

Jewishness left the area. It just became an ordinary candy store after a while. That's why my uncle closed up the store on Second Avenue.

The last batch of syrup was made by my Uncle Mendy about 1974. Someone did me a favor where I was working. When I asked him how I could pay him back, he asked me if he could have some egg-cream syrup. I asked my Uncle Mendy. It was difficult. He had to use a substitute cocoa and one other substitute. He made around eight quarts, and he gave me two. It was delicious, but not exactly the way it was. The soda didn't have enough pressure.

But there was something else. The egg cream is not only a great drink, but it's associated with a certain camaraderie or folksiness among people. Just having an egg cream alone today is not the full flavor of it. It's having an egg cream with a group of people. It's having an egg cream with a pretzel. It's having an egg cream while talking about various things. Nobody ever sat down to have an egg cream. People usually drink it while standing and kibitzing, and those days were long gone.

The Gem Spa, on the corner of Second Avenue and St. Mark's Place, is the last remaining original venue of egg creams. The store is now owned by Pakistanis, as most New York City newsstands are today, but they surely know how to mix a good egg cream. This was the last of the several Auster candy stores, and it is possible that the fountain that pumps the seltzer is original, although it does not make a soda more carbonated than any other.

"Two cents plain was what people ordered when they wanted seltzer from a fountain. For three cents got you syrup, too," says Seymour Kaye, the last of the Lower East Side restaurateurs (see page 127). Kaye also notes, "When Auster moved from East Third Street and Avenue D to Second Avenue, he had to raise the price from a nickel to seven cents. The two cents extra kept the customers away. It was sort of the end of Auster's."

The Gomberg Seltzer Works in Brooklyn is one of the last filling stations for old-time seltzer bottles. Kenny Gomberg operates the pump; wooden cases ready for home delivery.

HOW TO MAKE AN EGG CREAM

A well made egg cream is an elixir beyond understanding. It is made with only three ingredients: chocolate syrup, milk, and seltzer. As with all very simple recipes, those ingredients must be just so, and you should have extremely careful technique. The perfect egg cream has a head as white as the milk in it and a body of cocoa-colored soda. It's not just a visual goal. There must be a taste and textural contrast between the soda and its head.

Egg creams are best made, served, and appreciated in clear Coca-Cola glasses, the classic ones that curve up from a narrow, cylindrical base to a voluptuous upper basin or a fountain glass shaped as the one below. Some of New York City's corner candy store soda fountains used paper cones that fit into stainless steel holders, but syrup sticks in the points of those, and it isn't nearly as pleasant to drink from paper as from glass. In the old days, at fancier fountains, they might, in fact, have used a Coca-Cola type fountain glass placed in a *zarf*, which is a metal holder with a cup-like handle. At better fountains, milkshakes and malteds were often served in glasses like these, too.

It may be more fun making an egg cream with an old-fashioned seltzer siphon bottle but using bottled supermarket seltzer may, in fact, give a better result because it has stronger carbonation. It is bottled under pressure more like that of a commercial fountain, perhaps even as mighty as the famous pressure at Louis Auster's candy store, where the egg cream was invented, or at least became famous (see page 130).

Fox's U-Bet chocolate syrup is the classic egg cream flavoring, but sometime during the 1960s, vanilla egg creams came along. Then there were coffee egg creams and other flavors too inventive to mention. Many believe that the only egg cream is a chocolate egg cream. (I am also

Stanley Zimmerman of Sammy's, the last of the Roumanian Steakhouses, is an egg cream showman.

one to insist a Martini be made with gin.) Fox's U-Bet will give your egg cream a real New York City flavor, but the drink can be delicious made with other chocolate syrups. Try it with Bosco or Hershey's.

Pour about ¾ inch of Fox's U-Bet chocolate syrup into a 12-ounce glass.

Top the syrup with about 1 inch of very cold whole milk.

Fill the glass about halfway with seltzer. Stir, but only at the bottom of the glass, to mix the chocolate with the milk. Fill the glass with more seltzer, being careful that the foam doesn't run over the side.

You should have a fairly sweet chocolate soda with at least an inch of milk-white head.

WHY JEWS LIKE CHINESE FOOD

There's an old joke:

If, according to the Jewish calendar, the year is 5764, and, according to the Chinese calendar, the year is 5724, what did the Jews eat for 40 years?

The fact that Jews have an affinity for Chinese food is no secret in New York City. The Jews know it. The Chinese know it. Everyone knows it. Until the dispersal of middle-class Jews to the suburbs was complete in the 1970s and Chinese take-out shops opened on every corner of the city in the 1980s, it was said that you could tell how Jewish a neighborhood was by the number of Chinese restaurants.

Going out to eat Chinese continues to be a Sunday ritual for many Jewish families; including kosher families now that there are many kosher Chinese restaurants. (In Brooklyn, there's one called Shang Chai, a play on the Hebrew for "life," chai.). Any Sunday evening at 6 o'clock, step into Bill Hong's on East Fifty-eighth Street and Third Avenue, one of Manhattan's last old-time Cantonese-American restaurants, or Shun Lee West on West Sixty-fourth Street, the Upper West Side's upscale Chinese restaurant. You'd think they were holding bar mitzvah receptions.

Actually, embarrassingly, until we learned better, Jewish people would say they were going for "Chinks," not even knowing that the word was derogatory. At least in my family's circles, it was merely the food that was "Chinks," not the people.

What do Jews do on Christmas? They eat Chinese and go to the movies.

Eat Chinese because those are the only restaurants open on Christmas. Go to the movies because all the Christians are at home and it's easy to get into the theater without waiting on line.

That the Chinese are not Christian is important to understanding the appeal of the Chinese restaurant to Jews. If you went to an Italian restaurant (from the 1930s through the 1950s), which, besides the coffee shop, the luncheonette, or the deli, was likely the only kind of restaurant in your neighborhood, you might encounter a crucifix hanging over the cash register, or at least a picture of the Madonna or a saint. That was pretty intimidating even to a non-observant Jew. The Chinese restaurant might have had a Buddha somewhere in sight, but Buddha was merely a rotund, smiling statue—mere decoration to us, and perhaps even looking like your fat uncle, and therefore not intimidating at all.

Important, too, was that the Chinese were even lower on the social scale than the Jews. Jews didn't have to feel competitive with the Chinese, as they might with Italians. Indeed, they could feel superior. In addition, as Philip Roth points out in *Portnoy's Complaint,* to a Chinese waiter, a Jew was just another white guy.

The first great wave of Jewish, Chinese, and Italian immigrants came at about the same time— from the 1880s to the 1920s—and the three groups settled in the same area, the Lower East Side of Manhattan. They weren't all on the same streets, but lived close enough to be able to observe each other, and certainly close enough to see what each other ate, and what was in each others food stores and street markets.

Italians didn't go out to eat as much as Jews, however. Italian Americans spent Sunday afternoons gathering in large family groups, eating Italian food. The Italians and Jews continued to live together when they left their immigrant ghettos on the Lower East Side and started moving to the other boroughs. The Chinese that lived among them were the owners of the restaurants and the hand laundries.

The Jews' proximity to Chinese restaurants was important, and let's not discount the fact that Chinese food tastes good and costs little. When I asked my parents why when they were courting in the 1940s their dates always ended up with a Chinese meal, and why we continued to eat in Chinese restaurants as a family more often than at other kinds of restaurants, the answer was simple: they could afford it. In their youth, a classic combination plate of egg roll, fried rice, and usually chow mein, cost twenty-five cents. Value is important to Jews.

The forbidden aspect of Chinese food—the attraction of the forbidden—should not be underestimated either. Although both Italian and Chinese cuisines feature many foods that are proscribed by the Jewish dietary laws, such as pork, shrimp, clams, and lobster, there are two big differences. The Chinese don't combine dairy and meat in the same dish, as Italians do. The Chinese don't eat dairy products at all. And the Chinese cut their food into small pieces before it is cooked, disguising the non-kosher foods—called *trayf* in Yiddish. This last aspect seems silly but it is a valid point as far as the forbidden element goes. My late cousin Daniel, who was kosher, along with many other otherwise observant people I have known, happily ate roast pork fried rice and egg foo young. "What I can't see won't hurt me," was his attitude.

Even Jews who maintained kosher homes often cheated by serving Chinese take-out on paper plates. I had one neighbor who would only let her family eat Chinese on paper plates in the basement, lest the neighbors across the ten foot alley should look into her kitchen window and see those tell-tale white containers on the table.

Eating forbidden foods validates you as a true American. It is an assurance to yourself that you have fully assimilated. Not to mention urbane and sophisticated. It is an indication that you have "arrived."

Bernstein's on Essex, a Lower East Side deli, was the first to specialize in kosher Chinese food.

MATZOH BALLS

There's an old burlesque-style dumb blonde joke that was foisted on Marilyn Monroe when she married the great American (and Jewish) playwright Arthur Miller. The story goes that the couple went to Miller's mother's home every Friday night for Shabbat dinner, and after several months of dining at her mother-in-law's, Marilyn said, "Mother Miller, I see you cook the matzoh balls in chicken soup. Tell me, how do you prepare the other parts of the matzoh?"

You know that a food is a beloved and perhaps a simultaneously dreaded part of a culture when there are jokes about it. In the case of matzoh balls, it is usually about how heavy they are, how they cause heartburn and indigestion, how they are belly bombs, or worse. But a great matzoh ball, flavored lightly with chicken fat, either airy or firm, but always savory, in a bowl of steaming, strong chicken broth, is a primal and iconic food for Jews of European heritage. We eat it not only when we're under the weather—you've no doubt heard it called "Jewish penicillin"—but as a comfort food, or when we need to feel in touch with our Jewish-ness or New York-ness.

Indulging in a bowl of chicken soup with matzoh balls has become a veritable tourist attraction in New York. Today, people don't even say "chicken soup with matzoh balls." They simply say, "matzoh ball soup." To a traditionalist, however, chicken soup is also eaten with *kreplach*. These are meat-stuffed dumplings, like Polish pierogi or Chinese wonton, that are traditional for the Jewish New Year. And chicken soup can be eaten with *lukshun*, which are fine egg noodles. In fact, some of New York City's delicatessens serve chicken soup with both matzoh balls and noodles.

I always used to wonder how restaurants and delicatessens made perfectly round matzoh balls that keep their shape for hours and hours while waiting to be immersed. My matzoh balls always come out misshapen at best, and they often deflate while they await their fate. These would be my grandmother's matzoh balls, although her recipe is no different than a million other Jewish mothers' and grandmothers', or for that matter not any different than what is even today printed on the back of the matzoh meal box. But it's not about the recipe when it comes to matzoh balls. The same formula can come out light in one cook's hands, leaden in another's. There is mystery—call it karma—in matzoh balls.

The late Abe Lebewohl, founder of the Second Avenue Delicatessen, one day confided the deli man's secret to me: baking powder. In the old days, matzoh balls were mainly for Passover, and so you would never use baking powder because it was forbidden to use leavening during the eight days of the holiday. Traditional matzoh balls were and still are leavened only by eggs, like most dumplings. Abe was able to use baking powder all year—the deli is closed for Passover—and somehow, recently, after what must have been some pretty intense Talmudic arguing, there is baking powder approved for Passover use. Very observant Jews still will not use it, but many others will. The rest of the year, I suggest you do. Baking powder makes matzoh balls well-risen and light, while allowing you to make a stiff enough batter to form gorgeously round dumplings.

Makes about 12

Salt

4 eggs

⅓ cup Schmaltz (Rendered Chicken Fat, page 139)

¼ teaspoon freshly ground black pepper

1 tablespoon baking powder

1⅓ cups matzoh meal

Fill a large, wide pot three-quarters full of water, add 1 tablespoon salt, and bring to a boil.

While the water is boiling, crack the eggs into a large bowl and beat with a fork to mix thoroughly. Beat in the schmaltz, ¼ teaspoon salt, the pepper, and the baking powder. Slowly stir in the matzoh meal, then mix vigorously with a wooden spoon until completely blended, and very stiff. If the mixture is not stiff enough to form easily into balls, let it stand for as long as 30 minutes.

Wet your hands with cold water so the batter doesn't stick to them, then, holding and rolling the mixture between your palms, shape it into perfect balls about 1¼ inches in diameter. They will double in size when cooked.

Gently place the matzoh balls in the boiling water, reduce the heat to a simmer, cover, and cook for 25 minutes.

Remove with a slotted spoon. Serve immediately in hot chicken soup.

To hold matzoh balls for serving at a later time, remove them from the water and place on a platter or tray. Keep covered. Just before serving, reheat them by putting them in the simmering chicken soup.

LATKES

To demonstrate how Jewish New York City can be, even when it is not Jewish, the prestigious James Beard Foundation has been running an annual Hanukkah Latke Lovers' Cook Off since 1995. Forget their fancy dinners by rising star chefs. It's the Latke Lovers' Cook Off that attracts the media around here.

The contest further proves how sometimes—may I say, more often than not—innovation on staunchly traditional foods doesn't pay off. Carrot or zucchini latkes have yet to prevail. A traditional potato latke of one sort or another always wins the Cook Off—"traditional" if you are willing to admit that there is more than one legitimate style, and there are some who wouldn't.

The following recipe won the third annual Cook Off. It is the family recipe of Steve Gold, marketing director of Murray's Chicken. Coincidentally, his family recipe is nearly identical to my family recipe. We both go for the same proportions of potato and onion, and finely grate them, as opposed to coarse shredding or chopping. In the old days, when a little knuckle blood was considered a seasoning, both our families did this on the medium side of a box grater. Nowadays, we use the food processor. And we both add small amounts of flour and egg and large amounts of salt and pepper. Gold's family adds a little baking powder, though, and Steve's own innovation is to grate the potatoes in the food processor with their skins, which somehow manages to help keep the potatoes white for longer. Did I say innovation doesn't pay? I lied.

By the way, latkes are the Eastern European Jewish expression of Hanukkah, the eight-day festival in December that commemorates the miracle when, after the Second Temple was desecrated by the Syrian Greeks, then rededicated by the Jews, one day's worth of sacred oil for the altar's eternal lamp lasted eight days, just in time to get more. The celebration of Hanukkah is therefore supposed to include fried foods. In Central and Eastern Europe potato pancakes were fried in poultry fat—schmaltz—because potatoes were plentiful, and since December was the season for slaughtering geese and ducks, poultry fat was the most readily available fat. The New York City Hanukkah tradition is potato pancakes, too, although today we fry in vegetable oil. In the Mediterranean, dough of some kind is deep-fried, sometimes in olive oil, which happens to be pressed around the time of Hanukkah, and which very likely was the oil used in the Temple lamp.

Makes about 24, serving 3 or 4

Keeping the potatoes mixed with the onion helps the potatoes stay white longer. My grandmother stirred her batter with a large, tarnished, silver-plated spoon that she'd inherited from her mother that has since made its way to me. When not stirring, it was left in the bowl. I used to think the ancestral spoon had some magic, but it is only the tartrates on the surface of the silver that prevent the potatoes from turning dark. Short of a silver spoon, use a pinch of cream of tartar.

1 pound Russet potatoes, unpeeled, washed well,
cut into large chunks
1 large yellow onion (½ pound),
cut into quarters
2 eggs
¼ cup all-purpose flour

½ teaspoon baking powder
2 teaspoons salt, or more to taste
½ teaspoon freshly ground white pepper, or
more to taste
About ¾ cup vegetable oil

In a food processor fitted with the metal blade, process about one third of the potato chunks. At first pulse the motor, then let it run for longer intervals until the potatoes are coarsely granular. Pour them out into a large bowl.

Process half of the onion until very fine, then stir it into the potatoes in the bowl.

Process another third of the potatoes. Stir into the potatoes in the bowl.

Process the remaining onion, then the remaining potatoes.

In a small bowl, with a fork, beat the eggs. Stir them into the potato mixture.

Sprinkle the baking powder, salt, and white pepper over the surface of the potatoes, then stir in.

Heat about ⅛ inch of the oil (not all of it) in a 10-inch skillet until moderately hot. Make a test latke: Drop the batter off a large serving spoon, or half-filled kitchen utility spoon. If the pancake starts frying furiously, the heat is too high. If the fat doesn't sizzle immediately, the fat is not hot enough. If the pancake breaks up, or is too thin, or too lacy at the edges, add more flour—start with another 1 or 2 tablespoons.

After adjusting as necessary, continue to fry batter. Serve immediately. Potato pancakes do not hold well.

Schmaltz

The aroma of chicken fat rendering on the stove is one of those sensory cues that brings back memories of cuddly Jewish grandmas. It was the most important cooking fat in old time Jewish kitchens, and a defining flavor. Although we rarely fry with it today, preferring less saturated vegetable oils, it is still a necessity for flavor. A matzoh ball is just any old dumpling without it. Chopped liver needs it. Kasha Varnishkas *is so much better with it. In the old days, it was even used as a spread—on matzoh on Passover, challah on the Sabbath, and rye bread any other day of the week.*

The word for rendered chicken fat in Yiddish is schmaltz, *but the word is also used figuratively to mean something that is overly sentimental or overblown in a less than tasteful way, such as an orchestral piece with an excess of strings, or a tear-jerker movie.*

SECOND AVENUE DELICATESSEN'S HEALTH SALAD

The Second Avenue Deli still serves this sweet and sour slaw in the traditional stainless steel bucket. Alongside it is a bucket of dark and brownish sour pickles, pale and green half-sours, and pickled green tomatoes. People linger at delis, but the food comes fast.

At a deli, this type of cole slaw was called health salad. Compared to the other salty, fatty foods that are the hallmarks of a Jewish delicatessen, it was a veritable tonic. But you could get the same salad at the appetizing store. With black olives and bits of pickled herring, it was called Greek Salad.

Makes about 1½ quarts

1½ pounds cabbage (1 small head)
2 medium carrots, peeled
1 small green bell pepper
1 large rib celery
¾ cup distilled white vinegar

2 tablespoons olive oil
½ cup sugar
3 teaspoons salt
½ teaspoon freshly ground black pepper

Cut the cabbage into quarters. Cut out the core in each section. Shred the cabbage as finely as possible into a large bowl.

Using the coarsest side of a box grater, shred the carrots into the cabbage.

Cut the green pepper in half. Remove and discard the seeds and ribs and stem end. Wash and dry. Cut the green pepper into the finest strands you can, and add them to the slaw.

Cut the celery into thin slices, then add them to the slaw.

In a small bowl, whisk together the vinegar, oil, sugar, salt, and pepper. Pour the dressing over the slaw. Toss well.

Place the slaw in the refrigerator for at least 8 hours. The slaw will not wilt. It should remain crisp and fresh tasting for 2 to 3 weeks.

PICKLES

My paternal grandfather, Barney, was a professional pickle man at one point in his life. He sold pickles, along with coleslaw, potato salad, and Manhattan Clam Chowder (see page 40) from a pushcart to bars and grills in Manhattan. Later in life, he continued to make all of these for his family and friends. One of my strongest childhood memories is making pickles with him. Always given the most menial job in the kitchen, I washed them. My more important work was stuffing them into gallon-size and half-gallon glass jars. The cucumbers need to be firmly packed so they don't float to the top. My grandfather did the seasoning, using mixed pickling spices that you can buy in the supermarket and adding extra bay leaves, whole cloves of garlic, and either dill seed or sprigs of fresh dill that were going to seed. (I still like eating the pickled garlic.) The jars would be left with their covers ajar to allow for air circulation and lined up in the dark pantry at the back of his kitchen. After a few days, they would be ready as half-sours, which some people call green pickles. We liked them best at this light stage of pickling, but you could leave them at room temperature longer if you wanted a full sour. Once they were where you wanted them, they needed to be refrigerated. They never lasted long enough to spoil, but they will eventually. Well, they will get so sour and soft that they may not be to your taste—they weren't to ours.

By the way, there is nothing intrinsically kosher about pickles, but people call them kosher because they are a famous item of Jewish delicatessens.

Makes 3 quarts

Making pickles is easy but tricky. Because this style of pickle is naturally fermented, naturally things can go wrong. I once accidentally left my jars ajar sitting in the sun, and they became bitter and overly salty. A bitter cucumber will also make a bitter pickle. Taste one from your batch raw to make sure that it has a cool, refreshing flavor. Large cucumbers will, of course, take longer to pickle than small cucumbers, so try not to mix sizes in one jar.

1 gallon water
½ cup kosher salt
20 (3-to 4-inch) Kirby cucumbers for three 1-quart jars or 6 pint jars
12 to 16 cloves garlic, unpeeled

2 tablespoons mixed pickling spices
6 bay leaves
1 or 2 dried hot peppers, coarsely chopped
1 large bunch fresh dill, preferably going to seed, with tough stems

Bring the water to a boil. Add the salt, and stir until dissolved. Remove from heat, and allow to cool to room temperature.

Scrub the cucumbers. (There's no need to dry them.)

Lightly crush the garlic cloves, leaving the skins on.

To prepare the jars, either run them through a hot cycle of the dishwasher, or pour boiling water into them, then pour the water out. Pack the jars with cucumbers, packing them in tightly so they won't float to the top when the brine is added. Distribute the garlic, pickling spices, bay leaves, and hot pepper equally among the jars.

Pour in enough of the brine to cover the cucumbers. Add the sprigs of dill, pushing them in wherever you can. If they have woody stems, place them across the top of the jars, jamming them into the shoulders of the jars, to help keep the cucumbers in place.

Cover the jars loosely or with a piece of cheesecloth held on top with a rubber band. Keep in a cool and dark place. After 3 days, the cucumbers may be pickled enough to your taste. After 4 or 5 days, they should definitely taste like green pickles. For sour pickles, let them ferment for about 6 days.

Once the pickles are at the stage you like, refrigerate them. They will continue to become more sour as time goes by, but at a slower pace.

KNISHES

Knishes as we know them today were probably created in New York City, modeled after an unknown European prototype. According to Eve Jochnowitz, a culinary ethnographer, in a piece by Erica Marcus of Long Island's *Newsday*, the knish probably had its origins in Western Europe and it accompanied the Jews eastward when, in the fourteenth century, they were expelled from France. This dating, says Jochnowitz, explains why early European references to knishes have them stuffed with meat or cabbage: The potato didn't make its way from the New World to Europe until after Columbus's journey in the late fifteenth century.

Whatever their origin the word itself is related to the Italian word *gnocchi*, the Austrian word *knoedle*, and the Yiddish word *knaidlach*, all of which are kinds of dumplings. (Some sketchy etymological research on this produced the word "lump" as the meaning of the "gn" and "kn" root.)

The New York City knish is a kind of dumpling, too—a baked dumpling, much as people call apples baked in pastry apple dumplings. It is stuffed pastry. The traditional New York City fillings are potato and kasha (buckwheat groats), although the old-timers of my youth also liked dusty dry liver knishes. That palate and that taste are gone, and today we have flavors like spinach and broccoli, usually blended with the potato. I'm told the popularity of broccoli is about to exceed pure potato. Sweetened cheese knishes have been around for decades—Yonah Schimmel started making them in his bakery on Houston Street. But, as Erica Marcus remarks, at least there are no sun-dried tomato knishes—yet.

In the classic knish, the pastry encloses only the bottom and sides of the filling, leaving the top of the filling exposed. But there are various styles, including a strudel style in which the filling is made into a pastry-wrapped roll, then sliced. The first knishes were baked, as most delicatessen knishes are today.

Schimmel, a Romanian immigrant, began selling knishes from a pushcart in 1890, just as Eastern European foods were being introduced into the previously German-style Jewish delicatessen. In 1910, he opened the bakery (he called it a knishery) where it stands today, on Houston Street, near the corner of Chrystie Street.

Schimmel's knishes have had their ups and downs over the years. When I was a boy in the 1950s, it was a regular pit stop for my father and me on our Sunday morning food adventures, but we stopped as much for the glasses of cold borscht and "sour milk," a kefir-like drink, as for the knishes, which were not as good as those we could buy at our local Brooklyn delicatessen. Today, the knishes are back to delicious form thanks to the current proprietor, Alex Volfman.

In 1921, Elia and Bella Gabay created a different kind of knish, a square knish totally enclosed by a heavier, thicker casing and deep fried. The company, Gabila & Sons Knishes, which is still going strong, now produces more than one and a half million knishes a year, and says it is "The Original Coney Island Square Knish." The operative word in the claim, however, is "square." Many other knishes were sold on the beach, and Gabila & Sons' were not the first.

Knishes for some strange and unknown reason became popular on the Atlantic Ocean beaches and boardwalks of Brooklyn early in the twentieth century. Not just in Coney Island, but in Brighton Beach, which is the residential and beach area next to Coney Island, and all the way out to the boardwalk of Long Beach, which is in Nassau County on Long Island. How a hot item like a knish was deemed appropriate food for stifling New York City summer days is one of the mysteries of the universe. Could it be its manageable size, and that it is self-contained? They were enormously popular, one of the enticing features of going to the beach. Knish stands, often selling hot dogs as well, lined the boardwalks. And hawkers even walked the sand to sell them to the beach-blanket crowd.

The last of the Brighton Beach knisheries, Mrs. Stahl's, opened in 1935 and closed in 2003, although the knishes are still made and sold wholesale. Les Green, the current owner, explained that the Russian community of today's Brighton Beach (often called Little Odessa, see page 363) doesn't eat knishes. Most of his customers were coming from far away to stock up. So he sells them now to delicatessens, restaurants, and take-out shops in the suburban diaspora.

That Gabila & Sons knishes were made to withstand reheating—and that knishes go so well with a hot dog—does, however, explain how potato knishes came to be one of New York City's most popular street foods, split and spread with mustard or not. Knish carts were common on the streets of Manhattan before World War II, and after the war Gabila & Sons knishes were sold from the same carts as Sabrett's hot dogs. For supposed health reasons, Mayor Rudolph Giuliani's administration banned them from the hot dog carts in the mid 1990s, leaving hot dogs bereft of their traditional starch accompaniment, and New Yorkers just plain bereft. We never lost a New Yorker, or even, more importantly, a tourist, to a knish. But go fight City Hall.

Makes about 4 dozen

It doesn't pay to make just a few knishes. This is a party amount. If you want to freeze them, add ½ cup instant mashed potatoes to the real mashed potatoes. It will stabilize the filling and prevent it from becoming too wet when defrosted. The directions here are for making knish rolls that can be cut into individual finger-food servings after they are baked. These will have open sides, like pieces of strudel. To make a small knish with closed sides, use a plastic bench scraper to pinch the dough together at 1½-inch intervals. Press straight down as if you were trying to cut the dough, but do not use a sawing motion. Just press. Even if the dough does not pinch to a seal, it will be more enclosed when you cut the roll after it is baked.

For the potato filling:
5 pounds Russet (baking) potatoes
⅓ cup vegetable oil, or rendered chicken fat (page 139) for an old-time deli taste
6 cups coarsely chopped onions (about 2 pounds)
4 teaspoons salt, or more to taste (divided)
½ teaspoon freshly ground black pepper, or more to taste

For the dough:
½ cup hot tap water
½ cup canola, peanut, or other vegetable oil
2 eggs
1 teaspoon salt
¼ teaspoon freshly ground black pepper
3½ cups all-purpose flour (divided)
1 teaspoon baking powder

For the egg wash:
1 egg, well beaten

Make the filling:

Peel the potatoes, cut them into chunks, and place them in a large pot, covered with cold water by about an inch. Bring the water to a boil. Cook the potatoes until very tender, about 15 to 20 minutes, depending on the size of the chunks. Drain immediately in a colander.

Using a food mill with the medium blade or a ricer (do not use a food processor), work the potatoes into a smooth puree. Stir in 3 teaspoons of the salt (1 tablespoon) and the pepper.

While the potatoes cook, fry the onions. In a 12-inch skillet, heat the oil over fairly high heat. When the oil is hot but not smoking, add the onions and fry over medium-high heat, stirring regularly, until the onions are well wilted, about 8 minutes. Lower the heat to medium, and continue to fry, stirring only occasionally, until the onions begin to brown. (This could take as long as another 20 minutes.) As they cook, season the onions with the remaining 1 teaspoon salt.

Stir the onions into the mashed potatoes. Taste, and adjust the seasoning with salt and pepper (I like mine peppery). Cover and refrigerate until chilled.

Make the dough:

In the bowl of a food processor fitted with the metal blade, combine the water, oil, eggs, salt, and pepper. Process briefly to mix well.

Add 3 cups of the flour and the baking powder.

Process again until the dough is smooth.

Flour a work surface with some of the remaining flour, and scrape the dough out onto the surface.

Knead the dough briefly, just a minute or so, incorporating just enough additional flour to make a very slightly sticky dough. Wrap the dough in wax paper or plastic, and let it rest at room temperature for an hour before rolling it out.

Preheat the oven to 375 degrees.

Cut the dough into four pieces. Roll out one piece at a time to a rectangle about 18 inches long and 8 inches wide. The long side of the dough should be facing you.

Gather some of the potato mixture in your hand and make a long, approximately 2-inch wide roll of potato along the long side of the dough, about 2 inches from the bottom edge. Bring the bottom edge of the dough over the potato roll and brush the upper edge with egg. Bring the upper edge of the dough over the egg-washed edge.

Repeat with the remaining dough.

Transfer the rolls to lightly greased baking sheets, seams down. Brush the logs with the beaten egg.

Bake until golden, about 50 minutes.

To serve, cut the rolls into 1- to 1½-inch crosswise pieces. Or follow the instructions at the top of the recipe on page 143.

To form classic, open-topped knishes, make the rolls as instructed here, and cut into 2-inch pieces. Take the piece of dough that is overlapping on the side and twist it so that it covers one of the open ends of the slice. Dab the end with a bit of egg wash, and bring it back up to meet the side of dough. Push the knish into shape, and bake as directed.

OPPOSITE:
Alex Volfman
has brought
quality back to
Yonah Schimmel's
knishes.

REUBEN SANDWICH

Modern-day Reuben sandwiches are often open-faced and broiled, which dries out the corned beef and makes the cheese rubbery. Or, under the misguided belief that more is better, they are overstuffed. The main things to remember for a great Reuben are to keep the filling under control and in balance, so when you bite into it you get a harmonious and succulent mouthful; and to grill the sandwich slowly and under some pressure, so the bread gets toasty brown and buttery crisp, the meat gets warmed through, and the cheese is just melted enough to be oozy.

Makes 1

2 slices rye bread or pumpernickel

2 teaspoons butter, at room temperature

2 tablespoons Reuben's Russian Dressing
(recipe follows)

¼ cup well-drained, fresh-style sauerkraut

2 ounces thinly sliced Gruyère or Switzerland
Swiss cheese

¼ pound thinly sliced corned beef.

Butter each slice of bread evenly to the edges on one side.

Place one slice, buttered side down, in a small cold skillet: Build the sandwich in the skillet you'll grill it in.

Spread 1 tablespoon of the Russian dressing on the face-up, dry side of the bread. Then put on the sauerkraut, spreading it evenly.

Arrange the cheese in an even layer over the sauerkraut, then do the same with the corned beef.

Spread another 1 tablespoon Russian dressing on the dry side of the second slice of bread and place it, dressing side down, buttered side up, over the corned beef.

Place the skillet over medium-low heat and grill the sandwich slowly, pressing down on it a few times with a wide metal spatula. Grill until the bread is browned and crisped, then turn the sandwich over with the help of the spatula.

Now weight the sandwich down by placing a plate (or another small skillet) over the sandwich, then adding on a weight, such as a 28-ounce can of tomatoes. Grill until the second side has browned and crisped, then flip the sandwich over one more time to briefly reheat the other side.

Serve immediately.

REUBEN'S RUSSIAN DRESSING

It's possible that Reuben's was the first Jewish deli to make a corned beef sandwich with Russian dressing. So say some deli men. Mayonnaise-dressed deli coleslaw is good on a corned beef sandwich, too. The two together, Russian and coleslaw, is the best, though, and very New York. On the other hand, no New Yorker would dream of giving pastrami the same treatment. A pastrami sandwich only takes mustard.

It is said that for high-rolling or famous customers, Arnold Reuben would blend about a tablespoon or so of salmon roe (red caviar) into the dressing. The restaurant's eggs à la Russe were, in fact, hard-cooked eggs, cut in half and sauced with Russian dressing and caviar—Russian beluga, I suppose, if you could afford it.

Makes about ½ cup

½ cup mayonnaise

1 tablespoon chili sauce or ketchup

1 teaspoon finely grated onion

½ teaspoon horseradish

¼ teaspoon Worcestershire sauce

1 tablespoon finely chopped parsley

Caviar (optional)

In a small bowl or cup, combine all the ingredients and mix well.

Arnold Reuben probably did not create the Reuben sandwich, but he took the credit.

BLINTZES

Perhaps mainstream New York City's adoption of Jewish blintzes has something to do with the city's predisposition to love pancakes of any kind. Blintzes are, after all, nothing more than stuffed, folded, and pan-fried pancakes.

Blintzes were on mainstream menus from the 1920s to the 1950s, and they were introduced in New York City supermarkets as early as the 1950s; many home cooks counted blintzes as a specialty, my grandmother, Elsie, included. She made a whole two-day ritual out of their preparation. On the first day, she would put every leaf in the dining room table, cover it with cloths, then spend the day doing nothing but making the crepes—*frendele*—and laying them out in stacks on clean dish towels.

The next day she would make the fillings. She didn't go for sweet fruit fillings. She made only mashed potatoes seasoned with salt, pepper, and onions browned in butter, the same as knish filling (see page 142) and a filling of slightly sweetened pot cheese blended with egg and sour cream. After carefully rolling the fillings into the crepes, making neat, tucked in packages (a job I was often enlisted to help with), the blintzes were fried in butter, then eaten topped with sour cream. As she made hundreds of blintzes at a time, a lot were stashed in the freezer and many were given away.

I never realized how really easy it is to make blintzes because my grandmother made it into such a grand cooking project. I found out only late in her life that the reason she did it in such large quantity and only once a year (for the Jewish holiday of *Shavuot*) was her very long nails and perfect manicure. Her nails were so long that they would make holes in the pancakes as she cooked them, and she was only willing to take her manicure down once a year.

Makes 10 blintzes, either potato or cheese, serving 2 to 4

For the crepes:
1 cup all-purpose flour
1 cup milk
½ cup cold water
½ teaspoon salt
2 eggs
2 tablespoons melted butter

For the potato filling:
See knish filling, (see page 143)
OR
For the cheese filling:
2 cups pot cheese
½ cup sour cream
2 tablespoons sugar
1 egg, lightly beaten

For frying and serving:
(½ stick) unsalted butter
¼ cup sour cream

Make the crepes:

Combine all the crepe ingredients in a blender jar. Process for a few seconds to mix well. Stop the blender, scrape down the sides with a rubber spatula, then process again for about 30 seconds.

The batter should be very smooth and the consistency of very heavy cream. You'll know if it is right when you make the first crepes. For a thinner crepe, add 1 to 2 tablespoons more water.

Heat a 7- to 8-inch skillet. Holding the pan with one hand, pour in the batter with the other while rotating the pan to cover the bottom with a thin film of batter. Cook over medium heat for about a minute.

With the aid of a spatula, fork, or tip of a table knife, carefully pick up the crepe with your fingers and flip it over. Cook 30 seconds more.

Turn the crepes out onto a clean kitchen towel.

If preparing ahead, you can stack the crepes, but to insure they do not stick together, put pieces of waxed paper between them.

Make potato filling, see page 143, or make the cheese filling:

Combine all the cheese filling ingredients in a mixing bowl. Mix well. Set aside.

Assemble the blintzes:

Place a few teaspoons of filling just below the center of the crepe. Fold the crepe upward to enclose the filling, then fold in the sides to enclose the ends. Roll the crepe up to completely enclose. Place seam side down on a platter.

Fry the blintzes:

In a skillet large enough to hold at least half the blintzes, heat 2 tablespoons of butter over medium heat. (If you want to fry all the blintzes at once, use a 12-inch skillet, and double the butter.) When the butter is sizzling, arrange the crepes in the pan seam-side down. Fry until nicely browned. Carefully turn the blintzes over and fry the second side.

Serve immediately with a dollop of sour cream on each.

VEGETABLE CUTLETS

I get requests for a Jewish dairy restaurant–style vegetable cutlet recipe all the time, but the old-time taste, as nostalgic as it is to those who remember Rappaport's, Ratner's, and the Garden Cafeteria, doesn't fit our contemporary palates at all. At Ratner's, for instance, which published a cookbook, the popular vegetable cutlets were made with canned vegetables. There is some charm in the perfectly cubed carrots that come in a tin, but assuming most of us would rather eat fresh today, the following contemporized cutlets fill the bill.

Serves 4

¼ cup vegetable oil, olive oil, or margarine (divided)

1¼ cups finely diced red and/or yellow bell peppers

1¼ cups grated carrot

1¼ cups tightly packed chopped raw spinach

2 cups mashed potatoes (3 medium potatoes, peeled, boiled, and riced)

6 tablespoons grated raw onion

3 eggs

1½ to 2 teaspoons salt

½ teaspoon freshly ground black pepper

1¼ cups matzoh meal

Sour cream blended with horseradish (optional)

Ratner's Vegetarian Gravy, or tomato sauce (optional)

In a skillet, warm 2 tablespoons of the oil or margarine. Lightly sauté the peppers.

Place all the vegetables in a large bowl, along with the eggs, salt and pepper, and matzoh meal.

Mix well. Let stand for 30 minutes.

Using about ⅓ cup for each cutlet, form the mixture into neat, ¾-inch thick, hamburger-like patties. You should have eight.

In a medium skillet, over medium heat, heat the remaining 2 tablespoons oil or margarine. Fry the patties, turning several times, until well browned on both sides.

If desired, serve with sour cream blended with horseradish to taste, or a light tomato sauce.

BREADED FRIED VEAL CHOPS

Roumanian broilings may be what the signs and menus said at the old Jewish restaurants. But my favorite main course was always the Breaded Fried Veal Chop, the gargantuan slab of meat, bone, matzoh-meal breading, and, let us not forget, nearly melted and therefore sublimely succulent clumps of veal fat. In fact, fat boy that I am, I always tried to convince myself that the heavy breading on these chops was mainly there to disguise the areas of fat. This way you could bite in without guilt—fooling yourself that it was meat—but get that fabulously flabby fat instead.

The veal chops at Jewish restaurants were huge, but then Jewish restaurants created the concept of supersizing. (In delicatessens, the sandwiches were always said to be *ungeschtupped* or overfilled. And that was a good thing.) The chops were veal arm shoulder chops, a cut that is big enough to cover a large dinner plate. These are still sold in New York City, even in the supermarket. A veal arm shoulder chop, at about half an inch thick—it can be no thinner if it's to remain juicy—usually weighs more than a pound. It has a few small bones, often including a marrow bone, but even with the bones it is a lot of meat. In theory, it should be enough to feed two people, but at Roumanian steakhouses each chop was meant for one and generally consumed by one.

With shared side orders of mashed potatoes seasoned with onions fried in chicken fat, kasha varnishkas seasoned with onions fried in chicken fat, and perhaps some stuffed *derma*, which is essentially a starch sausage flavored by onions that are not fried in chicken fat, there was good reason that seltzer and antacids were considered the most appropriate finish to a meal. Now that was smart food and beverage pairing!

The chops can be single-breaded or double-breaded. In either case, a rest in the refrigerator will ensure that the breading solidifies and sticks to the meat as it is frying.

For each chop:
Salt and freshly ground black pepper
1 egg

1½ cups matzoh meal for dredging
Peanut oil or other vegetable oil for frying

Season the chops with salt and pepper.

In a large pie plate or deep platter, beat the eggs with a fork until well mixed.

On a large plate, platter, or a piece of waxed paper, spread about half of the matzoh meal to the size of the veal chops.

Prepare one chop at a time: Pass the chop through the egg, coating well on both sides. Then, still dripping with egg, place the chop on the matzoh meal. Pour the remaining matzoh meal on top of the

chop and, with a fork, press it down to make a good coating.

Turn the chop, spoon some of the matzoh meal on top of the chop, and press again. Be sure to press matzoh meal onto the edges of the chop.

When the chop is well coated, place it on a platter or baking sheet. Set aside to let the breading set. Repeat with the remaining chops. Refrigerate the chops for at least 30 minutes.

If a thick breading is desired, repeat the whole

process. Dip the chops in egg then press on more matzoh meal. Let dry again.

In a large skillet, over medium-high heat, heat about ¼ inch of oil. When hot (375 to 385 degrees), slide a chop into the pan. It is unlikely you will be able to fry more than one at a time, although you could work 2 or 3 pans at a time. Fry until golden brown, 3 to 4 minutes.

Turn the chop and brown the second side, another 3 to 4 minutes.

When cooked, keep the chop(s) warm in a 200-degree oven until all the chops have been fried.

KARNATZLACH

Hardly anyone knows what *karnatzlach* are anymore, but they are so delicious they are worth saving from oblivion. They are sometimes called "sausage" in English, and *karnatz* does indeed mean "sausage" in Romanian. But they have no casing and are less a sausage than a variant of Middle Eastern *kofta*, which is seasoned ground meat grilled on a skewer. *Karnatzlach* is a very old-fashioned Romanian Yiddish word, the suffix "lach" makes it mean "dear little sausages."

In modern day Romania these are called *mititei*, and in the burgeoning post-Ceauçescu Romanian immigrant community in Sunnyside, Queens, they are sold in the butcher shops already mixed and shaped, to take home and cook. And they are served in their restaurants. The only kosher-style Roumanian Steakhouse left, Sammy's on Chrystie Street, makes great ones.

Makes about 20, serving 6 to 8 as an appetizer, 4 to 6 as a main course

Make sure your meat is not overly lean. You need some fat to give the *karnatzlach* succulence. Besides a strong garlic presence, *karnatzlach* have a slightly funky "high" taste created by the action of seltzer and baking soda and a ripening period in the refrigerator. Skip the ripening period for a fresher, although less authentic taste.

These are best cooked over a charcoal grill, but are well worth making indoors, too. If cooking them in an oven broiler, make sure to preheat the broiler tray on the rung just below the highest, the one closest to the heat source.

(By the way, genuine Romanian *mititei* are made with beef and pork.)

1 pound not-too-lean stew beef, cut into
    ¾-inch cubes
1 pound stew veal, cut into ¾-inch cubes
½ cup club soda
½ teaspoon baking soda

8 to 10 large cloves garlic, minced
2 teaspoons coarse salt (kosher or sea)
1 teaspoon freshly ground black pepper
1 teaspoon sweet paprika
½ cup finely chopped parsley

Mix the two meats together.

Put about ½ pound of the meat in a food processor fitted with the metal blade. Pulse the machine until the meat is finely minced, but not a paste. Scrape the meat into a mixing bowl, and repeat with the remaining meat.

In a small bowl or cup, combine the club soda and baking soda. Pour the mixture into the meat.

Add the garlic, salt, pepper, paprika, and parsley. Stir with a wooden spoon, or mix with your hands. The meat should be very well blended.

Cover the bowl with plastic wrap and place it in the refrigerator for at least 2 hours, but preferably for about 8 hours.

Wet your hands with cold water and form the meat mixture into tapering rolls about 3 inches long and 1 inch in diameter. Every couple of rolls, you will have to re-wet your hands. Place the *karnatzlach* on a platter or baking sheet.

Prepare a charcoal fire, or preheat the broiler.

Place the *karnatzlach* on the hot grill or hot broiler tray and cook for 8 to 10 minutes, turning the rolls a couple of times to brown them on all sides. The lesser time is for rare, the longer time for medium-well.

Serve hot.

CHAPTER **9**
THE ITALIANS

NEW YORKERS' FAVORITE FOOD

Immigrants never believed that the streets of America were paved with gold. Instead, they expected that its tables were covered with food.

—HASIA R. DINER *in* Hungering for America

TECHNICALLY, YOU COULD SAY THAT AN ITALIAN DISCOVERED NEW YORK CITY. It's a technicality that the city fathers acknowledged when the Port Authority of New York and New Jersey named the bridge that spans the mouth of the Hudson the Verrazano Narrows Bridge. Unfortunately for Italian-American pride, Giovanni da Verrazzano (the Port Authority changed the spelling of his name, dropping a "z"), who came in 1524, eighty-five years before Henry Hudson, and was in any case sailing for the French, never went any farther than this narrow passage between what is now Brooklyn and Staten Island. He never even got off his ship. He thought he was in a great lake. He was looking for a passage to the East, but, when a storm came up, he didn't attempt to navigate the river that was proverbially "around the bend." He drew a map of the coast and went on his way.

There were other Italians in New York City from its earliest days, although they were of no cultural consequence.

It wasn't until the 1880s, when they started immigrating in great numbers, that Italians changed the culture and cuisine of New York City. For forty years, until 1924, when new immigration laws put a virtual end to this massive movement, they came mostly from south of Rome—from Campania, which is the region around Naples, and from Puglia, Calabria, Basilicata, and Sicily. They emigrated for economic reasons, although politics, as always, played a part in their poverty.

After the so-called unification of the Italian peninsula into the modern nation of Italy in 1861 by the Savoy monarchy in Milan, all those southern regions that were once part of the Kingdom of the Two Sicilies (also called the Kingdom of Naples) found themselves in more miserable conditions than when they had been controlled and oppressed by the Borboni, their previous monarchy.

Mostly unskilled, landless agricultural workers, they began flooding East Coast urban centers, mainly through the port of New York. The southerners formed communities in New York City, Boston, and Philadelphia, but more stayed in New York than went anywhere else. Many intended to make their fortunes here, then return to Italy—and many did. But so many more stayed, or went home only to find that they could not live in Italy once they'd had a taste for America. By the 1930s, nearly twenty percent of New Yorkers were of Italian background, and about twenty-five percent of all Italian Americans lived in New York.

OPPOSITE:
At Mike's Deli, on Arthur Avenue, the Little Italy of the Bronx

Food and the familial ritual of eating together are of prime importance in Italian culture, although the immigrants had been deprived of the best foods in the old country. They often subsisted on beans and other legumes, greens that they could forage, and a few vegetables that they were able to grow on small plots next to their homes. They had bread, which was eaten until the last bit was hard—hence the various southern Italian dishes that utilize stale bread. Pasta was a mainstay for some who were slightly better off, but not factory-made pasta. It was pasta made at home from only flour and water: *orecchiette*, little disks of dough with thumbprint indentations; *cavatelli*, a kind of dumpling; *fusilli*, a tubular or spiral type of macaroni formed on an iron rod; and a short, flat ribbon called *lagane*. They worked the fields, tended the sheep, goats, and pigs, gathered the olives, and harvested the grain that provided food for their rich landlords and those who lived in the cities, but they didn't have it for themselves. In other words, they knew all about the finer things of the table—good olive oil, cheese, cured meats such as prosciutto and salame, factory-made macaroni and spaghetti—but they were deprived of them, and ached for them. Meat was scarce in the Italian south, even for the better off, and a family would be lucky to have it three or four times a year, on feast days. Chickens were useful for their eggs, but only when the hens weren't laying anymore, and on the occasion of a feast day, could they be killed for their flesh, and to make some broth. Fishermen sold the better sorts of fish and shellfish to the rich. The poor who lived near the sea ate mussels and clams, octopus and conch.

One of the first things Italians did upon arriving in New York City was to find the foods that they had heard were available across the ocean. There was work for everyone in New York, perhaps not steady work or well-paid work, but work to make life better than in the old country. No matter how dingy and overcrowded the tenement ghettos were, here at least they could eat well.

The first unskilled Italian settlers did manual labor, working in construction and, literally, digging ditches. Those with building skills, and artistic skills, found work building the mansions, hotels, clubs, and pleasure palaces of the new American rich. It was the Gilded Age, and southern Italian craftsmen did much of the gilding. Italians were also famously instrumental in the building of the Lexington Avenue subway line, which was under construction at the beginning of the twentieth century.

The Italians also opened food businesses soon after they arrived. They established groceries on the Lower East Side, soon to be called Little Italy, and in Greenwich Village, where they also formed a community. They started import businesses to bring in the olive oil, cheeses, and factory-made macaroni that they had been deprived of in Italy. They started manufacturing pasta, too. Olive oil was one of the foods that became emblematic of their good fortune in a new land. At home, lard had been the fat of the poor, and olive oil was a luxury.

OPPOSITE: Savino Santomauro (Sam Di Paulo), in front of Di Palo, his store in Little Italy. His children still run what is now the best Italian market in the city.

Those who didn't have the wherewithal to open stores became street peddlers. According to Barry Lewis, a New York City historian, Italian peddlers were instrumental in bringing fresh produce into the neighborhoods of the city. At the end of the nineteenth century, most produce was still distributed at several markets at the perimeter of Manhattan and in Brooklyn.

The Italian peddlers and greengrocers carried it into the Italian residential areas of downtown Manhattan, including Greenwich Village. Not long after World War I, Italian immigration was at its peak and the borough housing boom began. The vegetable stores and Italian groceries moved with the Italians to Brooklyn and the Bronx, as well as to the East Side of Manhattan north of 116th Street, to what became known as East Harlem, a new Italian enclave.

The Italian habit of planting food near home was made possible with the move to the boroughs. Wherever Italians settled, they planted fig trees. It was almost like putting the Italian flag in the soil. Brooklyn is still full of them and they are now often huge trees that have lived to see their neighborhoods become predominantly Indo-Pak, Middle Eastern, or Chinese. The Italians grew tomatoes, eggplant, peppers, zucchini, and basil, too. They made wine in their basements with grapes brought east from California. These were sold at local wholesale markets, such as Brooklyn Terminal Market, which became famous as a source for imported Italian foods.

As recently as the early 1960s, before public housing was built on them, large tracts of land in Brownsville and East New York, on the Queens border, were cultivated by Italians who lived nearby. These were not simple backyard gardens. The Italians took over "vacant lots," as they were called in the days when such things still existed, and turned them into small farms. From the rear window of my grandmother's home in East New York, a mixed Jewish and Italian community largely built in the 1920s, one could see the Italian gardens tended on the weekends by men who worked in the building trades during the week. It was their greatest pleasure to grow food. In winter, the fig trees wrapped in canvas became Italian totems in the snow.

The custom of foraging was not forgotten either. Every spring, older Italian women—many dressed in the black of perpetual mourning—could be seen with their eyes toward the earth in Van Cortlandt Park in the Bronx, Cyprus Hills Park on the Brooklyn-Queens border, and Prospect Park in the heart of Brooklyn, and probably other places in the city, too. They found dandelions, chicory, and wild leeks (ramps), greens that were all familiar from the old country.

At first, Italian restaurants, like those of other ethnic groups, were meant to service the Italian community itself. Many men came without wives and gathered at the coffeehouses and restaurants of their community. Little Italy and Greenwich Village were famous for their small restaurants, which became appreciated by outsiders for their perceived romantic atmosphere. They weren't meant to be romantic, however. They were decorated to remind the owners and their Italian customers of the family-run trattorias they couldn't even dream of going to when they were back in Naples or Palermo, Potenza, Bari, or Reggio di Calabria. That style became a cliché: red-checked tablecloths, candles stuck in the necks of straw-covered Chianti bottles (ironically a wine from Tuscany, not from the south), plastic grapes hanging from indoor arbors. What may have made little Italian hideaways seem romantic was that their pace was slower, and their focus was on enjoyment of the meal with wine. Unlike the frenzied feeding pens of the Wall Street district, the old oyster bars of Canal Street, the uptown (now midtown) restaurants where the social scene and entertainment were more important than the meal (the Lobster Palaces), or Delmonico-style haute French cuisine with prices so grand that regular citizens could not afford them, the small Italian restaurants had waiters who offered warm hospitality and kitchens that prepared exotic, satisfying, inexpensive food. The Italian restaurant was also an alternative to the Jewish delis and restaurants proliferating at the time. The Italian restaurateurs had grace, and they cultivated the business of outsiders with charm. One of the first Italian restaurants to attract non-Italians was Mamma Leone's, opened in 1905 by Louisa Leona, who married Gerolamo Leone. It became so popular that Mamma kept adding rooms. Eventually the restaurant could serve twelve hundred, and was no longer the quaint place where Mamma cooked more food than you could eat. It became a tourist attraction.

The arrival of Enrico Caruso in 1903 also helped promote Italian food. Caruso had been booed off the stage in his hometown of Naples, but became a sensation in the United States after his debut at New York's Metropolitan Opera. The press covered his every movement, and he loved to frequent Italian restaurants.

Italians were naturals in the hospitality sphere, and they soon owned restaurants that did not serve Italian food. The most famous early example would be the Colony, which was opened in 1918 by an Italian and with an Italian staff (except for the French chef). The staff soon bought the business and made the restaurant one of the most glamorous in the world.

By the early 1920s, more elaborate Italian restaurants meant to attract non-Italians had opened in the Times Square area. The location took advantage of the growing number of tourists, who came to New York partly for food adventures, theatergoers, and the local theatrical community itself, a group that was much worldlier than the general population, who, in any case, couldn't afford these places. Like other types of ethnic restaurants opening in the area, the Italian restaurants supplanted the Lobster Palaces that were closing due to Prohibition.

LEFT AND RIGHT:
The Jewish Teitel family still sells Italian foods on Arthur Avenue in the Bronx .

RIGHT:
Zeppole at Manhattan's Feast of San Gennaro.

FROM UPPER-LEFT CORNER, CLOCKWISE:
A display of limoncellos;
stockfish on Arthur Avenue;
Mike Greco of Mike's Deli, the unofficial
mayor of Arthur Avenue;
New York City–made dried sausage;
Ronzoni used to be New York City
metro's local pasta company;
Mario Borgatti rolls pasta at his shop
on Arthur Avenue;
a variety of marzipan;
stuffing cannoli at the Feast of
San Gennaro, circa 1955 taken by Jerry Dantzic.

Although the food served at these restaurants was a variant of southern Italian cooking, Americans came to identify this food as the food of all of Italy, a country with twenty regions and at least as many different styles of cuisine. Tomato sauce ruled. Garlic was an important seasoning. Oregano was the dominant herb. Today, Italian-American food is often ridiculed as a bastard cuisine that is heavy and crude. In truth, this new Italian-American cuisine was not that dissimilar from its prototype, and had a lot more finesse than it is given credit for. True, the Italian immigrants adopted new ingredients that were more available here, such as meat, and worked around ingredients that were not so easy to get, which truly were not many.

What is also true is that as the Italian immigrants and their descendants got richer, so did their food, and richer could easily be interpreted to mean heavier. The southern Italian diet was based on vegetables and pasta. The easy availability of meat here, and the lower quality of the vegetables, turned the cuisine upside down. In America, instead of eating meat three times a year as they did at home, even a working-class immigrant family could afford to eat meat three times a week. Meatballs got larger, with less bread to extend the meat—and consequently became heavier. Where eggplant was fried and layered with tomato sauce and mozzarella back in Naples, veal (and eventually chicken) was treated the same way here. Where a few leaves of parsley would suffice to season a big pot of meat sauce in Italy, in the new country parsley joined oregano and basil. Where a little onion or garlic would do to start a sauce in Italy, in America both were used in the same dish. There was cross pollination of Italian cuisines, too. Although at first Italians clustered on streets with people from their same community in the old country, eventually Neapolitans had Sicilian neighbors (for example) and swapped recipes and culinary customs.

Strangely, as popular as the little Italian restaurant was in the neighborhoods, attracting those outside the Italian community, Italian food did not make inroads into mainstream menus the way Jewish food did, especially after World War II, when dishes like blintzes, chopped liver, and gefilte fish could be found on menus that also listed grilled ham steak and shrimp cocktail. You could always get your spaghetti Italienne, even at Schrafft's, but that was sort of it. At the same time, Italian restaurants that clustered in midtown felt obliged to serve dishes that were not Italian. On an early 1960s menu from the Grotto, which was at 224 West Forty-sixth Street, along with the veal cutlet parmigiana, pork chops pizzaiola, and spaghetti with clam sauce, was roast duckling with grape sauce, "shrimps a la Newburg [sic]," and a hot turkey sandwich.

Pizza, however, did assimilate. The first pizzeria opened in 1905, but pizza's popularity boomed after World War II. It is often said that the GIs who served in Italy came home with a taste for it. (See opposite page.)

Today, Italian is the most popular and important cuisine in New York City. (It's nearly the most popular in the United States, barely superceded by Mexican.) Every neighborhood, no matter the ethnicity, has a pizzeria, if not a pizzeria on every other corner. There are more Italian restaurants in the city than there are of any other kind, and they are of every type, from casual to formal, and from nearly every region, serving food from Sicily to Liguria. Regional Italian restaurants are a fairly recent phenomenon, but they are on the rise.

Borough neighborhoods still have friendly places to get the old-time Italian-American specialties, but these are rare these days. Meanwhile, in Manhattan, Italian restaurants are now called *trattorias*, or *osterias,* or *enotecas*. Manhattan also boasts Italian restaurants that are branches of restaurants in Italy and attract an international clientele.

The breakout in Italian restaurants and cooking started in the 1970s. The worldly Craig Claiborne, food editor of the *New York Times*, wrote about dishes from places other than the south of Italy, and he promoted the career of Marcella Hazan, then a Manhattan housewife who gave cooking lessons in her tiny apartment. In about 1968, Restaurant Associates, the big restau-

The Feast of San Gennaro takes place in Little Italy the week surrounding September 19.

rant operators, opened Trattoria in the new PanAm building (now the MetLife building). Alfredo Viazzi, an enterprising and theatrical restaurateur from Genoa, opened several small places in Greenwich Village, all of which served unfamiliar and very delicious food from regions north of Rome. (See page 168.)

Soon, southern Italian restaurateurs put up signs proclaiming they served "northern" Italian cuisine. Generally, this meant they had sauces based on butter and cream instead of oil and tomatoes. They weren't truly "northern" at all, but the marketing worked: New Yorkers, including Italian Americans themselves, were hooked.

PIZZA

New Yorkers are passionate about pizza. Within the parameters of "New York–style" pizza, which all New Yorkers would agree is the only legitimate style of pizza in the United States (fuhgetaboutit, Chicago), we have many styles to choose from, and we are choosy.

We argue: thin and crisp crust versus thin but pliable crust, blistered or not, coal oven versus gas oven, brick oven versus ordinary oven, sparingly topped versus a topping of cheese so thick you could skate across it—oh well, there I go showing my prejudices. It is simply not possible for a New Yorker to talk about pizza without voicing an opinion. But let's start at the beginning.

The first pizza in New York, and, I venture to say, the first pizza made in America, was baked by a Neapolitan immigrant, Gennaro Lombardi, in 1905. He had come to New York City in 1897, so he wasn't very distant from the prototype for all pizza: Neapolitan pizza. He had a grocery in the northern reaches of what was becoming Little Italy. Surrounded by hungry fellow Neapolitans, for whom pizza is not just food but a way of life, he decided that baking pizza would be a good way to supplement his income. Or something like that.

Back to New York: Because a Neapolitan-style, wood-burning oven was not then an efficient or economical way to bake pizzas in the middle of Manhattan, Gennaro Lombardi built a coal-burning oven, coal being the common heating fuel of the day. Hence, the real and true New York pizza should be baked in a coal oven, as many are today. And somewhere along the line, instead of baking individual pizzas, as they do in Naples, Lombardi's began baking large pies that were cut into wedges to make it easier to eat. (Everything in America gets bigger, richer, sometimes heavier than in the homeland.) Today, in Naples, most people use knife and fork to eat their pizza, but one way of maneuvering the pie into the mouth in the old days was to fold it in half (called a *libretto*, meaning "like a book"). So eating pizza out of hand was not unfamiliar to Lombardi.

Some pizza "historians," such as Ed Levine, author of *New York Eats* and a regular contributor to the *New York Times*, say that Lombardi himself didn't bake the pies. He was a grocer. Instead, he hired pizza makers, also recently off the boat: John Sasso, Patsy Lancieri, and Anthony (Totonno) Pero were three of the first. Eventually these three men opened their own pizzerias, all in burgeoning Italian neighborhoods. Anthony Pero opened Totonno's on Neptune Avenue in Coney Island, Brooklyn, in 1924. John Sasso opened John's on Bleecker Street in Greenwich Village in 1929. Patsy Lancieri opened Patsy's on First Avenue and 116th Street, in East Harlem, in 1933. All three pizzerias are still at their original locations.

The original Lombardi's, which evolved into a full-scale Italian restaurant, closed in 1984. But, ten years later, it was reopened as a simple pizzeria by Gennaro Lombardi's grandson and namesake, and the great quality is now carried on by John Brescia, a Lombardi cousin.

Totonno's has a branch in Manhattan now, on Second Avenue and Eighty-first Street, although it is not nearly as atmospheric (or as good, some would say) as the original in Coney Island. John's, besides its original Greenwich Village location on Bleecker Street, has several satellite pizzerias in Manhattan, including one in the Theater District in a deconsecrated church on West Forty-fourth Street. The name Patsy's has since been licensed to an outsider, Nick Tsoulis, a Greek, who operates four Patsy's locations in Manhattan.

After years of working as a waiter and only dreaming of being a pizza man, a nephew of the original Patsy, Patsy Grimaldi, opened a pizzeria on Old Fulton Street in Brooklyn, the area by the foot of the Brooklyn Bridge that is now called DUMBO (Down Under the Brooklyn Bridge Overpass). This newest of the old-style pizzerias caused quite a commotion when it opened. It was at first called Patsy's, but pressure from Patsy's licensee, Tsoulis, forced Grimaldi to change the name to Patsy Grimaldi's. A lawsuit ensued. Now the name is simply Grimaldi's.

OPPOSITE:
The first pizza in New York City was baked at Lombardi's grocery in 1905.

·LOMBARDI'S *in* 1905·

As fabulous and authentic as all these New York pizzerias are (or aren't), none of them serves pizza by the slice, which is another New York City contribution to the world of pizza. It used to be that every New York City neighborhood had a decent if not very good pizzeria. The sauce or tomatoes were sweet and flavorful. The cheese was made from milk, not chemicals. The dough had yeast flavor—it wasn't as bland as supermarket sliced bread. Indeed, I used to be able to say that when I am not near the pizza I love, I love the pizza I'm near. Not so today. There are still pizzerias that serve pizza by the slice in every neighborhood of the city—no matter the ethnicity—but quality varies dramatically.

Totonno in Coney Island is one of the city's original coal oven pizzerias.

SAUSAGE AND PEPPERS

A sausage and peppers sandwich is one of the main gastronomic attractions of the Feast of San Gennaro, which is held on the streets of Little Italy for the week surrounding September 19, the day when the saint's blood is said to liquefy (or not) in the Duomo (cathedral) of Naples, Italy.

Sausage and peppers have no special significance to the feast. They are not symbolic or traditional in the old country. They are merely something delicious and Italian that can easily be cooked on a truck. Indeed, in Naples, there is no street fair-type feast at all, and the only food of significance is the *torrone* (nougat) sold outside the church. The candy is shaped like a bishop's hat because San Gennaro was the bishop of Benevento.

In New York City, street vendors selling sausage and peppers are not even exclusive to San Gennaro anymore. Nowadays, you are likely to find sausage and peppers trucks at many other venues—at the street fairs held for no good reason in the summer (which tourists apparently like, but New Yorkers find annoying because they botch up traffic), and at the entrances to parks and sporting events. New Yorkers love a good sausage and peppers sandwich anywhere at any time, and you can always get one at the local pizzeria, too.

ALFREDO VIAZZI

Alfredo Viazzi may have been the first restaurateur in New York City (nay, America) to use the word trattoria to refer to a real trattoria, Trattoria da Alfredo. (Joe Baum and Gerald Brody used the word several years before for their huge and very un-trattoria-like Restaurant Associates operation in the PanAm building, which is now called the MetLife building and houses Naples 45.) More important, Viazzi was also the first to serve genuine Italian food: simple dishes made from great ingredients. His restaurant was down to earth and real, while it broke out of the red-sauce Italian-American mold. He wasn't a slave to "authenticity," meaning his dishes didn't always follow traditional recipes. He liked to invent. But they always had Italian attitude, and tasted truly Italian.

Viazzi was Genovese, but a man of the world, so his cooking wasn't from any particular region of Italy. Most customers probably didn't know he was even involved in the particulars of the kitchen. Always dapper, welcoming, flamboyant, usually wearing an ascot or scarf, he spent most of the dinner hour in the dining room, perhaps running back to the kitchen to check on things occasionally, but always hosting with expansive good humor and charm. Like many a great restaurateur, he had a knack for befriending powerful people, from all the New York worlds, and catered to many of them in the restaurant. Wall Street financiers might be seated next to people from the fashion world. Society ladies would come for lunch. Theater people loved the place. Alfredo's striking wife, and sometime co-host, was the actress Jane White. At night, limos and Bentleys could be seen waiting outside the modest storefront. It became a place to be seen, while the gastronomic crowd was just thrilled to have somewhere to eat genuine Italian food.

The uptown French chefs would come to Alfredo late at night. André Surmain, André Soltner's early partner at Lutèce, was a regular. Helen McCully, the very influential food editor of *McCall's*, was a friend of the Viazzis. The graphic designer and artist Milton Glaser, then the "Underground Gourmet" of *New York Magazine*, was a pal of Viazzi's, and Glaser designed and illustrated Viazzi's 1979 cookbook.

James Beard was also a close friend of Viazzi's, as well as his Greenwich Village neighbor, and a regular customer. Beard's longtime companion, Gino Cofacci, baked one of the trattoria's desserts, the same hazelnut-mocha dacquoise that he baked for the Coach House (see page 273).

Once, in about 1980, I had an afternoon-long lunch with Alice Waters at Alfredo's. She chose the restaurant; Viazzi was one of her early inspirations. On the gossipy side, Viazzi had a young mistress, Judy Himmelfarb, as well as a wife, and after the huge success of his trattoria, he set Judy up in a second restaurant, Tavola Calda da Alfredo, on Bleecker Street. There was also a third Alfredo restaurant, Caffe da Alfredo, which was run rather unsuccessfully by his children.

FROM UPPER-LEFT CORNER, CLOCKWISE:
Alfredo Viazzi by Milton Glaser;
the famous Gino's restaurant in
Manhattan, still extant;
The Lemon Ice King of Corona, in Queens,
features another major Italian-American
contribution to New York City gastronomy;
enjoying Italian ices at Ralph's, Staten Island;
Caffe Reggio, one of the
last Greenwich Village coffee houses;
enjoying spaghetti in the early 1920s;
Umberto's in Little Italy is famous for clams
and scungilli (conch) in
spicy tomato sauce;
elephants sculpted out of cheese.

SPAGHETTI AND MEATBALLS

The quintessential Italian-American dish is spaghetti and meatballs. It is often said that this is not a dish that exists in Italy, but that's not quite true. What is true is that a southern Italian would find it gross to have a giant, American-sized meatball on top of his pasta. But in some places in Italy you might really find small meatballs and spaghetti on the same plate. Meatballs, from Rome to Sicily, are often used in composite dishes with pasta, but they are as small as cherries or olives, and certainly no larger than walnuts. Large meatballs—with or without sauce—are eaten as they are, as a meat course, with a vegetable, not with pasta but after a pasta course.

Be that as it may, for Americans there is no Italian dish as satisfying as spaghetti and meatballs together in the same bowl, and Italian émigrés tended to adopt it immediately. For the first six years of my life I lived in the same house with a Neapolitan extended family that was right off the boat. Even they served spaghetti and meatballs, although some nights it was meatballs with macaroni, usually ziti.

Meatballs underwent the immigrant experience. In the old country, where meat was scarce and expensive, moistened stale bread was used as filler, which also gave the meatballs a light texture. When Neapolitan and other southern Italian immigrants arrived in the United States, the land of beef, they naturally used more meat and less bread. Beef was not only significantly less expensive and vastly more available in their prosperous new land than in Italy, but they associated bready meatballs with their Italian poverty. Today, you may see meatball recipes with a mere few tablespoons of breadcrumbs. These are a vestige of the soaked bread of old. Unfortunately, without a good portion of moist bread, meatballs are dense and heavy.

Serves 4

Ann Amendolara Nurse is a first-generation Italian Brooklynite whose family is from Bari, in Puglia. For many years, she taught cooking in various venues. Nowadays, she is the earth-mother force of New York's professional food world. She organizes cooking workshops with chefs for the culinary students at New York City Technical College and Saturday workshops at the Beard House. Every year, she pulls together one of the most popular feasts in New York, her brunch to benefit the Beard Foundation's scholarship fund. Her meatballs are really more Italian than American, although there is an American touch in her use of white bread as the filler. Because American sliced bread is so moist already, there's no need to soak it.

1 pound ground beef chuck

2 large cloves garlic, finely minced

2 eggs

½ cup freshly grated pecorino

½ cup chopped parsley

Scant ½ teaspoon freshly ground black
    pepper

3 slices high-quality supermarket white bread,
    with crusts, made into crumbs in a blender

Olive oil, for frying

3 to 4 cups tomato sauce (see opposite page)

12 to 16 ounces dried spaghetti, cooked

In a large mixing bowl, combine the beef, garlic, eggs, cheese, parsley, pepper, and breadcrumbs. Mix very well. (There's no need for salt, because pecorino is salty.) Shape the meat into 12 meatballs.

In a 10-inch skillet over medium heat, heat about ½ inch of oil. When hot, fry the meatballs, in two batches, until they are well browned on all sides.

In a saucepan, heat the tomato sauce to bubbling. Add the meatballs and heat through for 10 minutes.

Serve over the pasta.

ITALIAN-AMERICAN TOMATO SAUCE
(Marinara Sauce)
4 cups

3 tablespoons extra-virgin olive oil
1 small onion or ½ medium onion,
    finely chopped (about ½ cup)
1 or 2 large cloves garlic, finely chopped
2 (28-ounce) cans imported (from Italy)
    plum tomatoes

1 teaspoon salt
Hot red pepper flakes or freshly ground black
    pepper to taste
½ teaspoon dried oregano
4 leaves fresh basil, chopped, shredded,
    or torn

In a 3-quart saucepan, combine the oil, onion, and garlic. Cook over medium heat, stirring frequently, until the onion is tender, 8 to 10 minutes.

Drain the tomatoes and reserve the juice. If the juice is thick and there is no more than ½ cup in each can, then use in this sauce; if the juice is watery and plentiful, use it in another recipe, such as a soup or stew—the juice can be frozen.

Turn the tomatoes into a food mill and puree the tomatoes directly into the pan. Add the salt and hot red pepper flakes. Stir well. Increase the heat slightly and bring to a brisk simmer.

Adjusting the heat as the sauce cooks down, and stirring frequently, simmer briskly for about 12 minutes, adding the herbs in the last few minutes. The sauce should have thickened and reduced. If it needs to be thicker, continue to simmer briskly for a few more minutes. Taste and adjust the salt and pepper, if necessary.

Note: The yield will depend on how much liquid is in the can. Tomatoes imported from Italy yield the most sauce.

VEAL PARMIGIANA

In Italy, when you say "parmigiana" it is understood to be eggplant parmigiana, because these days there hardly is any other form of this classic Neapolitan dish. In times past in the Italian south, cooks might have prepared artichokes alla parmigiana, zucchini alla parmigiana, or some other vegetables alla parmigiana, but these are so rare today that they hardly count.

"Veal parmigiana? What can that be?" an Italian might well ask. It is strictly an American invention. I propose that it is a New York City invention. Few other American cities had as plentiful a supply of veal as New York City, and they still don't. The city has always been a consumer of veal because New York State was, at one time, the top dairying state in the nation. All you have to do is look at New York City restaurant menus from the late nineteenth century and through the mid-twentieth century and you can see all the veal products—calf's liver, veal sweetbreads, veal tongue, veal chops, and, of course, at least one dish featuring a scaloppine of veal. Interestingly, French chefs who started working in New York City in the 1960s say they had trouble getting milk-fed veal. I think the veal all went to the ethnic market, especially the Italians.

Serves 4

1 pound veal scaloppini, cut from the leg (should be 8 slices)
Salt and freshly ground black pepper
3 eggs
1 cup all-purpose flour

1 ½ to 2 cups breadcrumbs
Peanut or canola oil for frying
½ cup freshly grated Parmigiano-Reggiano
3 cups tomato sauce (see page 171)
1 pound fresh mozzarella

Season the meat on both sides with salt and pepper.

Break the eggs into a pie plate or other deep plate that the scaloppini can fit into. Beat with a fork to mix well. Spread the flour on a sheet of wax paper. Spread the breadcrumbs on another sheet of wax paper.

Draw each slice of veal through the egg, coating well, then dredge in the flour. Repeat the egg bath, then dredge in the breadcrumbs, pressing the crumbs into the veal to coat thoroughly.

Set each breaded veal slice on a plate or platter, placing wax paper between them. Refrigerate for at least 30 minutes, or for several hours.

In a 12-inch skillet, over medium-high heat, heat about ¼-inch of oil. When the oil is hot enough for a pinch of breadcrumbs to sizzle instantly, add two or three slices of the breaded veal. Do not crowd the pan. Cook for about 90 seconds on each side, until browned on both sides. Set aside on a wire rack to drain.

When almost ready to serve, preheat the oven to 400 degrees.

Arrange the fried veal slices on a baking sheet. Top each with a light dusting of the Parmigiano-Reggiano. Spoon some tomato sauce over each to almost entirely coat them. Place a few small slices of the mozzarella on top of the sauce.

Bake until the mozzarella is melted and the sauce is bubbly, about 10 minutes.

Serve immediately.

VEAL MARSALA

Of the triumvirate of Italian-American veal dishes—veal francése, veal parmigiana, and veal Marsala—veal Marsala is the most popular in Italian-American restaurants today. It is an easy dish to make at home if you get organized for it.

Serves 2 or 3

1 pound veal scaloppini
Salt and freshly ground black pepper
Flour, for coating
4 tablespoons extra-virgin olive oil
2 cloves garlic, lightly smashed
Big pinch of hot red pepper flakes

8 ounces white or cremini mushrooms, thinly sliced
¼ teaspoon salt
Pinch of freshly grated nutmeg
½ cup dry Marsala wine
Chopped parsley (optional)

If the butcher has not pounded out the scaloppini, you must do it yourself: Use a meat pounder meant for the job, or the bottom of a very heavy, flat-bottomed tumbler. The pounding is not just in a downward motion, but also out to the edges for very thin slices that will cook up tender and quickly.

Season the meat lightly with salt and pepper on one side. Set aside.

Place some flour on a plate and set aside.

Put 2 tablespoons of the oil, the garlic, and hot red pepper flakes in a 10-inch skillet. Place over medium-low heat, and nurse the garlic along, squashing it a bit in the oil, turning it a few times, until it is soft.

Add the mushrooms. Season with the ¼ teaspoon salt and the nutmeg. Increase the heat slightly and sauté, tossing the mushrooms for the first minute or so, until they start giving off their liquid. Cook for another minute or so to reduce the mushroom liquid. While the mushrooms are still a little juicy, scrape them into a bowl and set aside.

In the same pan, heat the remaining 2 tablespoons oil over medium-high heat.

While the oil is heating, dust a few of the veal slices lightly in the flour, shaking off any excess.

When the oil is hot, add the floured meat slices to the pan, never overlapping the slices. They should sizzle immediately. Fry for about 30 seconds on each side, until tinged with brown. As the slices are done, remove them to a platter. Continue with the rest of the meat, flouring the slices just before you add them to the pan.

When all the meat has been cooked, immediately add the wine to the pan. Let the wine boil furiously for about 1 minute to reduce it by half, scraping up any browned bits that may have stuck to the pan.

Once the wine has reduced, return the mushrooms, along with any liquid that has accumulated with them, to the pan. Boil for a few seconds, stirring.

Return the meat, along with any juices that have accumulated with it, to the pan. Turn each slice in the pan sauce to coat. After a minute or so, the sauce should be thickened into a glaze on the meat slices. Remove from the heat and transfer to a platter.

Serve immediately, garnished with the parsley, if you like.

CHICKEN FRANCESE

All of the dishes dubbed *francese*—which is to say those plates of veal, chicken, fish, or shrimp that are fried with a light, eggy batter and dressed with a lemon sauce—were probably created in New York City. Only after they became established here were they disseminated across America by Italian cooks and waiters moving to other parts of the country. The concept of *francese* which is still a very popular preparation in New York City's Italian-American restaurants, has all the hallmarks of an old-country Italian dish that's gone through either a glamour makeover or what I like to call the immigrant experience, a process in which old dishes get enriched by the new availability of ingredients not common or attainable in the homeland.

In any case, *francese*, meaning "in the French style," is a little-known name for a preparation that many southern Italians might refer to as *indorati e fritti*: gilded and fried, referring to the golden color of the batter and how the food is cooked. In Neapolitan cuisine, the only dish I've ever seen called *alla francese* (in an early-twentieth-century cookbook) is flour-and-egg-dipped then fried scamorza (which is, in essence, aged mozzarella), served with wedges of lemon. But you'd be hard-pressed to find a southern Italian today who's heard of *alla francese*. This is not to say that the preparation isn't popular anymore: Without calling it *alla francese*, vegetables, even seafood, are cooked this way, but not veal and chicken. The Italian-American dish puts meat in place of the cheese or vegetable, good meat being so much more plentiful and affordable in the new country. Instead of a mere sprinkling of lemon juice, the new dish is made grander by turning the pan drippings into a full-blown lemon sauce. It turns out "Continental style," which is what the crossbred French-Italian fare on transatlantic ships was called.

Which came first, the veal, chicken, fish, or shrimp? Veal francese was most certainly the original innovation. Sometime in the 1950s, Italian-American cooks started making fish fillets in that style. Chicken francese, made with chicken cutlets, didn't exist until the mid-1960s, when boneless and skinless breasts became popular. And the first time I ever saw shrimp francese on a menu was the late 1960s. It was considered extravagant.

Serves 4

Because this is a restaurant dish and usually made in single portions, the following recipe is a slight compromise. In order to prepare enough for four, you have to keep half the recipe warm while cooking the rest. Or you could use two separate pans. Use the same ingredients and method for preparing veal or shrimp or a fish fillet, keeping in mind that the cooking times will vary slightly according to the item cooked.

4 skinless, boneless chicken breasts
    (about 1⅓ pounds)
Salt and freshly ground black pepper
Flour, for coating
2 eggs
¼ cup vegetable oil
¼ cup unsalted butter (½ stick)
¼ cup dry white wine or vermouth
6 tablespoons chicken broth
¼ cup freshly squeezed lemon juice
Lemon wedges, for garnish

Note well: Make sure to have all the ingredients measured and lined up before starting to cook. You will have to make the chicken in two batches of two cutlets each, so the frying fats and the sauce ingredients will be used half at a time. Before beginning, preheat the oven to 200 degrees so you can keep the first batch of two cutlets warm while cooking the second.

Between two sheets of wax paper, using the side of a can, a heavy jar, or a meat pounder, pound the breasts until about ⅓ inch thick (or have the butcher do this for you). Season well with salt and pepper. Set aside.

Place some flour on a dinner plate or a piece of wax paper. In a wide, shallow bowl or a deep plate with a rim (I use a pie plate), beat the eggs with a fork. Set aside.

In a 10-inch skillet, over medium-high to high heat, heat the oil and butter together until sizzling.

Just before placing the breasts in the hot oil, dredge two of them on both sides in the flour, coating heavily by pressing it on. Pass the breasts through the egg, making sure they are thoroughly coated, then dredge them in the flour again, again coating heavily.

Place the coated breasts in the pan and fry for about 2 minutes or slightly longer per side, until the batter is golden and the cutlets are just done

through. If the fat in the pan starts smoking before the cutlets are done, turn down the heat slightly or add just a touch (1 teaspoon or so) more oil. Do not let the fat (or the flour that has migrated into it) burn.

As the cutlets are done, remove them to a serving platter and keep them warm in the oven while making the sauce.

Immediately add half of the vermouth, stock, and lemon juice to the pan. Boil over high heat for about 1 minute, until reduced by about half and slightly thickened. The sauce will be brown.

Pour the sauce into a cup and set aside while repeating the whole procedure with the remaining cutlets and ingredients.

When you have made the second batch of sauce, add the first to it, in the skillet, to reheat.

Pour the sauce over the cutlets, garnish with lemon wedges, and serve immediately.

MANICOTTI

Manicotti, stuffed pasta tubes, is another one of those dishes that no one in Italy has ever heard of. Manicotti in Italy today are the exhaust pipes of a car, whereas a dish like this would be called cannelloni or crespelle, and it would be made with crepes, not pasta tubes. At one time, manicotti, which literally means "cooked hands," might have referred to a woman's fur or quilted muff or hand warmer. These were fashionable as recently as the 1950s, but were very much in style in the late nineteenth century, when many southern Italians were emigrating to the United States. Maybe that's where the word comes from.

No matter the name, manicotti is a popular dish among New York City's Italian Americans, and the pasta tube version may well be a New York Italian idea and term. Until very recently, Ronzoni, which used to be a strictly metro New York brand, was the only maker of them.

Manicotti are often made for a midweek meal using "Sunday gravy," what Italian Americans often call their long-cooked meat sauce or ragu. Short of making Sunday gravy, you can use a plain, quickly cooked tomato sauce (see page 171); or use *sugo finto*, "fake gravy," a tomato sauce made with wine and vegetables in imitation of a meat sauce (the recipe follows).

Makes 12

2 (15-ounce) containers or 1 (32-ounce) container whole milk ricotta

4 ounces fresh mozzarella, chopped or shredded

1 cup freshly grated Parmigiano-Reggiano, Grana Padano, Pecorino Romano, or a mixture of pecorino and one of the others

1 egg

3 tablespoons not-too-finely chopped parsley

½ teaspoon salt

½ teaspoon freshly ground black pepper

4 cups tomato sauce (see page 171), Neopolitan ragu, or *sugo finto* (recipe follows)

12 dried manicotti pasta tubes or fresh crepes (crepe recipe follows)

To make the filling, in a large bowl, stir together the ricotta, mozzarella, ½ cup of the Parmigiano-Reggiano, the egg, parsley, salt, and pepper. Cover and refrigerate until you are ready to fill the pasta tubes or crepes.

If using dried pasta tubes, boil them in plenty of salted water until barely tender, using the package directions as a guide. As soon as they are cooked, drain them in a colander and place them under cold running water to stop the cooking. Drain them on a clean dish towel.

Preheat the oven to 350 degrees.

Spoon ½ cup of the sauce evenly over the bottom of a 13-by-9-by-2-inch baking dish. It should make only a thin layer.

If using pasta tubes, fill them well, using a spoon or a pastry bag (which makes the job easier) with ¼ to ⅓ cup of the filling.

If using crepes, place about ⅓ cup of the filling just below the center of the crepe, keeping it at least ½-inch from the edges. Roll up from the bottom to enclose the filling. Continue with the remaining tubes or crepes and filling, placing them close together and seam side down in the prepared dish.

Spoon on about 2 cups of the sauce, reserving the remaining sauce to serve at the table, for those who like a lot of sauce. Sprinkle evenly with the remaining ½ cup of Parmigiano-Reggiano.

Bake for about 30 minutes, or until the sauce is bubbling and the manicotti are heated through.

Let rest for 10 minutes before serving.

MANICOTTI CREPES (Makes 12)

3 large eggs
½ teaspoon salt

1 cup all-purpose flour
Olive oil

In a large bowl, whisk together 1 cup water, the eggs, and salt. Whisk in the flour until smooth. Cover and refrigerate for at least 30 minutes.

Heat a 6-inch omelet or crepe pan or a nonstick skillet over medium heat.

Brush the pan lightly with olive oil.

Holding the pan in one hand, and using a measuring cup for the batter, pour in a scant ¼ cup of the crepe batter. Immediately rotate the pan to completely cover the bottom.

Cook for 1 minute, or until the edges of the crepe turn brown and begin to lift away from the pan.

Flip the crepe over and brown lightly on the other side. Don't be alarmed if the crepe puffs up. It will flatten as it cools.

Transfer the cooked crepe to a dinner plate and cover with a damp kitchen towel.

Repeat with the remaining batter, stacking the cooked crepes, separating them with pieces of wax paper, and keeping the plate covered with the damp towel.

When all the crepes are cooked, cover with plastic wrap and refrigerate until ready to use. (The crepes can be made up to 2 days ahead. They can also be frozen for up to a month, wrapped well in plastic or in a zippered plastic bag.)

SUGO FINTO (Makes about 4 cups)

½ cup olive oil
1 cup finely minced onion (1 medium onion)
1 cup finely minced carrots (2 small carrots)
2 cloves garlic, finely chopped
½ teaspoon hot red pepper flakes

½ cup dry Marsala wine
½ cup dry white wine
2 (28-ounce) cans imported (from Italy)
    plum tomatoes, drained
1 teaspoon salt

In a large saucepan, combine the oil, onion, carrots, garlic, and hot red pepper flakes. Cook over medium heat, stirring occasionally, until the vegetables are very tender and beginning to brown, about 15 minutes.

Add the wines and bring to a boil, stirring constantly, and boil for 3 to 4 minutes.

Pass the tomatoes through a food mill directly into the pan. Add the salt, stir well, then bring to a simmer.

Adjust the heat so that the sauce simmers gently. Cook for 30 minutes, stirring occasionally, until the sauce is the right thickened consistency.

You can use the sauce immediately on pasta or other foods, but it is better reheated several hours later.

BISCUIT TORTONI

Long before the tiramisu explosion, two frozen desserts, tortoni and spumoni, were the most popular desserts in New York City's Italian-American restaurants. You still encounter almond-flavored tortoni from time to time, still served in the fluted paper "soufflé" cups that charm children so much. Spumoni has metamorphosed into "Neapolitan" ice cream, the strawberry, vanilla, and chocolate-striped blocks you can buy in the supermarket.

No one in Naples—indeed, no one in Italy—has ever heard of tortoni. While researching my last book, *Naples at Table: Cooking in Campania*, I searched for its Italian prototype, convinced that it must be Neapolitan. After all, the Neapolitans claim to have invented frozen desserts, and they definitely make almond-flavored ones very much like tortoni. They even freeze them and serve them in small individual cups (called *coviglie*).

Finally I ran across this tidbit: In the mid-eighteenth century, a Signor Tortoni (I haven't found his first name yet), a Neapolitan, opened one of the first ice cream cafes in Paris. It's anyone's guess how his name got on a dessert served in Italian restaurants in New York City. Could it have been carried here by an Italian waiter who stopped in Paris on his way to the United States? A bigger mystery yet is why it is called biscuit, which means "twice cooked" in French, just as *biscotto* means "twice cooked" in Italian. The dessert, however, is entirely uncooked, and so unbelievably easy to prepare that you may be making it all the time.

Makes 8 (4-ounce) servings

Michele Scicolone who grew up in Brooklyn and is this country's foremost expert on Italian-American cooking, loaned me this recipe. It is in her book *Italian Holiday Cooking* and it is perfect: It tastes exactly like the old days. It never goes near a real almond, except for the topping of chopped toasted almonds. And actually, I remember toasted coconut on top of the tortoni I enjoyed as a boy.

2 cups heavy cream
½ cup confectioners' sugar
1 teaspoon vanilla extract
½ teaspoon almond extract

2 large egg whites
Pinch of salt
½ cup toasted almonds, very finely chopped
   (see Note)

In a large bowl, whip the cream with the confectioners' sugar and the extracts until soft peaks form.

In a medium bowl, with clean beaters, beat the egg whites together with the salt on low speed until foamy. Gradually increase the speed and beat until soft peaks form. With a rubber spatula, gently fold the beaten whites into the whipped cream.

Spoon the mixture into 8 wine goblets or ramekins (custard cups or, if you can find them, the authentic fluted paper cups). Sprinkle with the toasted almonds. Cover with plastic wrap and freeze for at least 4 hours, or overnight.

Remove the tortoni from the refrigerator 15 to 30 minutes before serving.

Note: To toast almonds, spread blanched almonds (they can be whole, sliced, or slivered) on a baking sheet. Place in a preheated 350-degree oven for about 10 minutes, tossing them a couple of times. They should be a medium brown. Chop very finely to make the topping. Alternately, Michele says if you make the tortoni in cups in which the cream comes to the top of the cup or mounds slightly above it, you can roll and press the almonds into the top after it has been frozen.

"...WHAT STREET COMPARES WITH MOTT STREET?"

I bet the Chinese food here is terrible.
—MARISA TOMEI, *as Brooklynite Monalisa Vito in* My Cousin Vinny,
referring to a rural town in Alabama

TYPICAL. NEW YORKERS LAUGHED HARD AT THAT LINE BECAUSE THE LAUGH
was on us. Ridiculously, we always judge the general sophistication of other places by the quality
of their Chinese food. By that standard only San Francisco and Honolulu are up to snuff among
American cities. London passes muster. Forget Paris and Rome. Okay, in the 1980s, New Yorkers
started to concede that Paris had good Vietnamese restaurants. Vietnamese is almost Chinese.

New York City bluster aside, there was good reason that Chinese food might be better here
than most anywhere. New York City has had a Chinese population since the beginning of the
nineteenth century. It's not true, as some accounts have it, that New York City's Chinese didn't
arrive until the transcontinental railroad was built in the 1860s. By 1830, there was already a tiny,
budding Chinatown on Mott Street, where, it is speculated, Chinese sailors who had jumped ship
to remain in New York City had settled into a small bachelor society. They took up quarters on
the second floors of crumbling buildings. Without women to cook for them, they did it themselves. Without women to do their laundry, they did it themselves. You can see where this is leading. When, for reasons of racial discrimination, their job possibilities were restricted later in the
century, many made cooking and doing laundry their livelihood.

These few Chinese settled in what was the infamous Five Points section so colorfully depicted
in the Martin Scorsese film *Gangs of New York*. At one time, the Five Points, thus named because it
was the junction of five street corners, was considered the worst slum and most depraved neighborhood in the country. The Chinese were certainly at the bottom of the socioeconomic heap, and
many of them married Irish women, who were next up in the heap, leading to rumors of white
slavery. Chinese women didn't begin arriving in New York until the 1860s or 1870s.

Starting in 1849, when the California Gold Rush began and while the transcontinental railroad was being built, Chinese began flooding both the West and East Coasts. For a time, there was
plenty of work.

Hard economic times arrived in the United States in the 1870s, however, and with them the
racial scapegoating of the Chinese. They held the low-level jobs that the new European immigrants wanted. Pressure to deny Chinese immigration was particularly strong on the West Coast,
where there were riots. Finally, in 1882, Congress passed the Chinese Exclusion Act, which

OPPOSITE:
Dim sum lunch is
an extraordinarily
popular meal in
New York City's
several Chinatowns
today.

virtually ended Chinese immigration for sixty-one years. The law was repealed in 1943, but even then the regulations allowed for only inconsequential numbers of Chinese to immigrate compared to Europeans. It wasn't until 1965 that a greater number of Chinese were legally allowed to make a home in the United States, and that change significantly colored the complexion of Chinese food in New York City, as it must have in the rest of the country, too.

The Chinese Exclusion Act, however, didn't stop the Chinese who were already here from working toward the American dream of financial independence. They opened restaurants, and monopolized the laundry business. They educated their children and the children were quick to assimilate. Mark Twain, writing in *Roughing It* in 1872, noted that "All Chinamen can read, write and cipher with easy facility—pity but all our petted voters could." He also wrote that "They are quiet, peaceable, tractable, free from drunkenness, and they are as industrious as the day is long." Twain said they were already growing their own vegetables in California, as they may have been near New York City, too, when the season permitted.

In 1896, the Chinese-American dish chop suey, made at first with chopped organ meats and vegetables, was supposedly created in New York City for the visiting Chinese dignitary Li Hongzhang (also spelled Hung-Chang). True or not, Li Hongzhang's visit to New York City created a new curiosity about China, and all things Chinese were considered a marvel and a mystery. Businessmen in Chinatown did their best to cash in on the new interest. They printed menus in English. They put signs outside to entice uptown customers to taste chop suey. These usually advertised the dish as the one the Chinese viceroy loved, which, by the early twentieth century, had turned into a pale dish of stir-fried vegetables with chicken, pork, or beef, your choice, no animal innards—perhaps specifically to attract Caucasian business. Chow mein found

OPPOSITE: Both Chinatown and midtown Chinese restaurants glamorized themselves to attract non-Chinese and tourists.

> *I was in a taxi with a young cabbie from Ghana. As I often do when riding with a driver from a country I know little about, I asked about the food of his homeland. The driver was dressed rather preppy, in a yellow Ralph Lauren polo shirt with the collar up, and he was very well spoken. After he told me about what people eat in Ghana—mainly starchy root vegetables—I asked him, "And what's your favorite American food?"*
>
> *"I'm a real New Yorker now," the driver told me, "so I have to say my favorite American food is Chinese."*
>
> *He laughed. He knew exactly what he was saying.*

Chinatown
New York

Port Arthur Restaurant
Chinese Restaurant
IMPORTERS SOY KEE CO. EXPORTERS

BANQUET HALL & PRIVATE DINING ROOM

PORT ARTHUR
RESTAURANT
7 & 9 MOTT STREET
NEW YORK CITY

In the Heart of Chinatown
Near Chatham Square -:- Tel. Worth 2871

RESTAURANT CROSSROAD INN

18 PELL STREET
NEW YORK CITY
IN THE HEART
CHINATOWN

GAPORE

ADWAY AT
h STREET
YORK CITY

NEW YORK'S
MOST EXOTIC
CHINESE
RESTAURANT
AIR-CONDITIONED

YANK SING
CHINESE RESTAURANT

a Caucasian audience, too. It is, after all, essentially the same dish as chop suey, except that it's served on a bed of crunchy deep-fried noodles, not rice.

Until the 1890s, Chinatown was a ghetto with about eight hundred residents, according to an 1890 survey, and it was notoriously, if unfairly, labeled as the epicenter of depravity in the city. It was supposedly full of opium dens and a home to white slavery.

While the food was still mainly geared toward Chinese customers, a few Caucasians, for the most part quirky downtown personalities, were said to frequent the restaurants. For instance, in the 1890s, a personage of the Bowery, "Chuck" Connors, was famous for giving uptown swells tours of Chinatown. He even spoke some Chinese himself, or at least faked it well enough to fool his slumming clients. It was also said that he started every evening with a plate of chop suey.

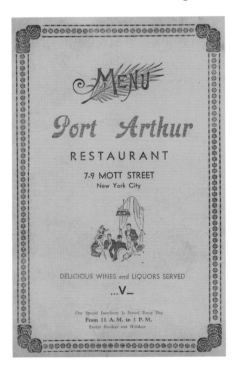

By the beginning of the twentieth century, there were really two Chinatowns, the tourist-oriented Chinatown that played into the Caucasian concept of the mystical Orient, and the real Chinatown, which gave a place to live and sense of community to its hard-working citizens. Starting in the 1920s, some Chinese restaurants were so popular they moved closer to their customer base. They moved north to Times Square, in the Theater District, where there was a ready audience among open-minded show people. They moved to Brooklyn and the Bronx, where the housing boom of the early 1920s was also drawing Jews and Italians out of the Lower East Side immigrant ghettos. Neighbors before, the Jews, Italians, and Chinese became neighbors again as the Chinese restaurateurs and laundry men moved into the new borough neighborhoods.

In the 1930s, Port Arthur, at 7-9 Mott Street, was among the most famous of the Manhattan Chinatown restaurants frequented by Caucasians. Its menu in the 1930s featured the combination plate dinners that were so popular then—soup, egg roll, an entree served with rice, plus tea and dessert, all for 95 cents, or 65 cents if you could live without the egg roll. There were also more expensive and elaborate table d'hôte dinners and family dinners. For a Chinatown restaurant, Port Arthur made huge concessions to American taste with a whole list of "American Dishes," such as "Fried Spring Chicken, Chicken Salad, Live Lobster Salad, Egg Salad, a Club Sandwich, and a Ham and Egg Sandwich."

"Chinese Delmonico's" was, no joke, the name of the other very popular Chinatown restaurant of the 1920s and 1930s, although Rian James didn't think much of it in his 1930 restaurant guide, *Dining in New York*. He wrote, "For some reason that has escaped us on each of three visits, the Chinese Delmonico's is famous through the city—and that is why it gets its name in this book, and that's the only reason. Personally, we like the uptown Chow Meineries heaps better; we find they are cleaner and much more accessible."

Around Times Square, Chin's and Ruby Foo's Den were the famous places. Ruby Foo's menu had a list of thirteen kinds of chop suey and nine kinds of chow mein. In parenthesis, the menu defined wontons as "kreplach," the Yiddish word for a similar dumpling, a nod to the restaurant's Jewish clientele. After all, Jews had an affinity for Chinese food (see page 133), and Broadway culture was heavily influenced by Jews.

On the surprisingly exotic side, Ruby Foo's also offered bird's nest and shark's fin. On the other hand, there is only one mention of "soy bean cake," otherwise known as

Chop suey restaurant, Chinatown, 1905

tofu, which is considered a staple Asian ingredient today. Ruby Foo's had a smaller list of American dishes than Port Arthur, but they included an expensive sirloin steak.

Ruby Foo's also had a few exotic dishes listed under "Suggestions," but, for the most part, Chinese dishes in those days were all created from the same limited palette of ingredients. Besides onions and celery, fresh vegetables were limited to bok choy (sometimes spelled "bok toy"), snow pea pods, and, because they could be easily grown in the kitchen, mung bean sprouts. Water chestnuts, bamboo shoots, and several types of mushrooms came from cans. Using chicken, beef, duck, and especially red-roasted pork, adding almonds, pineapple, and a mite few other condiments and seasonings (of course, there was soy sauce, and even a touch of garlic) the dishes were all variations and permutations of each other. For instance, if you ordered chicken chow mein you'd get a bed of vegetables topped with strips of white-meat chicken. But you could also order "cubed" chicken chow mein, a separate listing, the only difference being how the poultry was cut. Until the late 1960s, Chinese food in New York City may have been better than elsewhere, but, by today's standards, it was never exciting.

Then, in 1965, the laws were changed to allow a new flood of Chinese immigration. Chefs who had fled the Communist People's Republic and landed in Hong Kong, Taiwan, even South

America, were now coming to New York City. The new chefs brought new life to old Chinatown, and dazzled the jaded palates of power in a few uptown locations.

The Chinese food that these chefs found in New York City was unrecognizable to them. It was a variant of Cantonese—bland food that had precedent in the homeland but that was trans-

formed into a cuisine palatable to Americans, partly by force of limited ingredients. This food was served mostly in plain rooms downtown and in the boroughs, and in a flashy, kitschy, almost nightclub atmosphere in midtown Manhattan. That was about to change.

By the mid-1960s, New York City had also been exposed to so-called Mandarin cooking. That was a catch-all term used for northern Chinese cooking, as opposed to the "southern" cooking of Canton, the province from which most Chinese Americans hailed. Chef T. T. Wang, who was born in Yang Chow province but was trained in Taiwan, had been in service to a Chinese diplomat in Tokyo, and when his boss was moved to Washington in the early 1960s Wang came, too. He introduced the city to such dishes as pot-sticker dumplings and moo shu pork, a dish that is

wrapped in wheat pancakes called Peking doilies. Wang eventually opened a restaurant on the Upper West Side, a new bastion of "Mandarin" restaurants serving Peking-style and Shanghai-style dishes to Columbia University intellectuals and other open-minded eaters. Wang's establishment, on Broadway and Ninetieth Street, was "authentic, but not fancy, although he had an upscale vision," according to people who ate there at the time. That upscale vision became reality when Wang opened, in 1966, Shun Lee Dynasty, his dream restaurant, on Second Avenue and Forty-eighth Street. It was designed by Russell Wright, an important designer of the day who is now considered an icon of mid-century design, and it served dishes that no one in New York City

Chinatown markets are a great place to shop for roasted ducks and chickens **(ABOVE)** and all kinds of produce, Asian and not.

had eaten before. Beef with hoisin. Chicken soong. New York City never looked back to chow mein.

In 1967, Craig Claiborne awarded Shun Lee Dynasty four stars in the *New York Times*. This not only gave new respectability to Chinese food in New York City, but created new interest in it, and ensured a future for Chinese food served in elegant surroundings at higher than the cheap neighborhood and Chinatown prices. Claiborne actually was obsessed with Chinese food, considering it to be among the greatest cuisines of the world. In 1972, he even wrote a Chinese cookbook, co-authored with Virginia Lee, who, along with Grace Zia Chu (see page 190), was one of the first teachers of Chinese cooking in the city.

Some experts date New York City's Chinese food revolution specifically to 1969 and the opening of Hwa Yuan Szechuan Inn on East Broadway in Chinatown. But there were other pioneering new Chinese restaurants. Also in 1969, Restaurant 4, 5, 6, serving Shanghai food, opened on Chatham Square. And, at the same time, a chef named Uncle Lou was cooking in a restaurant called the Four Seas, a small space on the second floor of a building just a few blocks outside of Chinatown proper, just south of the Brooklyn Bridge entrance. Uptown big shots, such as Nelson Rockefeller and the Chinese architect I. M. Pei, were among Uncle Lou's devotees. Among his waiters was a young man named David Keh, who saw new possibilities for Chinese food uptown, where those customers lived.

Uncle Lou had spent his adult life cooking for an internationally famous Chinese painter who lived in São Paolo, Brazil, where many Chinese had gone to escape the Communists when the United States would not let them immigrate. Uncle Lou had no idea of how to cook for two hundred in a restaurant. The Four Seas had just a few tables. But the savvy David Keh found

A 1940s menu from the original Ruby Foo's

LEFT: In Flushing, Queens, the street signage makes the Asian shopping streets look like Hong Kong.

backers and opened a restaurant for him in 1970, on Chatham Square, in Chinatown. It was called Szechuan Taste. Later in 1970, David Keh also opened a restaurant called Szechuan on Ninety-fifth Street and Broadway, this time without Uncle Lou; it was the first Szechuan restaurant uptown. Then, in 1971, Keh opened yet another restaurant, on Second Avenue and Eightieth Street, called Szechuan East. That Danny Kaye, the singer and actor, was a cooking student of Uncle Lou, and a friend of David Keh, helped promote the restaurants to the right sophisticated and powerful uptown crowd.

Hunam, the first Hunanese restaurant in the city, opened in 1972 on Second Avenue and Forty-third Street. Uncle Tai's Hunan Yuan, another David Keh production, opened with a bang in 1973 at 1059 Third Avenue. So it was that in 1974 Hunan and Szechuan food became the rage in New York City. Orange flavor beef, which is strips of beef cooked with whole dried hot peppers and orange rind, and General Tso's chicken, which is deep-fried chunks of chicken that are then stir-fried with vegetables and sweet and spicy sauce, are examples of what was then the new style of Chinese food. This is also when the city and the nation were introduced to Lake Tung Ting shrimp, hot and sour soup, chicken with candied walnuts, and those slim northern Chinese—style spring rolls—as opposed to big American-style egg rolls.

With more and more legal immigrants coming in, New York City's Chinese population boomed in the late 1970s, and continues to grow to this day. While many Chinese were already well assimilated into the middle-class suburbs, and continued to move up the socioeconomic ladder, Manhattan's Chinatown started to expand north, eventually taking over most of Little Italy. It continued to grow as a Chinese community and as an attraction for tourists.

Then a second, more affluent Chinatown emerged, in Flushing, Queens. The Flushing community also absorbed a growing middle-class Korean population, which started arriving in the late 1960s and took over the city's neighborhood produce markets and groceries, filling the vacuum left by the Italians and Greeks, whose children were now educated and were no longer interested in such small retail business that required hard physical work and long hours (see page 365).

Now, in just the last decade, a third Chinatown has developed, along Eighth Avenue in the Sunset Park section of Brooklyn. It has been called "the other, other Chinatown." And yet a fourth Chinatown is beginning to bloom on Avenue U in Brooklyn, near Sheepshead Bay.

The dominant style of Chinese food in the various Chinatowns comes from Hong Kong. As Hong Kong money and population started coming to New York City in the late 1980s through the mid-1990s, in anticipation of the People's Republic takeover in 1997, new restaurants that specialized in Hong Kong's flashy seafood cuisine opened. Shrimp now needed to be live and shown to you in the dining room before they were cooked in the kitchen. Fish needed to be swimming in tanks in the walls before they met their fate. Often doing double duty as venues for private and public celebrations, the new Hong Kong restaurants are vast, heavily decorated in gold and red phoenixes and dragons, all good luck in the Chinese culture.

Although there has been a tea and dumpling parlor in Manhattan's Chinatown for more than fifty years—Nom Wah, on Pell Street—dim sum didn't become accessible or popular until the 1980s. Now, late morning through early afternoon on any weekend day, all the city's Chinatowns are packed with both Chinese and Caucasians gathering for dim sum. The kitchens send carts out to the dining room, and eaters just point and pick from dozens of kinds of dumplings in steamer baskets, plates of stewed dishes, and fried savory and sweet treats.

Ironically, with so much truly authentic and unusual Chinese food in the various Chinatowns of New York City, the Chinese food in other neighborhoods has declined badly. "True, today, there is no corner of the city not serviced by a Chinese take-out shop—the neighborhood wok," many New Yorkers call it—but, in general, the food is not good. New Yorkers put up with it because they can get it delivered, within minutes, to their door, even in a blizzard. The standard take-out Chinese is ostensibly Szechuan-Hunan (no one ever proudly claims to serve Cantonese food anymore), but today's Szechuan-Hunan food lacks fire and conviction.

GRACE ZIA CHU

Grace Zia Chu, who always let it be known that she was the wife of a general under Chinese Nationalist leader Chiang Kai-shek, was the first person to teach Chinese cooking in America. She did it at home and through the Chinese Institute in America on Lexington Avenue. By all accounts, Madame Chu, as she was usually known, was a better teacher than a cook.

She was a teacher's teacher, in fact. Gloria Zimmerman, who, among other accomplishments, cowrote the first Vietnamese cookbook in America, *The Classic Cuisine of Vietnam*, remembers her class with Grace Chu. "There were five of us in my group, including Marcella Hazan and Karen Lee [now a well-known cooking teacher in New York City]. Grace was always saying 'You gals should teach.' Then suddenly there was an article about Julia Child in the *New York Times* and I realized that yes, that's what I should do, teach. Grace was educated in China, then she went to Wellesley. She liked to brag about her husband, but in fact she left him and came to New York with her sons. She never went back, except to visit Madame Chiang in Taiwan."

Later, Grace Chu taught Chinese cooking through the Good Cooking School, which was organized by James Beard, Milton Glaser, and Burt Wolf after the success of their book, *The Cook's Catalog*. She traveled the country with Gloria Zimmerman and Karen Lee alternating as her assistants. "We'd set up school in a department store or some auditorium," says Zimmerman now. "When Marcella Hazan started teaching, in about 1970, she modeled herself on Grace Chu and taught at home, just the way Grace did."

> *In the 1920s, Chinese food you bought in Chinatown. There were no Chinese restaurants uptown. There was one place down by the Williamsburg Bridge called Lum Fong's that a lot of theatrical people used to go to. Mostly agents, like Abe Lastfogel of the William Morris Agency, would go down there for lunch. After a while they realized that they were spending two and a half hours a day just to get Chinese food. So they all got together and went to Lum Fong and said, "Listen, if you would open a restaurant on 52nd Street, we'll put up the money." They put up about ten thousand bucks each and Lum Fong opened on 52nd, just off Seventh, where he was for years and years.*
>
> —RUTH GORDON, *on Lum Fong, the first Chinese restaurant uptown, from* Manhattan Menus

CHINESE PEPPER STEAK

Chinese pepper steak was a standard home-cooked dish of my youth in Brooklyn in the 1950s. Jewish, Irish, Italian, even kosher moms made it, if they were hip homemakers. That's why I found it surprising that it is nearly impossible to find a recipe for it in an American cookbook.

Serves 4

Make sure to use a tender cut of meat here. The quick, high-heat cooking can toughen a marginal cut. If you only enjoy extremely tender meat, it wouldn't hurt to use strips of filet (beef tenderloin). Supermarkets in New York City still sell "beef for pepper steak," and it is usually strips of bottom round. A well-marbled piece of bottom round may be just fine, but it is iffy.

1 tablespoon dry or semidry sherry

3 tablespoons soy sauce

1 teaspoon sugar

2 teaspoons cornstarch

1 pound steak, trimmed of fat and sliced into ½-inch-thick strips about 3 to 4 inches long

3 tablespoons vegetable oil

1 heaping teaspoon minced garlic

1 medium green bell pepper, washed, cored, and cut into ½-inch strips

1 medium red, yellow, or orange bell pepper, washed, cored, and cut into ½-inch strips

1 medium onion, sliced thickly through the root end, then separated into pieces

3 or 4 (⅛-inch-thick) slices peeled fresh ginger

1 medium firm but ripe tomato, cut into 6 or 8 wedges

Place the sherry, soy sauce, sugar, and cornstarch in a medium bowl. With a fork, stir to combine.

Add the steak strips to the marinade and toss to coat. Refrigerate for 30 minutes or for several hours, until ready to cook.

Heat a 12-inch skillet or wok over high heat. Add 1 tablespoon of the oil and swirl to coat the pan. Add the garlic, peppers, and onion. Stir-fry for 3 minutes. With a slotted spoon or skimmer, remove the vegetables from the pan and set aside in a bowl.

Return the pan to high heat. Add the remaining 2 tablespoons oil and swirl as before.

Add the ginger and stir-fry just a few seconds. Toss the meat in the marinade one final time and add it to the pan with all the liquid in the bowl (which should be very little). Stir-fry until the meat is no longer pink, about 2 minutes. Discard the ginger, if desired (I don't).

Return the vegetables to the pan, along with the tomato wedges, if using, and stir-fry for 1 minute or so, tossing constantly.

Serve immediately, with plain white rice.

PEARL'S LEMON CHICKEN

This is from the *New York Times Style and Entertaining Magazine*, March 24, 2002. It was written by screenwriter and director Nora Ephron. It was headlined "As Pearl's Twirled."

To: Nora

From: Style & Entertaining

    Nora, are you inclined, do you have time, to write something about Pearl's? It seems as if there would be no new clothes on the runways if designers stopped referencing the 70's. And every time we read about the 70's, we keep hearing about Pearl's, on West 48th Street. People would eat there before going to Studio 54 or, before Studio happened, to Hurrah's or Le Jardin. Pearl Wong was the owner and hired Charles Gwathmey and Robert Siegel in 1973 to design the first modern Chinese restaurant. She felt the traditional ones were too kitsch. Was it good?

To: Style & Entertaining

From: Nora

    Oh, I wish I could write about Pearl's. It started as a *Time* magazine thing (where I never worked) and then suddenly became widely chic largely because of the lemon chicken. The lemon chicken was an amazement. Anyway, I was never a regular there. Then it moved, and I went a couple of times and realized there was enough MSG in the food to keep a battalion awake all night. At a certain point, by the way, Craig Claiborne printed the lemon chicken recipe in the *New York Times Magazine*. Lee Lum's Lemon Chicken, Lee Lum being the chef at Pearl's. Everyone cooked it. This is the part I really remember—Craig Claiborne would print a recipe in the *Sunday Times*, and everyone would cook it. When I think about it, I feel like one of those grannies talking about the days of horse-drawn buggies. You can't imagine how obsessed and diligent we were about cooking. Everyone made pilgrimages to Chinatown (or to a store on East 58th Street that carried Chinese groceries) to buy the water-chestnut flour you absolutely had to dip the chicken pieces in before frying them up. The recipe Craig printed wasn't really a good one, it had canned crushed pineapple in it, which was nowhere in evidence at Pearl's—but it was easy to figure out how to make a version closer to the one in the restaurant, which was, as far as I eventually ascertained, crisp-fried chicken on a bed of sliced-up iceberg lettuce absolutely saturated with a bottle of lemon extract and about six pounds of MSG. It was, as I said, an amazement and kept you up for days.

LEE LUM'S LEMON CHICKEN

When Craig Claiborne offered this recipe in the *New York Times Magazine* in 1969, he called this dish a triumph. For this adaptation, the MSG can be omitted.

Serves 4

For the chicken:

4 whole chicken breasts, boned and skinned

2 tablespoons light soy sauce

¼ teaspoon sesame oil

1 teaspoon salt

1 tablespoon gin or vodka

3 egg whites, beaten until frothy

1 cup water-chestnut flour or powder
    (available at Chinese grocery stores)

Peanut or salad oil for frying

For the broth:

¾ cup sugar

½ cup white vinegar

1 cup chicken broth

1 tablespoon cornstarch, mixed with
    2 tablespoons water

1 teaspoon MSG (optional)

Grated zest and juice of 1 large lemon

3 small carrots, julienned

½ large green bell pepper, julienned

3 scallions, trimmed, and julienned

3 rings canned pineapple, drained and
    shredded

1 (1-ounce) bottle lemon extract (see Note)

For serving:

¼ head iceberg lettuce, finely shredded

Make the chicken:

Place the chicken breasts in a shallow dish.

Combine the soy sauce, sesame oil, salt, and gin. Pour over the chicken. Turn to coat, and let sit for 30 minutes.

Drain the chicken and discard the marinade. Add the chicken pieces to the egg whites, and turn to coat. Pour the water-chestnut flour onto a plate and dredge the chicken in the flour.

Preheat the oven to 200 degrees.

Pour the peanut oil into a 10-inch skillet to ½ inch in depth. Heat to 350 degrees. Fry the chicken in batches: brown one side, turn, and brown the other. Set aside to drain.

Make the broth:

In a small saucepan, combine the sugar, vinegar, broth, cornstarch mixed with water, the MSG, if using, the lemon juice, and lemon zest. Bring to a boil. Stir until thickened.

Cut the chicken breast crosswise into 1-inch-thick slices, and place on top of lettuce on a serving platter. If necessary, keep it warm in the oven.

Add the vegetables and pineapple to the sauce. Remove from the heat and stir in the lemon extract. Pour over the chicken and serve immediately.

Note: The amount of extract is accurate. It should be added at the very last moment.

COLD NOODLES WITH SESAME SAUCE

Cold noodles with sesame sauce was cutting-edge Chinese in 1969, and New York City's food adventurers were going to Chinatown to eat them at Hwa Yuan Szechuan Inn at 40 East Broadway, one of Chinatown's first Szechuan restaurants. It was opened by Chef "Shorty" Tang, who became famous for the dish. Tragically, Shorty died in 1971. His family carried on for nearly a decade without him, but to their credit, the food remained as good as it was when Shorty was alive, and Shorty's reputation continued to grow. In 1977, Milton Glaser and Jerome Snyder, in their *Underground Gourmet* guide to New York City, note that Shorty "is reputed to be the culinary teacher of almost every Szechuan chef in town." They seemed not to know that he had been dead for six years.

The noodles were, in fact, just one among many other more ambitious and totally exotic Szechuan delights that Shorty would no doubt have preferred to be remembered by. I was a poor newlywed at the time he opened and remember frequenting the restaurant for a few other things—somehow braised duck sticks in my memory. Besides serving food that was breathtakingly spicy, the complete opposite of the subtle, if not downright bland, Cantonese-style cooking that ruled the day, Hwa Yuan was affordable.

Cold noodles with sesame sauce is very much part of New York City today. Every so-called salad bar has them. Every Chinese take-out menu lists them. Hardly anyone still associates it with the rage for hot and spicy Hunan-Szechuan cooking that was so popular in the 1970s. Indeed, it doesn't even have the pepper bite that it had when it was introduced back then. The following recipe suggests a range of pepper to suit your taste.

Serves 6

I have served this as a sort of salad base to receive additions of, say, strips of roasted chicken, pork, or shrimp, or steamed vegetables such as broccoli, string beans, carrots, fennel (could be raw)—you name it. The sauce, apart from the pasta, is also good as a salad or vegetable dressing.

1¼ pounds fresh Chinese egg noodles, or 1 pound linguine or spaghetti
1 tablespoon vegetable oil
7 tablespoons Chinese sesame paste or 100% natural peanut butter
⅔ cup warm water
6 tablespoons soy sauce
2 tablespoons rice wine vinegar
2 tablespoons sesame oil

½ to 1 teaspoon ground cayenne pepper, or more to taste
1 tablespoon sugar
1 teaspoon salt
1 tablespoon finely chopped garlic
3 to 4 whole scallions, finely chopped
1 cucumber, peeled, seeded, and julienned
Fresh coriander leaves (optional)

In about 5 quarts of boiling water salted with 1 rounded tablespoon salt, cook the noodles until done to taste. Drain immediately and rinse under cold running water until cooled. Place in a large bowl, drizzle with the vegetable oil, and toss well. Refrigerate until ready to serve.

If the sesame paste or peanut butter has separated, drive a chopstick repeatedly into it so you can mix the oil in sufficiently to stir, although it needn't be perfectly smooth at this point.

In a small mixing bowl, with a fork or small whisk, beat the sesame paste or peanut butter together with the water until fairly smooth. Add the soy sauce, vinegar, sesame oil, cayenne pepper, sugar, and salt. Beat again until smooth.

Add the garlic and scallions, stir well, and let stand for at least 30 minutes, or until ready to serve.

(The sauce may be made several days ahead. Allow to return to room temperature before tossing it with the noodles.)

Toss the noodles with about 1½ cups of the sauce.

Serve topped with the remaining sauce, the cucumber, and coriander, if using.

MRS. FAN'S CABBAGE

Auntie Yuan, at 1191 First Avenue, on the affluent Upper East Side of Manhattan, was a groundbreaking Chinese restaurant. In 1983 it made going out for Chinese food once again stylish enough to attract New York's power elite. That the restaurant was in or near their rich neighborhoods helped, but the menu also boasted new dishes, food never seen in the United States before, from all regions of China, which attracted anyone in the city willing to pay French prices for Chinese food. The "Auntie" conceit was double-edged: The word sounds appealingly lighthearted to Americans, even connoting home-cooked food. But like the word Uncle, used as a title for male Chinese chefs, Auntie is an honorific title for a woman chef. In this case it referred to the team of Taiwanese women cooks who were supposedly preparing your dinner.

What was really important here, however, was that the food was presented with glamour. Except for the wood floors and white tablecloths, the room was black and hung with large, striking red-on-white Chinese calligraphy pieces executed by the owner, David Keh. Keh was well known for his Chinese restaurants featuring the latest dishes. In the early 1970s, he had introduced Szechuan food to the Upper West Side, then the East Side, taking it out of Chinatown and making it more physically accessible to the uptown audience.

At Auntie Yuan, Keh combined contemporary drama with new Chinese cuisine. Each table was illuminated by a pin spot focused on a single orchid in the middle, with just enough light spilling over the vase to highlight two small bowls with salads meant to be nibbled while the diners were getting settled, contemplating the menu, and sipping an aperitif. It was more elegant by far, but along the same lines as the pickles and coleslaw on the table at a Jewish deli. Sure enough, Eddie Schoenfeld, New York City's foremost Jewish authority on Chinese food, was the manager and host. This salad recipe is from him.

Auntie Yuan was a short-lived phenomenon. In 1984, the first mention of it in the Zagat survey called it "The most important Chinese arrival of the last five years. Taiwanese women chefs produce an original menu in lovely surroundings; anyone who cares about Chinese food should try this place." Only three years later, however, the 1987 Zagat survey said, "We hear reports of 'complacency,' service lapses and 'pushiness'; the place is beginning to look a bit seedy, too." Auntie Yuan closed in 1988.

Serves 4 to 8

Do not toss this salad until the moment before you serve it. The cabbage wilts quickly, and without its refreshing, light crispness, the salad loses its point. With or without the dried shrimp, the salad is full of flavor, but the shrimp do add an exotic note. This would be a great accompaniment to broiled or grilled fish, or with a bowl of any Asian noodle soup.

1 head Napa cabbage
½ cup coarsely chopped and loosely packed coriander leaves
1 tablespoon finely chopped garlic
1½ teaspoons salt
1 teaspoon sugar

½ teaspoon MSG (optional)
2 tablespoons dried shrimp (optional)
6 to 8 scallions, finely sliced
Juice of 1½ lemons, or a little more to taste
2 tablespoons toasted sesame oil

Cut off the green part of the cabbage that is above the white (basically, cut off the top quarter of the cabbage), reserving it for another use. Cut the cabbage in half lengthwise. Cut out and discard the triangular core of the cabbage at the base of each half.

Lay the cabbage halves flat on a cutting board and cut them lengthwise into ½-inch-wide strips. Put the strips in a large salad bowl.

Add the cilantro and toss to mix.

Sprinkle the garlic, salt, sugar, and the MSG, if using, over the cabbage.

If using the dried shrimp, grind them in a mini food processor or blender, then, through a sieve; sprinkle the powder over the salad.

Add the scallions and toss again to combine.

Sprinkle with the lemon juice and drizzle the sesame oil over the salad. Toss again. Taste for seasoning, and adjust the salt and lemon juice to taste.

Serve immediately.

CHAPTER 11

GRAND HOTEL DINING

CENTERS OF SOCIAL LIFE

BECAUSE NEW AMSTERDAM WAS A TRADING POST WITH BUSINESSMEN COMING and going constantly, New York City has always had eating and sleeping accommodations for visitors and locals alike—taverns, inns, and boarding houses. However, the first European-style luxury hotel didn't open until 1836. It was built by real estate mogul John Jacob Astor and he called it Astor House. Built in the Greek Revival style at 223 Broadway at Vesey Street by architect Isaiah Rogers, it featured a great innovation: every one of its three hundred rooms had hot running water.

OPPOSITE:
The Starlight Roof when it opened in 1931 at the second Waldorf-Astoria on Park Avenue

By the 1830s, New York City was a booming business town and it became necessary, not just pleasurable, to dine out. As the city's more affluent population moved north, and the business center remained at the southern tip of the island, it became too time-consuming and difficult to travel home for lunch, still the big meal of the day. Although it is true that at the beginning of the nineteenth century most meals were cooked at home, luxurious dining, although not always the best, was found in the large hotels.

For some time, the hotels continued the custom of the earlier taverns and inns, giving everyone set meals, all paid for by the guests whether eaten or not, and served at long communal tables at fixed hours. The entire meal was placed on the table at once, and the guests helped themselves. It wasn't until Delmonico's opened its first full-scale restaurant in 1830 that some degree of order and pace was imposed by offering a la carte and table d'hôte meals in courses. Some of the larger hotels discarded the fixed courses in favor of menus from which each guest ordered separately. This became a general feature at major hotels by the 1850s. French cuisine was particularly favored in these establishments, although a number of hotels were openly American in their offerings.

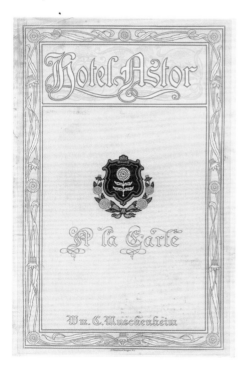

Some city restaurants equaled or excelled the great hotels as centers of good cooking. Two in New York City created a certain awe among all but the most sophisticated diners. The ostentatious Taylor's flourished during the 1850s. Less showy, but more concerned with good cooking, was Delmonico's, founded in 1827, a restaurant that for almost a century was to be the great example of culinary excellence. A growing number of city restaurants sprang up to serve midday meals to businessmen, particularly the numerous oyster saloons that existed in all the principal towns and cities of the East Coast. After New York State's abolition of slavery in 1827, many of these were owned by African Americans.

After the Civil War came the Gilded Age. New money was more plentiful than old money and the nouveau riche looked to European manners and material culture for guidance on how to spend their fortunes, how to behave in public, how to build and decorate their homes, how to dress, and how to eat and drink. By now, the Astor House was in decline, but the Fifth Avenue Hotel was thriving, and after a few years in which everyone seemed to retreat to their homes to eat—public transportation had improved and it became easier to go home from work—some new hotels attracted public attention and new business. The Hoffman House opened in 1864, but it took a decade, say Arianne and Michael Batterberry in *On the Town in New York*, "for it to become one of the most celebrated hotels in the city."

The Fifth Avenue
Hotel, 1836

Another famous hotel of the era was the Brunswick on Fifth Avenue and Twenty-sixth Street. It was famous for its French cuisine, which is said to have vied with Delmonico's in quality, but it was also well known as the spawning ground of great hoteliers and restaurateurs. Some accounts say Oscar Tschirky of Waldorf fame (see page 204) started as a busboy there.

As a teenager, the legendary Louis Sherry worked at the Brunswick. Sherry, one of the few U.S.-born restaurateurs of the grand dining era, grew up in St. Albans, Vermont. A social climber by nature, he befriended his rich customers who set him up in business in 1881. His confectionery store near the Metropolitan Opera house soon expanded into a catering business. The success of that, in turn, allowed Sherry to open a restaurant and apartment hotel in 1890 at Fifth Avenue and Thirty-seventh Street. Sherry specialized in staging over-the-top dinners and events, which gave his establishments plenty of press and notoriety. He fancied himself the chief competitor to Delmonico's, which still was the gold standard at the end of the nineteenth century, and when Delmonico's moved uptown, so did Sherry. He opened, in 1898, a Stanford White–designed restaurant and hotel diagonally across the street from Delmoncio's on Fifth Avenue and Forty-fifth Street. It was in this restaurant that Sherry produced one of the most outrageous dining events in New York City history: a dinner for the New York Riding Club at which all the guests ate while on horseback. Sherry's closed in May 1919.

The Holland House, now familiar as the brand name for supermarket-sold cocktail mixers, was another grand hotel of the era, opened in 1891 on Fifth Avenue and Thirtieth Street. It served meals on the European plan—meaning they were not included in the price of the room, and the guest had a choice of dining in or out of the hotel. Although introduced by Delmonico's in 1830, was still unusual. Its hallmark of luxury, however, was its tabletop accoutrements—Royal Worcester china and Gorham silver—and the Herzog Teleseme, a device that allowed guests to summon services from their rooms.

It is often said that New York City is never finished. Buildings are continually torn down to make space for new ones. A corollary to this is that New Yorkers love newness. We are fickle, particularly when it comes to restaurants. This could not be more true than it was at the end of the nineteenth century, when old hotels were being demolished and new citadels of gastronomy and comfortable living were being built. The Waldorf Hotel opened in 1893 and was followed by the Astoria in 1897. In 1899, John Jacob Astor IV opened the St. Regis Hotel, named for Lake St. Regis near the Astors' Adirondack Mountains lodge. By 1900, the Plaza, the Netherlands (later the Sherry-Netherlands), and the Savoy had been built. In 1902, the Ritz-Carlton opened on Forty-sixth Street and Madison Avenue. Caesar Ritz was the grand hotelier of Europe. Auguste Escoffier was Ritz's chef, and it was for Ritz's expanding hotel empire that Escoffier developed the brigade system, in which chefs are trained in their master's style and, when they can duplicate his food, they are sent out to duplicate it at other locations. Escoffier sent Louis Diat to head his brigade at the first Ritz hotel in the United States. For the next fifty years, Diat was a prime mover in New York City gastronomy, creating now-classic recipes (such as Vichyssoise), writing cookbooks, and eventually becoming one of the first columnists of *Gourmet* magazine.

It was during this era of the grand hotels that rooftop dining became popular. At the German beer gardens of the earlier part of the century, some of which were still going strong, New Yorkers had developed a liking for eating and drinking outdoors. So even with limited space, hotels fitted out their roofs for fine dining and entertainment. The Knickerbocker Hotel on the corner of Forty-second Street and Broadway (now a Gap) had one, as did the Hoffman House and the Waldorf-Astoria. The most famous rooftop establishment of all, however, was the one on top of the original Madison Square Garden (in Madison Square). It was here that the great architect Stanford White was murdered in a fit of jealousy by Harry K. Thaw, who had married White's former mistress, the Floradora and Gibson girl Evelyn Nesbit.

WALDORF-ASTORIA

The Waldorf-Astoria Hotel has odd roots in a family rivalry. It was originally two hotels. The first was the Waldorf, which was opened on the corner of Fifth Avenue and Thirty-third Street on March 14, 1893, by William Waldorf Astor. (Waldorf is the town in Germany from which the original Astor, John Jacob, emigrated in the late eighteenth century.) He built it because, first, he wanted to leave the country for Europe, and putting a hotel where his mansion was seemed like a convenient and profitable idea. Second, he wanted to irritate his aunt, whom New York City viewed as the one and only Mrs. Astor, although William Waldorf was by then the male head of the family, and married. His aunt, was, however, the Mrs. Astor who determined who was who in New York City society, who was in and who was not. Her famous "400" consisted of the names that she and her "Svengali," Ward McAllister, deemed grand enough. The exact number was determined by how many could fit into the ballroom in her mansion, which was next door to her nephew's, on the corner of Fifth Avenue and Thirty-fourth Street.

The Waldorf Hotel, at eleven stories, towered over Mrs. Astor's mansion, but it was not merely bigger, it was grander. The commercial commotion right next door to her was intolerable to Mrs. Astor. She moved farther up Fifth Avenue, and her son, John Jacob IV, built the Astoria Hotel on the site of the family manse. It opened in 1897 and, at sixteen stories, it was even taller and more magnificent than the Waldorf. Money and power being everything in New York City, superceding even family rivalries, John Jacob's and William Waldorf's intentions were to have the two hotels run as one. But just in case that didn't work out, John Jacob built his hotel in such a way that every passage between the two could be blocked so that the hotels could be run separately as well. The narrow, three-hundred-foot gallery that connected the hotels came to be known as Peacock Alley because it was the place for New Yorkers to show off their sartorial finery.

Arianne and Michael Batterberry, in *On the Town in New York*, wrote that Peacock Alley "teemed with wide-eyed life from breakfast time until the middle of the night, when both the fascinating foreigner in her Worth gown and the small-town housewife ruched to a fare-thee-well by the local seamstress collected their gloves and fans, their reticules and men, and promenaded off to bed. Preachers in every state of the Union were sure to include the Waldorf-Astoria and its spiritually pestilential Peacock Alley in their tirades against New York and its unholy fleshpots, its palaces of material lust." There is still a Peacock Alley in the Waldorf.

The original Waldorf-Astoria was demolished in 1929 to make way for the Empire State Building. The current hotel, a masterpiece of Art Deco architecture on Park Avenue and Forty-ninth Street, was designed by the firm of Schultze & Weaver and opened on October 31, 1931. It

COPYRIGHT BY
EO. P. HALL & SON. N.Y.

The original
Waldorf-Astoria
was where the
Empire State
Building is now.

was the city's first skyscraper hotel, and it carries on many of the culinary traditions established by its original operator, the legendary George C. Boldt, and its first maître d'hotel, Oscar Tschirky, known as "Oscar of the Waldorf."

OSCAR OF THE WALDORF

Oscar Michael Tschirky was born in Lode, Canton de Neuchâtel, Switzerland, in 1866. He arrived in New York City in May 1883, the day before the opening of the Brooklyn Bridge. According to Ward Moorehouse III in his 1991 book, *The Waldorf-Astoria*, Tschirky started as a busboy, then served an apprenticeship as a waiter at the revered Hoffman House on Broadway and Twenty-sixth Street. He was not a chef. It is said he'd never even boiled an egg. But he knew about food and service, and, at a time when the rich really wanted to learn about the good life, he guided New Yorkers to a new understanding of the graciousness of wining and dining in the European manner.

His fame grew in New York City's restaurant and hotel circles—his knowledge of cuisine, his ability to manage the difficult personalities in the kitchen, in housekeeping, and so on—and in 1892 he was approached by George C. Boldt, who had been hired to operate William Waldorf Astor's Waldorf Hotel, slated to open the next year.

It was, claimed Tschirky, the difficulty in pronouncing his name that made him known as "Oscar of the Waldorf." He presided over the operation of the hotel from its opening on Fifth Avenue in 1893 until 1943, by which time the hotel had moved to Park Avenue and Forty-ninth Street. During those fifty years, he was not merely the maître d'hotel of the Waldorf-Astoria, but a character about town. He is credited with creating Thousand Island Dressing (maybe not true; see page 206), Waldorf Salad (page 207), and Veal Oscar, in which veal is topped with crabmeat and a Mornay sauce. Even though he was not a cook himself, he wrote a cookbook, published in 1896, *Oscar of the Waldorf's Cookbook*. His collection of more than two thousand menus from the Waldorf is housed in the library of Cornell University's School of Hotel Administration.

Oscar Tschirky was called many complimentary things in his lifetime. Although he was short, portly, and not particularly attractive, the newspapers loved writing about him. "A friend to gourmets and epicures, and a confidant of swelldom" sums him up pretty well.

CARTE DU JOUR

Monday, November 8, 1909

Oysters and Clams

Blue Point 25   Cocktail 30   Cape Cod 30   Cocktail 35   Lynnhavens 35
Shinnecock Bay Clams 25   Cocktail 30   Clams à la Bourguignonne 50

Hors d'Oeuvre Varies (per person 40)

Stuffed Olives 30   Queen Olives 15   Mangoes 25   Salted Almonds 20
Carciofini 50   Saucisson de Lyon 40   Astrachan Caviar (p.p.) 90   Canapé of Caviar 60
Sardines marinés 40   Mackerel in oil 40   Brat Herring 50
Filet of Herring, Antipasto, Smoked Salmon or Spanish Angulas 50

Soup

Consommé Carmen 40 25   Crème Sévigné 50 30
Clear Green Turtle 90 50   Chicken Okra 50 30   Vermicelli, Tomato or Julienne 40 25
Petite Marmite 50   Strained Gumbo Chicken Consommé or Clam Broth, cup 25

Fish

(Ready) **Filet de Sole, Américaine 75 45**

English Sole, fried 1 25   Marguery 1 50   Halibut 60 40
Smelts 60 40   Pompano 75   Oyster Crabs 1 00 60   à la Newburg 1 25
Fried Scallops 75 45   Whitebait 60 40   Fried Frog Legs 1 00 60   à la Newburg 1 25

Terrapin à la Maryland or Travers 3 50

Entrees (Ready)

Philadelphia Squab en casserole, Montpensier 1 25
Braized Beef à la mode, potato pancake 1 00 60
Lamb Steak sauté, Robinson 1 25
Virginia Ham, timbale of spinach 90 50
Rail Birds sautés, Vénitienne (3) 85
Game Pâté à la gelée (cold) (per person) 75   Imported Veal au sautoir 1 50

Poultry and Game

Mallard Duck 2 25   Ruddy Duck 2 00   Bluewing Teal Duck 1 50   Redhead Duck 3 50
Canvas-back Duck 4 75   Golden Plover 1 00   *Partridge 4 50   Grouse 4 50
Woodcock 2 25   English Snipe 1 00   Virginia Soras (2) 75
Crow-Blackbirds (3) 85   Quail 1 00   Manx Poularde 7 00   *Hamburg Squab Chicken 1 50
*Guineahen 2 00   *Spring Turkey 3 50 2 00   Spring Chicken broiled 1 75 90   *roasted 1 75
*Spring Duckling 2 50   *Squab Chicken 1 25   *Royal Squab 1 00

GAME, ETC. PRECEDED BY (★) ARE ROASTED ON THE SPIT

Vegetables (Fresh)   String Beans 50 30   Fried Oyster Plant 40 25
Artichoke 50   Spinach 50 30   Mushrooms 1 25   Hothouse Asparagus 1 75
Egg Plant 40   Lima Beans 50 30   Cauliflower 50   New Peas 60
Canned—Flageolet Beans, French Peas, French String Beans 50 30   French Giant Asparagus 1 25
German Riesenspargel 1 25   Cardons à la moëlle 60   Truffles en serviette 1 75
Artichoke Bottoms 50   Cèpes Bordelaise 60   Brussels Sprouts 50 30   Hop Tips 60
Imported Italian Tomato sauté 40

POTATOES—Fried, Hashed browned, à la crème or sautées 20   au gratin 30
Sweet Potatoes— Fried or sautées 25   Soufflées or broiled 35

Salads   Chicory 50 30   French Endive 60 40
Kuroki, Grape Fruit or Orange 75 45   Escarole, Lettuce, Romaine or Tomato 50 30
Chiffonnade or à l'Astor 50   Cucumber 50 30   Field, Beet and Celery 50 30
Tomatoes stuffed with cucumbers 65   Lobster or Chicken 1 00 60

Dessert

(Hot) Apple Charlotte, brandy sauce 25   (Cold) Egyptian Cream 25
Champagne Jelly 20   Chestnut Cake 20   Apricot Squares 20   Chocolate Alma 20
Moka Cake 20   Plum Cake 20   Peach Pie 20   Pumpkin Pie 20
Grape, Apple or Pont Neuf Tartlets 20
Hickoryisques 25   Coffee, Vanilla or Chocolate Eclairs (2) 20   Soufflé à la vanille 75
Omelette à la Célestine 60   Crêpes Suzette 60

Ice Cream

Glace Monumentale, Henry Hudson 1 00   Horse Show Souvenirs 1 25, 1 00 and 50
Plain 25   Nesselrode Pudding or Parfaits 30   Biscuit Tortoni or Tutti Frutti 35
Asparagus, Biscuit or Meringue glacée 35   Biscuit Astor or Coupe Venus 40
Coupe St. Jacques 40   Parfait Tosca 50   Soufflé Alaska 50   Plombière Astor or Peach Melba 60
Pudding Sans Gênes 30   Parfait Tutti Frutti 30

Sorbets   Raspberry 25
Lemon, Pineapple or Orange 25   *Roman, Cardinal, Lalla Rookh or Yvette 30

Fruits   Coupe rafraichie 50   Pears (1) 20
Imported Hothouse Melon (per person) 75
Concord Grapes 40   Hothouse Grapes 1 50   Malaga Grapes 50
Oranges (1) 15   Assorted Fruit 50   Astor Cup 75

Cheese   Assorted, (per person) 20   Astor 30   Bar-le-Duc 40

Coffee   Demi-tasse 15   Diable 40   Turkish Coffee 20
Special 25   à l'Astor 30

HALF PORTIONS SERVED TO ONE PERSON ONLY

An extra charge of 10 cents will be made for each
portion or half portion served in rooms

Note the many varieties of game birds on this Astor Hotel menu.

THOUSAND ISLAND DRESSING

This is a deservedly famous recipe with a much-published history that is quite unlikely. Its story follows an all too typical urban legend form: The cook runs out of ingredients and concocts something that is so delicious it lives forever in the appetites of mankind. For instance, Caesar salad. For instance, Cobb salad. For instance, Thousand Island Dressing.

George C. Boldt was the multimillionaire proprietor of the Waldorf-Astoria from its opening as the Waldorf Hotel in 1893 until his death in 1916. He often spent his vacation time in the Thousand Islands, in the St. Lawrence River, between upstate New York and Ontario, Canada. His wife, Louise, loved the area.

The Boldts often entertained their rich friends when they went north, and they frequently took with them Oscar Tschirky, the Waldorf's maître d'hotel, the famous "Oscar of the Waldorf," to preside over their parties. On one such trip, the family and friends were aboard the Boldts' yacht *Louise*, and Oscar discovered that the noon meal's salad fixings had been left sitting on the dock. As quickly as you can say "wedge of iceberg," Oscar had concocted Thousand Island Dressing. The legend ends with Boldt serving the dressing at all his hotels and the dressing becoming a standard of the American kitchen.

A second legend is that a chef at the Drake Hotel in Chicago created it. That story has the wife of the chef commenting that the lumpy dressing reminded her of the Thousand Islands, which they had just visited.

There is, however, a third and most likely version of the Thousand Island Dressing story. This one has it invented in the early 1900s by Sophia LaLonde, the wife of George LaLonde, a Thousand Island fishing guide. According to St. Lawrence legend, George served his wife's dressing to clients as a sauce for their catch, which he would cook for them. One of those clients, the actress May Irwin, liked it so much that she passed the simple recipe on to George Boldt, who told Oscar Tschirky to put it on the menu. Boldt is said to have been the first to say "the customer is always right."

Whichever story is true, the dressing held enough appeal that a simplified version was included in Ida Baily Allen's 1917 *Mrs. Allen's Cook Book*, an indication of its wide acceptance. It is still a popular dressing in the Thousand Islands, too. St. Lawrence yacht fishing guides serve it on iceberg lettuce and on tomatoes, and the Thousand Islands Inn in Clayton, New York, manufactures a bottled version.

Makes about 1½ cups

In as much as they are both essentially mayonnaise blended with ketchup or Heinz tomato-based chili sauce, the difference between Thousand Island Dressing and Russian Dressing is minimal. Still, there's enough of a difference that both recipes are in this book. See page 147 for Russian Dressing.

1 cup mayonnaise
½ cup chili sauce or ketchup
2 tablespoons finely minced pimento-stuffed olives
1 tablespoon finely minced green pepper

1 tablespoon minced chives
1 chopped hard-cooked egg
2 teaspoons finely chopped fresh parsley

In a small bowl, blend all the ingredients together.

TRUFFLED WALDORF SALAD

Peel two raw apples and cut them into small pieces, say about half an inch square, also cut some celery the same way, and mix it with the apple. Be careful not to let any seeds of the apples to be mixed with it. The salad must be dressed with a good mayonnaise.
—Oscar of the Waldorf's Cookbook, *1896*

You may be struck by the absence of nuts in the original recipe for Waldorf Salad. They were a later addition that proved popular. So they remained. Oscar, it is said, didn't like the variation on his recipe and he became enraged when he saw a Waldorf Salad coming out of the kitchen with nuts on it. He would say, "Well, nuts!"

Serves 8

Today, this is what you get when you order the namesake salad at the Waldorf, embellished by current executive chef John Doherty, now the longest-running chef in the Waldorf's history.

⅓ cup mayonnaise
⅔ cup crème fraîche
Juice of ½ lemon
2 Granny Smith apples, cored and cut into
    thick julienne
2 Red Delicious apples, cored and cut into
    thick julienne
6 ounces celeriac, peeled and cut into fine
    julienne
1 teaspoon shaved fresh or frozen black
    winter truffles
1 head thinly shaved fennel (kept in ice water)
¾ cup toasted walnuts, roughly chopped

In a large bowl, stir together the mayonnaise, crème fraîche, and lemon juice.

Add the apples, celeriac, and truffle. Toss gently until well coated.

Spread the thinly sliced, iced fennel on paper towels and pat dry thoroughly.

To compose individual salads, spread slices of fennel in a semicircle at the center of each plate. Neatly arrange the apple salad in the center of the fennel. Garnish with the walnuts.

CRAB REMICK

The Plaza Hotel, like all the great New York City hotels, has hosted an incalculable number of important dinners and receptions. In 1920, Chef Albert Leopold Lattard created this dish for a dinner in honor of William H. Remick, then president of the New York Stock Exchange.

The combination of mayonnaise and Heinz ketchup or Heinz chili sauce first became popular around the turn of the century, and the vogue continued through the 1920s. According to the Heinz company, although its ketchup was introduced around 1880 (the company's first product was horseradish), it didn't become popular until 1914. So those early dishes using ketchup were, in their day, cutting edge.

The chili sauce, which is essentially a more highly seasoned and insignificantly coarser version of the ketchup, came a little later. In 1940, on the fiftieth anniversary of the opening of the Plaza, *New York Times* food reporter June Owen profiled the luxury hotel and included this recipe for the Plaza Hotel classic.

Serves 6

Although the original dish appears to have had crumbled bacon sprinkled on top, as follows, you may want to integrate the bacon into the crab by tossing it through before dividing the crab among the ramekins and putting them in the oven. Another minor variation in keeping with the tastes of the 1920s, and in the spirit of the dish, is to add ½ teaspoon of celery salt to the mayonnaise.

1 pound (about 2 cups) fresh crabmeat, in large flakes, picked over thoroughly to remove any bits of shell or cartilage
1 teaspoon dry mustard
¾ teaspoon sweet paprika

½ teaspoon Tabasco sauce
½ cup Heinz chili sauce
2 teaspoons tarragon vinegar
1¾ cups mayonnaise
6 slices bacon, fried until crisp, crumbled

Preheat the oven to 350 degrees.

Pile the crabmeat into 6 buttered individual scallop shells (the kind meant for serving coquilles St. Jacques) or porcelain ramekins. Heat in the oven for about 10 minutes.

Meanwhile, thoroughly blend together the mustard, paprika, Tabasco sauce, chili sauce, vinegar, and mayonnaise.

Remove the crabmeat from the oven. Turn on the broiler. Working quickly so the crabmeat doesn't cool much, sprinkle it with bacon, then top with the sauce, divided equally among the ramekins.

Place under the broiler, 5 to 6 inches from the heat, until bubbly and tipped with brown, 2 to 3 minutes.

Serve immediately.

CREAM VICHYSSOISE GLACÉ

Louis Diat, the great French chef of the Hotel Ritz Carlton from 1910—after its opening on Madison Avenue and Forty-sixth Street in 1902—and until his retirement in 1951, would be proud to know that today he is mainly associated with a soup.

As a boy, the first dish Diat ever cooked was soup. His first job, as a teenager, was as chef potager (soup chef) at the Paris Hotel Ritz, working under Auguste Escoffier. In 1906, at the age of twenty-one, he held the same position at the London Ritz, also under Escoffier, as all the Ritz hotels were. Indeed, in *Cooking à la Ritz*, Diat's 1941 cookbook, he singles out Vichyssoise as his greatest culinary invention and explains how he happened to devise it:

I recall clearly the boyish pride I felt when my first dish was set on the table. It was Potato Paysanne, the recipe for which I have included in this book. Another dish which has since become well-known throughout this country had its origins also in my mother's kitchen. She used to make a hot soup of leeks and potatoes which was liked very much by her children. But in the summer when the soup seemed to be too hot, we asked her for milk with which to cool it. Many years later, it was this memory, which gave me the inspiration to make the soup which I have named Crème Vichyssoise.... A cup of cream, an extra straining, and a sprinkle of chives, et voilà, I had my new soup. I named my version of Maman's soup after Vichy, the famous spa located not 20 miles from our Bourbonnaise home, as a tribute to the fine cooking of the region.

Diat went on to write several other cookbooks, *French Country Cooking for Americans*, *Menus Classiques*, *Sauces: French and Famous*, and, for *Gourmet* magazine, *Gourmet's Basic French Cookbook: Techniques of French Cuisine*. He died in 1957.

Serves 8

4 (large) leeks, white part
1 medium onion
¼ cup unsalted butter (½ stick)
5 medium potatoes (about 2 pounds)
1 quart water or chicken broth

1 tablespoon salt
2 cups milk
2 cups medium cream (or half heavy cream
    and half whole or reduced fat milk)
1 cup heavy cream

Finely slice the white part of the leeks and the onion, and brown very lightly in the sweet butter, then add the potatoes, also sliced finely. Add the water or broth and salt. Boil from 35 to 40 minutes. Crush and rub through a fine strainer. Return to fire and add 2 cups of milk and 2 cups of medium cream. Season to taste and bring to a boil. Cool and then rub through a very fine strainer. When soup is cold, add the heavy cream. Chill thoroughly before serving. Finely chopped chives may be added when serving.

Variation: Diat notes that for *Cream Glacée à la Ritz* one should add 1 cup of tomato juice to each 3 cups of Cream Vichyssoise.

CHAPTER 12
THE LOBSTER PALACES

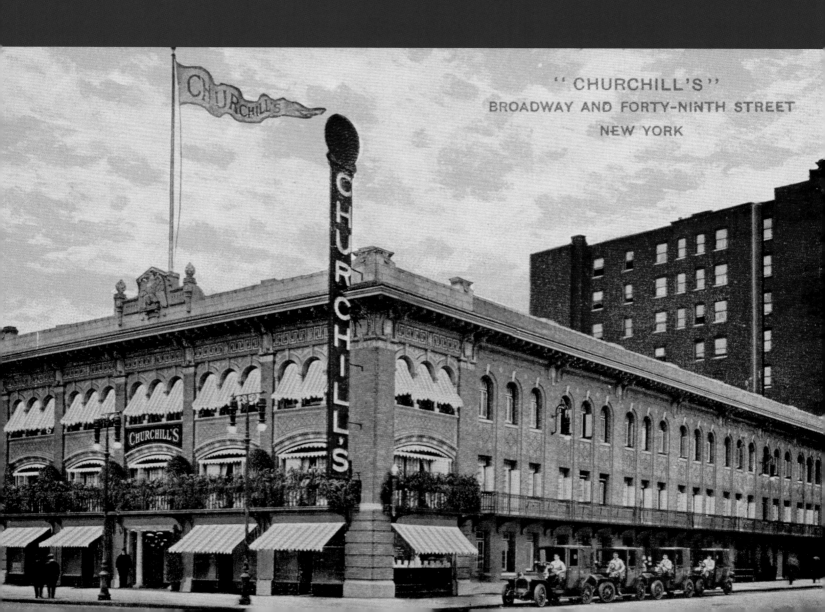

"CHURCHILL'S"
BROADWAY AND FORTY-NINTH STREET
NEW YORK

DIAMOND JIM AND HIS HAUNTS

THE SO-CALLED GAY OR NAUGHTY 1890S ACTUALLY STARTED IN THE 1880S AND lasted nicely into the twentieth century. It was also known as the Gilded Age, with the wealth trickling down to the middle, poorer, and immigrant classes. With ever more tax-free wealth being generated by the post Civil War/Industrial Revolution economy, there were new legions of self-made men and their women.

Prime among them—the most famous example of the conspicuously consuming, nouveau riche gentleman—was Diamond Jim Brady, a railroad equipment salesman. His platonic friend and regular dining companion, Lillian Russell, was an actress and a great, full-figured beauty. And the figure got famously fuller as time went on. You could say that Diamond Jim and Russell were among the first New York celebrities to be famous for being famous—and having gargantuan appetites. It is said Charles Rector claimed that Diamond Jim was his best twenty-five customers.

The prime institutions of vulgar consumption and gaudy wealth were the so-called Lobster Palaces. These were restaurants—but more than restaurants—often of staggering size, always of ornate gilt and crystal decoration, with menus that included every luxury of the day. The menus were not as extensive or as ambitious as those of the grand hotels or Delmonico's or Sherry's, but there was no dearth of caviar, truffles, and pâté de foie gras. Champagne flowed freely. It remained New York's wine of choice through the Roaring Twenties and Prohibition (then made a comeback in the 1980s.)

Lobsters were the ultimate luxury food. Until the late nineteenth century, Maine lobsters had been as plentiful as cockroaches. Then, in the mid-1870s, the catch diminished to such an extent that the crustacean became expensive, with demand being at a pretty high level—after all, they had always been cheap and plentiful. Consumption continued to rise as the century wore on, and the country's wealth and pretensions skyrocketed. In 1919, Julian Street, in his book *Welcome To Our City*, a New York City Baedeker, reported that "the available supply [of lobsters] has shrunk more than fifty percent within the past three years." Certainly, by the Gay nineties, the lobster had come to represent wealth and the good times. A popular graphic image of the day was a standing, prancing, or dancing lobster with a top hat, claw in arm with a gorgeous babe. It was meant to depict the sugar daddy, the big spender and his mistress. In a famous burlesque poster of the day, a lobster dances with a showgirl on top of a table while three seated male admirers salute them with their champagne glasses.

Along those lines, another less polite name for a Lobster Palace was a Bird and Bottle Joint, meaning a sport could take a very appreciative girl there for the cost of a bottle (champagne, naturally).

The Lobster Palaces were clustered around what was, until 1904, called Longacre Square. Then the *New York Times* built its high-rise headquarters and the area became Times Square. The intersection of Forty-second Street, Broadway, and Seventh Avenue was already a hub for the city's swells. The Knickerbocker Hotel, on the southeast corner of Broadway and Forty-second Street (still standing, but with a GAP on the street level and offices above) had a cafe that was a watering hole for Lobster Palace society. The mural, *Old King Cole*, by Maxfield Parrish, that now hangs in the St. Regis Hotel bar, was once the centerpiece of the Knickerbocker Hotel's bar, which was affectionately called the Forty-second Street Country Club.

Two blocks away, on the west side of Times Square, at Forty-fourth Street, was the Astor Hotel, which boasted the first revolving doors in New York City, and a dining room menu that vied with Delmonico's in breadth and high-style French cuisine (see page 47). Before the end of the century, the theaters had started clustering at the eastern edge of what was then called the

Tenderloin, around Longacre Square, and the Lobster Palaces catered to theatergoers before and after the performances. This was the beginning of Broadway as we think of it today.

High life and low life mingled in these gilded halls, society couples and men-about-town with their women, the rich and respectable gawking at the flamboyantly dressed and possibly, deliciously disreputable. And vice versa. Grand entrances were part of the show. For some people, reservations were hard or impossible to get, while others simply strolled in.

Here's something else that hasn't changed in New York City. Julian Street reported in 1919 that one way a new Lobster Palace could generate a buzz was by having the maître d' say, even when the books were empty, that he didn't have a table for the night. "The minute that person [who couldn't get a table] thought he might not be able to get in, he was obsessed with a mad desire to do so. He went up to see about it, and when, at last, he was promised a table, a great elation filled his bosom. Such tactics started people coming, and, once started, the movement soon became an avalanche."

Rector's, which opened in the mid-1890s on Broadway between Forty-third and Forty-fourth Streets, was the most famous of the Lobster Palaces, attracting everyone who was anyone in New York City, along with all the important visitors. "Rector's had the unique prestige that Mrs. Astor's palace had for the society of Fifth Avenue. It was the supreme shrine of the cult of pleasure, and the privilege of occupying a table there for after-theater supper certified that you had arrived, that you were worthy of sharing the highest rite celebrated by Broadway's elite," said Street.

And it was at Rector's, after all, that architect Stanford White met the Floradora Girl, Evelyn Nesbit—the most famous of the Gibson Girls—over whose favors he was shot by Nesbit's husband, Harry Thaw, in 1906.

In its day, however, Churchill's was the largest and possibly grandest of the Lobster Palaces, as well the most democratic. Murray's Roman Gardens was the most fantastically and vulgarly decorated. Bustanoby's Café des Beaux Arts was the most daring socially, and was renowned for its French cuisine. Café Martin, which was not near Forty-second Street but in the old Madison Square Delmonico's building, and Shanley's were also considered Lobster Palaces.

SOLE MARGUERY AND RECTOR'S

Sole Marguery is no longer on New York City menus. Its heyday was the Gay nineties way up through World War II and into the 1950s, by which time it was nothing like the grand dish of haute cuisine that sent Diamond Jim Brady into legendary paroxysms of grandness, and led Charles Rector to take drastic measures to please him.

Diamond Jim Brady got whatever he wanted, or at least whatever his vast fortune could buy. Obsessive eater that he was, sometime in the first decade of the twentieth century, Brady decided he wanted to eat Sole Marguery whenever he wanted, and he didn't want to travel to the Café Marguery in Paris to eat it.

There are many versions of this legend, varying only in the details. But according to an account in *Duet in Diamonds: The Flamboyant Saga of Lillian Russell and Diamond Jim Brady in America's Gilded Age*, by John Burke, it was at a dinner at Rector's attended by his dear friend Lillian Russell, the Broadway producer Sam Schubert, the composer Victor Herbert, and "other theatrical luminaries" that Diamond Jim challenged Rector. Why, he wanted to know, didn't Rector's serve Sole Marguery, which was all the rage in fin de siècle Paris?

"Charles Rector explained that the secret of its preparation was known only to the fish chef of the Café Marguery . . . and it was as closely guarded as the French general staff's plans for a counteroffensive across the Rhine if and when the Germans became obstreperous."

Rector couldn't resist Brady's dare, though. He would get the recipe. But who could he trust to go undercover in a Paris restaurant kitchen? The story goes that Rector pulled his son out of Cornell Law School, where the young George Rector was in his third year. (George never became a lawyer). He got a job as a dishwasher at the Café Marguery in Paris, then snooped and learned how to make Sole Marguery. The young Rector learned so well that it is said he eventually earned The Cordon Bleu, or passed muster before a jury of French chefs, or successfully tested the recipe on a panel of Broadway producers and other high-living people, including Marshall Field of the Chicago department store fortune and the St. Louis brewer Adolphus Busch. The story varies here in regard to his accomplishments.

There is probably a scintilla of truth to this legend but not much more. Diamond Jim's question to Rector was more likely a jab at his restaurant's menu, which was much more American and plebeian than Delmonico's (where you could certainly get Sole Marguery). And yes, George Rector did leave Cornell. He reportedly had no aptitude for law, whereas he had always enjoyed working at the family restaurant on summer vacations. Most likely, George didn't get a dishwashing job at Café Marguery. His father, Charles, would have certainly set him up in an apprenticeship of sorts, to educate him before taking him into the family business. Perhaps Charles wanted to upgrade his menu and make it more French, so he could compete with Delmonico's on cuisine, not just fancy customers. Charles was likely embarrassed about his son not doing well in law school, yet simultaneously pleased to have him in the business. George may not have had legal aptitude, but he turned out to be a legendary restaurateur.

There is an oft-repeated recipe for Sole Marguery that was first outlined in Rector's *Naughty Nineties Cookbook,* by Alexander Kirkland, but if you follow it you will end up with a disastrously overcooked fish in an uninteresting sauce. It is, in any case, only vaguely like the recipe for Sole Marguery as published in 1894 in Charles Ranhofer's *The Epicurean,* the way it must have been served at Delmonico's at the same time Charles Rector was sending his son to Paris to learn it. Ranhofer's complex sauce, way beyond the abilities of any home cook, sounds like something the discerning Diamond Jim would have swooned over.

CHARLES RANHOFER'S SOLES À LA MARGUERY

Raise the fillets from four medium-sized soles weighing about a pound each; remove the skin, pare them neatly and fold in two. Put them on a buttered baking sheet, season with salt, pepper, and chopped onions and moisten to their height with white wine and mushroom broth or else court bouillon. Let the liquid come to a boil, then set the pan in a moderate oven to leave until fish is well cooked, basting frequently with the stock. Drain off the fish and strain the stock, then reduce it with some velouté and thicken with raw egg yolks, cream, and fresh butter. Dress the sole fillets in a circle on a dish and garnish the inside border half with circular-shaped croutons three-sixteenth of an inch thick and an inch and a quarter in diameter; heat the dish slightly, dip the flat side of the crouton in beaten eggs, stick it to the plate, besprinkle with melted butter and color in a hot oven. Around the fillets of sole arrange some quenelles molded in a coffeespoon, some mussels or oysters from which the hard parts have been removed, and channeled and turned mushroom heads, then cover the whole with the sauce.

M. H. COX - VICE PRESIDENT, MORTIMER M. KELLY - MANAGER

1. MURRAY'S ROMAN GARDENS, NEW YORK CITY.

BUSTANOBY'S

Bustanoby's Café des Beaux Arts was the Lobster Palace perhaps best known for its fine French food and wine cellar. Its owners were legitimately French—four brothers from Pau—and they catered to the top names in New York City, including both society and upstarts. Roosevelts and Vanderbilts hobnobbed with Lillian Russell and Diamond Jim Brady. In 1915 F. Scott Fitzgerald declared it his favorite place to drink.

The family was also famous for its own liqueur, Forbidden Fruit, a grapefruit-based brandy concocted at a time when grapefruit was still considered an exotic fruit (and still called shaddock). According to Bustanoby family lore, "no respectable establishment was without this shaddock [grapefruit] brandy, so ironically, even if you were dining at the exquisite New York dining comparables like Maxim's or Delmonico's, or across the ocean in London or Paris, you were still sampling Bustanoby splendor."

Another claim to Bustanoby fame is that it was the first restaurant in New York City to offer dancing with dinner. Sigmund Romberg, the renowned operetta composer of *The Desert Song*, *Maytime*, and *The Student Prince*, was, earlier in his career, the conductor of Bustanoby's in-house orchestra. He convinced the Bustanoby brothers that it would be a popular attraction to allow dancing between courses.

The restaurant also pioneered an all-women's bar to match the popular men's cafes (that were really bars). It was a failure. Soirées Artistiques were a hit, however, and Lillian Russell, Anna Held, Maxine Eliot, Douglas Fairbanks, David Warfield, Vernon and Irene Castle, Isadora Duncan, and many other celebrities of the day would gather for them.

A MEAT AND POTATOES TOWN

BECAUSE NEW YORK CITY IS SUCH AN UNABASHEDLY GLAMOROUS PLACE, and possibly the most ethnically diverse city on earth, the rest of the world thinks we revel in stylish, cutting-edge, chef-owned boutique restaurants, palaces of French haute cuisine, and innumerable esoteric ethnic joints. Well, we do. But the dirty secret is that New York City is really a meat and potatoes town.

OPPOSITE: Peter Luger's famous Porterhouse steak

No matter what the city's circumstances—when stocks are up, when hems are down, when carbs are in, when meat is out—the steakhouses fill up. The supermarket meat cases carry more steaks than hamburger meat, and the steaks here are thicker, fatter, and older—all of which are very good traits.

New Yorkers have craved steak since the English sailed into the harbor in 1664. The English were big meat eaters, and renowned as grillers and roasters. Here they found a plentiful supply of beef to meet their appetites. The Dutch had already brought domestic cattle. The English brought more. It was raised in New Jersey, and Brooklyn and Queens (then simply Long Island), and ferried across the Hudson and East Rivers. Cattle drives came from the north, too, although today it is hard to imagine cattle ranges in the Bronx and Westchester. Perhaps second only to the English mutton chops, juicy steaks, and large roasts were the basic fare of eighteenth-century taverns and early-nineteenth-century English chop houses, one early form of New York eating house.

New Yorkers relish all kinds of steak, but mainly thick slices of the short loin, which is behind the rib section. The first two steaks of this primal cut, those closest to the rib, were called Delmonico Steaks at Delmonico's (see page 65). These days all the top loin pieces are variously referred to as New York Steaks outside of New York City, and either Shell Steak, Sirloin Strip, or simply Strip Steak in New York City. (Sirloin is actually a misnomer. In the eighteenth century, however, the true sirloin steak was indeed the common cut.) They can be had either boneless (the usual) or on the bone. With the muscle that is on the other side of its bone, which is the tenderloin or fillet, and with the bone itself, short loin steaks are called either Porterhouse, a term coined in New York City (see page 221), or T-bone, for the shape of the bone.

The classic, contemporary New York City steakhouse meal is modeled on the Steakhouse Row meal of the 1920s. These were the restaurants gathered around the big slaughterhouse on the East Side of Manhattan where the United Nations is today. Palm and Pietro's are the last of them. Long gone are Christ Cellar and Bruno's Pen and Pencil. The original Smith and Wollensky's (formerly Manny Wolf's) is still in the neighborhood, and a relative newcomer, Spark's, serves not only great meat but has one of the city's best wine lists. There were and are famous steakhouses downtown, too, near Gansevoort Street in the Meat Packing District, which is now turning into yet another fashionable neighborhood. The Old Homestead dates itself to 1868. Frank's, now on Fifteenth Street and Tenth Avenue, used to be in the middle of the market, on Fourteenth Street, and served as a steakhouse for workers in the meat houses.

The now-classic steak dinner starts with a salad, usually a unique salad. For instance, Peter Luger, in the Williamsburg section of Brooklyn, one of the city's oldest and most famous steakhouses, serves alternating slices of tomato and sweet onion, served with Peter Luger's house dressing on the side in a sauceboat. The most ordered dish at Palm, which has become a national chain, isn't the steak, it's the Gigi Salad, a chopped salad with green beans, shrimp, onion, and tomato.

After the salad, or perhaps a shrimp or other seafood cocktail, it's simple. You order steak, the house potatoes—either hash browns (see page 225), cottage fries, or something proprietary—and—creamed spinach. For dessert, it's probably New York cheesecake. That's overkill, but that's New York.

THE STORY OF PORTERHOUSE

The Porterhouse steak got its name in New York City. Apparently, until 1814, the short loin was not butchered into steaks. It was used as a roast. Here's an account of the naming of the steak from Thomas De Voe, a New York City butcher who wrote *The Market Assistant*, published in 1867. De Voe's hobby was to record and describe all the foods he found in the markets of Manhattan, Philadelphia, Boston, and Brooklyn. The book is the result of his interest, and provides insights into what people were eating in the mid-nineteenth century. The term "porter-house steaks" originated in about the year 1814, in the following manner:

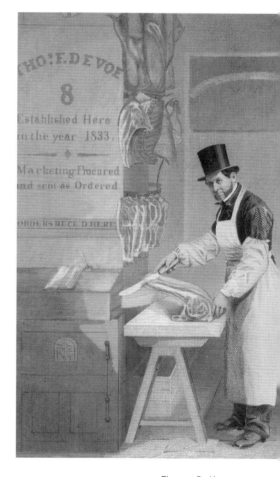

Thomas De Voe, the butcher who wrote *The Market Assistant*.

Martin Morrison was the proprietor of a long-established and well kept "porter-house," located and known at that period at No. 327 Pearl-street (New York), near the "old Walton House." We introduce him in 1803, where we find he opens a "porter-house" at No. 43 Cherry-street, which became a popular resort with many of the New York pilots for his prepared hot meals, at any hour, at their call, they being occasionally detained on shipboard until their vessels were safely moored.

The "porter-houses" in those days were not so devoted to tippling, dram-drinking, and the common nests for the loafing, or the manufacturing of politicians and corrupt officials as at the present day, but rather to accommodate the hungry and thirsty travelers, old and young bachelors, seamen, and others with a cold lunch after the English custom—"a pot of ale" (or porter) and a bite of something. Some "porter-houses" prepared a hot meal of one or two dishes, among which was Morrison's, who must have been quite famous for his excellent broiled beefsteaks, which were universally called for at his place.

On one occasion (at the above period, 1814), Morrison having had an unusual call for steaks, he had cooked his last steak, and, as fortune would have it for all future partakers of beefsteaks, an old-fashioned but a rough pilot, made him a late visit, both hungry and thirsty, having been several hours without food. Not caring for the salt junk aboard the vessel which he had piloted in, he concluded to wait until he got on shore, that he might cast his anchor at Morrison's where he could enjoy his "hot steaks and mug of porter."

In his honest language the pilot gave his usual order. Morrison had nothing but his family dinner for the next day which consisted of a sirloin roasting-piece, of which he offered to cut from if the old pilot would have it. "Yes, my hearty, any thing—so long as it is a beefsteak—for I am as empty as a gull!"

exclaimed the pilot. Morrison cut off a good-sized slice, had it dressed and served, which the pilot ravenously devoured, and turning to the host (who had been expecting a blast from the old tarpaulin, but who, to his astonishment, received an order): "Messmate, another steak just like that—do you hear?" Having finished his steaks and the second mug of porter, the old pilot squared himself towards his host, loudly vociferating. "Look ye here, messmate, after this I want my steaks off the roasting-piece!—do ye hear that?—so mind your weather-eye, old boy!"

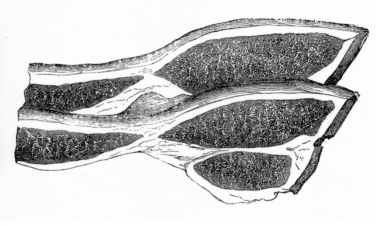

Small Loin, or Porter-House Steaks.

It was not long after this when the old pilot's companions insisted upon having these "small loin steaks" served to them. Morrison soon discovered that these steaks were more suitable in size to dish up for single individuals, and he ever after purchased the sirloin roasting-pieces, from which he cut off these small steaks as they were called for, the large sirloin-steaks becoming less in demand. Morrison's butcher—Thomas Gibbons—in the Fly Market, one morning put out the question, after he (Morrison) had selected several sirloin pieces , "Why he had ceased purchasing the usual quantity of sirloin steaks?" Says Morrison, "I will tell you a reason: I cut off from the sirloin roasting-pieces a small steak which serves my pilots and single patrons best; but as it is now cold weather, I wish to have these roasting-pieces cut up as I shall direct every morning." After this, Morrison's sirloins were daily cut up by Mr. Gibbons, with his order to "cut steaks for the porter-house;" hence the sirloin was changed into "cut the porter-house steaks." Their appearance attracted the attention of the other butchers and keepers of porter-houses, who admired their appearance and convenient size; in a few years their name and character became quite common to the butchers of the Fly Market, from which the name has spread to the several principal cities of the United States, and I doubt not that the name, porter-house steak, has reached across the Atlantic.

THE BEEFSTEAK

The New York City "Beefsteak" can best be described as a dining event that was very popular in the late nineteenth century. In *Up in the Old Hotel*, the 1938 collection of Joseph Mitchell stories, mainly written for the *New Yorker*, he describes it better than I ever could.

The New York steak dinner, or "beefsteak," is a form of gluttony as stylized and regional as the riverbank fish fry, the hot-rock clambake, or the Texas barbeque. Some old chefs believe it had its origin sixty or seventy years ago, when butchers from the slaughterhouses on the East River would sneak choice loin cuts into the kitchens of nearby saloons, grill them over charcoal, and feast on them during their Saturday-night sprees.

In any case, the institution was essentially masculine until 1920, when it was debased by the Eighteenth and Nineteenth Amendments to the Constitution of the United States. [The Amendments that made drinking illegal—Prohibition—and gave women the vote.] The Eighteenth Amendment brought about mixed drinking; a year and a half after it went into effect, the salutation "We Greet Our Better Halves" began to appear on the souvenir menus of beefsteaks thrown by bowling, fishing, and chowder clubs and lodges and labor unions.

The big, exuberant beefsteaks thrown by Tammany and Republican district clubs always had been strictly stag, but not long after the Nineteenth Amendment gave women the suffrage, politicians decided it would be nice to invite females over voting age to clubhouse beefsteaks. "Womenfolk didn't know what a beefsteak was until they got the right to vote," an old chef once said.

It didn't take women long to corrupt the beefsteak. They forced the addition of such things as Manhattan cocktails, fruit cups, and fancy salads to the traditional menu of slices of ripened steaks, double lamb chops, kidneys, and beer by the pitcher. They insisted on dance orchestras instead of brassy German bands. The life of the party at a beefsteak used to be the man who let out the most ecstatic grunts, drank the most beer, ate the most steak, and got the most grease on his ears, but women do not esteem a glutton, and at a contemporary beefsteak it is unusual for a man to do away with more than six pounds of meat and thirty glasses of beer. Until around 1920, beefsteak etiquette was rigid. Knives, forks, napkins, and tablecloths never had been permitted; a man was supposed to eat with his hands. When beefsteaks became bisexual, the etiquette changed. For generations men had worn their second-best suits because of the inevitability of grease spots; tuxedos and women appeared simultaneously. Most beefsteaks degenerated into polite banquets at which open-face sandwiches of grilled steak happened to be the principal dish.

STEAK À LA STONE

Steak à la Stone, which is slices of Strip Steak on toast with smothered onions, pimento, and a drizzle of butter, is a specialty of Palm. The restaurant is now a national chain but it used to be merely one of many rough-and-tumble steakhouses near the old East River slaughterhouse, a site now occupied by the United Nations complex.

But New York City is really a small town. When I was bemoaning the fact that I couldn't find out who Stone was to Jean-Claude Baker, the owner of Chez Josephine, he got all excited. He knew that film director Oliver Stone's father was Lou Stone, a Wall Street financier, and that Jacqueline Stone, who is one of Baker's best friends, would be certain to know if it was her late husband who "suggested" the dish. "Yes, Palm was his spot," said Jacqueline Stone, "but I don't know why they call that dish after him. It doesn't sound like my husband. He was strictly a meat and potatoes man. That dish would not have been his cup of tea."

Serves 6

At Palm, Steak à la Stone is still made with pimentos out of a jar. These days, if you want to keep it easy but make it better, use a good brand of imported roasted peppers. Better yet, take the trouble to roast a couple of fresh red bell peppers.

½ cup vegetable oil, preferably corn (or, even better, olive oil)

4 medium onions (about 1 ½ pounds), peeled, cut in half through the root end, then cut into ½-inch-thick slices

1 (12-ounce) jar imported whole pimentos or roasted peppers, cut open, seeded, and flattened or cut into large sections, or 2 large red peppers, roasted, peeled, seeded, and each cut into 3 sections

3 (16-ounce) Strip Steaks, cut about 1 ½ inches thick, at room temperature

Salt

6 slices of white bread, crusts removed, toasted, and cut in half on the diagonal

Freshly ground black pepper

8 tablespoons (1 stick) unsalted butter, melted and warm

⅓ cup chopped fresh flat-leaf parsley leaves

Preheat the broiler.

In a 10-inch skillet, heat the oil over medium-high heat, then cook the onions, stirring them constantly, until they are wilted and beginning to brown very slightly, about 5 minutes.

Reduce the heat to low, and continue to cook, stirring only occasionally, until the onions are soft, about 15 minutes.

Remove from the heat. Spread the pimentos or roasted pepper sections over the onions in a single layer. Cover the pan to warm the peppers slightly and keep them warm while preparing the steaks.

Season the steaks with salt. Broil the steaks until nicely browned on one side, 6 minutes. Turn and cook the second side for another 5 minutes. The steak is now rare. For medium-rare, turn the heat down and cook another 3 minutes. For medium, cook an additional 4 to 5 minutes, turning twice. Transfer to a cutting board and let stand 3 minutes.

Place 2 toast triangles on each of 6 plates. Arrange onions and pimentos on the toast.

Carve the steaks into ½-inch-thick slices and place them over the vegetables and toast. Season with salt and freshly ground black pepper. Spoon melted butter over the steak slices. Sprinkle with the chopped parsley.

Serve immediately.

STEAKHOUSE HASH BROWNS

The classic New York steakhouse menu consists of the steak, creamed spinach, and—instead of a baked potato, which is most of America's favorite starch side dish—either hash browns, home fries, cottage fries, or what Peter Luger calls German fried potatoes, basically French fries that have been broken up and re-cooked with onions. Every New York City steakhouse has its potato specialty.

Serves 6

In New York City steakhouses, potatoes like these may be served in crusty discs, or on oval metal sizzle platters in mounds doused with butter and browned under the broiler.

3 pounds boiling or all-purpose potatoes
2 to 4 tablespoons unsalted butter (divided)
2 to 4 tablespoons vegetable or olive oil (divided)

1 pound yellow onions, coarsely chopped
Salt
Freshly ground black pepper

Put the potatoes in a pot with enough cold water to cover well. Bring to a boil, and boil for 20 to 30 minutes, or until the potatoes are tender but not soft.

Drain. When cool enough to handle, peel them, and cut them into roughly 1-inch cubes.

In a large skillet, heat 2 tablespoons of the butter and 2 tablespoons of the oil together over medium-high heat. When sizzling, add the onions, and sauté until just beginning to brown, 5 to 8 minutes.

Add the potatoes, and mix them in with the onions. Using the side of a metal spatula, break the potatoes up a little. Fry over medium-low heat, without mixing, for about 10 minutes. Then scrape the potatoes up to mix them. Some should be a little crusty by now. Mix well. If you like, you can break them up a little bit more.

Let the potatoes fry 10 minutes more, without mixing.

Crusty pieces will develop faster if you add more fat. If you intend to serve the potatoes loose (as diners and coffee shops do) add a few tablespoons more of either butter or oil or both, and raise the heat.

To make a crusty steakhouse-style disc of potatoes, use a 6- or 7-inch nonstick skillet. Heat it with 1 tablespoon each of the butter and the oil. When the oil is very hot, transfer some of the potatoes to the smaller pan. Fry until crusty, without turning, tamping the potatoes down a few times.

Once a crust has formed on the bottom, turn the potato cake onto a pot cover. While holding the potato cake on the pot cover, pour another tablespoon of oil into the pan. Turn the potato cake back into the pan, crisped side up, and fry the second side until crusty.

Serve immediately.

FELTMAN'S

CHARLES FELTMAN, A GERMAN IMMIGRANT, STARTED OUT AS A PIE PEDDLER IN 1867, and, in 1871, he may have created the frankfurter on a bun and the hot dog cart as we know it. One thing is for sure: By the end of the 1880s, he owned the largest German beer garden in Coney Island, and it was built on his frankfurter business. Jimmy Durante, Eddie Cantor, and Irving Berlin were singing waiters at Feltman's in the 1910s, and Sophie Tucker entertained there during the same period.

OPPOSITE: Umbrella hot dog carts are an icon of New York City streets.

According to legend, Feltman was delivering pies to the inns and lager-beer saloons that lined Coney Island's beaches when some of his customers asked him to carry hot sandwiches, too. His wagon was ill-equipped for such business, but he thought perhaps he could manage hot sausages served on a roll if he could figure out a way to heat the wagon. He presented his problem to someone named Donovan (whether that was a first name or a last name no one knows—it's a legend), a wheelwright on Howard Street in East New York, in Brooklyn, who had built his pie wagon. (These legends always have specifics to give them more veracity.) Donovan created a tin-lined chest to keep the rolls fresh and rigged a small charcoal stove inside to boil the sausages. They were quite similar to today's hot dog carts, if the story is to be believed.

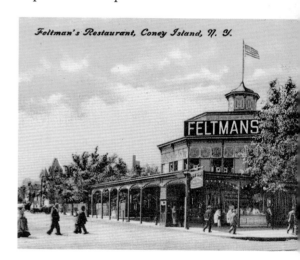

Feltman's Restaurant, Coney Island, N. Y.

In 1871—now the story becomes more fact than legend—Feltman subleased a plot on one of the big shore lots. He served hot dogs to 3,684 patrons that first season (here goes the legend again), and after a few summer seasons he was successful enough to buy his own shore lot at West Tenth Street and Surf Avenue. Here he built his famous octagonally shaped Ocean Pavilion. Feltman placed huge grills around the beer garden and sold frankfurters on buns by the thousands.

By the time Prohibition came in 1920, Feltman's beer garden had expanded to take up the entire block, but of course now the lager beer had to go. The only thing that saved the restaurant from extinction was the subway, which was extended to Coney Island in 1921. With mass transit came the masses. Millions of New Yorkers could now conveniently get to the beach, and thousands of customers were delivered to Feltman's door. It's said that in the first year of the subway extension, he served 3,500,000 customers. In 1922, the number grew to 4,100,000. In 1923, more than 5,230,000 customers went to Feltman's for hot dogs. Those numbers are almost certainly overstated; more likely, they represent the number of hot dogs that he sold, and still they seem quite high.

Whatever the numbers, the volume of business Feltman attracted was impressive enough to encourage competition. Feltman's chief rival became Nathan Handwerker, a former employee. But that's another story. (See below.)

During the Depression, Feltman's business began to decline. Coney Island had become the playground of the poor. They could barely afford the subway token to get there, much less a Feltman's sausage on a bun. At any rate, Nathan's was underselling Feltman's, whose heirs finally closed the restaurant in 1946. The property is now Astroland.

NATHAN'S

One of my most vivid childhood memories is the crush of people trying to buy hot dogs and French fries at Nathan's. In the days before ubiquitous air-conditioning, when everyone migrated to the beach for relief from the heat, thousands of people—no exaggeration—would crowd the deep sidewalk on Surf Avenue, trying to muscle up to the outdoor counter to put in their order. They screamed, pushed, and fought over their position in the throng.

"Eight well done, with four fries!" I can hear them now. The grill men could not have moved faster, using big tongs to turn over a dozen dogs at a time, loading them into the buns, piling them onto paper plates. Meanwhile, the fry guys piled the thick, rippled, salted potatoes into cones. At one time, the fries went into bags, but bags needed to be opened to be filled. Nathan's switched to cones so the countermen could bypass that step and keep those fries coming.

On hot summer evenings—especially Tuesday nights, when there was a fireworks display from a barge offshore—we'd go to Coney Island to catch a breeze on the boardwalk and eat a few hot dogs at Nathan's. Officially, on the sign, they were called frankfurters. Early in the century, there were some people who were made squeamish by the name hot dog, so a regulation was passed stating that they had to be called frankfurters. In print, anyway.

Nathan's got its start in 1916, when Nathan Handwerker, a roll slicer at Feltman's, was encouraged by his friends Jimmy Durante and Eddie Cantor, who were entertainers at Feltman's, to undersell Feltman's on his frankfurters on a bun. Handwerker rented a corner down the avenue from George Tilyou, the owner of Steeplechase, the amusement park, and started selling five-cent hot dogs. Feltman's franks were a dime. The plan backfired, however. Frankfurters were already a suspicious product, and selling them so cheap made the public even more suspicious of their content. Handwerker came up with a clever marketing idea. He invited interns from nearby Coney Island Hospital to eat free at his hot dog stand as long as they came dressed in their hospital whites. Seeing that doctors were willing to eat the cheap hot dogs assured the public that the sausages were wholesome.

When the subway came to Coney Island in 1921, Nathan's business bloomed. It was the hot dog stand of the people, while Feltman's was still relatively elite—at least it was more expensive. According to Nathan's son Murray, the hot dog stand didn't have a name until 1925. People used to say, "Nathan, why don't you put up a name? I tell people to go down there, and I can't tell them what name," Murray Handwerker relates in the book of oral history *It Happened in Brooklyn*. "So, in 1925, he incorporated. The word famous was being used a lot then. He put the sign up: Nathan's Famous."

Although Nathan's hot dogs are now sold all over Manhattan in concessions mostly owned by the Riese Corporation, which controls almost all the fast food licenses in midtown, the hot dogs remain about the same. Maybe they are a little smaller than they used to be, but they are still made only with beef, they still have their hearty spicing, a closely guarded formula developed by Nathan Handwerker's wife, and they still have snap from their natural skins, bursting with juiciness when you bite in. (Nathan's hot dogs are sold in the supermarket, but there are two types—look for the ones with skins for the authentic experience.)

No man can hope to get elected in New York State without being photographed eating hot dogs at Nathan's Famous.

 —NELSON ROCKEFELLER, *former governor of New York*

There was so much ritual in Catholic life [in the 1940s and 1950s], *it spilled over into your social life. When I was a kid, Catholics weren't allowed to eat meat on Friday, and so we developed a ritual for Friday night, which was our date night: a whole crowd of guys and gals would jump into the car and drive from downtown Brooklyn to Coney Island. We had it timed so that we got there as close to midnight as possible. At the stroke of midnight, we'd be standing at Nathan's hot dog counter. A minute later, meatless Friday was over, and we'd be devouring franks.*

 —TOM BOORAS, *in* It Happened in Brooklyn

PAPAYA DRINK AND HOT DOGS

When did the frankfurter meet the papaya drink? This uniquely Manhattan combination (okay, there is one hot dog–papaya stand in the Bronx) was created in 1939 when Gus Poulos added hot dogs to his Hawaiian Tropical Fruits stand on Third Avenue and Eighty-sixth Street. At least this is what Papaya King claims in its official history, which anyone can reference on its eponymous website.

I sort of doubt it, but here's their version of the story anyway. Gus, a Greek immigrant who owned a deli of some kind in Yorkville, went on vacation to Florida. Loving the tropical fruits and drinks he had there, he decided to open a tropical fruit and drink store near his deli. The exotic produce didn't go over all that well in his working-class German and Eastern European neighborhood, so he put women in grass skirts out on the street to attract business. To a degree, that helped. Then Gus fell in love with a neighborhood German girl. Trying to impress her with his roller-skating ability, he became overly ambitious and fell, badly injuring his ankle. Birdie, as the girl was called, nursed him through his recuperation, feeding him the German specialties of the neighborhood. Of course, Gus married the girl, and also decided to sell frankfurters at his tropical fruit stand.

The problem with this story is that only a few years later there were hot dog and papaya stands all over Times Square, and not one was a Papaya King. You can see them clearly in the background of pictures taken in the early 1940s. There is, in fact, a much published VE-Day picture, in which a huge Elpine papaya drink and hot dog stand is visible right on the corner of Broadway and Forty-second Street.

Besides a great and cheap hot dog and papaya drink, Papaya King and Gray's Papaya also offer coconut, and alcohol-free piña colada drinks. It's a mystery why the concept never spread to the other boroughs, but Papaya King is, as of this writing, trying to go national.

HOT DOG ONION SAUCE

Nobody seems to remember when onion sauce, based on ketchup or its more piquant equivalent, Heinz chili sauce, first appeared at hot dog carts as an alternative to mustard. Could it have been an Italian hot dog vendor who thought tomato sauce might be good on the German-American sausage?

Whatever the origin, the sauce has changed in my lifetime. It is sweeter, less tomato-rich, and exceedingly gloppy now. My taste is obviously in the minority, however. Sabrett's anemic onion sauce is sold in jars at the supermarket these days, and the same insipid sauce can be found at most street carts.

In the old days, each vendor prepared his own sauce and was proud of his product's special character. Personally, I prefer mustard and sauerkraut on a hot dog, but if you prefer tomatoes and onions, this recipe makes a much better sauce than you can buy.

Makes 4 to 4 ½ cups

1 tablespoon vegetable oil
3 large sweet onions (about 2 ½ pounds), cut into ¼-inch dice or thinly sliced
¾ cup Heinz chili sauce
12 ounces tomato juice
1 teaspoon paprika

¼ teaspoon dried oregano
Pinch of sugar
¼ teaspoon salt, or to taste
⅛ teaspoon hot sauce, or to taste (or use hot red pepper flakes)

In a 3-quart saucepan, heat the oil; add the onions and sauté for 10 to 15 minutes, tossing the onions constantly.

When the onions are well wilted, but not browned, add the remaining ingredients and stir to combine. Let simmer, partially covered, for 30 minutes.

Taste for seasoning, adding salt and more hot pepper as desired. If using hot red pepper flakes, remember that they will need to simmer for a few minutes before they give their heat to the sauce.

Photographer Jerry Dantzic captured this New York City moment in the mid-1950s.

PROHIBITION

"The old Broadway dimmed its house lights . . . on January 16, 1920, when the Eighteenth Amendment took effect and Prohibition began. Without being able to sell liquor, the restaurants and cafes and cabarets . . . were forced to close their doors. Some tried to resist the law but were harried into bankruptcy by federal agents. Wrecking crews soon demolished Louis Martin's, Maxim's, Bustanoby's, Shanley's, Churchill's, Reisenwebber's, even Rector's. Murray's Roman Gardens, which had been celebrated for its revolving dance floor and lavish décor, was taken over by Hubert's Museum and Flea Circus. The elegant old Knickerbocker Hotel at Broadway and Forty-second Street was converted into an office building. Before the decade was out, the old Waldorf-Astoria with its Peacock Alley and stately dining rooms was demolished to make way for the Empire State Building. Very soon the places where well-heeled people could eat and drink with leisurely elegance were replaced by establishments such as the Bombay Bicycle Club and a hundred places known simply as Tony's—speakeasies where booze could be tossed down furtively, swiftly, and at an untold amount of damage to internal organs. By 1929, there were 32,000 speakeasies in New York City, double the number of old-time saloons."

— *from* Duet in Diamonds, *by* JOHN BURKE

PROHIBITION WAS VERY GOOD FOR DRINKING. WHAT PROHIBITION KILLED WAS fine dining in public. According to John Kobler, in an essay titled, "How Prohibition Failed in New York":

The city's reputedly wettest street was Fifty-second Street between Fifth and Sixth Avenues, and while it is apocryphal that liquor could be bought in any building there, certainly nobody had to take many steps along the brownstone-lined thoroughfare to slake a thirst. Robert Benchley once counted 38 speakeasies on Fifty-second Street. Such was the street's reputation that a lady who occupied a guiltless brownstone between two speakeasies was obliged to post a sign: "This is a private residence. Do not ring."

Given how disastrous Prohibition was for one large segment of the restaurant business, it's astounding how many new restaurants opened in the 1920s, and how many of them remained important well after the repeal of Prohibition in 1933. The Colony, Sardi's, '21' Club, and Leon & Eddie's all opened during the dry period, and only Sardi's didn't serve alcohol, although Vincent Sardi did allow regular customers to bring their own booze as long as they drank it from coffee cups. This was also the period when small Italian restaurants started opening in Times Square. Mamma Leone's was already a success, which encouraged others, such as Zucca's and the Caruso chain of restaurants. Small French restaurants opened in midtown, many operated by the kitchen and waitstaffs of the closed palaces of haute cuisine.

Prohibition coincided with women getting the vote, which was no coincidence. The women's temperance and suffrage movements deemed the women political equals of men and women felt freer to eat, drink, smoke cigarettes, and carouse in public just as men did, and they broke the law with equal gusto. It was the convergence of these social and political events that fueled the Roaring Twenties. It would take the economic disaster of the 1929 stock market crash and the following Depression to quiet down the city.

A NIGHT ON THE TOWN IN THE 1920s

The great actress, playwright, screenwriter, and wit, Ruth Gordon, spoke into a tape recorder for *Manhattan Menus* 1983 edition, a book of menu reproductions that was published for about six years in the 1980s. She describes the time, during Prohibition, when the expression "doing the town" meant something. On the tape she says the following is a typical itinerary for dinner to dawn in the 1920s. I'll add that she must have been thinking of the early 1920s, because Delmonico's and Churchill's closed soon after Prohibition began:

For a really swell night out in the Twenties you'd probably start out at an elegant place like the Crystal Room in the old Ritz-Carlton on Madison Avenue. Oh, did they have wonderful food there. You ordered a la carte of course. Anything you wanted. You'd start off with the oysters, then you'd have a lovely soup with croutons on the side. Then, if you were truly eleganza you'd have some fish, and then you'd have the game, if it was in season. (That was Fanny Brice's great restaurant line—"Give me anything, as long as it's out of season.") Or you'd have the gigot—which was a big thing all by itself. Nobody thought too much about salad. Salad, in those days, was Lobster Salad or Chicken Salad. And the desserts were paradise—Baked Alaska and profiteroles! Nobody cared about diets. Everybody ate chocolates and cakes and whipped cream. Adele Astaire [sister of Fred], a friend of mine, had a chocolate soda every day of her life, as I did for the most part, and once I said to her, "Why don't we ever get fat?" She said, "We are just fortunate that we are blessed with poor assimilation." I don't know what she meant by that, but it's true that we ate anything that we wanted to and we certainly did not get fat.

After a lovely late dinner at the Crystal Room you'd go over to Harry Richmond's Wigwam Club. Of course it was during Prohibition so you'd have to order something like Chicken à la King just to hold the table, but actually you were there just to have more illegal drinks. Depending on how you felt at two or three in the morning, you'd make your way up to Harlem and go to Small's Paradise or The Savoy to hear the great bands. Then you might have a snack at one of the little Harlem bistros where you would eat what we now identify as "soul food." At seven or eight in the morning you'd arrive at Reuben's, which was on Fifty-eighth Street between Fifth and Madison, where you would have breakfast. And everybody who was anybody was always there.

Going out in the Twenties was so glamorous, so dazzling. Everybody was beautiful and everybody was sexy and nobody was economical. If you weren't glamorous and beautiful you stayed home. But the whole idea was to have money, to be striking. Nobody was concerned about being cultured or being talented.

'21' CLUB

'21' is the freshest old restaurant in town. Joe Baum, the famous restaurateur (see page 308), once defined a successful New York City restaurant as one that lasts as long as its lease. By that standard, '21' is the most successful restaurant in town, always renewing itself so it can find new people to appreciate its vintage virtues and often excellent food. The story of its beginning as a speakeasy in the Roaring Twenties is famous. There is a bank vault in the restaurant's lower depths where the alcohol stash was kept. Since Prohibition ended in 1933, the several different owners keep cashing in on that feature. It's been written about in magazines, shown off on television, and used as the centerpiece of a private dining room. If '21' had merely been any speakeasy, however, it would be long gone. From the beginning, there was much more to the place than illegal booze.

Jack Kriendler and Charlie Burns, cousins and pals, always wanted their place to serve the best fare and the best alcohol to the "best" people, and everyone who has run the establishment since has carried on that tradition. In 1922, Kriendler was enrolled in Fordham pharmacy school, Burns was working toward a business degree at New York University. Kriendler's uncle, Sam, who owned the most fastidious bar on the Lower East Side when alcohol was legal, was making big money with a speakeasy in Greenwich Village. The cousins thought this would be a good way to earn their next semester's tuition, so they opened the Red Head, also in the Village, on Sixth Avenue near Washington Place. Like everyone else during those early days of Prohibition, they sold their illegal booze in dollar-an-ounce flasks that customers poured into teacups; the boys also paid protection money to the police. In addition they provided music for dancing. It was the beginning of the Jazz Age, which also meant the beginning of flappers. My maternal grandmother, the daughter of a rabbi no less, told me she would leave the house dressed demurely, but on the subway, would powder her face, rouge her cheeks, gloss her lips, hike up her dress, then go out on the town with her girlfriends. The Red Head attracted that type of crowd, as well as New York University students, and the bohemian artists, writers, and actors who lived in or frequented Greenwich Village. F. Scott Fitzgerald is said to be the most famous habitué. There was so little respect for the Eighteenth Amendment (and the Volstead Act that enforced it) that Kriendler's mother didn't mind being enlisted to help supply the boys with alcohol. She distilled it in her Lower East Side apartment—to keep her son and nephew in school, of course.

After only one year, Kriendler and Burns moved around the corner to 88 Washington Place and opened Club Fronton. It was the stereotypical speakeasy. The bar was just a plank of wood held up on saw horses. There were only four kinds of booze—scotch, bourbon, rye, and gin—and they were poured out of pitchers. If Prohibition enforcers came the booze was poured down a drain in the floor. There was a peephole in the door to check on who came in, and a buzzer to warn the customers to hightail it out the back door in case of a raid. Nearly everyone flouted the law. Even the Mayor of New York City, James J. (Jimmy) Walker was known to frequent the speakeasies. But of course no one wanted to get caught.

In 1926, Kriendler and Burns moved the business, this time because their property near Sixth Avenue was condemned to make way for subway construction. By now Kriendler had given up on pharmacy school, although Burns finally did get his business degree. They opened at 42 West Forty-ninth Street and they called the new place the Puncheon. Then they had to move again in 1928. This time it was to make way for Rockefeller Center. Their final destination, a brownstone townhouse at 21 West Fifty-second Street, opened on the New Year's Eve that rang in 1930. It was discreetly called Jack and Charlie's '21'. There were reportedly thirty-eight speakeasies on Fifty-second Street at the time, some of which were jazz clubs, or became jazz clubs in the 1930s. That's why it was unofficially known then, and is officially now called, Swing Street.

Kriendler and Burns moved there for other reasons, however. First, they were able to buy the building; no more renting for the guys who had outlived their lease twice. Second, they were already well known to that neighborhood's well-paid-off police precinct. Finally, with the Puncheon only three blocks away, their customer base was from the neighborhood.

The jockeys at '21' sport the stable colors of regular customers.

New Yorkers, then as now, are unbelievably provincial; we don't like to leave our own neighborhoods. When a favorite restaurant or bar moves to another part of the city, it might as well have moved to Antarctica.

One reason that '21,' although raided, was never found to have violated Prohibition, was that it had a system in which all the bottles and booze could be dumped into a deep well as soon as the feds appeared at the door, and its stash of reportedly two thousand bottles of wine was kept in that famous vault in the basement of the brownstone next door—not in '21,' but in 19 West Fifty-second Street. In addition, that vault door was camouflaged behind a brick wall. Altogether there were eighteen inches of metal and brick between the booze and the feds. To unlatch the door and open it, you needed a wire commensurately long to push through a crack in the bricks and beyond the metal. There was one very famous raid of '21,' however—famous because it was incited by gossip columnist Walter Winchell, who, after having been snubbed by Jack and Charlie, noted in his column that the joint had never been raided. Naturally, the feds pounced on the place the next day.

Exclusivity was always one of the guiding forces of '21,' so although it was never a true club that required paid membership, many people thought it was. For one thing, Kriendler and Burns always made sure their prices were so high that undesirables didn't even try to get in. As late as the 1970s, customers were carefully scrutinized, and unless you were known to the house, you didn't feel comfortable even when they admitted you. Today, as long as you are dressed appropriately, which means a jacket and tie for men, you are greeted warmly.

FROM TOP: Me at the '21' bar; booze was safeguarded behind the thick brick door during Prohibition; Richard Nixon's stash is still aging.

LEON & EDDIE'S

In 1928, Leon Enker and Eddie Davis opened a speakeasy supper club at 33 West Fifty-second Street, between Fifth and Sixth Avenues, a few doors closer to Sixth Avenue than '21'. The street was then filled with speakeasies, but it became known colloquially as Swing Street (see page 236).

Leon & Eddie's must have been some joint. All through the 1930s and 1940s, it attracted the biggest names in music and comedy. If the talent wasn't on the stage, it was in the audience. Not all the clientele could you brag about, however. Big names in the underworld loved Leon & Eddie's too. Al Capone's mob enjoyed the place, including Capone himself, who felt it was safe enough to bring his wife. Other infamous names that history records as regulars were Louis Lepke of Murder Incorporated and Legs Diamond.

On the entertainment side, Milton Berle used to go to Leon & Eddie's to see the new comic talent. That's where he got the reputation of stealing material, and that's where he met sixteen-year-old Alan King, who was, in his own words, "part doorman and part comic."

"Milton came in and saw me," said King in a tribute to Berle after he died, "and the first thing he did: He called me over to the table; he put a foot-long cigar in my mouth. He says, 'kid, if you're going to be funny, you better start smoking these.'" From that day, Alan King was known as Milton Berle's protégé.

It is not clear exactly when Leon & Eddie's closed, but by the early 1950s, Eddie was running a Leon & Eddie's in Reno, Nevada, and Leon had a club in Miami, Florida. Leon & Eddie menu covers are now highly collectible because they were always risqué. Inside, the menus were typical, if not downright stereotypical of their day, offering many different cuts of broiled meat, a limited list of baked and fried fish, corned beef and cabbage, always one pasta, always an Italian-style veal dish, a sweetbread preparation, and such New York City classics as Vichyssoise, Lobster Newburg [sic], and Chicken à la King.

LINDY'S

Have you heard this gag?

Customer: *"How come the rice pudding with raisins costs one dollar and the rice pudding without is a dollar and a quarter?"*

Lindy's waiter: *"It costs us twenty-five cents in labor to take out the raisins."*

Here's another:

Customer: *"I haven't come to any ham in this sandwich yet."*

Lindy's waiter: *"Try another bite."*

Customer (taking a huge bite): *"Nope, not yet."*

Lindy's waiter: *"You must have gone right past it."*

Lindy's may be remembered for cheesecake today (see page 276), but it also is said to have been the first New York City Jewish delicatessen-restaurant with wisecracking waiters—a feature that later became an annoying (or amusing, depending on how you look at it) aspect of Jewish restaurants all over town. "Wisecracking" is putting it mildly and kindly, however. Having grown up with a grandfather who was a wisecracking Jewish waiter of the Lindy's era—although not at Lindy's—I can testify to the great disdain these waiters had for their customers. The so-called wisecracks were not jokes. They were meant to be insulting. It was a case of the customer is rarely right.

There are still a few restaurants called Leo Lindy's in New York City (the Riese Corporation owns the name), and they still produce the supposedly original cheesecake recipe, but that's where the similarity ends.

Wisecracking waiters, great cheesecake, and altogether good food in large portions made Lindy's the most popular hangout on Broadway from its earliest days and well into the 1950s. Lindy's was not a classy place, as Arnold Reuben liked to think his was, and it was immortalized by Damon Runyon, who turned it into "Mindy's" in his stories about the Broadway underbelly of gamblers, lesser lights, outright gangsters, and other less-than-social register characters that frequented the place. The real restaurant was opened in 1921, at 1626 Broadway near Fiftieth Street (and later at 1655 Broadway), by Leo Linderman, a German Jew who, when he was fourteen, left school to apprentice in a Berlin delicatessen. Or so the story goes.

Before it was famous for cheesecake, not to mention strawberry shortcake (see page 358), Lindy's was famous for overstuffed sandwiches. In Yiddish, one would say *ungeschtupped* sand-

A DICTIONARY OF JOINTS

CAB JOINT — *A place the cab drivers would take you because they got a kick back*

CARPET JOINT — *A fancy restaurant*

CHEAT JOINT — *Where married men and women would go to meet each other and other single, adulterous partners. Could be one and the same as a Cinderella Joint.*

CINDERELLA JOINT — *Where women would come in dressed demurely, then change into more provocative clothes in the ladies' room*

CLIP JOINT — *A place where they were likely to cheat you*

CONSCIENCE JOINT — *A place where you added up your own bill*

CUP JOINT — *During Prohibition, a place where they served alcohol in a coffee cup*

GRAB JOINTS — *Cafeterias*

JEW JOINT — *What non-Jews called Jewish restaurants, such as Ratner's (dairy) or Gluckstern's (meat)*

wiches, using a word that also has sexual connotations. (I told you it wasn't a classy place.) The Lindy's Special was roast turkey, smoked tongue, and Swiss cheese piled with Bermuda onions, coleslaw, and Russian dressing—on rye, or, for a small surcharge, on twin rolls, a concept original to Lindy's. A couple of the other Lindy's original sandwiches were the G-Man Special (referring to the Prohibition enforcers), which was chopped raw steak, chopped onions, and capers; and the Tongue Temptation, which was ox tongue, Swiss cheese, tomato, and India relish.

The Lindy's menu was much more Jewish than most restaurants of its ilk, but it did list Long Island scallops and creamed chicken on toast (a necessity on any menu of the day), alongside scrambled eggs with Nova smoked salmon and onions, cheese blintzes with sour cream and blackberry preserves, and chicken in the pot with matzoh balls and noodles. The famous dessert list offered Nesselrode pie (see page 300), rice pudding (see page 101), and Danish pastry with the famous strawberry shortcake and cheesecake.

Linderman didn't invent cream cheese cake, what we now call New York Cheesecake. In fact, it looks like he stole the idea from his chief competitor, Arnold Reuben, who did claim to have created the prototype for this now iconic item. The fact is that Linderman lured away Reuben's Swiss-trained pastry chef, Paul Heghi, who then baked the cake for Lindy's with just one obvious change: He put strawberries on top. The cookie crust may also have been a Lindy's innovation.

ORIGINS OF NEW YORK CHEESECAKE

New York cheesecake, which is ironically always made with Philadelphia cream cheese, is a variant on the Eastern European cheesecakes that were made in the old country with fresh "curd cheeses"— cheeses on the order of pot cheese and cottage cheese. Think Russian *pashka*, the Easter cheese dessert formed into a four-sided pyramid, and you've got an idea of the ancestry, although the original cheesecakes of Jewish Eastern Europe were probably much poorer and drier than the rich, festive *pashka*.

Cream cheese was the ingredient that turned a dry cake into a much beloved, iconic food of New York. According to Kraft foods, which now makes Philadelphia-brand cream cheese, the product "originated in the United States in 1872 when a dairyman in upstate Chester, New York, developed a 'richer cheese than ever before,' made from cream as well as whole milk." The new cheese was supposed to imitate French Neufchâtel. Then in 1880, a New York cheese distributor, A. L. Reynolds, first began distributing cream cheese wrapped in tin-foil wrappers, calling it Philadelphia Brand.

But why Philadelphia? Says Kraft, the name "Philadelphia Brand cream cheese" was adopted by Reynolds for the product because, at that time, top-quality food products often originated in or were associated with a place of origin; Maryland capon, and Jersey pork chops; for example.

There was, in fact, a much earlier cream cheese from Philadelphia, pointing to the inspiration for the name. In Thomas F. De Voe's *The Market Assistant*, an 1867 treatise on the markets of New York, Philadelphia, Boston, and Brooklyn, the author notes that there was a kind of cream cheese "sometimes found in our markets, but more particularly in those of Philadelphia."

He even describes how it was concocted: "It is made from rich sour cream tied up in linen cloth to drain, then laid on a deep dish, still covered around, and turned every day, and sprinkled with salt for ten days or a fortnight, until it is ripe." This sour cream could not have been the cultured sour cream that we know, but a more natural product.

De Voe also says "there is another article much used called Smearkase, a German name for churds [sic]. It is made into pies, cakes, spread on bread, and also eaten with pepper and salt. I ate some in Philadelphia made into cake, which I found was very good."

New York Cheesecake as we know it, however, didn't appear until the twentieth century. It is possible that, as he claims, Arnold Reuben of Reuben's delicatessen was the first to serve such a cake to the public. He also claimed his family developed the first cream cheese cake recipe, but Reuben had a tendency to make spurious claims (to put it politely) so it is hard to say if that one is true. It is at best unlikely, because at about the same time that Reuben claimed his family invented cheese-cake, Kraft ran a promotion for its cream cheese with a recipe called "Philadelphia Supreme Cheesecake."

SARDI'S

It is typical of New Yorkers to label Sardi's as a tourist trap. But if it ever closes, you'll hear plenty of wailing. New Yorkers would be bereft, and they'd kick themselves for not having supported it more. Fortunately, the tourists love it—as well they should—and keep the place hopping.

After more than eighty years in business, Sardi's remains as synonymous with Broadway theater as the Playbill program you're handed on the way to your seat. It may no longer be the site of every Broadway opening party, as it used to be. It may no longer be the place where anxious actors, directors, and playwrights wait for their reviews in early editions of the *Times*, the *News*, and the *Post*. It may no longer attract the biggest stars for after-theater supper. But the food is good, and sometimes terrific. The hospitality is still as genuine as it was when Vincent Sardi, Sr., and his wife, Jenny, opened their doors in a brownstone townhouse at 246 West Forty-fourth Street in 1921. And you don't have to merely imagine the theater ghosts. Their caricatures are on the walls.

Sardi, who was born Melchiorre Pio Vincenza Sardi, had an unusual ambition from the moment he arrived in New York City from London, his first stop after having left his family home in the Piedmont region of Italy. He wanted to cater to the theater crowd, which is what he had done so well as a waiter in London. With his wife, who was born Eugenia Pallera and called Jenny by the Broadway crowd she came to befriend, he wanted to open a small place where theater people would feel at home. It was the beginning of Prohibition. The lobster palaces of Times Square were failing because they couldn't serve alcohol. The city was changing. Restaurants were getting more personal. Broadway, bright with theater lights, had become the Great White Way.

At first, Sardi called his place the Little Restaurant, not because of its size but because it was next door to the Little Theater. "After a while," Sardi wrote in his 1953 memoir, *Sardi's*, "we changed the sign to read Sardi's for that is what our regular customers always called the place. In the front was a tiny bar, which we used as a coffee counter, and from which we served ice cream and salads. Naturally, at the time, we could not use it as a bar, for Prohibition had already been made the law of the country. Behind it were tables, and if I am not mistaken forty was the largest number we could take care of at one time. The walls were green, and I had hired an artist to paint romantic country scenes on them. We had a few potted palms scattered about here and there."

Sardi's quickly became a watering hole for the Broadway crowd, not only actors and directors and musicians, but producers, theater owners, and the "angels" with money. In 1926, however, Sardi's landlord, Vincent Astor, gave an option on his building to A. H. Erlanger, who was planning to build a new theater on the site (now the St. James). Erlanger had already bought the adjacent brownstones, and he was ready to tear them all down. Sardi had to move.

Sardi considered a space on Forty-fifth Street. Schubert Alley, named after the theater-owning family, connected Forty-fifth and Forty-fourth Streets, and Sardi figured his old customers would easily be able to find him and Jenny. But then he was approached by a representative of Lee Schubert, who had been keeping his eye on the Sardis. He had intended to build another theater on Forty-fourth Street, on a vacant lot he owned, but instead he had decided to build a restaurant. Sardi and his wife were so well liked by the theater community that Schubert was willing to build to suit.

It took more than a year to build what ended up as a five-story structure, and by the time Sardi's reopened, at 234 West Forty-fourth, on March 5, 1927, Vincent and Jenny had lost most of their customer base. The custom of hanging celebrity caricatures started as an act of desperation. When, after several months, business was still dead, he and his wife searched for something other than their hospitality, good food, service, and location to attract customers.

Sardi found caricaturist Alex Gard, a Russian refugee, through an artist who lunched at the restaurant. To Sardi's relief, Gard did not want pay. He was willing to barter his services for one meal a day for himself and a guest. To his dying day, on June 1, 1948, through twenty-one years and more than seven hundred caricatures of both the enduringly famous and the flash-in-the-pans, Gard had dinner every night at Sardi's.

He was a notoriously mean caricaturist, always exaggerating a subject's ugliest characteristic. But part of his deal with Sardi was that he never had to make any changes. Sardi couldn't complain about the drawings and Gard couldn't complain about the food. The only exception to Gard's rule was the picture he made of the great actress Katherine Cornell, one of his first subjects. She hated that he'd drawn her with a cigarette dangling from her mouth. He agreed to remove the offending butt, but only because Mrs. Sardi had appealed to him. To give an idea of how cruel Gard could be, Boris Karloff signed his picture with the quip, "He said I looked like Boris Karloff."

After Gard died, several other artists took up the custom of drawing the Broadway stars of the day. It took more than a year for Sardi to replace Gard. John Mackey was the next artist. Sardi was not impressed with his work, and he didn't last long. Then Jack Kirkland (who wrote the stage version of *Tobacco Road*) recommended his son-in-law, Don Bevan, who had drawn caricatures of enlisted men for the combat room during his time in the service. War correspondent Walter Cronkite had fed these drawings to his wire service. Bevan was shot down and imprisoned in Stalag 17, where, along with fellow prisoner Edmund Trzcinski, he wrote the play *Stalag 17*. After the war, Bevan turned out approximately a caricature a month for Sardi's while working for the *Daily News* and the *Baltimore Sun*. He retired from his Sardi's caricaturture work in 1974. Richard Baratz replaced Bevan after a public competition, and he continues to mock the stars with his pen. The Sardi's caricature collection is now part of the Billy Rose Theatre Collection of the New York Public Library at Lincoln Center. The walls are still lined with caricatures of current stars of stage, screen, and television.

LONGCHAMPS

New York City restaurant, Longchamps, transformed food from the profane to the sacred. The design of the restaurant focused one's attention on the central display of food. The bare interior detached the food from its surrounding, while the island on which the food was exhibited isolated it, drawing all attention to this shrine of edible delights. Through the design of its interior and its treatment of food, Longchamps . . . [transformed] food into art. The sculptural shrine made food untouchable, precious objects. The formality of space took on a sacred quality, similar to an art museum. The removal of people from the picture dissolved all possible pretense about humans eating, preserving the holy qualities of the food. The Longchamps Restaurant metamorphosed food from a daily substance to a divine manifestation.

—YASHA BUTLER, Architectural Forum, *1935*

Yasha Butler may have been referring to the first Longchamps restaurant, opened by Henry Lustig in 1920, or perhaps the next Longchamps, opened in 1927 on the ground floor of 55 Fifth Avenue, on the northeast corner of Twelfth Street. Lustig had been in the produce business before he opened his first restaurant: He started out with a produce pushcart on the Lower East Side. At Longchamps, he made the fruits and vegetables of the day—of the season—not only the focus of his menus but the design focus of his restaurants. Walking by a Longchamps restaurant must have been something like walking by Tiffany today. Small display windows looking onto the street featured artful still lifes of produce, much like the Tiffany displays of jewels.

Longchamps quickly became a pricey but widely popular chain, and by 1937, when Lustig opened the first restaurant in the five-year-old Empire State Building, there were twelve. Situated on the corner of Fifth Avenue and Thirty-fourth Street, where the old Waldorf-Astoria had stood, it was the largest location. It originally seated a thousand people on two floors. And it was the last in the chain to close.

In its final days, the Longchamps chain, down to nine outlets, was owned by a Swedish-born restaurateur and Café Society dapper don, Jan Mitchell, who also bought Luchow's, another landmark restaurant. He had various designers strip the Longchamps of their signature red, gold, and white décor and redesign them with kitschy themes. For some unknown reason, the Empire State Longchamps was given a totally inappropriate Mississippi riverboat décor by set designer Oliver Smith, who did the Broadway sets of *My Fair Lady* and *Camelot* with much more sensitivity than he gave this historic location. More appropriately, but no less campy, the City Hall Longchamps was decorated in Dutch style, and the one on Forty-second Street and Lexington Avenue (most recently a Houlihan's), across from Grand Central Terminal, looked like an old Pullman car.

In its heyday, the Longchamps chain was highly regarded. "The food is perfection, the portions are good size to large, and the service is impeccable—which is remarkable, for the no-tipping rule is rigidly enforced, a ten percent charge being added to the bill instead. The Longchamp's restaurants cannot be too highly recommended," said a critic in 1940. But founder and operator Lustig came to a bad end. In March 1945, Lustig and four associates were indicted for federal tax evasion to the tune of nearly three million dollars. Asking for clemency, Lustig's lawyer pleaded that Lustig had himself revealed the evasion and had already paid $1.8 million to the government. Nevertheless, in June 1946 he was found guilty of twenty-three counts of tax evasion. He was sentenced to four years in prison and fined $115,000.

The liquor licenses of the nine remaining Longchamps were suspended for five months, until the restaurants were sold to another operator, Theodore T. Mets, president of the Exchange Buffet cafeterias. Jan Mitchell seized control of the chain in 1959, saying that he wanted to own it because he had come to admire Longchamps when he lived in the Waldorf Towers in the 1940s:

My appetite stimulated by the fresh fruits and vegetables . . . I was never disappointed. The linen would be immaculate and smooth. The glassware and silver and china would sparkle. The knives would be sharp. The plates would be of generous size. The lighting would be bright, but not too bright. The chairs would be wide enough to accommodate that portion of the anatomy for which chairs are made. And the service was something which I came to applaud as "impersonally personal."

THE COLONY

All it took was one Vanderbilt to change the Colony from a sleazy hangout for gamblers and adulterers—and their less than respectable women—to the most glamorous restaurant of its day. It was 1920, and, as Iles Brody said in his 1945 book *The Colony*, "If a man of good repute ventured there alone, he was at once classified—either he wanted a girl, or a little strip-poker or crap-shooting. . . . And if a man appeared at the Colony with his wife or girl, well, then the lady was immediately and neatly catalogued, providing she was pretty." Rarely did anyone actually eat in the restaurant. They went to the upstairs room where all the action was (most importantly, illegal booze), only occasionally ordering a bite from the kitchen.

A guy named Joe Pani was the owner. He had a staff consisting of the French chef Alfred Hartmann (from Alsace), the maître d' Ernest Cerutti, and a waiter named Gene Cavallero. By all accounts, Hartmann was a fabulous chef. Cerutti must have been a master of his craft too. When Pani decided to turn the Colony into a nightclub, an idea (loud music while dining) Cerutti found reprehensible, Cerutti quit, and Pani hired another Italian to take his place, M. Achille Borgo. Meanwhile, Gene Cavallero became the manager when Cerutti left, and his instincts about people helped make the Colony what it eventually became—the most famous restaurant in the world.

Success didn't come immediately for the Colony. The night before New Year's Eve 1922, a certain socialite called to ask if there was any room for her party of six for the New Year's festivities. Perhaps word of Hartmann's impeccable cuisine had gotten to her, and certainly the location was fashionable. The Colony was at 667 Madison Avenue, with a door that opened onto Sixty-first Street. In any case, she was promised there would be a crowd of fine people and that a good time would be had by all. When she arrived with her party the restaurant was empty. The staff hadn't even been able to scramble together a few friends to come by for New Year's Eve. As the story goes, a few days into 1922, the socialite, Mrs. W. K. Vanderbilt, returned for lunch. "I suppose I should have made a reservation," she joked when she saw the place was again empty.

Naturally, the staff was embarrassed and had never expected her to show up again, so they treated her like royalty. Borgo sent her a bottle of champagne—1902 Roederer Brut, according to Iles Brody. Realizing that they might be able to make more of the place than Pani ever could, Hartmann, Borgo, Cavallero, and Cerutti, who was now at the Knickerbocker, conspired to buy the Colony by going behind Pani's back and making a deal with the landlord.

To their great fortune, Mrs. Vanderbilt told her friends about her good experience at the Colony, how good the food was, how they had made up for the fiasco of New Year's Eve. Suddenly, names from the society pages started turning up. Eventually, Mrs. Vanderbilt brought her husband, a picky gastronome. With his stamp of approval, the Colony was on the map. As Brody tells it, "The wealthy playboys who used to take only their pro-tégés to the Colony began to be coaxed by their wives to take them there, too—the ladies were dying to see the place where their husbands' unmarried men friends took their sweethearts."

"Cafe Society" at the Colony, in the 1940s

The regulars included European nobles (the Duc d'Orleans, the King of Siam), Broadway and Hollywood royalty (George S. Kaufman, Preston Sturges, Louis B. Mayer), and New York aristocracy (Astors, Vanderbilts galore, Franklin D. Roosevelt). Society/gossip columnist Cholly Knickerbocker wrote about them all. The clientele became known as "Cafe Society."

Hartmann and Cerutti left the Colony in the mid-1920s, and Cavallero took his headwaiter, George Fiorentino, as a new partner. The crash of 1929 and the ensuing Depression didn't help business, but Cavallero allowed some of his regulars to build up tabs during those hard times. That policy would pay off in a big way in later years; when those people made it big again they couldn't have been more loyal to the Colony. Another reason the Colony was such a huge success, and was so for many years—it didn't close until 1972—was Cavallero's attitude toward his customers. He greeted everyone. He said good-bye to everyone. And he wasn't servile. He treated his highfalutin customers as if they were equals and he was entertaining them at home. It's a lesson that Sirio Maccioni learned well when he was the maître d' at the Colony in the late 1950s through the 1960s. It's a manner that made his Le Cirque such a success and a true successor to the Colony.

Although the food may have been very good at the Colony, it wasn't really the reason everyone was there. The kitchen always bought the best ingredients, but the clientele, for the most part, demanded cooking that was relatively simple. As Brody points out, at lunch women outnumbered men by at least six to one and "they are not flocking here to gourmandize." Cavallero catered to the diet conscious and actually got together with some of his doctor customers and devised the Colony Diet. It was heavy on protein (eggs, minute steaks, and lamb chops were daily fare) and devoid of all white carbohydrates (bread, rice, potatoes, and sugar)—except for a slice of Melba toast at lunch allowed only from the fourth day on—and included some fruit (grapefruit every morning) and vegetables. Sound familiar?

Still, one could always get a dish that was elaborately sauced, or a bouillabaisse like the one you had on the Riviera, or the osso bucco you enjoyed in Milan. It was also one of those places where, especially if you were the Duke of Windsor, Bernard Baruch, or Frank Sinatra, you could get whatever you wanted even though it wasn't on the menu.

PATRICIA MURPHY'S

Say Patricia Murphy's and New Yorkers of a certain age say popovers. No one remembers what else they ate at Patricia Murphy's, but everyone can wax nostalgic about the popovers, which were carried from table to table in baskets, on the arms of fetching teenage Popover Girls, all dressed in long gingham skirts.

This was all part of the atmosphere that Patricia Murphy carefully cultivated at her Candlelight restaurants.

Why popovers? Why Candlelight?

Murphy came to New York in 1929 from a small fishing village in Newfoundland. She was seventeen years old and her father had sent her to his brother in Staten Island so she could study piano in preparation for a career in music.

After just a few weeks, she decided that if she was going to live in New York City it was not going to be on Staten Island. She put sixty dollars of the money her father had given her in the bank. It was her stash just in case things didn't work out and she needed to get back to Canada. She got a job playing piano in a student's cafeteria restaurant near Columbia University. This was before the stock market crash, and, as she says in her autobiography, *Glow of Candlelight*, "Money was easy and people were friendly."

She realized that they always needed extra kitchen help at this restaurant, so she started coming in early to earn a few extra bucks. Meanwhile, she hung around Columbia University, where she knew she would meet people her own age and make friends. She did. To earn even more extra money, she hand colored postcards—"at three dollars a hundred."

She liked the restaurant business and dreamed of being a hostess, but at only five feet tall, she wasn't hostess material. Instead, she got a job as a cashier in another restaurant, but that didn't last long because the owners realized she wasn't very good at giving change.

At the end of 1929, she was living in a rooming house on Henry Street, in Brooklyn Heights, not a good neighborhood at the time; the stock market had crashed, and the Great Depression had begun. She had been taking her meals at a very cheap tearoom-type restaurant down the street from where she lived, but one day in early 1930 she found it closed. She banged on the door. The owner, who knew her, explained that he couldn't keep up with the rent and was going out of business.

Where she got the gumption to take over this little tearoom, Murphy doesn't say. But she did, using her sixty-dollar stash to bankroll the business. The landlord, who lived down the street and liked frequenting the restaurant, was cooperative. He agreed to wait until the

*S*he's always active—has been since the days when she chugged back and forth between her first two restaurants, delivering food and wondering if her customers could really afford her 75c lamb chop luncheon.

end of her first week to collect the rent. She redecorated, and came up with a simple menu that she could produce at a price that was competitive with what the homemaker herself would pay for ingredients. She got some of her Columbia student friends to help her, and even got one to cook. Then she opened, and at last she was a restaurant hostess.

At the time, it was popular for tearoom restaurants to serve specialty breads, for instance, Schrafft's had its famous cheese bread (see page 82). The decision to serve popovers, she says in her book, "did not come to me in a blinding flash. I went through lists of hot breads, knowing that hot bread was an item that people who were dining out were not likely to have at home. I rejected all sorts of buns, muffins, and rolls, and chose my popovers because they were tasty, slightly exotic and not too hard to make."

The decision to light the restaurant with candles was simpler. The tearoom she took over was lighted by unsightly bare bulbs hanging from the ceiling. With the restaurant lighted by candles, no one would notice she couldn't yet afford chandeliers. From the first night, the restaurant was a huge success. Everyone loved the popovers. Everyone loved the candlelight.

Patricia Murphy made a meteoric rise in the restaurant business. After Brooklyn Heights, a restaurant that lived on into the late 1960s, Murphy opened on East Sixtieth Street near Madison Avenue. Then she opened places in Manhasset, on Long Island, then in Westchester. Eventually, after she married, she opened one in Fort Lauderdale, Florida. At one point, she had a dispute with her sister Lorraine, who then went into business for herself, calling her restaurants Lorraine Murphy's. Lorraine is nowhere mentioned in Patricia's autobiography. Now in her nineties, Lorraine lives in Florida. Patricia never had children, but the sons of her siblings now operate the Milleridge Inn on Long Island, a restaurant that carries on the family formula of serving simple American fare at very reasonable prices in a country-like setting. And they serve popovers.

JUNIOR'S

It's easy to make both too much and not enough of Junior's. In one form or another, it has been part of Brooklyn's life since 1929. Just the fact that it is still there, and that it thrives against all odds, can be construed as a metaphor for Brooklyn itself. On the other hand, it's just a family restaurant that serves the people well. It makes good hamburgers. Some days the pastrami is truly excellent. They sell everything from dinner to doughnuts. They even have a retail bakery where among the many gaudy goodies is one of New York City's purest pleasures, the item for which Junior's has become internationally famous: cheesecake.

It is a classic New York cheesecake, very smooth and creamy, thick but not heavy. It's baked on a moist, buttery sponge layer, a Junior's innovation. Other cheesecakes come with either a cookie crust or graham cracker crust. It can be had in many flavors—strawberry, pineapple, chocolate swirl—and in several innovative forms—as a filling for chocolate cake layers, for instance. But to a traditionalist there's nothing like the unadorned, completely unembellished, pure vanilla and cream cheese flavor of the hardly plain, "plain" Junior's cheesecake.

Junior's history mirrors the history of Brooklyn since 1929, long before founder Harry Rosen could have any idea that cheesecake would be his legacy. Harry, the grandfather of the currently ruling Rosen generation, started the business with his brother Mike as a sandwich shop called Enduro's. It was the name of a stainless steel fabricator who supplied restaurants and was used only because Harry liked the name. Harry saw how Brooklyn was booming. In the early 1920s, Brooklyn had more housing starts than any other city in the nation. By the end of the decade, the busy Downtown corner of Flatbush Avenue Extension and DeKalb Avenue already had the very grand Paramount Theater, as well as subway lines coming from all directions. Nearby were the genteel department stores of Fulton Street, like Martin's, where the merchandise was brought to the white-gloved ladies, so they didn't have to leave their perches on high stools. Another elaborate movie palace, the Brooklyn Fox, was about to open down the block. And the booming civic center of courts and municipal buildings brought hundreds of thousands of people to Harry and

The beloved Camille Russo retired from the bakery counter at Junior's in 2004.

Mike Rosen's corner almost every day. It was about this time that Brooklyn's population exceeded 2.8 million, making it the most populous borough (which it still is) and the fourth largest city in the country—that is, if it were split from New York City (which it joined in 1898), as many Brooklynites would have liked.

You might say Enduro's was a Jewish delicatessen, although it wasn't kosher. In fact, Rosen was looking to fill a delicatessen void in Downtown Brooklyn. The borough may have had a large middle-class Jewish population by the end of the 1920s, but the Jews were not yet culinarily served downtown. At this time no restaurant sold thick sandwiches of corned beef, pastrami, rolled beef, tongue, and brisket, on either rye bread, challah, and what the Jewish delis called "club" bread, a soft-crusted, yard-long loaf that was cut into segments for sandwiches. Later, one of Junior's specialties would be a fabulous innovation on this: onion-rye club bread.

Almost as soon as Enduro's opened, the stock market crashed and the Great Depression began. Somehow, Enduro's endured, although Harry and Mike Rosen had to close their Manhattan properties to keep their most promising location going. At the height of the Depression, in November 1933, Prohibition was repealed and that provoked Harry Rosen to rethink his operation. By expanding to adjacent space that he could now rent from his landlord, the Dime Savings Bank, he decided to open a full-scale restaurant and cafe with a bar surrounding an elevated bandstand. It was quite the place, all in the latest Art Moderne style. The new menu now included steaks and chops, a full compliment of side dishes, and desserts.

The new Enduro's did just fine through World War II. My grandfather was a wait-

er there and always reminisced about the Brooklyn swells he waited on, including the local politicians, lawyers, and judges who made it their club. After the war, Brooklyn began changing again. Downtown shopping began to decline. This time the middle class was leaving for the suburbs, many of them to homes purchased with GI loans. Poor black people from the south, with no extra money for eating out in restaurants, were moving to New York City for jobs and settling into Brooklyn's older neighborhoods of Bedford-Stuyvesant and Fort Greene (among others), which bordered the Downtown area. Then, a final blow: Robert Moses, officially the New York City Commissioner of Land Management, the regional planning guru who was responsible for some of the best and worst urban/suburban planning ideas of the twentieth century, built court houses and a wide, moatlike avenue (Adams Street) that functionally cut off the affluent and historic Brooklyn Heights neighborhood from the business center of

The predecessor of Junior's

the borough. Enduro's needed rethinking.

In 1949, Harry Rosen's idea was to downsize slightly—get rid of the bar and bandstand—and turn the swank moderne Enduro's into an upbeat family-style restaurant for all occasions and tastes, serving from morning to night everything from eggs and omelets, pancakes and French toast, their original deli sandwiches, as well as dinner entrees, and baked goods.

Harry called the new restaurant Junior's, because it was to be a restaurant for his sons, Walter and Marvin, who had just returned from war. Junior's Most Fabulous Restaurant Caterers and Bakers [sic] opened on election day 1950, with full fountain service and orange vinyl upholstered booths.

Part of the plan was to have a great bakery, and to that end Rosen hired Danish-born baker Eigel Peterson to develop his line of products. It wasn't until the late 1950s, however, that Eigel, under Rosen's supervision and to Rosen's taste, developed Junior's famous cheesecake. Lindy's, Reuben's, and the Brass Rail were all famous for their cheesecakes, but they were fading institutions. By the early 1960s, everyone—in Brooklyn, at least—knew that the reinvented Junior's had a superior product.

The cheesecake's broader fame didn't come until the summer of 1973. That's when Ron

Rosenbaum wrote an ecstatic story about it in the *Village Voice*. That story then encouraged *New York* magazine to have a blind tasting of cheesecakes from around the city, and in early 1974 the magazine declared Junior's cheesecake the best in town. Based on that one tasting and magazine story, Junior's has had a marketing hook for more than thirty years. Junior's cheesecake is now sold coast to coast through mail order. With or without cheesecake, Junior's is a miracle place. Through the decline of Brooklyn in the 1960s and through the 1970s, it managed not only to serve good food and stay alive, but it attracted an amazing cross-section of the borough's people. To this day at Junior's, at any given meal on any given day, you can find at least one of every kind of person who lives in Brooklyn there, now that the borough can again boast that it is the most diverse municipality on earth. The politicians, lawyers, and judges still go there. The shoppers go there. Everyone who goes Downtown meets at Junior's.

RAINBOW ROOM

It was called the Stratosphere Room when it first opened in 1934. Strangely, it was managed by Union News, which owned newsstands all over the city and also operated snack bars and restaurants in train and bus stations, including the Oyster Bar in Grand Central Terminal. The name was changed to the Rainbow Room shortly after it opened because organ recitals were held there at lunchtime and the organ was hooked up to a rainbow of lights in the ceiling. Michael Whiteman researched the room's history when he and partners Joe Baum and Dennis Sweeney were about to restore the facility in 1987, and he discovered that the first chef was a woman, which is even stranger for the day than having Union News as the operator.

New York City, and in fact the world, had never seen anything like it. Located on the sixty-fifth floor of 30 Rockefeller Center, it had large windows with views of the entire city, which only a few years earlier had been graced by the two tallest buildings in the world, first the Chrysler Building in 1930, then the Empire State Building in 1931. Besides the organ with the coordinated light show, it had a revolving dance floor. It had the best swing bands for dancing. The room was the latest in Art Deco design. It virtually defined modern glamour—the kind of place Fred and Ginger would dance in—and, with the city's new skyscrapers, it made New York City the most glamorous place on earth.

The Rainbow Room had to close during World War II. It was hard to have a nightclub at the top of a skyscraper when there were regular blackouts. Excepting that time, Union News ran Rainbow until the early 1960s. In 1964, Jerome Brody, the founder and president of Restaurant

Associates, took it over with a ten-year lease. Sometime during that period, for reasons insiders only speculate about, Brody lost the lease, and the Rockefeller family, who built and then owned Rockefeller Center, turned the remainder of it over to Bryan Daly and Tony May. May now owns San Domenico, a luxe Italian restaurant on Central Park South. May and Daly ran the Rainbow Room for a few years, but when the Rockefellers heard that they had installed a Las Vegas–type show with scantily clad showgirls, they objected. The lease was canceled for that and other reasons. Leases on large blocks of office space were also coming due, as well as the massive lease on the NBC studios in the building. The Rockefellers thought the building needed some improvements to get the best tenants, and that a once-again classy Rainbow Room could be a symbol of the building's renewal.

That's when the Joseph Baum-Michael Whiteman Company was hired. They had consulted on the mammoth World Trade Center food service facilities, including creating the successful Windows on the World, but were no longer responsible for the operation of those restaurants. The mandate from the Rockefeller family was to replan Rainbow, which, with its private party rooms, occupied forty thousand square feet (over an acre) on two floors, and again make it the most glamorous restaurant, nightclub, and party venue in the city. Baum-Whiteman agreed to do the job, but their contract stipulated that if they were not ultimately to be the operators, they had to be paid a royalty for their consulting work—in addition to their handsome fees. It was apparently more financially agreeable to the Rockefellers to make them the tenants.

Hugh Hardy, an architect famous for his restoration work, was hired to refurbish and replan the space. Everything was demolished and rebuilt at a cost of twenty-six million dollars. Carpeting was custom made to the original design, as were the fabrics and papers on the walls. The Rockefellers, insisting on the best, even spent an extra three hundred dollars per chair to have them covered in real leather instead of imitation. The silver lamé tablecloths were a new idea, however. It added the necessary glitz a nightclub needed, according to Whiteman. And the china designs and graphics were conceived by the famous designer and illustrator Milton Glaser.

From its inception, the food and beverage service of the Rainbow had many ups and downs. Five years after it opened, the 1939 restaurant guide, *Dining Out in New York* by G. Selmer Fougner, declared that John Ray, "the man who presides over its destinies . . . has always paid particular attention to the cuisine, which is on a par with the best and towers . . . above all other places where a floor show is provided."

In 1964, Craig Claiborne damned the food. He wrote: "There is one thing to be said for certain about the Rainbow Room. The windows on a clear night open onto some of the most glorious views of the city. The food is another matter." Still, in 1971, the editors of *Cue* magazine (since incorporated into *New York* magazine) thought "the food, for a supper club, was 'excellent.'"

When Baum-Whiteman took over, they tried to upgrade the cuisine. During one period of consistent high notes, it earned three stars from the *New York Times*.

The bar, the Rainbow Promenade which was under the direction of Dale De Groff, reintroduced New York City to classic cocktails. We have De Groff to laud or blame for popularizing the Cosmopolitan (see page 91), and for bringing back the martini—and all those other drinks now poured into cocktail glasses and called martinis of one sort or another.

THE STORK CLUB

Sherman Billingsley, the owner of the Stork Club, the premier celebrity watering hole of the 1940s and 1950s, is usually described as a mild-mannered Oklahoman, a generous man with his customers, a non-smoker, and a teetotaler. Curious! The signature of the restaurant, which can be seen in almost every photograph taken there—is an ashtray, now a collectible. Billingsley himself was usually photographed with a cigarette in his hand, and often there was a glass of something brown in front of him (Scotch, Bourbon?), or Champagne. It was Coke. One must suppose that the private abstainer thought it was important to his glamorous image to look like he indulged. He did, indeed, cut a handsome, dashing figure, and he did like to treat his most famous customers to dinner or Champagne—it kept them coming back. It's telling, too, that for a long time he dated Ethel Merman, a notorious ball buster. Either he knew how to control her or he took orders from her—no one ever knew which. It is known, however, that he controlled every detail at the Stork Club; for instance, he had only urinals put in the men's room because he didn't want there to be any telltale odor from the other use of a men's room. For a proper toilet, the men had to go to the third floor. Apparently, it was fine if the ladies' room smelled.

The Stork Club was the most exclusive restaurant cum nightclub of its day. There was always a good band for dancing, although with no musical or comic performances like a full-fledged nightclub. Billingsley invented the bouncer and velvet rope combo to keep out the gawkers and other undesirables—except Billingsley's rope wasn't velvet. He put a solid gold chain across the entrance of the Stork Club. He also created the first of what we would now call a VIP room. His inner sanctum for superstar customers was called the Cub Room. Here, J. Edgar Hoover felt secure enough to regularly dine with the love of his life, Clyde Tolson; Bing Crosby was allowed to smoke his pipe; Damon Runyon observed the scene; the Roosevelts, Rockefellers, and Vanderbilts could slum; Irving Berlin was allowed to play poker; and Walter Winchell, the most powerful newspaperman of his day, could gather items for his gossip column and radio broadcasts from the famous Table Fifty.

Card playing became a problem during Fiorello LaGuardia's first term as mayor of New York City in the 1930s. The populist politician decided to put a stop to illegal gambling, and he picked on the Cub Room patrons, who he appropriately thought were too elitist for their own good. Billingsley won him over, however, plying him with food and drink, deference and hospitality.

The kitchen pretended to be French—salads were *salades*, fish were *poissons*—but the specialties had international scope, in the Continental mode. Irving Berlin, who was of Russian descent, loved the popular chicken burgers because they were really Russian *cutletin pajorsky* (see page 271). John Wayne ordered Beef Bougeoisie [sic], a not especially French pot roast with a not especially French spelling. Frogs' legs came Provençal style, but they were listed next to chicken potpie, sliced turkey, and shrimp curry. Perhaps the oddest part of the menu was the long list of "Chinese specialties." One of these dishes, Billingsley Chop Suey, had no Chinese connection whatsoever (see page 268). The others were typical Chinese-American dishes of the day, including chicken chow mein and moo goo gai pan.

JAMES BEARD

Meeting James Beard was my first goal as a food journalist. I was twenty-two, and it was 1970. I had just gotten a job as assistant food editor of *Newsday*, the Long Island newspaper, when I called James Beard at his home in Greenwich Village. I told him I wanted to write a story about him shopping at his favorite neighborhood stores, then go back to his house and cook something with him.

Beard liked young men as much as he liked publicity, so the next week I found myself meeting Beard and being introduced by him to Annie Faicco of the Faicco sausage store that is still on Bleecker Street.

Beard then took me to Ottomanelli, his local butcher shop, which is still there. We bought bread at Zito's, which closed in May 2004, and biscotti a few doors down at Rocco's, which is still there, if not quite the same. He picked vegetables at Balducci's, which was then run by the original Andy Balducci. We stopped in at the Jefferson Market, which is now much expanded but still doles out personal service to everyone, as it did to Beard that day.

Beard was a quintessential New Yorker, even though he was born May 5, 1903, in Portland, Oregon, and didn't come to the city until he was thirty-two. Like so many Americans even today, Beard came to New York City to become a star. He had been expelled from the elite Reed College in Portland. He had done a little theater in Oregon. He traveled around Europe for a couple of years. Finally, in 1935, with the encouragement of his mother, Elizabeth, who ran a boarding-house and had inspired her son's interest and eventual career in food and cooking, he moved east for a final stab at stardom, as an opera singer.

At this time, his culinary skills were not as well honed as his social skills, which were formidable. He made friends quickly, and one of his new friends, Jeanne Owen, was key to his later success in the food world. Owen was a wine connoisseur, a highly placed member of the Wine and Food Society. In the beginning, to support his theatrical and opera aspirations, he began to cater parties. Large, stylish, even somewhat eccentric, Beard, with Owen's help and mentorship, charmed his way into some elite social circles, his customer base. It was only a few years after the repeal of Prohibition and New York City was just getting back on keel.

Owen introduced Beard to Bill and Irma Rhode, with whom Beard bonded over their mutual passion for food. With the financial backing of a rich, high-living friend, Jim Cullen, Beard and the Rhodes started a company that specialized in providing cocktail party foods to wealthy clients. It was called Hors d'Oeuvre Inc. and it was located in a former carriage house on the Upper East Side, in the neighborhood where their potential customers lived. With the Rhodes' culinary sophistication, Beard's apparently innate talent for presenting food temptingly, and the social contacts of their well-placed friends, the company succeeded immediately.

In 1940, Beard's first cookbook was published. Predictably, it was on cocktail party food, *Hors d'Oeuvres and Canapes*. Ironically, it precipitated the breakup of the business. In any case, the war years, and the eventual food rationing and servant shortage that they brought, put a damper on the party business.

Patriotically, Beard tried to join the armed services, and he spent some time studying cryptography. But he was thirty-eight years old and was told he would never be sent abroad, which is really what he wanted. Instead, he joined the United Seamen's Service, which was part of the War Shipping Administration, a non-military organization charged with entertaining servicemen while they were far away from home. Beard was hoping to be stationed in Europe, but he was sent first to Puerto Rico, then to Rio de Janeiro, and briefly to Panama. Finally he was sent to to Casablanca. Later he was stationed in Marseilles; from there he traveled around Provence. All along, of course, he was learning about the foods of these places.

Beard's *Fowl and Game Cookery* was published while he was in the Seamen's Service, and although he got no attention, Beard was set on becoming a food writer.

As the legend goes, Beard was walking down a street in New York City one spring day in 1946 when he ran into a friend who told him that—knowing Beard was both an actor and a cook—producers from NBC were looking for him to star in a television cooking program. The show was sponsored by Borden and it was called "Elsie Presents James Beard in 'I Love to Eat,'" Elsie being Elsie the Cow, the Borden mascot. It wasn't successful enough for Borden to sponsor it beyond a year, however, and the other sponsor, Birds Eye Frozen Foods, pulled out the year after. The concept was a television breakthrough, nevertheless.

Still, Beard was after a regular food writing job, and he managed to get one in 1949, at five-year-old *Gourmet* magazine. He was in great company since everybody in the New York City food world wrote for *Gourmet*. After only three months, it became apparent to his editors that Beard couldn't construct a proper sentence. Ann Seranne was given his job and Beard realized that if wanted to write about food he needed to find a professional writer with whom he could work.

All during the 1950s, Beard continued to increase his social circle and circles of influence. He befriended or was befriended by everyone who counted among New York City's arbiters of gastronomy. Among Beard's accomplishments in the 1950s, actually starting in 1949, was the publication of *The Fireside Cookbook*, for which he was paid a fee with no royalties. The decision to do this was difficult, according to Evan Jones in his biography of Beard, *Epicurean Delight*. But, even though Beard needed money, in the end he felt he had made the right decision. The book was the most elaborately presented cookbook to date, with, according to the title page, "1217 recipes and over 400 color pictures," and period-style illustrations by Alice and Martin Provensen. It was a huge success and it made Beard a nationally known figure. Its rewards were more than money could buy.

It was in 1955 that Beard started his cooking school, which would exist for nearly thirty years in various locations, including classes each summer near his hometown of Portland. His friend André Surmain, whom he met in 1953 while running a restaurant on Nantucket, owned a townhouse at 249 East Fiftieth Street, where he lived and also had a kitchen in which he devised meals for Varig airlines. Surmain, who was from Provence, invited Beard to start giving classes in his facility. It was another homerun for Beard, who was a generous and gregarious teacher, making his classes fun as well as educational. The classes lasted only a few years at that location. Surmain and Beard then came up with the idea to hire a French chef for themselves and make the space an exclusive restaurant; by all accounts it didn't start as a serious business. The chef was André Soltner, and the restaurant was Lutèce (see page 309).

the James Beard Foundation
167 West Twelfth Street
new york city

Although Beard had been writing restaurant reviews for *Apartment Life* magazine, the 1960s brought restaurants into his life in a new way. He was called by Joe Baum to help him open a restaurant at Newark Airport with Albert Stockli, who would later become the first chef at the Four Seasons. It was a challenge. No one had ever attempted a fine-dining restaurant at an airport. (They are still nearly non-existent.) That job led Beard to other positions advising Restaurant Associates, as the company pioneered themed dining experiences. Beard collaborated with Nika Hazelton and Baum on the restaurant Trattoria in the then-new Pan-Am building (now Met Life). He worked with Mexican cook and writer Elena Zelayeta at La Fonda del Sol. Finally, as a crowning accomplishment, he worked on developing the menus at the Four Seasons (see page 311).

By the time I arrived on Beard's doorstep in 1970, he was a nationally syndicated columnist,

> *My oldest brother is a lawyer. His senior partner is an urbane gourmet who has been taken into the army as a general to do lawyerly things for the War Department in Washington. He has made a list of the best restaurants in New York and what to order at them for officers going to the big city from Washington. My bride and I have the list. We go to the Grotta Azzurra for the lobster fra diavolo, to '21,' Divan Parisienne, Du Midi, Charles à la Pomme Soufflé, the Chambord (we like French restaurants; there are none in Houston), Dinty Moore's, Lindy's, and Reuben's. We have the corned beef and cabbage at Dinty Moore's, which is the general's recommendation. The only meal I don't like. The cabbage is too much like what I had cooked for my roommates at Stalag Luft III (in the army). The Chambord is supposed to be the most expensive restaurant in New York so I am not surprised or outraged when lunch is $6 each even though a multi-course dinner at the best restaurant in Houston is $2.*
>
> —DAVID WESTHEIMER, reminiscing about his honeymoon in New York in 1945

he was the spokesperson for numerous products (sauerkraut and turkey stand out), and he had written nearly twenty cookbooks. He was the god of American gastronomy, although his monumental work, *American Cookery*, wasn't published until two years later. His household entourage included Richard Nimmo, his personal assistant, and Josie Wilson, a food and wine writer in her own right, but also Beard's editor and ghostwriter. His longtime companion, Gino Cofacci (see page 273) puttered around in the background. Clay Tibbet, his household major domo, was there too, keeping the hundreds of glass jars and ceramic canisters well-dusted and ordered, the copper shined, and Beard comfortable. Tibbet still works at the Beard Foundation.

When Beard died at the age of eighty-one on January 21, 1985, he left his house to Reed College with the stipulation that Cofacci and the third-floor tenants could stay as long as they liked. His personal effects, kitchen equipment, Majolica collection, and other precious serving pieces were auctioned off. To paraphrase the creation story of the Beard Foundation, as Julia Child told it to me, "Peter Kump and I were standing outside the house and all I said was 'It's a shame they have to sell the house.' Then Peter got the idea to make a foundation. He found a friend to put up the money for the down payment. And that was it. The next thing I know my name is on the letterhead of the James Beard Foundation."

Now, the Beard Foundation runs the so-called Academy Awards of food, and celebrates Beard and his work the first weekend in May, near his birthday on May fifth. His house is host to chefs from all over the country, showing off their skills to New York City organization members. His sleeping platform at the front of the parlor floor—he didn't have a formal bedroom—is now set with dining tables and chairs. Fitting. And Beard would have loved the publicity.

TOFFENETTI'S

On the east side of Times Square at Forty-third Street where the Condé Nast tower now stands used to be a restaurant with the largest chandelier on Broadway. It hung from the ceiling of the ground floor, but hung low because it was over a grand, sweeping stairwell that led to the lower level, which put the chandelier practically at eye level as you walked by the big plate-glass windows. Toffenetti's wasn't remarkable for too much else, but that was quite enough. When Toffenetti's closed in the early 1970s, it became a huge Times Square branch of Nathan's from Coney Island, the first branch in Manhattan, and only the second at all—the first was in Oceanside, Long Island. The city rejoiced. In *New York* magazine Gael Greene nearly swooned over the idea that she now could get the world's best hot dog and French fries in the middle of town. And she commented on how glamorous it felt to walk down that sweeping staircase.

PATRICIA MURPHY'S POPOVERS

At the old Patricia Murphy restaurants the popovers were served with a relish tray holding pickled watermelon rind, apple butter, and cottage cheese. Some customers probably found this to be normal food, but for the many ethnics from the boroughs who would travel on a Sunday afternoon to the suburbs headed for Patricia or Lorraine Murphy's, pickled watermelon rind was as exotic as mango chutney. And who ate cottage cheese for fun, before dinner?

Makes 6

Patricia Murphy's popover recipe was very easy to get. At one point, she printed it on her cocktail napkins. The recipe also appears in Murphy's autobiography, *Glow of Candlelight*. It is actually a totally standard recipe.

I've tried making popovers in muffin tins, as some recipes suggest you can, but they will be misshapen and not popped as high as their potential. Pans made specifically for baking popovers are readily available. Usually they are ½-cup custard-cup-shaped individual pans welded onto a heavy-gauge rack. Similarly sized custard cups will do.

1 cup milk	1 cup all-purpose flour
2 eggs	2 tablespoons unsalted butter, melted
½ teaspoon salt	

Preheat the oven to 450 degrees.

In a mixing bowl, with a whisk, beat the milk, eggs, and salt together to combine well, but not to make the mixture foamy.

Add the flour and beat until smooth. Stir in 1 tablespoon of the butter.

(Alternately, mix the batter in a 4-cup measure, measuring out the milk first.)

Brush popover pans with the remaining 1 tablespoon butter, then place them in the oven to preheat for 5 minutes.

Pour ⅓ cup of the batter into each ½-cup popover pan.

Bake for 30 minutes.

Reduce the oven temperature to 350. (Do not open the oven.) Bake for another 15 minutes.

Serve immediately.

KATHERINE CORNELL SALAD

The legendary Broadway actress Katherine Cornell was a regular at Sardi's from the very beginning. She and her husband, Guthrie McClintic, who performed various off-stage functions (stage manager, producer, and so on) over his long theater career, were married in 1921 and became great personal friends of Vincent and Jenny Sardi almost from the moment Sardi's opened.

In his 1953 memoir, Vincent Sardi, Sr., reported that Cornell loved garlic and that this salad was created to please her. It is essentially coleslaw dressed with the Piedmontese *bagna cauda*, "warm bath," for seasoning vegetables, an après ski dip of anchovies melted into oil and butter—with a significant amount of garlic. Sardi was from the Piedmont region of Italy, so this dish was a natural for him, and he put it on the menu. It was the time when everyone was naming dishes after famous customers, so he called it "Katherine Cornell Salad" with the fair expectation that her name would sell it. The public's taste was not as advanced as Miss Cornell's, however. The salad had to be taken off the menu when customers complained it had too much garlic. After that fiasco, whenever Cornell ordered the salad, she joked, "With extra garlic."

Serves 4 to 6

This salad was prepared at the table for Miss Cornell, dressed the moment it was served. You should do the same. The cabbage is cold, crunchy, and a fresh green color, while the dressing is hot, a fabulously appealing contrast. It will still taste delicious if made in advance, even a day ahead, but it will be wilted and a much less appetizing color.

1 (2-ounce) can anchovy fillets
3 tablespoons unsalted butter
2 tablespoons olive oil
2 to 4 tablespoons finely minced garlic
2 tablespoons fresh lemon juice or wine
    vinegar (either red or white)

8 cups finely shredded green cabbage
    (½ a large head)
Freshly ground black pepper
4 to 6 strips bacon, cooked until crisp,
    coarsely crumbled

In a small skillet, over medium heat, combine the anchovies with all their oil, the butter, and the olive oil. When the butter has melted, add the garlic.

Stir the mixture until the anchovies have completely melted into the fat. Let the garlic sizzle for 30 seconds longer, then remove the pan from the heat and stir in the lemon juice.

Pour the hot dressing over the cabbage. Grind on pepper to taste and toss well.

Portion into individual servings and garnish with the bacon.

'21' CLUB'S STEAK DIANE

By the 1940s, Steak Diane was a standard of Cafe Society haunts. In January 1953, Jane Nickerson wrote in the *New York Times* that it was the most popular dish in the dining rooms of the Drake Hotel, the Sherry-Netherland Hotel, and the Colony restaurant. Nickerson also duly reported that "Nino of the Drake" took credit for introducing this dish to New York and "in fact, to the entire United States." Still no one knows who Diane was.

'21' is the last restaurant in New York City to serve Steak Diane. Except when the restaurant is exceedingly busy, it is still prepared tableside by one of the captains, some of whom have been working the floors for more than forty-five years.

Serves 2

As one might expect, every captain at '21' prepares Steak Diane slightly differently. They use varied amounts of the ingredients—more or less mustard, Worcestershire, or A-1 steak sauce, for example. The beef can be browned first then removed from the pan while the sauce is made. Or vice versa. No matter. As they do it—with drama and finesse—a large copper pan with brandy flaming and sauce bubbling, it is not only a great show, but very delicious. It will be a great show in your own kitchen or dining room, too.

1 (16-ounce) boneless shell steak (also called New York strip steak, short loin, or sirloin strip)
Salt
Freshly ground black pepper
2 tablespoons (¼ stick) unsalted butter (divided)
3 tablespoons finely minced shallot
6 tablespoons cognac (or other good brandy) (divided)

2 tablespoons dry white wine or dry vermouth
2 teaspoons Dijon mustard (preferably imported)
2 tablespoons A-1 steak sauce
½ cup beef broth
2 tablespoons heavy cream
2 tablespoons finely snipped chives

Trim all the outside fat off the steak. The steak should now weigh about 12 ounces.

Cut the steak in half horizontally, creating two 6-ounce steaks. Pound the steaks lightly to flatten them to ¼-inch thick. Season them liberally on both sides with salt and freshly ground black pepper.

Heat a 12-inch skillet until a drop of water dances on the surface. Add 1 tablespoon of the butter. As soon as the foam subsides, add the seasoned meat. Cook on each side for 1 minute. Remove to a plate.

Immediately adjust the heat under the pan to low. Add the second tablespoon of butter and the shallots. Sauté the shallots for 1 minute.

Increase the heat to high. Add 3 tablespoons cognac and flambé, if desired. Add the wine and with a wooden spoon scrape up any browning in the pan (deglaze the pan). Stir in the mustard and A-1 sauce. Cook for about a minute, or until the liquid is reduced to a syrup.

Add the broth and continue to boil for about a minute, until reduced to a few tablespoons. Add the cream and stir well to incorporate. Boil a few seconds. Taste for seasoning and add freshly ground pepper to taste.

Add the remaining cognac and ignite.

When the flames die down, stir in the chives, taste for salt and pepper, and adjust if necessary.

Add the reserved steaks and their juices (that have accumulated on the plate) to the simmering sauce. Turn the steaks in the sauce a couple of times, as the sauce reduces a little more.

Place the steaks on individual plates. Divide the sauce on the steaks.

Serve with mashed potatoes or rice, or at least some bread to mop up the sauce.

CHICKEN DIVAN

Chicken Divan, an iconic casserole dish of the 1950s, probably originated in the 1930s, at Divan Parisien, 17 East Forty-fifth Street, one of a group of small French restaurants that opened in Manhattan in the wake of Delmonico's closing in 1923. The restaurant was managed by some of the staff from Delmonico's but they didn't attempt to compete with the haute cuisine and extensive menus of their former employer. Divan Parisien, like its post-Delmonico's contemporaries, served simpler food from a shorter menu.

The original recipe for Chicken Divan is poached chicken on a bed of Parmesan-sprinkled broccoli, both of which are blanketed with a Hollandaise-enriched béchamel with whipped cream. Under the broiler, the sauce acquires a golden glaze. It became a much imitated idea, and turns up on New York City menus throughout the 1940s and into the 1950s with slight variations and under different names. For instance, in a 1955 review of Champs Elysees at 25 East Fortieth Street in *New York's 100 Best Restaurants* by Harry Botsford, chicken Champs Elysees is described as "delightful—generous pieces of white meat and a layer of broccoli, covered with an ingratiating cream sauce, lashed with grated cheese and run under the broiler to attain color."

By the 1950s, however, the dish had reached Middle America, and was served at restaurants, high end and low, all over the country. Over time, chicken Divan became one of those shortcut casseroles made with creamed condensed soup, promoted by Campbell's, and a popular recipe in the women's magazines of the era. It had an especially long life as a recipe for using up leftover Thanksgiving turkey, which happens to be an excellent idea.

THE DIVAN PARISIEN RESTAURANT

The dish was originally made by folding a half cup of hollandaise into the béchamel sauce. Given that hollandaise is basically butter emulsified with egg yolks, that combination seems unnecessarily rich for today, especially since egg yolks alone give a similar substance to the sauce. I use both white and dark meat here, but, as in the original recipe, you may want to use only the breast.

1 (4- to 5-pound) chicken
1 tablespoon whole black peppercorns
2 tablespoons salt
3 tablespoons unsalted butter
3 tablespoons flour
2 cups milk
½ teaspoon grated nutmeg
3 tablespoons sherry

1 teaspoon Worcestershire sauce
1 ½ tablespoons fresh lemon juice
1 large bunch broccoli, tops only, cut or
    broken into very small florets
1 cup grated Parmesan cheese, approximately
2 egg yolks
½ cup heavy cream, whipped

Place the chicken in a large pot. Cover it with cold tap water. Add the peppercorns and salt. Cover the pot, put it over high heat, and bring the water to a boil. As soon as the pot boils—you can listen, or watch for steam to escape from under the lid—turn off the heat and let stand for 3 hours. Uncover the pot. Remove the chicken. Reserve the broth for another use—it may be kept for several days in the refrigerator, or for several months in the freezer.

Meanwhile, make a white sauce: In a small to medium saucepan, melt the butter over medium heat. Stir in the flour with a wire whisk. Let bubble for about 2 minutes.

Remove from the heat, and let the bubbling stop. Beat in the milk all at once. Return the pot to the heat, and, stirring constantly with the whisk, bring the mixture to a boil, at which point it should be thickened and smooth. Stir in the nutmeg, sherry, and Worcestershire sauce. Simmer another minute. Stir in the lemon juice. Cover, and keep hot over a very low flame.

Remove the skin of the chicken and carve the breast, leg, and thigh meat into neat slices. Whatever you cannot slice neatly, save for another purpose.

Bring a large pot of well-salted water to a rolling boil. Cook the broccoli until tender, about 5 minutes. Drain the broccoli in a colander. Then, arrange it in one layer in a deep heatproof serving platter, or in a shallow casserole or gratin dish.

Preheat the oven to 400 degrees.

Sprinkle the broccoli with about half the grated cheese.

Arrange the chicken meat on top of the broccoli.

Whisk the egg yolks into the white sauce. Fold in the whipped cream. Pour the sauce over the chicken and broccoli.

Sprinkle with the remaining grated cheese.

Place in a preheated oven for about 15 minutes, to heat through.

For a final glazing, place the casserole about 5 inches below the broiler heat source, and cook until tinged with brown, about 3 minutes.

BILLINGSLEY CHOP SUEY

In the 1920s through the 1950s, and even to some extent today, chop suey was a word that was used for more than just the Chinese-American dish. Americans took the Chinese word literally. It means "this and that," and that allowed almost any concoction to be called chop suey. Sherman Billingsley supposedly concocted one especially for Margaret O'Brien, who was a child at the time. Her first movie was a Judy Garland and Mickey Rooney opus called *Babes on Broadway* that opened in 1941, when she was four years old. *Journey for Margaret*, made her a star at five.

Serves 4

Wild rice was extremely exotic and expensive when this recipe was created. By law, it could only be gathered by Native Americans in the traditional method of turning the tall grass over a small boat and beating it with a stick to dislodge the seeds. Today, wild rice is cultivated, and it can be found in the supermarket at a reasonable price. This is a great dish for a casual but festive dinner, and a very good buffet dish because it tastes great at room temperature as well as hot, and it is easily eaten with only a fork.

1 tablespoon butter
1 cup wild rice, rinsed three times and drained
3 cups beef broth
1 cup thinly sliced celery hearts (inner ribs of celery), with a few leaves

1 pound raw spinach, heavy stems removed, washed thoroughly, very coarsely chopped
Freshly ground black pepper
2 (14- to 16-ounce) boneless rib steaks (or shell steaks), broiled to taste

In a 3-quart saucepan or flame-proof casserole, melt the butter over medium heat. Stir in the wild rice, and sauté for 5 minutes.

Add the beef broth, and bring to a simmer. Simmer briskly, covered, for 20 minutes.

Stir in the celery. Then, turn the heat down to very low and cook at a gentle simmer, still covered, for about 30 minutes, or until the rice has opened up and the liquid has been absorbed. If, after 20 minutes of the second stage of cooking, there seems to be an excess of liquid, uncover the pot for the last 10 minutes.

Stir in the chopped spinach, and cook until well wilted, but still bright green. Season with freshly ground black pepper to taste.

Broil the steaks to taste.

When the rice is fully cooked, cut the steaks into 1-inch cubes, and toss with the rice mixture. Serve hot.

SARDI'S CANNELLONI

One of the several times that Vincent Sardi, Jr., put his restaurant up for sale, the Joseph Baum–Michael Whiteman Company offered to buy it. That was 1983. Inquiring about food costs and such, the Baum-Whiteman team was told, as a selling point, that there were essentially no food costs for the famous cannelloni, the biggest seller on the menu. The ingredients for the crepes—milk, flour, eggs—amount to nothing, and the filling was based on whatever meat leftovers were in the kitchen, all ground up with some economically inconsequential spinach, and a handful of Parmesan.

The deal never went through, but it came close enough for George Lang to send his friend Joe Baum a copy of the elder Sardi's 1953 book, *Sardi's: The Story of a Famous Restaurant*, written with Richard Gehman. Inside the book (the copy is in my possession now), George wrote, "To Joe Baum from George Lang, Congratulations! It's nice to own a place which is a bit older than we are."

Made with leftovers though they may be, Sardi's cannelloni are duly famous and continue to be one of the restaurant's most popular and delicious dishes. There are two kinds of cannelloni offered on the Sardi's menu today: a meat-stuffed version and a spinach version.

Neither of the current cannelloni recipes, however, follows the one sketched out in Sardi's memoir, which is cannelloni à la Ripley after the creator of Believe It or Not, a sideshow-style attraction on Broadway until the 1970s. "It was always the first thing that he would order when he came back to New York and took up his headquarters in our place," wrote Sardi.

Makes 12, serving 6 as an appetizer, 4 as a main course

For the crepes:
½ cup cold milk
2 eggs
¼ teaspoon salt
1 cup all-purpose flour
2 tablespoons unsalted butter, melted
Olive oil

For the filling:
2 tablespoons olive oil
½ cup finely minced onion (1 very small
    onion)
⅓ cup finely minced carrot (1 small carrot)
¼ cup finely minced celery (1 small rib celery)
½ pound sweet Italian sausage (3 links),
    casings removed
1 (10-ounce) package frozen chopped or leaf
    spinach, cooked according to directions

2 cups diced cooked chicken
6 tablespoons freshly grated Parmigiano-
    Reggiano or Grana Padano
A few gratings of nutmeg
Salt and freshly ground black pepper to taste

For the sauce:
5 tablespoons unsalted butter
6 tablespoons all-purpose flour
3 cups chicken stock
A few gratings of nutmeg (a bit less than
    ⅛ teaspoon)
Scant ¼ teaspoon freshly ground black pepper
½ cup freshly grated Parmigiano-Reggiano
    or Grana Padano
½ cup heavy cream
Salt to taste

269

Make the crepes:

Put ½ cup cold water, the milk, eggs, and salt into the jar of a blender. Cover and blend until mixed, just a few seconds.

Add the flour and butter. Cover and blend at top speed for 1 minute. If bits of flour stick to the sides of the jar, scrape them down with a rubber spatula, then blend for 2 or 3 seconds more. Refrigerate for at least 2 hours.

The batter should be the consistency of light cream, just thick enough to coat a wooden spoon. If, after making your first crepe, it seems too heavy and the crepe too thick, beat in a little more water, no more than 1 tablespoon at first.

Heat a 6-inch omelet or crepe pan or a non-stick skillet over medium heat. Brush the pan lightly with oil.

Holding the pan in one hand, and using a ¼-cup measuring cup for the batter, pour in 3 tablespoons of the batter. Immediately rotate the pan to completely cover the bottom.

Cook for 1 minute, or until the edges of the crepe turn brown and begin to lift away from the pan. Flip the crepe over and brown lightly on the other side. (Don't be alarmed if the crepes puff up; they will flatten as they cool.) Transfer the cooked crepe to a dinner plate. As you cook the crepes and remove them to the plate, cover with a damp kitchen towel.

Repeat with the remaining batter, stacking the cooked crepes, separating them with strips of wax paper, and keeping the plate covered with the damp towel.

When all the crepes are cooked, cover with plastic wrap and refrigerate until ready to use. (The crepes can be made up to 2 days ahead. They can also be frozen, for up to a month, wrapped well in plastic or in a zippered plastic bag.)

Make the filling:

In a 10-inch skillet, heat the oil over medium heat. Add the onion, carrot, and celery. Cook, stirring frequently, until the vegetables are very tender, about 10 minutes.

Add the sausage, breaking up the meat with the side of a wooden spoon as you mix and cook until the sausage is fully cooked, about 8 minutes.

In the bowl of a food processor, combine the spinach, the sausage mixture, the chicken, cheese, nutmeg, and salt and pepper. Pulse the mixture until very fine, stirring it once or twice.

Turn the filling out into a mixing bowl. Taste, and, with a wooden spoon, stir in more salt and pepper if necessary. Set aside.

Make the sauce:

In a medium saucepan, over medium heat, melt the butter, then stir in the flour with a wooden spoon; cook for 2 minutes.

Remove from the heat, and when the mixture stops bubbling, stir in the stock.

Return the pan to the heat and, stirring constantly, bring to a simmer.

Add the nutmeg, pepper, and cheese. Stir well.

Stir in the cream, then taste for salt, adding more to taste if necessary. Set aside.

Preheat the oven to 375 degrees.

Spread about ¾ cup of the sauce on the bottom of a large baking dish or gratin pan. Place about ¼ cup of the filling on one crepe, arranging it into a long sausage shape. Roll the bottom of the crepe over the filling and keep rolling to enclose entirely.

Place the rolled crepes in the pan. When the pan has been filled, top with the remaining sauce.

Bake for about 20 minutes, or until the sauce is bubbling.

Serve immediately.

STORK CLUB CHICKEN BURGERS

These were a favorite of Irving Berlin, according to Ralph Blumenthal's *Stork Club*. The recipe he gives, however, is pretty rough. This is my interpretation.

Makes 8 burgers

They were served with a simple tomato sauce at the Stork Club, but their elegant crumb crusts become soggy from the sauce. I think they are better without. I have made these burgers with ground turkey with equal success.

2 pounds ground chicken or turkey

2 tablespoons (¼ stick) unsalted butter, at room temperature

½ cup heavy cream

⅛ teaspoon freshly ground nutmeg

¼ to ½ teaspoon freshly ground black pepper

1 teaspoon fine salt

6 tablespoons (¾ stick) unsalted butter, melted

3 slices firm white bread, made into fine crumbs in a blender

Place the chicken or turkey in a large mixing bowl. Break it up a little.

Squish the 2 tablespoons of room-temperature butter in your hand, letting it ooze out of your fingers. With your clean hand, pour in the cream, and sprinkle on the nutmeg, pepper, and salt.

With your butter hand, knead and mix all the ingredients into the chicken. When thoroughly mixed, there should still be bits of butter visible. If they are large-ish, squish them smaller with your fingers, but do not attempt to make the mixture totally homogenous.

Form the meat into 8 burgers or cakes. Set aside on a platter. They can be made ahead and refrigerated, covered with plastic, for up to 1 day.

When ready to cook, pour the 6 tablespoons of melted butter into a shallow bowl just large enough to dip the burger. Spread the fresh breadcrumbs on a plate.

Dip the burgers in the melted butter. Then, dredge them in the fresh crumbs, making sure to coat the burgers thoroughly, even on the edges.

Arrange the burgers on a cold broiler tray. Broil 6 to 7 inches from the heat for 5 minutes. After three minutes, reverse the pan if the burgers are not browning evenly.

Remove the pan from the broiler. Carefully turn the burgers over. Broil the second side for another 5 minutes. They should be well browned and cooked through. They will feel firm to the touch.

Serve immediately.

JAMES BEARD'S ONION TEA SANDWICHES

These simple and sort of silly tea sandwiches may be Beard's best-known recipe. He and his partners in Hors d'Oeuvre Inc., Bill and Irma Rhodes, must have made and sold thousands of them in the few years they were in business. They're always the hit of a cocktail party, and besides Beard's New York City society clientele some very famous people enjoyed them. Maida Heatter, the doyenne of baking writers and daughter of Gabriel Heatter, the legendary radio news broadcaster (the Walter Cronkite/Tom Brokaw of his day), once told Beard that her parents' home was never without them. "During World War II there were many important people in government from both London and Washington in and out of their home constantly. The onion sandwiches were always ready. I wish you could have heard the raves."

In 1937, when Beard and Bill and Erma Rhodes were catering these, sliced bread was still a novelty convenience item and the women's magazines were giving recipes for crustless tea sandwiches fashioned into amusing shapes with cookie cutters. The commercial New York City bakeries—Silvercup, Bond, and Wonder Bread—published booklets on the subject. In that light, Beard's recipe is truly of its day, except that for his rich clients he changed the white bread to brioche.

Here are, word for word, Beard's directions from *Menus for Entertaining,* first published in 1963:

Cut brioche or challah (or in a pinch, good white bread) into thin slices, and cut these into rounds with a cutter. Peel and slice thinly about 6 or 8 small white onions. Chop finely 1 large bunch of parsley or more. Have a bowl of mayonnaise at hand. Spread the rounds of bread with mayonnaise, top half of them with slices of onion and salt them well. Top these with the remaining rounds, and press them together firmly. Roll the edges in mayonnaise and then chopped parsley. Chill in the refrigerator several hours before serving.

These are my notes on the above:

Good, firm white bread works better than very rich brioche and challah, which toughen at the edges when punched with a cookie cutter.

Make sure to use cookie cutters with sharp edges, or you will compress the edges. A 2-inch round cutter is about right. If the sandwiches are larger than that they become hard to eat gracefully.

The bread should be no more than ¼-inch thick, thinner if possible.

The point of "small" onions is that the diameter of the onion slices should be about the same as the bread rounds.

I don't find pressing the edges of the bread together to be necessary.

What is necessary is to get plenty of mayonnaise on the edges of the sandwich. Hold the sandwiches between thumb and forefinger and roll them in the mayonnaise.

Chilling in the refrigerator is not necessary, in fact it can make some breads toughen. To hold for up to several hours before serving, just wrap the serving platter in plastic wrap, or cover loosely with a barely damp towel.

GINO COFACCI'S HAZELNUT DACQUOISE

Who knows what happened between Gino Cofacci and James Beard? Who knows what makes lovers become merely dependents? Although he made disparaging remarks about Cofacci to friends, Beard was devoted to him, in his way, to the end. They had lived together for thirty-something years when Beard died. He allowed Cofacci to remain on the second floor of his house, along with their dog, a pug named Percy.

Cofacci—trained as an architect—earned some pocket money by baking a certain mocha-hazelnut dacquoise, which he sold to Beard's friends: Leon Lianides at the Coach House and Alfredo Viazzi at Trattoria da Alfredo. With a little publicity, Cofacci's dacquoise set off a rage for the dessert in New York City. The fad never became as intense or long lasting as crème brûlée, or tiramisu, but in the 1970s it was everywhere.

This recipe is adapted from the version Cofacci gave in the May 1978 issue of *Cooking*, which was published by Cuisinart. The magazine was a sort of vanity vehicle or, you might say, marketing device for George Sondheimer, the creator of the Cuisinart food processor, the first of its kind on this side of the Atlantic. (Sondheimer modeled his appliance after the French Robot-Coup.)

Serves 10

This is a masterpiece of contrasting textures and flavors. The mocha buttercream is silky smooth and a bit bitter, which plays against the crispness and sweetness of the meringue layers. That both are under a bittersweet chocolate frosting is an added attraction. You may well have a little extra meringue batter after piping out three layers. If so, bake it off in a layer and use it, crumbled, to press into the buttercream-covered sides of the dessert.

For the dry ingredients:
⅔ cup (3 ½ ounces) blanched hazelnuts
⅔ cup (3 ½ ounces) blanched almonds
1 cup sugar
2 tablespoons cornstarch

For the wet ingredients:
7 egg whites, at room temperature
Pinch of salt
¼ teaspoon cream of tartar
3 ½ tablespoons sugar
2 teaspoons vanilla extract
⅛ teaspoon almond extract

For the mocha buttercream:
3 tablespoons powdered espresso coffee
1 tablespoon hot water
¾ cup milk
4 egg yolks
1 ¼ cups confectioners' sugar
1 ½ cups (3 sticks) unsalted butter,
    at room temperature

For the chocolate icing:
6 ounces semisweet chocolate
½ cup sour cream

Prepare the dry ingredients:

In a food processor, pulsing the motor, chop the nuts to the texture of coarse sand. If necessary, shake the nuts in a strainer to remove any powder. Discard the powder or set aside for another purpose, although you should have very little, if any.

Preheat the oven to 350 degrees.

Spread the chopped nuts on a baking sheet, and toast in the preheated oven until golden, about 10 minutes. Set aside to cool.

In a large mixing bowl, combine the nuts with the sugar. Sprinkle the cornstarch over the mixture, sieving it into the bowl if it is lumpy. Mix thoroughly. Put the mixture in the freezer to cool it quickly.

Prepare the pans:

Using the bottom of a 9-inch round cake pan as a guide, cut out three 9-inch rounds of parchment paper. The layers can be baked directly on the backs of the cake pans. Or, line a baking sheet with parchment paper and trace 9-inch circles on the paper using the bottom of a cake pan as a guide.

Prepare the wet ingredients:

Use a stand mixer with the whisk attachment. Make sure the bowl and whisk are absolutely clean and dry. Start beating the egg whites at low speed until foam appears, about one minute.

Beat in the salt and cream of tartar. Gradually increase the speed, and beat until the whites are the consistency of mayonnaise. While still beating, gradually sprinkle the sugar over the egg whites. Add the vanilla and almond extract and continue beating on high speed until the mixture is stiff and shiny but not dry.

Make the layers:

Preheat the oven to 275 degrees.

Sprinkle the dry ingredients over the beaten whites. With a rubber spatula, carefully fold the dry ingredients into the whites until thoroughly combined.

Fill a pastry bag with the batter. Pipe a spiral design on each 9-inch parchment round until the circles are completely covered. Smooth out the tops with a metal spatula.

Bake on the backs of cake pans or on baking sheets, in the preheated oven, for 1 hour and 15 minutes, or until firm to the touch and tan to light brown. Cool on a rack.

When the meringues are cooled (about 10 minutes), peel off the paper.

(If the meringues didn't turn out with even edges, they can be trimmed: Place the baked layer over the bottom of the cake pan on which you based it. Use a serrated blade knife to slowly and carefully trim to size.)

Make the mocha buttercream:

Dissolve the instant coffee in the hot water.

In a small, heavy saucepan, bring the milk to a boil. Remove from the heat, and set aside.

By hand, in a small bowl with a wire whisk, beat the egg yolks with sugar just until combined. Gradually add some of the scalded milk, then pour the mixture into the small saucepan with the remaining hot milk. Cook over medium-low heat, stirring constantly with a wooden spoon, until the mixture has thickened and coats the spoon. (This would now be called a crème anglaise.)

Pour the hot crème anglaise into the bowl of a stand mixer. Using the whisk attachment, beat at a high speed until the bottom of the bowl is only warm to the touch. Reduce speed to medium, and gradually add the butter.

When the buttercream is smooth, and with the mixer still beating, add the dissolved coffee powder. Beat until blended.

Make the chocolate icing:

In a heavy saucepan over low heat, or over simmering water, melt the chocolate. Add the sour cream, and stir until smooth. Set aside.

Assemble the dacquoise:

Spread the buttercream between the three meringue layers and around the sides. Cover the top with the chocolate icing. If desired, press any extra, baked meringue, crumbled, into the buttercream on the sides.

Sprinkle confectioners' sugar over the top, if desired.

Refrigerate for at least 2 hours before serving.

LINDY'S CHEESECAKE

This is the genuine article, the very cheesecake recipe over which Nathan Detroit made a bet with Sky Masterson in the Broadway musical *Guys and Dolls*, the one whose name even today is world renowned. However, in its 1930s heyday, Lindy's cheesecake was not necessarily always the most famous in New York City. Reuben's cheesecake was incredibly famous, and many other restaurants featured famous cheesecakes. Lindy's recipe has come down to us, I think, because Leo Linderman understood the value of publicity and shared the recipe. One of those customers who asked for the recipe was Duncan Hines, who published it in 1955 in *Duncan Hines's Food Odyssey*. As the nation's first legitimate national restaurant critic, Hines had a huge following. He traveled from coast to coast inspecting the hygiene in kitchens and eating and evaluating food and service. "As I write this," he told readers of *Odyssey*, "gold is worth somewhere around thirty-two dollars an ounce. Lindy's cheesecake at forty-five cents a slice is somewhat less expensive, yet a good many people who've eaten at Lindy's famous Broadway restaurant consider it pure gold."

Makes one 9-inch cake

The crust, though authentic, is not necessary to make a wonderful, creamy cheesecake. And since it is difficult to assemble, I often make the cake without the crust—and with great success.

For the crust:
- 1 (2-inch) piece of vanilla bean
- 1 cup all-purpose flour
- ¼ cup sugar
- 1 teaspoon freshly grated lemon zest
- 1 egg yolk
- 8 tablespoons (1 stick) unsalted butter, cut into bits
- ¼ teaspoon salt

For the filling:
- 2 ½ pounds cream cheese, at room temperature
- 1 ¾ cups sugar
- 3 tablespoons all-purpose flour
- 1 ½ teaspoons freshly grated orange zest
- 1 ½ teaspoons freshly grated lemon zest
- ½ teaspoon vanilla extract
- 5 whole eggs
- 2 egg yolks
- ¼ cup heavy cream

Make the crust:

Preheat the oven to 400 degrees.

Split the vanilla bean lengthwise, and scrape the seeds into a bowl. Stir in the flour, the sugar, and the lemon zest. Add the egg yolk, the butter, and the salt, and knead the mixture until it forms a dough. Flatten the dough into a round, and chill it, wrapped in wax paper, for 1 hour.

Remove the sides of a 9-inch springform pan.

Oil the bottom of the pan lightly, and cover it with a ⅛-inch layer of the dough.

Bake the bottom crust in the middle of the preheated oven for 10 to 12 minutes, or until it is golden. Remove from the oven, let cool 10 minutes, then chill it in the refrigerator for at least 30 minutes.

Butter the sides of the pan, reattach them to the

bottom (the bottom has the baked crust), and cover the sides with a ⅛-inch layer of the remaining dough. Set aside.

To make the filling:

Preheat the oven to 550 degrees.

In a stand mixer (or in a large bowl, using a hand-held mixer), beat the cream cheese with the sugar, the flour, the zests, and the vanilla until the mixture is smooth.

Beat in the whole eggs and the egg yolks, one at a time, beating lightly after each addition.

When all the eggs have been incorporated, stir in the cream.

Pour the filling into the prepared crust and bake the cheesecake in the middle of the preheated oven for 12 minutes.

Reduce the heat to 200 degrees. Bake the cheesecake for 1 hour more.

Let the cheesecake cool in the pan on a rack. Still in the pan, chill it overnight.

Serve cool, but not well-chilled: Remove the cake from the refrigerator about an hour before serving.

JUNIOR'S CHEESECAKE

Truth be told, this recipe, from *Welcome to Junior's*, the restaurant's own cookbook, makes an even better cake than the one you can buy there, as great as that may be. That's understandable. Junior's now ships cakes all over the country. You can imagine that making one at a time with love is preferable.

Makes one 9-inch cake, about 2 ½- inches high

Make sure to have the cream cheese at room temperature. It will beat up lighter and higher and still produce a fabulously rich and creamy cheesecake. The thin sponge cake layer at the bottom is a distinctive feature of Junior's cheesecake, but if you don't want to bother making it, you can bake the cheesecake without it. If omitting the sponge cake layer, place a round of baking parchment on the bottom of the pan to ease removal of the cake.

1 Thin Sponge Cake Layer for Cheesecake
   (recipe follows on page 279)

Junior's can customize many of its cakes for special occasions.

For the filling:

4 (8-ounce) packages cream cheese (the regular kind, not light or Neufchatel) (divided)

1 ⅔ cups sugar (divided)

¼ cup cornstarch

1 tablespoon pure vanilla extract

2 extra-large eggs

¾ cup heavy cream

Make the sponge cake as the recipe directs.

Make the cream cheese filling:

Place one (8-ounce) package of the cream cheese, ⅓ cup of the sugar, and the cornstarch in a large bowl. Beat with an electric mixer on low until creamy, about 3 minutes. Then beat in the remaining three packages of cream cheese.

Increase the mixer speed to high and beat in the remaining 1 ⅓ cups of the sugar. Then beat in the vanilla. Add the eggs, one at a time, beating the batter well after each one. Blend in the heavy cream. Mix the filling only until completely blended. Be careful not to overmix the batter.

Gently spoon the cheese filling on top of the baked sponge cake layer.

Place the springform pan in a large shallow pan containing hot water that comes about 1 inch up the sides of the pan. Bake the cheesecake until the center barely jiggles when you shake the pan, about 1 hour.

Cool the cake on a wire rack for 1 hour. Then, leaving the cake in the pan, cover it with plastic wrap and refrigerate until it's completely cold, at least 4 hours or overnight.

Remove the sides of the springform pan. Slide the cake off the bottom of the pan onto a serving plate. (Or, if you wish, simply leave the cake on the removable bottom of the pan and place it on a serving plate.) If any cake is left over, cover it with plastic wrap and store for up to a week in the refrigerator.

THIN SPONGE CAKE LAYER FOR CHEESECAKE

Makes one 9-inch sponge cake, about ¾ inch high, enough for 1 cheesecake

Watch this cake carefully while it's baking. There's not much batter, so it needs only about 10 minutes of baking—just enough time for the cake to turn light golden and set on the top. The cake should not brown on top.

½ cup sifted cake flour

1 teaspoon baking powder

Pinch of salt

3 extra-large eggs, separated

⅓ cup plus 2 tablespoons sugar (divided)

1 teaspoon pure vanilla extract

3 drops lemon extract (optional)

3 tablespoons unsalted butter, melted

¼ teaspoon cream of tartar

Preheat the oven to 350 degrees.

Generously butter a 9-inch springform pan.

Into a medium bowl, sift together the flour, baking powder, and salt. Set aside.

In a large bowl, beat the egg yolks with an electric mixer on high for 3 minutes. Then, with the mixer still running, gradually add ⅓ cup of the sugar, and continue beating until thick light-yellow ribbons form in the bowl, about 5 minutes more.

Beat in the vanilla and lemon extracts.

Sift the flour mixture over the batter, and stir it in by hand until no more white flecks appear. Then blend in the butter.

In a clean bowl, using clean dry beaters, beat the egg whites and cream of tartar together on high until frothy. Less than a tablespoon at a time, add the remaining 2 tablespoons of sugar and continue beating until stiff peaks form.

Stir about ⅓ cup of the whites into the batter, then gently fold in the remaining whites (don't worry if a few white specks remain).

Gently spoon the batter into the pan.

Bake the cake just until the center springs back when lightly touched, only about 10 minutes (watch carefully). Let the cake cool in the pan on a wire rack while you continue making the cheesecake filling. Do not remove the cake from the pan.

HAUTE CUISINE AND HAUGHTY ATTITUDE

FRENCH USED TO BE THE BE-ALL, END-ALL CUISINE IN NEW YORK CITY. If it wasn't French, how good could it be? As in most of the rest of the Western world since the eighteenth century, French cooking and food presentation has been considered the best, the most refined, a model for civilized society.

OPPOSITE: The famous murals at La Côte Basque before it closed in 2004.

Delmonico's set the high-style pace when it opened as a full-scale restaurant in lower Manhattan in 1830 (see page 47). Even before then, however, the French-style cafe was where businessmen met each other in the downtown (Wall Street) commercial district. Until Prohibition began, Delmonico's remained the standard bearer, continually moving north, following the rich uptown. Then the Volstead Act killed it off, along with all its Gallic competitors—the other restaurants that depended on wine in the pot and, more importantly, wine sales at the table. During Prohibition, drinking hardly stopped; it actually increased. But fine dining in the grand French manner became virtually nonexistent. Some small, more modest French restaurants opened in the city, mostly operated by the kitchen and dining room staffs of the now defunct dining palaces. The Divan Parisien (see page 266), with a staff from Delmonico's, was chief among them. As Arianne and Michael Batterberry say in *On the Town in New York*, "A horde of Henri's and Pierre's and Robert's could be observed sweeping through the city's streets like expeditionary forces."

Then came the Depression. It didn't kill off high living, or dining out, as there was still plenty of money on Fifth and Park Avenues, but at this time the country was looking inward, not to Europe.

The New York World's Fair of 1939, whose theme was "The World of Tomorrow," brought optimism and French food back. The fair was both an economic and a culinary boost at the end of the Depression, and it spawned a French food revival spearheaded by a restaurant called Le Pavillon. By then, war had been declared in Europe and the fair's French-pavilion restaurant staff decided to stay in New York City to ply us with French cuisine in a haughty atmosphere presided over by owner and maître d' Henri Soulé, the snobbiest of French snobs. Only the rich, powerful social elite could go to Le Pavillon. The same could be said of the Brussels, a restaurant operated by the staff from the Belgian pavilion, also stranded in New York City because of the war.

By the end of the war, New York City was the capital of the world, and during and after it, French refugees opened bistros in Manhattan, mainly on the far west side of midtown, near the Hudson River piers; it is said that many of the owners opened shop and lived there because that's where they landed when they arrived on the ocean liners. All these restaurants had pretty much the same menu: pork pâté, onion soup, escargot (snails), frog's legs, coq au vin, beef bourguignon, tripe à la mode de Caen, veal medallions with mushrooms . . . you get the picture. Tout Va Bien at 311 West Fifty-first Street is the last of these bistros to survive, and it is still popular with tourists, although ignored by all but old-timer New Yorkers who may remember that Laurence Olivier and Vivian Leigh had assignations at a rear table while they performed on Broadway in the 1940s. Other similar restaurants in the neighborhood were the Café des Sports, Napoleon, Maude Chez Elle, Belle Munière, and Restaurant Robert.

During the 1940s and 1950s, the East Side of Manhattan also had its own cadre of small French restaurants. Le Café Chambord was at 803 Third Avenue near Forty-ninth Street and was considered to be one of the best of the lot. Le Coq Rouge, on East Fifty-sixth and Fifth Avenue, was the haunt of debutantes, their parents, and their beaus. Voisin, at 375 Park Avenue, attracted the same crowd. L'Aiglon, on Fifty-fifth Street and Fifth Avenue, attracted a who's who of Park Avenue. In 1955 La Caravelle opened on Fifty-fifth Street near Fifth Avenue; it closed in May 2004 but remained the grande dame of New York City's French restaurants until the end. "Madison Avenue," then synonymous with the advertising business, frequented the East Side French restaurants for lunch. It was at these restaurants that the two-martini lunch was indulged.

The famous Restaurant Marguery, at 270 Park Avenue, was named for the Parisian place that created the famous Sole Marguery, which in turn was named after the Marquis de Marguery, a famous eighteenth-century French gastronome. It was grand, with Louis XVI furnishing and details. In addition to the eponymous fish dish, the Marguery was known for its house appetizer, Canapé Marchisio, which sounds more Italian than French because the owner was Italian.

Many French restaurants of the post–World War II era were French in name and menu language only. The menu would list *huitres* instead of oysters. *Agneau de printemps* was roast lamb any way you pronounced it. *Ris de veau financière* were the same sweetbreads with mushrooms served at bar mitvahs. Some of the French restaurants were operated by Italians, or by Eastern European Jews. The famous Restaurant Crillon, on Forty-eighth Street near Fifth Avenue, was owned by Otto J. Baumgarten, a Viennese who could not resist putting Wiener Backhuhn, a breaded and fried chicken cutlet, on his menu. Meanwhile, old-time, classic dishes created in New York City by French chefs were now distant enough from their origins to be passed off as authentically French: Lobster à la Newberg (page 58), Chicken à la King, and Vichysoisse (page 209).

Some of the speakeasies of Prohibition days evolved into somewhat French restaurants. The Colony, owned by an Italian, Gene Cavallero (see page 246), boasted Frenchified dishes, as did Jack and Charlie's 21, owned by cousins who were Jewish. Both restaurants dazzled their celebrated regulars by flambéing food tableside, but their French credentials amounted to having a Frenchman in the kitchen. (The Colony's successor, Le Cirque, has a French name and always a French chef, but it is owned by an Italian, the Tuscan Sirio Maccioni, and serves Italian and contemporary Continental dishes mixed in with the French.)

Then, in 1961, along came André Surmain (née Sussman, a French Jew) and his pal, James Beard. They realized how hackneyed and poor French food was in New York City—the sauces were heavy, the ingredients often canned or frozen or simply not good—and they decided to change all that. They hired a young chef from Alsace, André Soltner, and opened Lutèce. Soltner's mandate was to use only fresh ingredients, in season, and to cook only genuinely French food—regional food, simpler food than was then in vogue—not the showy food that was popularized at Le Pavillon.

Lutèce remained New York City's most famous and popular French restaurant long after Surmain sold out to Soltner and until Soltner retired in 1994. However, a new French movement, La Nouvelle Cuisine, hit the city in a big way in the late 1970s. The new French food was touted as being lighter and more modern than classic cuisine. The presentations became more studied, incorporating Japanese-style restraint and careful placement of the dishes' elements. Color and artfulness began to supercede flavor. During the nouvelle period, the china plates became larger and the portions became smaller. Instead of flour-thickened sauces, food was dressed with butter emulsions. New, non-European ingredients were introduced. New Yorkers were stunned by the new food. Always loving the new and novel, we couldn't get enough of it, figuratively and literally. I remember going to a highly touted nouvelle cuisine restaurant and, on the way home in a taxi, my friends insisted we stop at McDonald's: They were still hungry.

Daniel Boulud's several French restaurants are considered among the city's best.

One famously enduring proponent of nouvelle cuisine is Jean-Georges Vongerichten, who came to New York City in 1988 to work under three-star Michelin chef Louis Outhier at Lafayette, the new restaurant in the Drake Hotel on Fifty-sixth Street near Park Avenue. His use of vegetable juices and purees as sauces was new, and they were really light. It was at Lafayette that Vongerichten also came up with a dessert that has become inescapable—the hot, molten chocolate cake. Vongerichten continues to reinvent himself every few years. His flagship restaurant is in the Trump World Tower at Columbus Circle, but he owns several other restaurants in New York City, around the country, and around the world.

By the late 1980s, nouvelle cuisine had been discredited, but it had an enduring impact. It made celebrities of French chefs—Bocuse, Troisgros, Guérard. These are all names that are still bandied about with reverence, which encouraged young American men and women to look at cooking as a respectable and potentially lucrative profession, and it opened American minds to the creative possibilities of cooking. Although it is often held up to ridicule these days, without La Nouvelle Cuisine there would be no New American cuisine.

Today, French food in New York City is often more exciting than it is in Paris—of course, this the opinion of a chauvinistic New Yorker. Daniel Boulud is certainly considered one of the foremost French chefs in the world, even though his various operations are strictly in the United States: New York City and Palm Beach, Florida. American chefs, who are trained mainly in classic French technique, produce French-style food with local ingredients. Italian is actually New York City's favorite food today—no French restaurant can be without a pasta dish—but now that we understand how informal and delicious French regional and bistro food can be, bistros are proliferating all over the city. Steak-frites reigns. Onion soup with melted cheese is as ubiquitous as chicken soup with matzoh balls used to be.

HENRI SOULÉ'S LEGACY

Henri Soulé was the "showman, snob, perfectionist, martinet, conman, wooer and wood master of haute cuisine," as restaurant critic Gael Greene called him in a profile of his internationally famous restaurant, Le Pavillon, that ran in the *New York Herald Tribune* Sunday magazine in 1965, the year before Soulé died. (It was the food piece that launched Greene's career. And the *Tribune* Sunday supplement was to mutate into the independent *New York* magazine.)

At age thirty-six, Soulé came to New York City for the World's Fair of 1939, where he served as a captain at the much-hailed restaurant of the French pavilion. However, while he and the staff of the restaurant, which included eighteen-year-old Pierre Franey working in the kitchen, were in Flushing Meadow, war broke out in Europe. The European situation was very bad when the fair closed, so Soulé and company decided to stay in New York City and dazzle the locals with high-style French cuisine. The city had not had a really top-flight French restaurant since Delmonico's and its ilk had closed in the early 1920s, when Prohibition started (see page 47), and New York City had an audience for French food, the money to buy the best, and just enough insecurity to take Soulé's often abusive behavior as something it deserved. He opened at 5 East Fifty-fifth Street, strategically located to be convenient to both the business luncheon crowd and the Park Avenue and Fifth Avenue residences of the city's rich and powerful, including "the ladies who lunch." Later he moved the restaurant into the Ritz Towers at 111 East Fifty-seventh Street. But that's another story. Keep reading.

The restaurant was an instant success. Soulé was a perfectionist. He also knew who was important and who was not. If you were not, he followed the lead of Sherman Billingsley at the Stork Club and Gene Cavallero at the Colony and seated you in "Siberia." Getting the right table at Le Pavillon was as much a status symbol as living at the right address.

Aside from the social aspects of the restaurant, which should not be underestimated, Le Pavillon was often called the best French restaurant in America, and, according to Gael Greene, occasionally "the only French restaurant in America." Craig Claiborne agreed that there was no better French restaurant in town, and that it was "the principal training ground for hundreds of chefs, waiters and the like." Craig's eventual friend, neighbor, and writing partner, Pierre Franey, was one of those chefs. Soulé said he considered Franey like a son, but in 1960, when Soulé reduced the kitchen staff's working hours from forty—with five hours' overtime— to thirty-five, Franey and his staff walked off the job. On March 3, the story made the front page of the *New York Times* and included a reproduction of the restaurant's menu. That's how important the restaurant was.

A "typical" meal at Le Pavillon, according to Craig Claiborne, started with "vodka and fresh caviar, followed perhaps by a mousse of imported fresh Dover sole with lobster sauce, a Chateaubriand with a Madeira and truffle sauce, and a gossamer soufflé made with out-of-season berries. Such a meal is the quintessence of dining well and the cost at Le Pavillon would be $50 to $60, depending on the choice of wine."

In 1958, Soulé decided he needed more space and moved the restaurant to Fifty-seventh Street. He then opened La Côte Basque in the Fifty-fifth Street premises. Rumor had it that he wanted to set up his mistress, the coat-check girl at Le Pavillon, a stern woman called Madame Henriette, with her own restaurant. He hinted at this when he told Gael Greene that La Côte Basque was his "contribution to illicit romance," although he explained that what he meant was that he needed two restaurants so that his male customers could take their wives to one and their mistresses to the other. He also called La Côte Basque his "Pavillon for the poor," which, of course, it was not. It was very expensive, although, with its gaily colored murals of the Basque countryside, it wasn't as austere as Le Pavillon, and it served some regional French dishes, such as bouillabaisse and cassoulet.

Madame Henriette ran the restaurant as autocratically as Soulé did Le Pavillon. In the early 1970s, she was one of the last restaurateurs to refuse admission to women wearing pants, even though pants with tunic tops were the style of the day.

La Côte Basque also gained notoriety when Truman Capote revealed some secrets of his socialite friends in a catty piece called "Answered Prayers" in *Esquire* magazine. It was supposedly an excerpt from his novel in progress, but after his death it was revealed that he had never gone further than that one piece. The loss of the society friends that he betrayed destroyed him. He became a sad and drunken caricature of himself on Johnny Carson's *Tonight Show*.

La Côte Basque changed hands in 1979. It was bought by chef Jean-Jacques Rachou, whose kitchen continued to turn out classic and contemporary haute cuisine, as well as French regional specialties. He trained numerous chefs over the years, many of whom became stars

BELOW: Restaurateur Henri Soulé

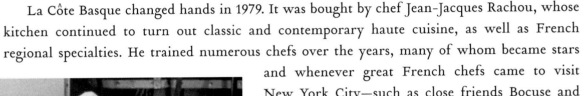

and whenever great French chefs came to visit New York City—such as close friends Bocuse and Guérard—Rachou's dining room was on their itinerary. They all considered him the grand master in New York City.

In 1995 Rachou moved the restaurant one block east to 60 West Fifty-fifth Street, pretty much recreating the look of the old restaurant, reinstalling the famous murals, and filling up the room with huge flower displays, as always. But, La Côte Basque closed in March 2004. The closing was big enough news to merit a *New York Times* feature. The day of such grand restaurants had passed, and as much as Rachou was an innovator—he was, for instance, the first chef in the United States to use the squeegee bottle to decorate plates with sauce, and one of the first

OPPOSITE: The murals at La Caravelle were placed in storage when the restaurant closed in 2004.

to build dishes high on the plate—New Yorkers viewed the restaurant as old-fashioned. That's usually the kiss of death. In place of La Côte Basque, at the same location, Rachou has just opened a brasserie, which is the style of French restaurant New Yorkers, and Americans in general, love now.

BEYOND BAGELS

IF, AS FOOD PHILOSOPHERS SAY, THE GASTRONOMY OF A PLACE CAN BE measured by its interest in bread, then by that criteria alone New York City must be judged the world's greatest gastronomic capital. Nearly every kind of bread in the world is baked in the city—not to mention a good deal of its cake, cookies, and pastries.

OPPOSITE: G. F. Corwin's bakery was, indeed, "Up To Date" in 1904.

In New York City, you can always tell the ethnicity of a neighborhood by checking out the bakeries. To give one vital example, Coney Island Avenue in Brooklyn used to be mainly a street of car repair shops and auto parts houses, but it has now become the shopping street for various ethnic communities. Traveling from where the avenue starts at the south end of Prospect Park to its final intersection at Brighton Beach Avenue (one block from the Atlantic Ocean), there are, in this order, a Mexican tortilla bakery, several Pakistani sweet shops, a kosher bagel bakery, an Eastern European–style Jewish bakery, an Israeli boureka shop, a Turkish bread bakery, a non-kosher bagel bakery, a store that sells kosher Middle Eastern pastries, and several Russian-Ukrainian grocery stores and bakeshops where black breads and poppy seed sweets hold sway.

As many bakeries as New York City has now, however, there used to be more. For most of the twentieth century, every neighborhood had a small bakery, if not several small shops (what we would now call artisan bakeries). And there were larger, more commercial bakeries, too, with fleets of trucks that delivered delicious baked goods door to door. The city's corner bakeshops didn't start to proliferate until the end of the nineteenth century, but a deep interest in bread and cake dates back to Dutch days.

The first laws governing baking—indeed, the first laws of any kind—merely required "just weights and good materials." In 1656, however, legislation was passed that required every bakery to bake at least twice a week, and to produce both white loaves and "coarse wheat" bread for both Indians and Christians. In Dutch days, bakers were not allowed to make sweets unless they also sold whole wheat bread. There is a record, in fact, of one baker who was prosecuted for having gingerbread in his window but no coarse bread on his shelves.

The Dutch were fond of sweet cakes and their three chief indulgences were, as Washington Irving described them, "the doughty doughnut, the tender *olykoek* [also spelled *olijkoeck*] and the crisp and crumbling cruller." According to Alice Morse Earle, who in 1897 quoted one of several possible Mrs. Vanderbilts in *Colonial Days in Old New York*, the New Englanders' love of doughnuts could be attested to the fact that they ate them "all the year . . . ," which came from the Pilgrims' soujourn in Holland, where "the English goodwives learned to make doughnuts from the Dutch *vrouws*." But Earle chalks this up to Mrs. Vanderbilt wanting to include doughnuts among "the other triumphs of 'Dutch colonial influence.'" In New Amsterdam and during the century of English colonization, there were also pie vendors, always women, besides the bakeshops.

The English had a sweet tooth, and French-style cafes abounded during the early nineteenth century. Delmonico's began as a patisserie and coffeehouse (see page 47). Places like it were where businessmen met downtown, to conduct their affairs and to take light meals at lunchtime when the residential sections of the city began to be too far uptown to go home for a midday meal. It was the Germans, however, who started arriving in great numbers in the 1840s and were the most formative influence on New York City's modern bakeries. The Germans had a great baking tradition, and they brought with them the knowledge to make their sturdy rye bread and pumpernickel, as well as a myriad of sweet baked desserts. They contributed the city's beloved crumb cake (see page 295), and were most likely responsible for introducing the city to so-called Danish pastries. Although one might well think that Danish pastries are from Denmark, the Danes call them Viennese. They are made with a yeast dough that is layered with butter the same way French puff pastry is made. As sold in New York City's bakeries, they are, at their most basic, filled with cinnamon-sugar and chopped nuts, or more elaborately with fruit jams, baker's cheese (a low-moisture fresh cheese), and, starting in the 1950s, with chocolate. Danish dough is also baked into rings—coffee cake—that are often drizzled with sugar icing or topped with crumbs. The German bakeries also made all sorts of buttercream-filled layer cakes and nut tortes.

The famous Ebinger's retail stores of Brooklyn and Queens, which sold cakes and other confections baked at a central bakery on Bedford Avenue in the Flatbush section of Brooklyn, became the most famous of the German-style bakers. It was such a wholeheartedly German operation that well into the 1950s even the women retail clerks had German accents. After World War II, many Jews refused to purchase cakes from Ebinger's, feeling that the clerks were somehow sympathetic to the Nazis. Ebinger's closed its last retail store in the late 1960s.

Other German bakers, such as Drake's, Cushman's, and Pector's, were famous for home delivery. Somehow a bakery with an Irish name got stuck in that group, too—Dugan's. All of them had trucks that roamed the quiet residential streets of the Bronx, Brooklyn, and Queens. Entenmanns, originally a Brooklyn-based bakery, also started with home-delivery trucks. But when the second generation Entenmanns came home from the war in Europe, they correctly saw that the supermarket and the suburbs were the future. They opened a huge commercial bakery in Bayshore, Long Island, which is still the company's base of operations.

Starting in the 1920s, when a housing boom hit the boroughs, predominantly Jewish neighborhoods, which included large areas of Brooklyn and the Bronx, as well as the Upper West Side of Manhattan, were famous for their bakeries. Then, after World War II, Queens got its share of

Jewish bakeries as that borough became populated by young families. These were not necessarily kosher bakeries, but they always carried the Central and Eastern European specialties that every ethnic group loved by then. Their crusty Kaiser rolls, undoubtedly adopted from the German bakers, became the city's everyday breakfast bread and sandwich vehicle. Until the 1940s, these crusty rolls were even more popular than bagels (see page 118). The Jewish bakeries also baked crusty German-style rye bread covered and studded with caraway seeds or nigella seeds. Before bagels went national in the 1980s, rye bread used to be the bread most associated with New York City, and very different from the fluffy, nearly white stuff that is sold in supermarkets nationally.

The bialy has a special place in the hearts of old-time Jewish New Yorkers, perhaps because it remains relatively unchanged, unlike it's cousin, the bagel, which has become fluffy and overblown. Kossar's Bialystoker Kuchen, at 367 Grand Street on the Lower East Side, opened in 1927 and is the last bakery devoted only to baking bialys. Like bagels, bialys are from Poland. But the flat, chewy, flour-dusted disks with a central indentation housing a scattering of toasted onions are still sold from many of the city's sidewalk coffee carts. And most of the breakfast counters in midtown Manhattan, near the still very Jewish Garment Center and jewelry exchange, split them and butter them or give them a schmear of cream cheese.

Drake's started as a home-delivery Brooklyn bakery.

Gentrification has taken its toll on New York City's bakeries. In Yorkville, the German and Middle European neighborhood on Manhattan's Upper East Side, there used to be bakeries with all sorts of Continental confections, including Hungarian strudel. These shops often had a cafe aspect, too, with tiny tables and chairs at which to enjoy their delicacies. In the Arab neighborhood that borders Brooklyn Heights, on Atlantic Avenue, there used to be several pita ovens, as well as several Middle Eastern pastry shops, including a storefront where you could watch the stretching of phyllo dough into a table-sized, paper-thin sheet. Now there is just one pastry shop and one bread bakery, although the Sahadi Middle Eastern grocery carries pastries and breads baked on less expensive real estate in other areas of the city. In Greenpoint, Brooklyn, young hipsters are starting to push out the Poles. Sushi bars are replacing pierogi restaurants. Still, one Polish bakery has recently become so popular that it has expanded to a full-blown cafe. The old Italian enclaves of Bensonhurst and Bay Ridge are moving across the Verrazano Bridge to Staten Island, and that borough now has more Italian bakeries than most cities in Italy. What is now called the East Village but used to be the northern reaches of the Lower East Side has become one of the artier sections of the city, but venerable Veniero's on First Avenue and Tenth Street, whose ricotta cheesecake is nationally known, is a holdout from when the area was largely Italian. Ditto for Cafe Roma and the touristy Ferrara's on Grand Street, which are among the last vestiges of old Little Italy.

The main Ebinger bakery in Brooklyn

FROM UPPER LEFT CORNER, CLOCKWISE:
Joe Generoso of Bensonhurst's
Royal Crown (Italian) bakery;
old-time New Yorkers have nostalgia for the
simple and disappearing Charlotte Russe;
Polish poppy seed strips at a Greenpoint bakery;
in New York City, challah, the Jewish
Sabbath bread, is even served in Greek diners;
Raven the Cake Man holds a carrot cake
at his bakery in Fort Greene, Brooklyn;
cheese Danish, a New York City breakfast staple;
black and whites at a bakery in the Bronx;
Nesselrode pie

BLACK AND WHITES

On February 3, 1994 (Season 5, Episode Number 77), Jerry Seinfeld, waiting on line in a New York City bakery, used Black and Whites as a metaphor for racial harmony and consequently made these cookie-cakes into a national sensation. Since then, everyone who comes to New York City needs to eat a Black and White. Meanwhile, native New Yorkers laugh to themselves. Black and Whites were never very good, and nowadays they're worse. A few bakeries would bake a tender, vanilla-and-lemon-scented cake, as the one below, but most would bake a dry and tasteless cake. Now they are sold in corner grocery stores.

Not a cookie, but sometimes called a cookie, Black and Whites are made with a stiff cake batter, baked into a mound, free-form on a cookie sheet. The curved top becomes the bottom. The flat bottom becomes the top and gets slicked, harlequin style—half with chocolate, half with vanilla fondant.

No one seems to know who invented the Black and White, or where it was first created. George Greenstein, a second-generation Jewish baker who has devoted his retirement to translating the old New York neighborhood bakery recipes into contemporary home recipes (*Secrets of a Jewish Baker*), feels they must have been invented at the beginning of the twentieth century by a baker looking for yet another way to use his standard yellow cake. They were clever. They caught on. They got copied all over town.

Makes 10 to 12 large cookies or 16 to 18 small ones

I worked on this recipe back in the 1970s when I was a food writer at *Newsday*. Marie Bianco of *Newsday* reworked the recipe slightly in the 1990s. I made a few more slight changes for this book.

1 ⅓ cups granulated sugar
1 cup solid vegetable shortening, at room temperature
½ cup (1 stick) unsalted butter, at room temperature
2 teaspoons light corn syrup
4 eggs, at room temperature
2 ¼ cups cake flour
2 cups all-purpose flour
2 teaspoons baking powder
½ teaspoon salt
⅔ cup milk

2 teaspoons vanilla
¼ teaspoon lemon flavoring
⅛ teaspoon orange flavoring

For vanilla icing:
1 ½ pounds confectioners' sugar, sifted
⅓ cup light corn syrup
¼ cup water
½ teaspoon vanilla extract
    For chocolate icing:
1 recipe vanilla icing
4 ounces semisweet chocolate, melted

Preheat the oven to 400 degrees. Cut parchment paper to cover a large baking sheet. If making large cookies, trace four 4 ½-inch circles on each sheet of parchment. If making smaller cookies, trace four 3 ½-inch circles. Place oven rack in the center of the oven.

In a large bowl, using a hand-held or stand mixer, cream together the sugar, shortening, and butter until light and fluffy.

Reduce speed to medium and add the corn syrup, then the eggs, one at a time, beating after each until just incorporated.

In another large bowl, combine the flours, baking powder, and salt.

On medium speed, beat the dry ingredient mixture into the creamed mixture, alternating with milk, and beginning and ending with dry ingredients. Add vanilla, lemon, and orange flavorings.

To make large cookies, place ½ cup batter in the center of each circle and spread evenly with the back of a spoon or rubber spatula to fill the outline.

Bake one tray at a time for 10 minutes, or until the bottoms are golden.

To make smaller cookies, spread ⅓ cup batter in each circle. Bake one tray at a time, for 8 minutes, or until the bottoms are golden.

To make the vanilla icing, combine the ingredients in the top of a double boiler over barely simmering water. Stir until well combined. The mixture will be thick. Cook to 100 degrees. If too thick, add a few drops of water. Remove from heat; keep icing over hot water.

Turn cookies over and frost one half of the flat side with vanilla icing. You can use a piece of wax paper as a guide for an even line of icing. Using a pastry brush (or paintbrush) instead of a spatula or knife gives the smoothest surface. To keep icing glossy, don't go over it too much. Place on a rack to dry.

To make chocolate icing, add melted chocolate to vanilla icing. Apply the chocolate icing when the vanilla icing dries.

CRUMB CAKE

A few years ago, Williams-Sonoma introduced a mix to make what they call New York Style Crumb Cake. The mix, sold in a can, is made by a family-owned bakery in the Bronx that claims it is "a heritage recipe brought to New York City by German bakers in the late nineteenth century."

This may well be. Certainly, crumb cake is German. But who knew it was particular to New York City? New Yorkers so much take this cake for granted that, until Williams-Sonoma said it was from New York City, we all thought everyone everywhere in America loved Crumb Cake.

I didn't dare doubt Williams-Sonoma, but I decided to do some checking anyhow. First I called Marion Cunningham in San Francisco. The reviser of *The Fannie Farmer Cookbook,* the cooking teacher and writer who has been called the grandmother of American gastronomy, said, she knew about crumb cake, but it wasn't something a West Coast person would crave. It's definitely an East Coast thing. In Kentucky, they'd never even heard of it. "We don't have a bakery culture down here," drawled a friend from Lexington. In Chicago, another friend said it wasn't a bakery item in the Midwest either, but she was familiar with Drake's Coffee Cake. That's when I remembered that Drake's was originally a Brooklyn bakery.

For the topping:

1 cup (2 sticks) unsalted butter

2 ½ cups all-purpose flour

1 ½ cups packed dark brown sugar

½ teaspoon salt

1 ½ teaspoons vanilla extract

2 tablespoons ground cinnamon

For the cake:

2 ¼ cups sifted all-purpose flour

2 teaspoons baking powder

¼ teaspoon baking soda

½ teaspoon salt

10 tablespoons (1 stick plus 2 tablespoons)
   unsalted butter

1 cup superfine sugar

2 eggs

1 teaspoon vanilla extract

1 cup sour cream

Make the topping: Melt the butter in a medium saucepan over low heat. Remove from the heat and let cool for about 5 minutes, but do not allow the butter to become cold.

Add the flour, brown sugar, salt, vanilla, and cinnamon. Stir with a fork until the mixture forms small crumbs. Set aside.

Make the cake:

Preheat the oven to 350 degrees with the rack in the lower third of the oven. Butter a 9-by-13-inch cake pan. Dust the pan with flour, then invert the pan over the kitchen sink and tap to remove excess flour.

Combine the flour, baking powder, baking soda, and salt in a large bowl, then whisk together. Set aside.

Cut the butter into 1-inch pieces. Place them in the large bowl of a stand mixer fitted with beaters or a paddle attachment. Soften the butter on low speed. Increase the speed to medium-high and cream until smooth and light in color, 1 1/2 to 2 minutes.

Add the superfine sugar, 1 tablespoon at a time, taking about 6 to 8 minutes to blend it in well.

Scrape the sides of the bowl occasionally.

Add the eggs, one at a time, at 1-minute intervals, scraping the sides of the bowl as necessary. Beat for about 1 minute longer. Blend in the vanilla.

Reduce the mixer speed to low. Add the flour mixture alternately with the sour cream, starting and ending with the flour. Mix until just incorporated after each addition, scraping the sides of the bowl as necessary. Mix for 10 seconds longer.

Turn the batter into the prepared pan, smoothing the surface with the back of a spoon or rubber spatula.

Take a handful of the crumb mixture and make a fist to press the mixture into a large clump. Then separate into smaller clusters, scattering them on the top of the batter. Repeat until all of the crumbs have been used. There should be enough to coat the cake all over.

Gently pat the crumbs into the batter with the palm of your hand, but do not press hard.

Bake on the lower rack of the oven for 30 minutes, or until the cake is golden brown on top and begins to come away from the sides of the pan.

TEA BISCUITS

What New Yorkers call tea biscuits are really what the English and Irish call scones, and they have been part of our neighborhood-bakery repertoire for as long as anyone remembers. The city's Jewish and German bakers carried on the tea biscuit tradition and put them in the same cases that housed their rugalach and crumb cake (page 295). These days tea biscuits are sold in coffee shops, and even from sidewalk coffee carts, along with crullers (see page 23), doughnuts, buttered or cream-cheese-schmeared bagels, bialys, and crusty seeded rolls. Most tea biscuits today are bigger and sweeter than they were in the old days. But so are muffins and bagels, and too many other foods to mention.

Makes 9 to 12 biscuits

My friend George Greenstein, who is a retired second-generation baker and the author of *Secrets of a Jewish Baker,* provided this recipe, along with some others for New York City bakery items. As he notes, tea biscuits taste best when served warm, but they can be kept for several days in a bread box or plastic bag and reheated. They freeze well, too: Reheat them, still frozen and individually wrapped in tinfoil, in a 350-degree oven until heated through. If you defrost them first, you can split them and lightly toast them. Make sure you use a sharp-edged cookie cutter or fine-rimmed drinking glass to cut the biscuits. If the dough gets pinched at the edge, the biscuits will not rise properly.

3 cups all-purpose flour
6 tablespoons sugar
4 tablespoons (½ stick) unsalted butter or
    vegetable shortening
1 ½ tablespoons baking powder
½ teaspoon baking soda

½ teaspoon salt
⅓ cup nonfat dry milk
1 egg, beaten
¾ cup dried currants or raisins (optional)
1 egg, beaten together with 1 to 2 teaspoons
    water, for egg wash

In a large bowl, combine the flour and sugar. Mix well. Cut or rub in the butter until the mixture resembles coarse meal. Add the baking powder, baking soda, salt, and dry milk and gently stir to distribute. Add 1 cup cold water and the egg. Stir to mix, then add the currants, if using, and stir until all the flour is absorbed.

Lightly dust your hands with flour. Turn the dough out onto a floured work surface and knead only until it all comes together. The less kneading, the more tender the biscuit.

Preheat the oven to 400 degrees. Lightly grease a baking sheet.

On a clean, floured surface, press or roll out the dough ½ to ¾ inch thick. Cut out with a 2 ½-inch-diameter biscuit cutter or the rim of a sharp-edged drinking glass. Knead the scraps together, roll out, and cut more biscuits. You should have 9 to 12 rounds.

Place the rounds evenly on the prepared baking sheet. Brush the tops with the beaten egg mixture. Let dry for a few minutes, then brush a second time.

Bake until well browned, about 15 minutes. Serve warm.

BLACKOUT CAKE

I consider my sister and myself the world experts on Blackout Cake; when we were teenagers and didn't have dates on a Saturday night we would consume an entire cake. The taste is still fresh in our memories. It was Ebinger's most famous chocolate cake—in fact the Brooklyn bakery's most famous cake of any kind.

Word of this sensational cake—dark, moist layers both filled and frosted with cool, shimmery chocolate pudding—has since spread from coast to coast. There are plenty of restaurants and bakeries outside of New York City that make a facsimile. Recipes for Blackout Cake, or Brooklyn Chocolate Cake, Brooklyn Decadence Cake, or Chocolate Pudding Cake, appear in cookbooks and magazines. None in my vast experience come close to the original.

The following formula pleased my sister, however. It also got the go-ahead from other New Yorkers who had strong memories of the cake. Like me. The easily mixed and cooked pudding is based on one developed by Lynn Stallworth for her version of Blackout Cake in *The Brooklyn Cookbook*. The fine crumbed cake itself is a recipe developed by Karen Barker, a Brooklyn native, who serves a more richly iced version of Blackout Cake at the Magnolia Café in Chapel Hill, North Carolina, where she is the pastry chef and owner.

Makes one 8-inch, 3-layer cake, serving about 10

The only hard part of this cake is patting on the cake crumbs, and children (or more patient bakers than I) might actually get a kick out of the job. If you want to make the cake in easy stages, instead of in one stressful swoop, the pudding can be made and refrigerated for several days, and the cake is moist enough to keep overnight, wrapped well (after it has thoroughly cooled) in plastic or under a cake dome.

For the pudding filling and frosting:
1 ⅓ cups sugar
4 tablespoons cornstarch
½ teaspoon salt
3 cups whole milk
6 ounces unsweetened chocolate, chopped
2 teaspoons vanilla extract

For the cake layers:
1 ½ cups plus 1 ½ tablespoons bleached
    all-purpose flour
¾ cup unsweetened cocoa (not Dutch process)
2 teaspoons baking soda
½ teaspoon baking powder
½ teaspoon salt
2 cups sugar
2 eggs
½ cup vegetable oil
1 cup buttermilk
1 cup brewed coffee, at room temperature
    (not espresso or a very dark roast)
1 teaspoon vanilla extract

Make the pudding filling and frosting:

In a heavy 2-quart saucepan, combine the sugar, cornstarch, and salt. Gradually add the milk, mixing thoroughly with a wire whisk. Add the chocolate.

Place over medium heat and cook, stirring constantly, until the mixture thickens and bubbles; continue to cook for 3 minutes.

Remove from the heat and stir in the vanilla.

Pour into a medium bowl and put plastic wrap or wax paper directly on the surface of the pudding, to prevent a skin from forming.

Chill pudding for at least 8 hours, or up to 2 days.

Make the cake layers:

Preheat the oven to 350 degrees. Butter two 8-inch cake pans. Line the bottoms with parchment, and butter the parchment. Through a fine sieve, dust the pans with cocoa. Tap out the excess and set aside.

Sift together the flour, cocoa, baking soda, baking powder, and salt; set aside.

In a mixer with a whisk attachment, beat the sugar and eggs at high speed until thick but still grainy, about 4 minutes. Reduce to medium speed, and beat in the vegetable oil. At low speed, alternately add the flour mixture and the buttermilk, then stir in the coffee and vanilla.

Divide the batter evenly between the prepared pans.

Bake for 40 minutes, or until a cake tester inserted in the center comes out clean. Let the layers cool in their pans for 15 minutes, then invert them onto a wire rack. Peel off the paper, and let cool completely.

Using a long serrated knife, split each cooled layer in half horizontally.

To make cake crumbs to coat the cake, crumble one layer, using your fingertips to make small pieces, and spread the crumbs on a baking sheet. Dry the crumbs in a 250-degree oven for 15 minutes, stirring twice. Crumble into finer crumbs and bake again for 15 minutes. It may be necessary to do this one more time, to make very dry, fine crumbs. Let cool, then crumble the cake again to make fine crumbs; set aside.

Assemble the cake:

Place one of the layers on a cake plate or stand. To prevent dirtying the plate while assembling the cake, put three folded pieces of wax paper partway underneath the cake, but not all the way under. Spread the chilled pudding on the first layer about ⅓ inch thick.

Place a second cake layer on top of the pudding and spread the second layer of cake with another ⅓ inch of the pudding.

Top with the third layer and cover the entire cake, including the sides, with the remaining pudding.

Press the cake crumbs into the sides and top of the cake, covering the pudding as completely as you can.

Remove the wax paper on the serving plate: Gently lift each side of the cake with a wide spatula while you pull the paper out.

Cut into wedges to serve.

NESSELRODE PIE

Nesselrode Pie is nearly extinct. No restaurant serves it. Only one bakery (in Brooklyn) makes it. But this great New York City dessert still lives vividly in the taste memories of many. For about twenty years, and until she closed the doors just before World War II, Hortense Spier owned a restaurant in a brownstone on Ninety-fourth Street between Columbus Avenue and Central Park West. Among other things, she was famous for her pies, including lemon meringue, banana cream, coconut custard, and the one that made Mrs. Spier really, really famous, Nesselrode. It is sometimes even referred to as New York Nesselrode because it apparently never existed anywhere but here.

Count Karl Robert Nesselrode was the French nobleman who, in 1856, negotiated the Treaty of Paris, which settled the Crimean War. For this occasion, Nesselrode's chef, a certain Monsieur Mouy, created Nesselrode pudding, a custard flavored with maraschino, chestnut puree, and chopped candied fruits macerated in Málaga wine.

Who knows how the French pudding became the New York City pie, but Mrs. Spier did well with it. When she closed her restaurant she went into the wholesale pie business, and her Nesselrode remained famous. When she died, her daughter, Ruth, and daughter-in-law, Mildred, continued the business.

Nesselrode pie was hugely popular in the 1940s and 1950s, and into the 1960s. It was listed on many menus, in all kinds of restaurants. All of the ones served in restaurants were made by Mrs. Spier, who had a delivery truck emblazoned with "Mrs. Spier's Pies" that you would see tooling around the city. But it became so popular that other bakeries made it too. For holidays, particularly Thanksgiving, my family would buy Nesselrode pie at Mrs. Maxwell's, a Brooklyn bakery that made great pies and sold them in returnable metal pie plates that required a deposit. The demand was so great, you had to order your holiday pie weeks in advance. (Mrs. Maxwell's is still there, on Atlantic Avenue, but the ownership and product line are totally different.)

By the end of its era, Nesselrode pie deserved to disappear. Instead of being a huge, rich, glorious mound of chocolate-curl-covered rum-, chestnut-, and candied-fruit-flavored Bavarian cream, it had deteriorated into a meringue-inflated pouf speckled with hard colored bits that purported to be candied fruit.

Makes one 9-inch pie, serving 6 to 8

One of the attractions of Nesselrode pie was its monumental size. It was a huge dome of cream. To achieve that height and volume of filling, you must shape the filling in a mixing bowl, which you then turn out into a prebaked pie crust. If you do not want to attempt this feat, halve the recipe for the filling to make just enough to generously fill a 9-inch shell.

Candied chestnuts packed in syrup are imported from Turkey at a very reasonable price and are available in Middle Eastern food stores and other specialty markets. There are French chestnuts in syrup too, but they cost more and are of the same quality. I do not include multicolored tutti frutti—bits of candied fruits—but you are free to add them. Substitute them for as much as half the amount of chopped candied chestnuts. If desired, soak the candied fruit in sweet wine before adding them.

6 tablespoons dark rum

2 envelopes unflavored gelatin

3 cups heavy cream

1 cup milk

4 eggs

2 egg whites

⅛ teaspoon salt

½ cup sugar

1 ½ cups coarsely chopped, drained chestnuts in syrup

1 prebaked 9-inch pie shell

A block of semisweet chocolate to shave into curls

In a cup or ramekin, combine the rum and 2 tablespoons water, then sprinkle the gelatin over the surface. Set aside. The gelatin will soften and absorb the liquid.

In a small saucepan, combine the cream and milk and place over medium-low heat. Stir occasionally. Remove from the heat when the mixture starts steaming, but before it begins to boil; this takes about 10 minutes.

Separate the eggs, placing the yolks in a medium mixing bowl and the 6 whites in another, immaculately clean medium mixing bowl.

Using a wooden spoon, stir the salt and ¼ cup of the sugar into the yolks. Slowly pour the hot, scalded cream mixture into the yolk mixture, stirring constantly. Pour this mixture into the top of a double boiler and place over simmering water (or put the mixture in a bowl set over a pot of simmering water) and cook, stirring constantly, until thickened. Do not allow the custard to boil or it will curdle.

Stir the gelatin mixture into the cooked custard. Chill, stirring frequently, until almost set. It should not be so set, however, that when you stir it, it breaks into clumps. You can put the mixture in the refrigerator or speed up the chilling process by placing the bowl of custard in a larger bowl filled with ice.

Beat the egg whites until they hold soft peaks, then add the remaining ¼ cup sugar, a tablespoon at

a time, while continuing to beat until stiff.

Stir the chestnuts into the nearly set custard.

Fold in the beaten egg whites.

To make the filling dome, line a mixing bowl with plastic wrap. Pour the filling mixture into the bowl. Place in the freezer until very well set, about 2 hours. (It is best to have the filling slightly frozen to make it easier to turn out into the pie shell. If not making the dome, pour the filling directly into the pie shell and chill well in the refrigerator.) Carefully turn the bowl of well-chilled cream filling into the pie shell, centering it as best you can. The filling, if slightly frozen, is less fragile than you expect, and it can be adjusted into the shell.

To make chocolate curls, use a swivel-bladed vegetable peeler to shave the block of chocolate. Decorate the top of the pie with the curls.

BABKA

Babka means "grandma" in Polish. It's said that this yeast cake is called babka because, in its original form, it was stout and round, just like grandmothers used to be before they went to aerobics classes and practiced yoga. At Gertel's Bakery, a kosher bakery on the Lower East Side and one of the last holdouts of the neighborhood's Jewish immigrant era, they still bake it that way. It is a giant streusel-topped cake from which pieces are cut and sold by the pound. However, for as long as I can remember, neighborhood bakeries have sold babka in rectangular loaves, each cake housed in pleated paper.

It wasn't so long ago that you could buy an authentically austere babka in New York City. It was a simple cake on the dry side, a coffee cake in the true sense in that it was best eaten with a cup of coffee or "a glass tea," as Yiddish speakers used to say. But today's cake is a prime example of the transformation that foods often go through after they arrive on our shores. They get either bigger or richer, or both.

No longer is it enough for babka to be baked from a rich yeast dough with a parsimonious filling of swirled cinnamon, sugar, and chopped nuts. Many babkas today are more like candy, with the cake part merely functioning as something to hold generous lacings of chocolate and/or almond paste. This recipe uses both, but it takes the middle road, providing plenty of cake to send down the coffee. It is adapted from *The Neighborhood Bakeshop* by Jill Van Cleave.

Makes two 5-by-8-inch loaves

For the dough:

1 (7-gram) package active dry yeast
   (1 scant tablespoon)
1 tablespoon nonfat dry milk
½ cup lukewarm water
3 ¼ to 3 ½ cups unbleached all-purpose flour
⅓ cup sugar
½ tablespoon salt
½ tablespoon vanilla extract
¼ teaspoon ground cardamom
2 large eggs, plus 1 egg yolk
8 tablespoons (1 stick) unsalted butter, melted
   and cooled

For the streusel:

⅔ cup all-purpose flour
⅔ cup packed dark brown sugar
2 teaspoons ground cinnamon
6 tablespoons unsalted butter, softened
½ cup almond paste
2 egg whites
6 ounces semisweet chocolate, grated
2 tablespoons unsalted butter, melted

Make the dough:

Prepare a sponge starter by dissolving, in a mixing bowl, the yeast and dry milk in the warm water. Add ¾ cup of the flour, stirring with a fork until smooth.

Cover with plastic wrap and set aside until the sponge has bubbled up and fallen back slightly, 45 minutes to 1 hour.

Stir in the sugar, salt, vanilla, and cardamom.

Mix in the eggs and egg yolk, blending well.

Add 2 cups of the flour, a little at a time, mixing to incorporate completely.

Pour in the melted butter in a slow, steady stream while mixing the dough.

Stir in ¼ cup more of the flour to form a smooth dough.

Turn the dough out onto a work surface and gently knead for about 5 minutes, adding ¼ cup or more of the remaining flour as necessary to produce a dough that is smooth and elastic but not dry.

Transfer to a clean bowl, cover with plastic wrap, and set aside at room temperature to rise until doubled in bulk, 50 minutes to 1 hour.

The dough can be covered and refrigerated for up to 24 hours.

Make the streusel:

In a medium bowl, combine the flour, brown sugar, and cinnamon. Using a pastry blender, cut in the butter until the mixture resembles fine crumbs. Set aside.

Assemble the babka:

Grease two 8 ½-by-4 ½-inch loaf pans. Set aside.

The almond paste may be hard. If it is, grate it and place it in a mixing bowl. Stir in the egg whites and mix until well blended. You may not be able to get it perfectly smooth. Do not worry if there are small lumps.

In another bowl, combine ⅔ cup of the streusel and about one quarter of the chocolate to make a topping. Set aside.

Place the dough on a lightly floured work surface. Divide it in half. Set one half aside.

Roll out the other half into a 14-by-10-inch rectangle.

Using a spoon, spread half of the almond paste mixture evenly over the rectangle, leaving about ½ inch empty along the long sides.

Sprinkle with ½ cup of the remaining plain streusel and half of the remaining plain grated chocolate.

Starting with the short end, roll the dough up tightly around the filling. Pinch the ends closed. Place the filled dough seam side down in the prepared loaf pan, pushing the dough down slightly to fill the pan.

Repeat the process with the second piece of dough.

Cover both pans with plastic wrap and set aside at room temperature to rise for 45 minutes, or until risen to the top of the pans.

Preheat the oven to 350 degrees.

Place the pans several inches apart on a baking sheet.

Brush the dough with the melted butter and sprinkle each with half of the chocolate-streusel topping.

Bake for about 40 minutes, until crusty and browned.

Let the loaves cool in their pans on a wire rack. Make sure they are at room temperature before removing the loaves. They can even be stored in their pans.

Cut with a serrated knife.

CHAPTER 18
COMING OF AGE

CRAIG CLAIBORNE

AS FOOD EDITOR OF *THE NEW YORK TIMES*, CRAIG CLAIBORNE BROUGHT WORLD-liness, new excitement, and new standards to New York's restaurants and home kitchens at a low point in the city's gastronomic history.

OPPOSITE: Solowey's, by the old Penn Station, had an ethnically diverse menu that was typical after World War II. BELOW: Craig Claiborne

It was 1957. Grilled ham steak with pineapple rings reigned on mainstream restaurant menus—to exaggerate only slightly. Modern young homemakers were succumbing to the temptations of frozen dinners and other conveniences. Curried whatever with "condiments" was considered the ultimate in elegant dinner-party fare. Home economists and socialite wannabes were still running most newspaper food pages. Then, the *New York Times*, the city's most influential newspaper, gave a 37-year-old man the job of food editor, making him the first male newspaper food editor in the country.

Claiborne was well-prepared. He grew up in a boardinghouse in Mississippi, eating his mother's good Southern cooking. He had a University of Missouri journalism degree. He'd spent years as an officer in the navy, in communications, then wined and dined clients as a public relations man in Chicago. Crowning all of this, he was a graduate of a top Swiss hotel school, an education in classical French cuisine and dining room service that he got courtesy of the GI bill. He knew about food and restaurants and he could write.

In 1954, after graduation from L'Ecole Hotelière in Lausanne, he came to New York to be a food writer. "Not without guile," as he pointed out in his sometimes shocking autobiography, *A Feast Made for Laughter,* he made a point of meeting Jane Nickerson, who was then the food editor at the *Times*.

Claiborne always talked about his insecurity, but he somehow found the muster—like the practiced p.r. man he was—to phone Nickerson and ask her if she was interested in writing a story about a young American who had studied French cuisine in Switzerland—himself. He took her to lunch at the Colony. She wrote the story.

The story helped him get a job at *Gourmet* magazine, acting as a receptionist and answering the mail. He did eventually graduate to a writing post, but was dismayed that his work didn't always get a byline. So he was eager to move on when word got to him in 1957 that Nickerson had decided to leave the *Times*. She had two small children and a happy marriage to a man who was making his fortune in Florida. She wanted to devote herself to her family. Claiborne called her, took her to lunch at '21,' and told her he was interested in the job. She didn't hold out much hope because, as she told him, no one had ever heard of a man being a food editor.

Claiborne went through the usual series of interviews at the *Times*, but it was probably Turner Catledge, the managing editor, who was ultimately responsible for his hiring. Catledge was another drawling boy from Mississippi and he and Claiborne immediately bonded.

Claiborne brought exactitude to the *New York Times* recipes—his recipes "worked"—and unquenchable culinary curiosity to the job. He interviewed and wrote about great home cooks and the world's most accomplished chefs with the same interest and respect. He would eat anything, and cook anything, and go any distance or to any length to do so. Stories by Craig Claiborne in the *New York Times* helped establish the careers of Marcella Hazan, Julie Sahni, Paul Prudhomme, Diana Kennedy, and Zarela Martinez, just to name a few who are still among the most prominent names in the food world. And he blew the horn in America for some of the century's top French chefs—Paul Bocuse, the Troisgros brothers, Michel Guérard—whom he would invite to his specially designed kitchen in East Hampton to cook and be interviewed for the *Times*. Here was a man who admitted he couldn't pass up a hot dog on the street, and at the same time could, with authority, critique the haute-est of French meals. He loved to travel and he loved it when he found genuine cooking from other cultures in New York.

In 1959 he was approached to write a book based on the *New York Times* recipe archive. Strangely, the *New York Times* gave Claiborne the right to use its name on a cookbook without asking for any of the proceeds from publication. No one could have predicted that the cookbook would become a huge bestseller and make its sole copyright owner—Craig Claiborne—a rich man.

A few years after joining the *Times*, Claiborne also became its restaurant critic and created the model for serious restaurant criticism that remains today. Before Claiborne, there was no such thing as serious restaurant criticism. Reviewers were guests of the house, received free meals, and were more cheerleaders than critics. Claiborne changed it all by going anonymously, or as anonymously as he could, so he could have the same experience as the general public. He went with several friends so he could try many dishes in each course and also to make the dinner seem as much like a normal one as possible. And he returned several times to check on a restaurant's consistency. He always paid the bill, so he wouldn't be beholden to the management. His ratings—no stars to four stars—balanced the food quality and cooking, the decor, the service, and, in those days, the "value."

Claiborne did not hand out stars freely, so it was a shock to the city when he gave Shun Lee Dynasty four stars in 1967 It was the first time, and the last until the mid-1990s, that an Asian restaurant got such a high rating from the *Times*'s restaurant critic.

Just before he started reviewing restaurants, in late 1959, Claiborne wrote a feature on Henri Soulé, the great restaurateur who owned Le Pavillon (see page 284), then the best French restaurant in the city. In the kitchen of Le Pavillon, Claiborne met Pierre Franey, Soule's chef. They were to remain nearly lifelong friends and professional collaborators. They even lived next door to each other in East Hampton.

In fact, Claiborne left his post as food editor of the *Times* in 1970 to write a newsletter with Franey. The business didn't work out and Claiborne went back to the *Times* in 1974. He wrote the Sunday magazine column with Franey, ghostwrote Franey's "60-Minute Gourmet" columns in the weekly food section, and they collaborated on several books.

Claiborne was not "out," as it is meant today, but he never hid his homosexuality from his friends and associates. Wags who didn't know them may have gossiped that Claiborne and Franey were a couple, even though Pierre Franey appeared to be and was happily married and with a family.

Those who did know Claiborne knew that Henry Creel was his lover during his early years in New York City. With Claiborne's guidance—and with a foreword by Claiborne—Creel even wrote a cookbook in 1976, *Cooking for One Is Fun*. In later years, Claiborne had "a gentleman friend," as he called him, who was a doctor in Atlanta.

It was not a public confession of his homosexuality in his autobiography that set New York City abuzz in 1982 but the disclosure of his incestuous relationship with his father. Worse yet, he didn't seem regretful. Indeed, the whole book, except for the recipes, is filled with things you'd say only on a psychoanalyst's couch. This public display embarrassed and infuriated Franey. It was the end of their friendship.

In 1996 Franey died suddenly on a cruise ship where he was doing cooking demonstrations. Claiborne died on January 22, 2000. He had been frail for a long time, but nearly to the end, continued to go out, often by himself, to restaurants not far from his apartment in the historic Osborne on West Fifty-seventh Street.

JOE BAUM

Jerome Brody founded Restaurant Associates, the huge, New York–based operator of both institutional and fine-dining establishments, but Joe Baum's creativity and theatricality is what turned it into the powerhouse it was and now is again under the direction of Nick Valenti. Called

Michael Whiteman, Julia Child, and Joe Baum at the second opening of Windows on the World.

on by Brody in 1953 to do almost the impossible, create a luxury restaurant at New Jersey's Newark Airport, Baum hired Swiss-trained Albert Stockli, who would eventually become the opening chef at the Four Seasons, bought fine china, and came up with a menu gimmick to grab the public's and the press's attention: "knife and fork oysters," which were Absecon oysters so large they couldn't possibly be eaten in one gulp. He served seven oysters to the half-dozen, the extra served on a separate plate to emphasize its presence and size, and the Newarker restaurant became known for its huge portions—a notable attraction in New Jersey, then and now. Baum always knew what his audience wanted and how to give it to them.

By 1955 the Newarker was a certified success, serving a thousand people a day, 90 percent of whom were not air travelers, and turning a good profit on a three million dollar gross. Baum rose quickly in the Restaurant Associates hierarchy. He had taken the company from being the operators of the Riker's coffee shops and snack bars to being a white-tablecloth restaurant company. His next assignment was to save the Hawaiian Room in the Hotel Lexington. From there, he was given his chance at a star turn—to create what would become the Forum of the Twelve Caesars, a restaurant inspired by a set of Caesar portraits purchased by Brody. With Brody and some other R.A. executives, Baum went to Rome, Pompeii, Naples, and London to research ancient Roman art and gastronomy. What ended up in the restaurant as décor, atmosphere, and cuisine, however, sounds like pure kitsch today: White wine and champagne were chilled in what looked like upturned centurians' helmets. The waiters wore togas of imperial purple and red. Some of the menu items were "Crêpes of the Mad Nero," "Pheasant of the Golden House on a Silver Shield in Gilded Plumage," and "Truffle-Stuffed Quail Cleopatra—Wrapped in Macedonian Vine Leaves, Baked in Hot Ashes." So many dishes were flambéed, according to Brody's biography, that the restaurant required an extra-strong air-conditioning system.

The theatricality of the staff uniforms, the flaming food, and the evocative menu language and décor were Baum trademarks. At La Fonda del Sol, his next project, the theme was Latin

American food because the location was the ground floor of the new Time-Life Building and the street in front of it was named Avenue of the Americas, a name New Yorkers still refuse to use. (We call it Sixth Avenue.) Even the carefully contemporary and restrained Four Seasons in the Seagram Building (see page 311) exhibited some of these flamboyant Baum touches: The plantings, waiters' uniforms—even the color of the typewriter ribbons—changed with the seasons. Baum is often credited with inventing the theme restaurant, and in a way this is true, but the food was always far above what one would expect in such theatrical restaurants.

Born into the hospitality business on September 17, 1920 (his parents owned the Gross and Baum Family Hotel in Saratoga Springs), by 1963 he had replaced Jerome Brody as president of Restaurant Associates; he then went on, with his own company, to create Windows on the World and all the food services in the World Trade Center (see page 340). He restored the Rainbow Room to its original glory (see page 253), then reinvented Windows on the World after the terrorist bombing in 1993. By developing food courts, slews of domestic and foreign restaurants and more *New York Times* three-star restaurants than anyone had or has yet, he changed the industry and got to do everything there was to do in the restaurant business—except for one thing: "To kick off New York restaurant week in 1995, Joe wanted to build a two-story replica of the Statue of Liberty out of chopped liver and put it in Rockefeller Center," says his partner, Michael Whiteman. "We had to veto that idea."

ANDRÉ SOLTNER

Lutèce, a relatively small townhouse restaurant on East Fifty-second Street was, almost from the beginning in 1961 and until chef-proprietor André Soltner's last day behind the stove in 1994, the highest rated and most popular French restaurant in the country, not just in New York. At its height, it was that rarest of New York destinations, a place that New Yorkers consider the tops even though it is full of tourists. It was, in its small-scale way, the Delmonico's of the twentieth century. It set new standards for French cuisine in New York, standards that we still agree on today.

It's no wonder that with that kind of track record, after the coming of La Nouvelle Cuisine in the 1970s, it was popular to say that Lutèce was the last bastion of grand classic French cuisine in New York. This wasn't true. The food was never grand, and Soltner never got the credit he deserved for being as contemporary as he really was.

In fact, Soltner and the creator of Lutèce, André Surmain, with whom he very soon became partners, were, for New York City, as much revolutionaries as the French chefs who came after them with nouvelle ideas. Soltner and Surmain's mission, as they saw it, was to embrace freshness, seasonality, and the simpler cooking of France, not the grand cuisine, not haute cuisine, not the heavy and clichéd food that was being prepared at every other French restaurant in New York City—namely Le Pavillon and Le Chambord. What Surmain and Soltner aimed for was, for the early 1960s, a truly contemporary take on French food.

"Surmain is my friend, but he is a snob," says Soltner now, pushing the tip of his nose into the air for emphasis on "snob." "He wanted to be as important as Le Pavillon. He wanted that clientele. So he made sure he was the most expensive. We were always the most expensive. And his orders were that I could use nothing canned and nothing frozen. Everything I cooked had to be fresh—which was expensive."

In 1961, cooking only with fresh ingredients in New York proved more difficult than the two thought it would be. "When I got here," Soltner says, "I went to see what the other French restaurants were cooking and I saw that, for instance, veal medallions with girolles was a very popular dish. But the quality of veal was so poor then. I couldn't use that dark meat. *Plume de veau* was still years away from being generally available. And the girolles were canned, from Germany. I couldn't use canned mushrooms."

Years later, when fresh wild girolles became available from Oregon, Soltner asked the source how it was that Oregon suddenly had fresh wild mushrooms. They must have been there before, he said, when all he could get was mushrooms in a can from Germany. There was no market for fresh wild mushrooms before, the man from Oregon told him. So he and his fellow mushroom gatherers sent their mushrooms to Germany. The Germans then sent them back in cans.

Surmain knew the New York market very well. He was a friend of James Beard and before there was a restaurant called Lutèce (an antique name for Paris) Surmain had started a cooking school with Beard in the East Fiftieth Street townhouse where he also lived, and which would eventually house the restaurant. Some old-timers who knew the two (Surmain now lives near Cannes, in the south of France, where he was born) say that Surmain and Beard hired Soltner on a lark. They thought it would be fun to have a French chef on the premises, to cater parties. Surmain at the time was already doing catering for Varig airlines, using the townhouse as his commissary.

Soltner says he came to the United States, after having met Surmain in Paris, mainly because he wanted to learn English, and also because his grandfather had come to America early in life and had always told wonderful stories about his adventures here. Born in Alsace, with German as his first language, he was twenty-eight years old and a chef in a good restaurant in Paris when he met Surmain. He was ready for another adventure. He didn't know that the adventure was going to be searching for fresh ingredients in New York.

In the 1970s, he was the first to fly in fresh Dover sole. At his country home near Hunter Mountain, where he still skis regularly, he foraged for the wild mushrooms that he couldn't buy. He made demands on his suppliers that brought New York rosier veal, free-range chickens, and freshly picked berries, among other things.

Soltner was a celebrity chef long before there were celebrity chefs, but he is perhaps proudest of the fact that, in more than thirty years, he never missed a day behind the stove. If he wasn't actually in his tiny kitchen with his small crew, he was in the dining room charming the pants off his regular customers.

By the late 1980s, New Yorkers' incessant demand for the new, not the tried-and-true, took its toll on Lutèce. In 1994, Soltner left his stove and leased the space and the name to a large restaurant operator who, even with a big-name chef, was never able to capture the old Lutèce glory or business. Lutèce closed for good in February 2004. André Soltner is now a dean of the French Culinary Institute in New York City, he is in demand as a lecturer and teacher, and he travels extensively. He says he doesn't regret leaving his restaurant kitchen behind.

THE FOUR SEASONS

The Four Seasons in the Seagram Building on Park Avenue is one of only two restaurant interiors in the city that is an official landmark. That's just the architecture, design, and furnishings. Although not officially designated, it is every bit as much a culinary landmark. It is probably safe to say that the team that put the Four Seasons together will never be matched, and that its food, style, and attitude were a breakthrough for American cuisine and restaurants. The term "New

American Cuisine" was, in fact, coined by restaurant chronicler Silas Spitzer in the December 1959 *Holiday* magazine to describe the food at the Four Seasons. It took nearly twenty years before that term to become fully realized.

Starting at the very top, the building, which was commissioned by Sam Bronfman—founder of the wine and spirits company Seagram, as its headquarters, was designed by Ludwig Mies Van der Rohe in 1957. It is considered a masterpiece of the severe "International" style of architecture, of which Mies was the master. He's the architect who said form should follow function, "less is more," and "God is in the details."

Heading the restaurant design team was Philip Johnson, now considered one of the greatest

The Four Seasons' famous chocolate cake.

American architects of the twentieth century, then an assistant to Mies on the Seagram project. The restaurant's chairs are an adaptation of Mies's Brno chair. The private party chairs were designed by Charles Eames, famous for molding plywood into comfortable forms. The tables and hassocks were designed by Eero Saarinen. Philip Johnson did the banquettes himself. The dishes, silver, and glasses were designed by Garth and Ada Louise Huxtable. Eighteen of their pieces for the restaurant are in the Museum of Modern Art. The carpets were hand-loomed. Everything, from the ashtrays and matchbooks to the now famous shimmering metal drapery, were obsessed over. Richard Lippold himself installed his masterwork sculpture of bronze rods over the bar in the Grill Room.

Heading the food and service team for Restaurant Associates was Joseph Baum, a thirty-nine-year-old restaurant showman, who had most recently created the Forum of the Twelve Caesars, and a team that now reads like a pantheon of twentieth-century restaurateurs. Jerome Brody, who was the founder and president of R.A., and the one who secured the project for his company, put his best men on the job: George Lang, Alan Lewis, Stuart Levin, and Roger Martin. James Beard was a consultant. Sometime after the opening, Mimi Sheraton, later the restaurant critic for the *New York Times*, became a consultant. Albert Stockli, who, with Baum, had created the first fine-dining restaurant in an airport, the Newarker, was the chef. Albert Kumin, who would later work with Baum on the Rainbow Room and who is now a professor at the Culinary Institute of America, was the pastry chef.

In accordance with the restaurant's name, which was meant to reflect not only the fresh, cyclical aspect of the cuisine, but also the changing mood and dynamism of New York, then clearly emerging as the world's capital, everything changed with the season. Every three months, the colors of the staff's uniforms changed, the trees and plantings around the reflecting pool in the main dining room, the Pool Room, changed. The matchbooks and ashtrays changed —the winter ones had bare brown trees, the spring ones pink trees, the summer ones green trees with leaves, the autumn ones trees with just a few red leaves.

Sam Bronfman's daughter, Phyllis Lambert, was in charge of the whole project. (She continues to be a major force in American and Canadian architecture and design circles.) And although it is said she was not a fan of Restaurant Associates or of Jerome Brody, whom she thought had taste at the opposite end of the spectrum from the modernist Mies, she did get her way on one thing. Originally she had wanted the restaurant to be an homage to Picasso—she even wanted to call it Picasso. What she got was the huge curtain Picasso designed for the Diaghilev ballet's 1920 Paris production of *The Three Cornered Hat*. It hangs in the hall space between the formal Pool Room and less formal Grill Room, and can be seen through glass in the lobby. She also felt comfortable about the project because Philip Johnson was there to guard Mies's aesthetic. It cost $4.5 million to build the Four Seasons.

When the restaurant opened on July 29, 1959, it naturally caused a sensation. Aside from all the design talent that went into it, no one had ever attempted an American restaurant of this scale. French restaurants reigned at the time. And even more than an American restaurant, Joe Baum wanted the Four Seasons to be a New York City restaurant, whatever that meant. "Baum sought to challenge every accepted notion about fine dining as developed since the nineteenth century according to Parisian models adapted by Delmonico's," wrote John Mariani and Alex Von Bidder in their deliciously detailed 1994 history, *The Four Seasons*.

The first menu of the Four Seasons was enormous, literally, both in size—it was something like two feet tall—as well as in the number of dishes offered. It was also more expensive than any other restaurant on the continent. I remember the size and prices well. In December 1959, my parents spent their fourteenth anniversary at the Four Seasons and were so bowled over by the experience that they awakened my sister and me when they got home. The menu listed twenty-six cold appetizers, twenty-two hot appetizers, twenty-five main courses, and numerous side dishes. Everything was à la carte. My father couldn't get over the nerve of charging a dollar fifty extra for string beans. The average dinner bill was forty dollars, before tax and tip; astronomical for the time.

As revolutionary as it was to serve foods only in season and from local sources whenever possible, the menu still offered steaks, chops, classic seafood dishes, and, for dessert, a great chocolate cake, Chocolate Velvet. It even gave a nod to the tastes of the time with a grilled ham steak, albeit from an Amish farm and served with hot rhubarb instead of the ubiquitous hot pineapple.

Craig Claiborne of the *New York Times* complained that many of the sauces were oversweet, yet, in general, he gave it high praise. Scared that Francophile Claiborne would not appreciate what they were trying to do, Jerome Brody took Claiborne to lunch before the opening. Claiborne was yet to formally review restaurants for the newspaper—that job wasn't created until 1963. But he was the food editor and certainly reported on restaurants, feeling no qualms about expressing his opinions. He opened his report by saying, "There has never been a restaurant better keyed to the tempo of Manhattan than the Four Seasons. Both in décor and in menu, it is spectacular, modern, and audacious . . . it is perhaps the most exciting restaurant to open in New York within the last two decades."

Not only Claiborne, but all the restaurant writers and architecture critics thought the Four Seasons was absolutely splendid. On the other hand, the general public, those that could afford the tab, found it cold. "A dentist's office," sneered an acquaintance of my parents. The Four Seasons was not supposed to appeal to such people in any case. In the late 1950s, it was businessmen on expense accounts that spent money in Manhattan's restaurants. The Four Seasons had a decidedly masculine feel. With that, it immediately became the seat of power in New York City. There is a famous story that the publisher of the *New York Times*, Arthur Ochs Sulzberger, was denied a table because he didn't have a reservation. Another story has James Rockefeller dimming the lights on his bank across Park Avenue because Jerry Brody complained to him that they glared through the restaurant's metal curtains.

By the mid-1960s it was apparent that the cool, International style and advanced "American" food was not catching on with the general public, and even the high-rolling power brokers were moving on. If the restaurant wasn't losing money, it wasn't making any either. George Lang took over its management in 1966 and tried to enliven the menu with elaborate French dishes and Continental favorites. He also added warmth to the place by being, as he always is, one of the most charming men on earth. Instead of the cool but polite greeting and service that the Four Seasons had become known for, Lang would make the rounds of the tables and tell delicious stories.

Meanwhile, the world had changed and Restaurant Associates was changing along with it. The company opened Zum Zum in the Pan Am building, an almost-fast-food, counter-service restaurant featuring sausages of all kinds. (Joe Baum gave it that name, entirely fabricated, because he thought it sounded fast.) It got the concession at the Orange Bowl in Miami, the cafe in the Museum of Modern Art, and opened Charley O's, a bar with middle-brow pretensions.

The Four Seasons still did not make money; in 1970, Joe Baum found himself deposed as president of R.A. Gael Greene, the restaurant critic of *New York* magazine wrote in a piece called "Restaurant Associates: Twilight of the Gods" that "The philistines sit in the driver's seat" and "excellence is frowned, nay, spat upon."

By 1972, things were so bad at the Four Seasons that the Bronfmans were embarrassed by its presence in their building. When George Lang left, his successor as director of the restaurant, the cultured and debonair Transylvanian Paul Kovi, tried to hold things together, and Tom Margittai, another sophisticated Hungarian brought into the corporate office by George Lang, was also trying to carry on with the standards set in the beginning by Joe Baum and crew. In 1973, they bought the restaurant.

Except for the first few years of its existence, when novelty and advanced, modern taste carried it, the glory days of the Four Seasons really started with the Kovi and Margittai years. They became completely devoted to the original concept of the restaurant, to creating a truly American restaurant, with the highest level of cuisine, wine, and service. They hired Swiss chef Seppi Renggli (then an executive chef with R.A., and today again an executive chef with the company, which has also renewed its dedication to quality) and his assistant Hitsch Albin. They restocked their wine cellar with California wines, one of the first restaurants in the East to feature them. And they knew how to cultivate the press, to get their message to the public. Starting in 1976, furthering the image of the restaurant as a place for fine wine and the food to go with it, the pair instituted the first-ever Barrel Tastings in America. Most appealing to wine lovers was the restaurant's pricing policy. They charged a 100 percent markup over retail plus $1, where other restaurants were (and still are) charging a whopping 300 percent over retail.

Kovi and Margittai also shortened and simplified the Grill Room menu, in the process attracting the power brokers again. They hired women for dining room jobs, which was revolutionary at the time. To cut costs and put the emphasis where it belonged, on the plate and in the glass, they discontinued the custom of changing everything every season, although the Pool Room was always kept fresh and seasonally appealing with new plants. In response to New York's obsession with slimness, they created "Spa Cuisine" to attract those with power and money. ("You can never be too rich or too thin," Babe Paley once said.)

All through the 1980s, the critics lavished praise on the Four Seasons and it became one of the most important restaurants in the world. For tourists with well-stuffed wallets, it became a must-eat on visits to New York City. Under the dedicated proprietorship of Alex von Bidder and Julian Nicolini, both of whom worked under Kovi and Margittai and bought the restaurant from them in 1995, it is still among the most popular New York City restaurants.

THE COACH HOUSE

It is interesting that the Coach House was considered an American restaurant, and even, in the 1950s through the early 1970s, America's best American restaurant. True, hot corn sticks were the bread specialty, and they gave the place an American first impression. But, among other foreign items, the menu offered shish kebabs, several dishes "provençale," duck "Bigarade," and fish prepared "à la Méditerranée." In the last couple dozen of its more than forty years in business, the two dishes that insiders, including James Beard, James Villas (of *Town and Country*), and Craig Claiborne, ordered most often were the famous seven-rib rack of lamb (seven ribs, count 'em), and the whole striped bass à la Grecque, in which the fish was brushed with olive oil, roasted, presented, filleted, then served with nothing more than good olive oil, lemon juice, and lots of fresh dill.

Yes, this was "American" food, and way ahead of its time, too. While most other restaurants with pretensions to gastronomy and elegance were cooking French or "Continental," and badly—using canned vegetables, turkey instead of veal, and frozen fish—the Coach House's owner, Leon Lianides, had a commitment to freshness and superior ingredients, and the understanding that cooking them in the simplest way was best.

Lianides was Greek, from Rhodes. Knowing that, you can see why he would have thought he had an American place. A restaurant like his could only happen in America, maybe only in New York City in 1949, when he bought the property, an 1850s Greenwich Village carriage or coach house that was once part of the John Wanamaker estate. The address, 110 Waverly Place, was called the Lane when it first opened as a restaurant in 1929, and it is now the home of Mario Batali's Babbo.

When Lianides took over, all of the carriage house's original details had long been stripped away. The only remnant of the old building was a half-story floor at the back of the building that Lianides named the Hay Loft. It was used on very busy dinner nights and for private parties. Lianides decorated to his own taste, which was heavy on red: red brick walls, red banquettes, red table linens, and red carpeting. The oil paintings that crammed the walls were once kindly referred to as "a highly personal collection."

As a foreign-born American, Lianides definitely had a more inclusive view of American food than, say, a third-generation Texan would have, but he did give menu space to a few true-blue American standards. He served a handsome chicken potpie at a time when chicken potpie had already been delegated to the frozen food case in the supermarket. His menu listed prime ribs of beef, and crabmeat cooked various ways. The favorite of these was simply lump crab tossed with bits of Smithfield Virginia ham, doused with butter, and put under the broiler.

Service was caring and correct, provided by a staff of African American waiters, kindly men who doled out the corn sticks with a knowing smile. But, at least in later years, Lianides's hospitality was dished out parsimoniously, only to those whom he felt were refined enough, rich enough, appreciative enough, or famous enough to deserve any attention. I remember him as a joyless, intimidating presence, pacing back and forth between the front door and his nearby reception podium.

As well he should have, he very much catered to James Beard, who lived a few short blocks away, at 119 West Tenth Street (not yet at the so-called Beard House at 167 West Twelfth Street). Beard shamelessly promoted his favorite neighborhood restaurant until it became nationally known as a mecca for American food. Not that it didn't deserve it. For me, as a young man and aspiring gastronome in the late 1960s, a visit to the Coach House was a

rite of passage. I was impressed. In 1977, Mimi Sheraton, the exacting restaurant critic for the *New York Times*, gave it the newspaper's highest rating: four stars.

Ten years later the Coach House's luster was beginning to wear thin. In 1987 Brian Miller, who was then the *New York Times's* restaurant critic, demoted it to two stars. By 1990 it was clear that time and fashion had passed the Coach House by. A frequent customer, noting the empty dining room one night, commented on how business must be slow. Lianides answered that it wasn't merely a slow night. "It's like this now," he said. "People seem more interested in the artistic cooking and smaller portions [referring to La Nouvelle Cuisine's influence] instead of food with flavor and substance." Soon after, in 1991, Marion Burros, acting as temporary *Times* restaurant critic, hammered the final nails in the coffin. Burros gave it no stars. The restaurant closed. Leon Lianides died on June 1, 1998, at his home in Riverdale in the Bronx. He was eighty-one or eighty-four, depending on which report you believe.

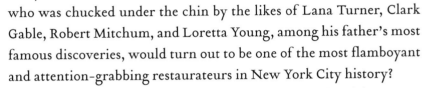

WARNER LEROY

Imagine having the real Toto from *The Wizard of Oz* as your very own dog, and a screening room with a popcorn machine in your house. These were just a few of the privileges accorded to Warner LeRoy when he was growing up in a mansion in Los Angeles. He was born on March 5, 1935, his father the Hollywood producer Mervyn LeRoy and his mother Doris Warner, which made him the grandson of Harry Warner of Warner Brothers Studios. Is it any wonder that a boy who was chucked under the chin by the likes of Lana Turner, Clark Gable, Robert Mitchum, and Loretta Young, among his father's most famous discoveries, would turn out to be one of the most flamboyant and attention-grabbing restaurateurs in New York City history?

His parents' divorce when he was seven years old took him away from the Hollywood hullabaloo: He was sent east to boarding school, and eventually to Switzerland for prep school, where, instead of Hollywood stars, his friends were the young Aga Khan and the future shah of Iran.

After graduating with a drama degree from Stanford University, LeRoy became a Broadway and Off-Broadway producer and director for ten years. In 1966, managing a theater on the Upper East Side and a little bored and not feeling terribly successful in the theater, he took over a coffee shop on First Avenue and Sixty-fourth Street. It was to become Maxwell's Plum, considered to be the first singles bar in New York—not just a bar for drinking and carousing, but a bar and restaurant people would go to for the purpose of meeting people of the opposite sex. It became a symbol of the Swinging Sixties.

At the time, the neighborhood was changing. It had been an ethnically diverse area of run-down tenement buildings and brownstones. Now the old buildings were being replaced with expensive high-rise apartment houses, many of them notoriously filled with airline personnel, in particular young stewardesses and secretaries. With its base of beautiful bodies, Maxwell's Plum attracted many celebrities of the day—Julie Christie and Warren Beatty are most often mentioned in stories about the place—which, in turn, attracted young athletes, models, Wall Streeters, the diplomatic crowd that lived on the East Side of Manhattan near the United Nations, and even what was dubbed the Bridge and Tunnel crowd, the young swingers from the boroughs who needed to take a bridge or tunnel to get into Manhattan for the evening. The menu had something for everyone, from hamburgers to foie-gras-stuffed squab. Before long, the city's first singles bar was the highest grossing restaurant in America.

LeRoy used all of his showmanship when decorating Maxwell's Plum. A huge mahogany bar anchored the center of the restaurant. (It now does the same at the Tribeca Grill.) A vast Tiffany-style stained-glass skylight was installed. And LeRoy himself became a decoration, dressing in Liberace-like brocade, sequined, bejeweled, or otherwise ostentatious outfits. His rotund figure was as much a symbol of the restaurant and bar as the Art Nouveau accessories and motifs he used on his menus, his dinnerware—everywhere.

In 1974 LeRoy acquired his second large property, Tavern on the Green, which had a sensational location at the edge of Central Park at West Sixty-seventh Street, but which had become a run-down eyesore with barely edible food. Built in 1870 as a sheepfold by architect Jacob Wrey Mould in the Victorian Gothic style, the Tavern originally housed a hundred South Down sheep that grazed in Central Park's Sheep Meadow. In the early 1930s, Parks Commissioner Robert Moses exiled the sheep to Brooklyn's Prospect Park and converted the building into a restaurant, which opened on October 20, 1934.

Over the forty years before LeRoy took over, the Tavern was operated by a succession of companies, the last being Savarins Management, Inc. Like their other operations, the Tavern was a glorified coffee shop, although it had a full menu of typical dishes of the day; seafood cocktails, steaks and chops, chicken in cream sauce, Lobster Newberg, ham steak with pineapple. The "Hot Savarin" sandwich was the signature dish: sliced white-meat chicken, tongue, and Swiss cheese on French toast, a variant of the French croque monsieur. With a good slathering of mustard it's rather good.

LeRoy had different ideas for the place. Over two years, and at a cost of more than ten million dollars, he totally renovated Tavern on the Green, which is still leased by the New York City Department of Parks. He decorated each room with a different fantastic theme. The showcase room, the room whose tables are most prized, is the Crystal Room, which is decorated with dozens of Baccarat crystal chandeliers that LeRoy supposedly bought from Indian maharajahs. (That was his claim to the press at the time, although I didn't see it in any of the restaurant's official literature.) It has glass walls with a view of the Tavern's terrace, which has trees strewn with tiny lights, and Chinese lanterns. In the summer there is dining and dancing on the terrace.

The new Tavern on the Green opened on August 31, 1976, and was an immediate success. LeRoy's over-the-top decorating skill had worked its magic again. Paul Goldberger, architecture critic of the *New York Times*, wrote: "It is all, on one level, absurd; and yet it is all, on another level, quite wonderful. Mr. LeRoy's creation, as a piece of design, goes beyond the conventional limits of taste to create a new and altogether convincing world of its own." Soon, Tavern became the largest grossing restaurant in the country.

LeRoy didn't have as much luck with some other projects. Apparently San Francisco was not ready for LeRoy's style. A branch of Maxwell's Plum that he opened there in 1981 failed quickly. Potomac, the largest and most glamorous restaurant Washington, D.C. has ever seen, closed after only one year. LeRoy had invested nine million dollars in the eight hundred and fifty-seat restaurant with twenty-four vast crystal chandeliers and a ceiling of jeweled glass.

Finally, he purchased the Russian Tea Room, but his partnership with chef David Bouley dissolved quickly and after much nasty gossip. When the restaurant finally opened it was ridiculed by the *New York Times* restaurant critic William Grimes, and never really recovered. That building, next to Carnegie Hall, is still empty. LeRoy's daughter Jennifer Oz LeRoy now operates Tavern on the Green.

After a long bout with lymphoma, LeRoy died at age sixty-five on February 22, 2001.

Tavern on the Green before the LeRoy makeover.

Tavern-on-the-Green, New York City in Central Park at 67th Street West

Tavern-On-The-Green
..."Up in Central Park"

CHICKEN SPAGHETTI

This is one of Craig Claiborne's mother's Mississippi boardinghouse creations, and one of the "One Hundred Favorite Recipes" he provides in his autobiography. Claiborne published the recipe several times in his career. One of those times, perhaps the first, must have been in the mid-1970s. I remember making it then, and it being served at many informal gatherings of my friends.

Serves 12

1 (3½-pound) chicken, with its giblets
Fresh or canned chicken broth to cover
Salt
3 cups imported Italian peeled tomatoes,
    1 (35-ounce) can, drained
7 tablespoons unsalted butter (divided)
3 tablespoons all-purpose flour
½ cup heavy cream
⅛ teaspoon grated nutmeg
Freshly ground black pepper
½ pound fresh mushrooms
2 cups finely chopped onion

1 ½ cups finely chopped celery
1 ½ cups chopped seeded green bell pepper
1 tablespoon or more finely minced garlic
¼ pound ground beef
¼ pound ground pork
1 bay leaf
½ teaspoon hot red pepper flakes (optional)
1 pound spaghetti or spaghettini
½ pound cheddar cheese, grated (about 2 to
    2 ½ cups)
Freshly grated Parmesan cheese for serving

Place the chicken with its neck, gizzard, heart, and liver in a kettle and add enough chicken broth to cover the chicken. Season with salt to taste. Partially cover the kettle with its lid. Bring to a boil, and simmer until the chicken is tender without being dry, 35 to 45 minutes. Remove from heat and allow to cool.

Remove the chicken, and take the meat from the bones. Shred the meat, cover, and set aside. Return the skin and bones to the stock in the kettle, and cook the stock down for 30 minutes or longer. There should be 4 to 6 cups of broth. Strain and reserve the broth. Discard the skin and the bones.

Meanwhile, put the tomatoes in a saucepan and cook down to half the original volume, stirring frequently. Set aside.

Melt 3 tablespoons of the butter in a saucepan, and add the flour, stirring to blend with a wire whisk. When blended and smooth, add 1 cup of the reduced hot broth and the cream, stirring rapidly with the whisk. When thickened and smooth, add the nutmeg, and season with salt and pepper to taste. Continue cooking, stirring occasionally, for about 10 minutes. Set aside.

If the mushrooms are very small, leave them whole. Otherwise, cut them in half or quarter them. Heat 1 tablespoon of the butter in a small skillet, and add the mushrooms. Cook, shaking and stirring until the mushrooms are golden brown. Set aside.

Heat 3 tablespoons of the butter in a deep skillet, and add the onion. Cook, stirring frequently, until the onion has wilted. Add the celery and green pepper, and cook, stirring, for about 5 minutes more. Do not overcook. The vegetables should remain crisp-tender.

Add the garlic, beef, and pork. Cook, stirring frequently, and chopping up any clumps with the edge of a large metal spoon to break up the meat. Cook just until the meat loses its red color. Remove from heat. Add the bay leaf and the red pepper flakes, if desired. Add the tomatoes, the white sauce made with the chicken broth, and the mushrooms. Set aside.

Cook the spaghetti in 3 to 4 quarts of boiling salted water until it is just tender. Do not overcook. (Remember that it will cook again when blended with the chicken and meat sauce.) Drain the spaghetti and run under cold running water. Set aside.

Spoon enough of the meat sauce over the bottom of a 5- or 6-quart casserole to cover it lightly. Cover with a layer of about one-third of the spaghetti. Add about one-third of the shredded chicken, a layer of meat sauce, and a layer of cheddar cheese. Continue making layers, ending with a layer of spaghetti topped with a thin layer of meat sauce and cheddar cheese.

Pour in up to 2 cups of the reduced chicken stock or enough to almost but not quite cover the top layer of spaghetti. At this point the dish may be left to stand, covered, for up to an hour. If the liquid is absorbed as the dish stands, add a little more chicken stock. Remember that when this dish is baked and served, the sauce will be just a bit soupy rather than thick and clinging.

Preheat the oven to 350 degrees.

Place the spaghetti casserole on top of the stove, and bring it just to a boil. Remove from heat.

Cover (with tinfoil if there is no lid to the casserole), and place it in the oven. Bake for 15 minutes and uncover.

Bake about 15 minutes more, or until the casserole is hot and bubbling throughout and starting to brown on top. Remove from the oven.

Let rest for 10 minutes before serving.

CHARLIE O'S SOUSED SHRIMP

The only bar and grill to ever get three stars from the *New York Times*, Charlie O's was created by Joe Baum and his team at Restaurant Associates in 1963. As of this writing, there is still a Charlie O's in Manhattan, on Eighth Avenue in the heart of the Theater District. It is owned by the Riese Corporation.

Needless to say, the last of the Charlie O's, as drearily and cynically tourist-oriented as can be, is nothing like the first of the Charlie O's, which was a glamorous addition to what was then a very staid Rockefeller Center. As Craig Claiborne, the legendary *Times* restaurant critic, wrote:

This is one of the most joyous, colorful and smartly contrived restaurants ever to open in New York. At noon the restaurant has an elbow-to-elbow ambiance, pretends to be an Irish saloon (which it isn't) and has the best shrimp on ice, herring in cream, corned beef sandwiches and foaming, old, delicious draught beer. Charley O's is a largish restaurant with a long, handsome and sturdy bar for beer and spirits and another equally sturdy bar where the sandwiches, including tartar steak, shrimp and so forth, are dispensed. Guests help themselves to forks and napery. The food in the main dining room is less festive, but at its best it is excellent. There is such interesting fare as pigs' knuckles with a vinaigrette sauce, soused shrimp and such main dishes (they vary every day) as boiled ham and cabbage, braised brisket of beef with egg barley, and roast ribs of beef with boxty pudding, made with potatoes. It must be noted that the pudding recently was tough, but the beef was first rank.

Serves 6 to 8 (possibly more) as an appetizer

These shrimp were sold by the piece at the bar. Attesting to their popularity, there are several published and word-of-mouth recipes for the shrimp. None of them is quite right, however, says Michael Whiteman, Joe Baum's business partner. He guided me in this recipe

1 tablespoon plus 2 teaspoons salt

3 pounds jumbo shrimp (about 24 to the pound), in their shells

4 lemons

1 pound onions (3 medium), peeled

1 cup extra-virgin olive oil (see Note)

1 rounded tablespoon whole black peppercorns

1 tablespoon tarragon vinegar

½ cup chopped fresh tarragon

6 large bay leaves, roughly crumbled

1 tablespoon Worcestershire sauce

10 drops Tabasco sauce

Bring 5 quarts of water to a rolling boil. Add the 1 tablespoon salt and the shrimp. Cook the shrimp for 1 minute from the time they've been added. The water will not return to a boil immediately. Drain well. Let cool without rinsing.

Use a mandolin to slice the lemons as thinly as possible, adjusting the mandolin's blade so that you can slice the lemon very, very thinly, but still have an intact, whole round lemon slice. Cut the onions in half through the root end, then slice, on the same setting of the mandolin, into half-moon slices.

Put the lemons, then the onion, into a very large bowl. Add all the remaining ingredients and the 2 teaspoons salt. Stir for several minutes, to combine thoroughly, but also to break down the onion and lemon slightly and to get their juices mingling.

Peel the cooled shrimp and add them to the marinade. Stir and toss to mix very well.

Chill for 12 to 18 hours, tossing and stirring every few hours. The onions and lemon slices are edible; in fact, some people think they are the best part, and at Charlie O's even an order of one or two shrimp got its complement of lemon and onion.

Note: Charlie O's would not have been using extra-virgin olive oil in the 1960s. But both the old published and word-of-mouth recipes do call for olive oil. Its deeper flavor may not be in keeping with the original dish, but condiment-quality extra virgin is delicious here.

TARTE À L'OIGNON

This classic tart from Alsace, the home region of Chef André Soltner, was only on the lunch menu at Lutèce. At dinner, however, it was sometimes offered, on the house, as a pre-dinner treat—what today would be called an *amuse bouche* or *amuse gueule*.

Serves 5 to 6 as a first course

At Lutèce, says André Soltner, he rarely added cheese to this tart. But today, as then, when he makes it at home for friends, he often sprinkles the top with grated Gruyere or Parmesan.

For the pastry:
2 cups bleached or unbleached all-purpose flour
1 ½ teaspoons fine salt
8 tablespoons (1 stick) unsalted butter, cut into
    1 tablespoon pieces
½ cup cold water

For the onion filling:
2 tablespoons lard or butter
1 pound onions, peeled and chopped
1 egg
½ cup heavy cream
½ teaspoon salt
¼ teaspoon freshly ground black pepper
⅛ teaspoon freshly ground nutmeg

Make the pastry:

In a small bowl, combine the flour and salt; mix well. Using a pastry blender, or your fingertips, cut the butter into the flour until the mixture looks like coarse meal with some small pea-sized pieces of butter.

Drizzle ½ cup of cold water over the flour mixture. Use a table fork to gently stir the dough together. If the dough is not sticking together, add water a few drops at a time until it does. Be careful not to add too much water; just enough to make the dough come together when stirred.

Gather the dough into a ball, pressing it together, then shape the dough into a disk. Place on a lightly floured surface and cover with an inverted bowl or a piece of plastic. Let rest at room temperature for at least 30 minutes. If making ahead, the dough can be wrapped in plastic and refrigerated, but let it return to room temperature before attempting to roll it out.

Prepare the onions:

In an 8- to 10-inch skillet, over medium heat, melt the lard or butter and sauté the onions until they are slightly browned and tender, about 8 minutes. Remove the skillet from the heat.

In a small bowl, beat the egg and cream together. Add this to the onions. Stir in the salt, pepper, and nutmeg.

Preheat the oven to 375 degrees.

On a lightly floured surface, roll out the dough to about a 14-inch circle.

Line a 10-inch, fluted, removable-bottom tart pan with the pastry. After fitting the pastry inside the pan, cut off the excess by rolling your pin over the top of the pan. The overlapping excess pastry will be cut off.

Prebake the pastry: Line the inside of the pan with aluminum foil. Fill the pan with beans or pie weights and bake in the preheated oven for

15 minutes. Remove the foil and pie weights, then return the pastry to the oven for another 10 minutes. Remove from the oven again and fill with the onion mixture. Return to the oven and bake for another 25 minutes.

Serve hot, warm, or at room temperature.

THE FOUR SEASONS' CRISP DUCK

The Four Seasons has been famous for its roast duck since Chef Seppi Renggli introduced this recipe in 1976. It was right after Tom Margittai and Paul Kovi bought the restaurant from Restaurant Associates, their former employer, and they had a new refrigeration system and a convection oven installed.

Says Chef Renggli now: "I saw the oven, and all this refrigerator space—rack after rack, and it had a fan —and I said to myself 'Oh, I can make Peking duck now.'"

Renggli's recipe is not truly the Chinese banquet dish. The Four Seasons serves its duck with orange sauce, not in the Chinese style, though Renggli is well-acquainted with Asian seasoning and cooking, since he is married to an Asian woman. His goal was not to create authentic Peking duck but seriously crisp duck skin. He achieved this by the Chinese method of letting the skin dehydrate through several days of air circulation in the refrigerator, then painting it with what amounts to a teriyaki glaze, a coloring and flavoring mixture of soy sauce and honey with spices. The drying is easily done in a home kitchen, if you are willing to monopolize a refrigerator shelf for three days. A convection oven is not needed. The following recipe is devised for a conventional oven.

Serves 4

Begin the preparation three days before serving. I am not offering the Four Seasons' orange sauce recipe. It is much too time-consuming and involved for a home cook. Suffice it to say, as roast duck for its own sake, this is sensational.

2 (4½- to 5-pound) ducks (if frozen, thoroughly defrosted), necks removed and reserved for a sauce, if desired

For the marinade:
½ ounce fresh ginger, peeled and thinly sliced
1 clove garlic, peeled and halved
Zest of ¼ orange, cut into thin strips

1 teaspoon lightly crushed coriander seeds
1 teaspoon lightly crushed black peppercorns
½ cup soy sauce
1 tablespoon honey

Plus:
¼ cup loose jasmine tea leaves
1 tablespoon Szechuan pepper (optional)

Cut the wing tips off the wings at the second joint. Cut or pull away all the fat from the ducks' cavities.

Clear a rack in your refrigerator and place the ducks on it, breast sides up and several inches apart. It is important that the air circulates freely around the ducks so the skin will dry. You can place a large baking pan below the rack with the birds to catch drippings. (There will not be many.) Leave the birds for 3 days without touching them.

To make the marinade, place all the ingredients in a jar or plastic container. Shake well to combine and refrigerate for 3 days, along with the ducks, shaking daily.

To roast: After 3 full days of drying and about 3 hours before you plan to serve the ducks, remove them and the marinade from the refrigerator.

Strain the marinade through a sieve into a bowl.

In handling the ducks, avoid pressing on the breasts since this will leave dark spots after roasting. I use a two-pronged meat fork placed inside the cavity to hold the ducks without touching their skins.

With the point of a small sharp knife, prick the skins all over, giving the thighs a few more pricks than the breasts.

Holding the ducks over a platter or pan, brush the ducks liberally with the marinade.

Place the ducks on a rack and let dry, breast side up, for about 15 minutes. Then brush them again and let dry again.

Meanwhile, preheat the oven to 350 degrees and arrange the racks so the ducks can be placed on the middle shelf and so there can be a rack under their rack to hold a roasting pan of water.

In the roasting pan, combine 3 quarts of water and the jasmine tea. Place in the oven while it preheats.

Spoon the remaining marinade into the ducks' cavities and carefully place them directly on the middle rack of the oven, breast side up, separated by a couple of inches, and positioned so they are directly over the pan of water and tea.

Let the ducks roast undisturbed for 1½ hours. The skin should be shiny, dark caramel in color, and very crisp.

Before removing the ducks from the oven, tip them to drain the liquid in their cavities, letting the juices run into the pan of water.

Place the ducks on a carving board. Sprinkle with Szechuan pepper, if using.

Let stand 10 minutes before carving. I use poultry shears to split the ducks in half the long way, then to cut the thigh-drumstick quarters from the breast quarters. Serve each person a half duck.

MRS. FOSTER'S FROSTY LIME PIE

Long before Chez Panisse in California, there was Mr. & Mrs. Foster's Place in Manhattan. Like Alice Waters's restaurant, Foster's had a market-driven menu, and only one a night. The only choice was take it or leave it.

Pearl Byrd was born in the late nineteenth century in Virginia, but spent her formative years on a farm in Oklahoma, when you could still plant on virgin soil. That's where she learned how food grows and how to prepare it, and preserve it, and to appreciate that cycle, she says in *Classic American Cooking*, a cookbook she wrote during her last days, after she had closed the restaurant.

Looking for a career on the stage, she came to New York, where she lived with an uncle, went to private school, and then to university. Only when she realized that she would never be a great actress did she turn to her love of food as a career. She got a job as a hostess in a restaurant. She admits, although not in so many words, that she was too bossy to work for others. So after several restaurant jobs, she married the boss. The restaurant owned by her advertising-executive husband, was called Foster. Under Pearl's direction, it evolved into a chain of four restaurants employing 250 people.

When the Fosters sold Foster, Pearl opened a restaurant called The Schooner, where she built a test kitchen for herself, and hired Louis Diat, the famous chef of the Ritz-Carlton Hotel, by then retired, to teach her the basics of French cuisine.

Mrs. Foster was an intimidating, stately figure in her later years. The restaurant was in a townhouse, and you had to ring the bell for the door to open. There would be Mrs. Foster waiting for you, looking you over to make sure you were dressed appropriately. You knew you had better behave. Her good friend James Villas, the legendary *Town and Country* magazine food writer, says he remembers her "swathed in Ultrasuede and hardly the image of one who had been cooking since noon."

Pearl Foster served true-blue American food, much of it based on her southern heritage, but informed by, if not fused with, her knowledge of French and other cuisines. In its heyday, during the 1960s and early 1970s, Mr. and Mrs. Foster's Place was certainly New York's premier American regional restaurant, and it has hardly been matched since.

Makes one 9-inch pie

This pie was one of the most popular desserts at Mr. and Mrs. Foster's Place. Tart and icy, it is incredibly refreshing. It can be served barely frozen—about two hours in the freezer—but you won't get the full "frosty" effect unless you leave it to firm up for several hours. I think a good deal of the pie's appeal is the contrast between the icy and tart filling and the soft and soothing whipped cream topping.

For the graham cracker crust:
1 ¼ cups graham cracker crumbs

¼ cup superfine sugar
6 tablespoon sunsalted butter melted

(continues next page)

For the filling:
5 eggs, separated
¾ cup superfine sugar, divided
⅔ cup freshly squeezed, strained lime juice
2 teaspoons grated lime peel
Pinch salt

For the topping:
1 ½ cups heavy cream, whipped
Thin slices of strawberries
Sugar

Preheat the oven to 350 degrees.

In a bowl, place the graham cracker crumbs, sugar, and melted butter. Blend well.

Press the mixture evenly into a 9-inch pie plate.

Bake 10 minutes. Cool to room temperature.

In a medium-sized bowl that you can place over a medium saucepan to create a double boiler, whisk the egg yolks until well mixed, then gradually beat in ½ cup sugar, beating until the mixture is pale and thick.

Stir in the lime juice and the rind with the whisk until well combined.

Place the bowl over a pot of barely simmering water. Stir gently and slowly with the whisk, scraping the sides of the bowl with the whisk, heating until the foam disappears from the surface of the mixture, it has thickened, and it will coat the back of a metal spoon. Do not allow to boil.

Place a sheet of plastic wrap directly on the surface of the custard and refrigerate until chilled.

When the yolk mixture is chilled, beat the egg whites with the salt until soft peaks form. Beat in the remaining ¼ cup sugar a tablespoon at a time and beat until the mixture is stiff and shiny.

Carefully fold the beaten whites into the cooled yolk mixture until evenly distributed.

Turn the filling into the cooled graham cracker pie shell.

Place the pie on a baking sheet and bake in a pre-heated 350-degree oven for 15 minutes or until tinged with brown.

Cool to room temperature (the top may crack slightly, but don't worry; it gets covered with whipped cream.)

Chill and freeze for 2 to 3 hours. If not serving then, cover with plastic wrap and keep frozen until just before serving.

Remove the pie from the freezer 10 minutes before serving. Cover with the whipped cream and garnish with lime slices dipped in sugar or fresh strawberries.

Note: The pie will keep frozen nicely for two to three weeks. If a sweeter pie is desired, cut down the lime juice to as little as ½ cup.

COACH HOUSE BLACK BEAN SOUP

Black bean soup was by far the most famous dish at the Coach House, and this recipe shows why. It is not at all a typical Cuban-style or other Latin-style bean soup. Unlike those relatively simple soups, this one has a base of long-cooked stock made from ham hocks and beef bones, which gives it a beautiful smoky flavor and a silky gelatinous texture.

Makes at least 12 servings

The stock should be simmered slowly the day before you plan to eat the soup.

For the stock:

4 tablespoons vegetable oil

2 large onions, coarsely chopped (about 3 cups)

3 medium leeks, well washed and coarsely chopped (about 3 cups)

2 large cloves garlic, lightly crushed

1 large rib celery, coarsely chopped (about 1 cup)

2 bay leaves

2 or 3 whole cloves

1 large or 2 small smoked ham hocks (with bone and rind)

3 pounds beef or veal bones

1 rounded teaspoon whole black peppercorns

For the soup:

2 cups dried black beans

Salt and freshly ground black pepper to taste

½ cup Madeira

Chopped parsley

2 or 3 finely chopped hard-cooked eggs

Very thin lemon slices

Make the stock:

In a large stock pot, over medium heat, heat the oil. Add the onions, leeks, garlic, and celery. Mix well, cover the pot, and, stirring once or twice, let the vegetables sweat until they are tender, about 10 minutes.

Add the bay leaves, cloves, ham hock, meat bones, peppercorns, and 5 quarts water. Bring to a boil. Reduce the heat and skim the scum from the surface and simmer, skimming occasionally until no more scum rises to the surface, partly covered, for 8 hours.

Let the stock cool somewhat, then strain it. Discard all the vegetables and bones. If you like, pick over the ham hock and save the meat for another use. Refrigerate the stock overnight, then remove all the solidified fat from the surface.

Make the soup:

Soak the beans overnight in water to cover by several inches. The next day, strain and reheat the broth.

Drain the soaked beans and add them to the broth and simmer, partly covered, stirring occasionally, until the beans are very tender, about 1 hour.

Remove from the heat, and put the soup through a food mill, or puree in a blender or food processor. You should have a very smooth and silky puree, not very thick, but so full of the gelatin from the bones that it has a mirrored surface. If you would like the soup a little thicker, let it reduce by simmering it gently, uncovered.

Taste, add the salt and pepper, then add the Madeira and bring to a boil.

Serve very hot, garnished with the parsley, eggs, and lemon slices.

CHITTERLINGS AND ALL THAT JAZZ

AMERICANS ASSOCIATE SLAVERY WITH THE SOUTH, WHERE CHEAP (OR FREE) labor supported the cotton plantations. But New York's dirty secret is that there were slaves here from the earliest days of the city. While the southern English colonies were importing slave labor from Africa, the Dutch West India Company in New Amsterdam was importing slaves from among those brought to work the sugar plantations of the Caribbean. When New Amsterdam was handed over to the British in 1664, there were fifteen hundred whites, three hundred black slaves out of a population of six hundred nonwhites, and a mere seventy-five freed black men. Then, in the eighteenth century, according to *Gotham*, the history of New York City, "more blacks came involuntarily to New York . . . than whites came voluntarily in the seventeenth . . . .[With an increase in trade with the West Indies], by 1746 African Americans comprised about 21 percent of the city's residents—more than 2,440 in a total population of 11,720. This was the highest concentration of slaves north of Virginia."

With about forty percent of the city's households depending on slave labor, and many of the city's businesses, too, in the nineteenth century New York City was divided on the question of slavery. Then, with the arrival of German and Irish immigrants in the mid-1840s, all looking for the low-level jobs that were held by recently emancipated blacks, racial strife and violence ruled the day. The Draft Riots of 1863, which began as a rebellion against the rule that three hundred dollars could buy you an exemption, quickly turned into a riot against the black people. The state of New York had given emancipation to the slaves in 1827, and immigrant groups saw these freed black men as competition for precious jobs.

Many freed blacks went into the food business. Largely, they owned the low-down oyster bars of Canal Street, although a few opened more respectable taverns. Samuel Fraunces could have been an inspiration to them all. He was a free black who, in 1762, opened his business, Fraunces Tavern, one of the city's premier gathering places. He later hosted George Washington when he gave his farewell address to his officers. Fraunces Tavern closed in 1785, but only because the building was appropriated as a headquarters for several federal agencies. A restored version of the tavern still stands and is a restaurant geared to Wall Streeters and tourists.

From 1900 to 1920, the city's population of African Americans boomed, increasing by four hundred percent. Most came from the South seeking better economic opportunities and an escape from Southern racism. The racism might not have been much better in New York City, but, as chance would have it, a real estate bust in Harlem, which, at the turn of the twentieth century was essentially a Jewish area, provided housing for many blacks.

OPPOSITE:
Unique Lunch was a highly regarded Harlem diner of the 1930s.

New York City has a large middle-class African-American population today. Soul food is how many of them refer to the cooking of the South that their parents or grandparents brought with them, but there are those who object to the term. The argument against the expression is that every group has its "soul food"—Italians their pasta with tomato sauce, Jews their delicatessen, and so on—and that their food should more properly be called African-American Southern food. This includes standard dishes of all Americans from the South—fried chicken, cornbread, greens cooked with smoked ham hocks—plus the dishes like chitterlings and macaroni and cheese that poor Southerners ate. Chitterlings, which are beef intestines, are a marginal food and so weren't eaten by the rich white overlords. In Harlem, to show how a poor food can be made into a celebration, they are paired with champagne in some restaurants. We no longer think of macaroni and cheese as a food for only poor people, but its popularity among African Americans most likely stems from the government handouts of processed cheese during the Depression and well into the 1960s. The handouts had a dual purpose: The inexpensive protein nourished the poor at the same time as it subsidized dairy farmers.

Soul food restaurants are usually neighborhood places serving their community, but a few have attracted citywide attention. The Pink Tea Cup, now at 42 Grove Street in Greenwich Village, has been a downtown gathering place for both black and white

Harlem's Hy Grade Restaurant in the 1930s

displaced Southerners for nearly forty years. In the early 1980s, Sylvia's, at 328 Lenox Avenue in Harlem, became a destination restaurant. Now, with Harlem becoming gentrified by young middle-class families, black as well as white, there are numerous media-touted restaurants that know how to smother pork chops, cook those collards, and pour big glasses of iced tea and lemonade.

CHICKEN AND WAFFLES

Everyone wants to get into the act, as Jimmy Durante used to say. Everyone wants to lay claim to the idiosyncratic combination of chicken and waffles. You'll read that it was created at Roscoe's in Los Angeles or at any number of other black-owned restaurants, jazz joints, and what have you. All these claims are clearly fabricated: Fried chicken and waffles is a Harlem creation. One plausible story has it that during the late 1940s, when bebop jazz musicians such as Miles Davis and Thelonius Monk would play at Harlem nightclubs the early hours of Sunday morning, they would breakfast at a local restaurant called Well's, on Seventh Avenue, which opened in 1938.

Harlem was hot in the 1930s, 1940s, and 1950s. White people went to the clubs, restaurants, and bars, and some black celebrities owned them. Sidney Poitier, the actor, had a rib place around the corner from Well's. Count Basie, the bandleader, had a bar and restaurant nearby. Roy Campanella, the baseball player, had a liquor store up the block. Sugar Ray Robinson, the boxer, had a barbershop, cleaners, and a bar. In fact, Sugar Ray owned a whole block of Harlem.

With what seemed like all New York City gathering at Well's after hours, Mr. Wells came up with the idea of chicken and waffles, a dish that was both dinner for those who hadn't had dinner and breakfast for those who were starting their day, not ending it. Another version of the story is just as likely: The jazz musicians created the combo themselves, ordering the breakfast waffles with a side of last night's fried chicken.

Another part of the legend has it that when Well's first put the combination on the menu it didn't sell, so he started to give it away, and, naturally, it caught on. It eventually became not only a restaurant item, but a tradition among Harlem blacks. Today, you can go to a breakfast prayer meeting, a Sunday gospel brunch, or a church supper and be served chicken and waffles. In the 1980s, there was even a black-owned discotheque and club downtown, in the east thirties, Mr. Leo's, that served chicken and waffles to the racially mixed crowd it attracted.

Roscoe's in Los Angeles was originally owned by a New Yorker, who carried the idea to California. Other restaurants around the country that are famous for the dish (Gladys Knight's and Ron Winans's places in Atlanta, for instance), just copied the idea.

For a great waffle to go with your fried chicken, use the batter for Childs' Wheat Cakes (page 78).

RED VELVET CAKE

Red velvet cake, a bright red, extremely moist and fine-crumbed cake that is barely flavored with cocoa, is also called $100 cake and Waldorf cake, and comes with a classic urban legend attached to it.

Here's how the story goes: Someone patronizes the Waldorf-Astoria for a meal, eats the cake, loves the cake, asks for the recipe, gets the recipe, but is charged for it. Then, in retaliation for what the purchaser considers an exorbitant bill for a recipe, she distributes the recipe to as many people as possible, sometimes in the form of a chain letter.

The price keeps getting higher as the story is repeated, but one hundred dollars was quite a lot of money in the mid-twentieth century, when this story is supposed to have taken place. (An almost identical story, is

also attached to a cookie recipe that supposedly comes from Neiman Marcus, as well as to something called Million Dollar Fudge.) In *The Vanishing Hitchhiker*, Jan Brunvald, a folklorist, confirms that the story of red velvet cake is, indeed, one of several American legends that pits a large, greedy institution against a consumer who feels she has been unfairly charged for a recipe.

Red velvet cake didn't become popular in New York City until the 1980s, which excludes the possibility that it was served at the Waldorf-Astoria. In the 1960s, it did enjoy a vogue on U.S. military bases, among whites and blacks, who, for the first time, began living next door to each other. The recipe appears in several community cookbooks written and published by military wives.

Nowadays, red velvet cake is made by a number of bakeries in Harlem; in Jamaica, Queens; and in Bedford Stuyvesant ("Bed-Sty") in Brooklyn. It is particularly popular as a birthday cake. Brooklyn's "Raven the Cake Man" (Raven Dennis) gets many requests for it as a wedding cake, too. (His three-layer version is pictured above.) For the obvious reason that it is red, it also pops up in mainstream Manhattan restaurants on Valentine's Day.

Makes one 9-inch, 2-layer cake, serving at least 10

Many recipes for red velvet cake have you mix the vinegar and baking soda together at the very end, then fold this tiny bit of seething liquid into the otherwise fully mixed batter. Here, making the mixing much easier, the vinegar goes in with other wet ingredients and the soda is mixed with the flour.

As for the amount of red food coloring, some recipes call for as much as two 1-ounce bottles. Some recipes ask for only 1 teaspoon, which merely tints the faintly chocolate-brown cake. One bottle will produce a vivid red color. Two bottles seem unnecessary, especially since food coloring now costs more than $2 an ounce or bottle, making it more expensive than cocoa and nearly as expensive as vanilla.

2 ¼ cups cake flour

1 teaspoon baking soda

1 teaspoon salt

¼ cup cocoa powder

1 ½ cups sugar

1 ½ cups vegetable oil

2 eggs

2 teaspoons to 1 bottle red food coloring
(1 ounce)

1 teaspoon vanilla extract

1 teaspoon distilled white vinegar

1 cup buttermilk

Cream Cheese Frosting (recipe follows)

Confectioners' sugar (optional)

Preheat the oven to 350 degrees. Prepare two 9-inch round cake pans: Grease them lightly then flour them lightly, or grease them then line the bottoms with parchment or wax paper. (There's no need to grease the paper.)

In a mixing bowl, combine the flour, baking soda, salt, and cocoa powder. Set aside.

In another mixing bowl, with a hand-held mixer on low speed, or with a wooden spoon, beat the sugar and oil until well blended.

Add the eggs, one at a time, blending well between additions.

Blend in the food coloring, vanilla, and vinegar. Scrape the sides of the bowl with a rubber spatula.

Alternately blend in the flour mixture and the buttermilk, using about one-third of each at a time and scraping the sides of the bowl a couple of times. Do not overbeat or use the electric mixer on high, as this will toughen the cake.

Immediately pour the batter into the prepared pans, dividing it evenly.

Bake for 25 to 30 minutes, until a toothpick inserted in the center comes out clean.

Cool the cakes in their pans on a wire rack for 5 minutes.

Remove the cakes from the pans and cool completely on the rack.

Fill and frost as desired, or not at all. For presentation, you may want to sprinkle unfrosted cakes with confectioners' sugar.

CREAM CHEESE FROSTING (Makes enough for one 9-inch, 2-layer cake)

1 (8-ounce) package cream cheese

8 tablespoons (1 stick) unsalted butter

1 pound confectioners' sugar

1 teaspoon vanilla extract

Milk, as needed

In a mixing bowl, beat the cream cheese until softened and smooth.

Add the butter and continue to beat until softened, smooth, and well incorporated with the cream cheese.

Beat in the confectioners' sugar a little at a time, then beat in the vanilla.

If the frosting is too thick to spread easily, beat in cold milk, 1 tablespoon at a time, until it is of spreading consistency.

CHAPTER **20**
CONTEMPORARY CLASSICS

LE CIRQUE

IT WAS GAEL GREENE, THE LONGTIME RESTAURANT CRITIC OF *NEW YORK* magazine, who first called Sirio Maccioni "the ringmaster" of Le Cirque, a sobriquet that has stuck for more than thirty years. From the night it opened in March 1974, Le Cirque became the watering hole for international society. There were always a few old-money social titans among them, with antique New York names like Astor, Whitney, Roosevelt, and Vanderbilt, but the nouveau riche and the power brokers, whom New York always worships above its aristocracy, were the life of the party. It was the most international, moneyed restaurant scene in New York City.

OPPOSITE:
Sirio Maccioni has been catering to the rich and famous since his days at the Colony.

Maccioni was well prepared to be its master. A self-described "poor boy" from Montecatini, in Tuscany, Italy, he was raised by his grandparents and two uncles after his parents died, when he was a boy. His father was a hotel concierge. "He wore a tie and jacket to work, and a gold key in his lapel," Maccioni remembers. In 1951, through a family friend—actually Yves Montand, whose Italian name was Livi—Sirio got a job at the Plaza Athénée in Paris. He thought he would learn French, a necessary language for hotel service, when he got there. "But when I arrived, they said come back when you know French," he says.

Maccioni changed plans and went to work in Germany, where he not only learned German, but French and English as well. He was on his way. He worked briefly on the Home Line, an Italian cruise ship line, and eventually, in 1956, he ended up in New York City, on the doorstep of the Colony, which was then Cafe Society's favorite spot.

He is often described as a John Wayne lookalike, but to Gene Cavallero, the owner of the Colony, he must have looked the part of a maître d', because he immediately put him on the door. It was a test that the tall, handsome, charming, and diligent Maccioni was born to pass. The maître d's tasks, such as guiding people to the table at which you'd like them to be seated (as opposed to the table where they'd like to be seated) and somehow making them think it more wonderful than their own choice, must be handled with great delicacy and requires a real talent to pull off.

It was, of course, at the Colony that Maccioni learned who was who in New York City, and the most important lesson of all: "If you say hello and good-bye to people they feel important. Even if they are already important, they need even more than others to feel they are important.

And if you treat them as an equal and important—hello, good-bye—they will come back so you can say hello and good-bye to them again."

When the Colony closed in 1973, Maccioni, its maître d', was a much-admired figure among the rich in New York City. He had taken care of them for so many years. William Zeckendorf, the real estate mogul, still craved Maccioni's attention, and, as the city was in a deep recession, he offered him a space for a new restaurant with a low rent and long lease; Maccioni could not refuse. In April 1974, with Jean Vergnes, who had been a chef at the Colony and knew what Cafe Society wanted to eat, he opened, essentially, a new Colony—Le Cirque.

The restaurant was in a ground-floor space of what was then the Mayfair Hotel, but it was entered through its own door, which later became the background of many a paparazzi picture. It was well received from the beginning, but not because of its cuisine—in fact, Gael Greene was not at all impressed. Some critics evaded the subject of the food but said good things about other aspects of the restaurant. Because they were "the boys from the Colony," everyone was predisposed and prepared to support Vergnes and Maccioni.

Malcolm Forbes, who then served as restaurant critic of his own magazine, said it was a "great addition to the New York posh restaurant plateau . . . a great oasis for the midtowners who need to talk business." Stendahl (William Bernal), then writing for the *New York Daily News,* gave Le Cirque a somewhat backhanded compliment: "There is something wonderful about Le Cirque that goes beyond wine and food."

It took a few years for Le Cirque to really find its own voice, one that was not merely an echo of the Colony, which had closed, after all, because its era was over. Maccioni realized almost immediately that in this new age food mattered. Vergnes was too old-fashioned. They parted ways, and Alain Sailhac became chef in 1978. He raised the standards considerably, making the food more contemporary. Still, you could always get a piece of plain grilled fish and a salad with the dressing on the side. "That's what society ladies like to eat, and what they make their husbands eat when they're with them," says Maccioni, confiding that the gentlemen are more self-indulgent when they come with each other. (Sailhac is now a dean of the French Culinary Institute in Manhattan.)

Daniel Boulud became the chef in 1985. He brought the kitchen to its highest level, then left to open his own restaurant in 1992. Sylvain Portay succeeded Boulud. When he returned to France in 1995, Sottha Kuhn, Boulud's former sous, took over. The Cambodian-born chef became a favorite of New York City's food press. When he returned to Cambodia, to a semi-retirement he still enjoys, Pierre Schaedelin became the chef.

The restaurant has gone through a number of pastry chefs as well, all of whom have become famous in their own right and have gone on to great personal success—Dieter Schoener, who introduced crème brûlée to America (see page 349) and now teaches at the Culinary Institute of America in Hyde Park, New York; François Payard, who owns the Payard Patisserie and Bistro on Lexington Avenue and Seventy-third Street; and Jacques Torres, who became a television personality and then opened a chocolate factory in Brooklyn.

Two of Sirio's three sons, Marco and Mauro, along with his wife, Egidiana (Egi), run a casual Le Cirque, Osteria del Circo. Another son, Mario, operates Le Cirque in the Bellagio Hotel in Las Vegas. And the family rotates duties managing a newer endeavor, a Le Cirque in Mexico City.

BARBARA KAFKA

Barbara Kafka was New York City's food muse for the last twenty-five years of the twentieth century. Her lasting contribution is that she inspired some greats and many not-so-greats of the food world—through her knowledge of history and gastronomy, her sheer intelligence, her good taste in the kitchen (and out), her writing and teaching, and not a small dose of New York City pushiness.

Among her many more concrete credits, she wrote and did much of the research for 1975's The Cook's Catalog, *a project credited to James Beard, Burt Wolf (of CNN fame), and graphic designer Milton Glaser. She worked with Joe Baum and Michael Whiteman at the original Windows on the World, buying the "table top" and setting up the ground-breaking wine cellar. She was a close friend of Beard, and became his teaching partner in his later years. She opened the first store to feature only American food products—Star Spangled Foods. She was a restaurant consultant. She wrote the first serious microwave cookbook, and many other cookbooks. See her story about presenting a restaurant concept to William Paley of CBS, on page 358.*

WINDOWS ON THE WORLD

Windows on the World is the restaurant in the World Trade Center that everyone remembers, but feeding the more than fifty thousand people that worked every day in the two 110-story towers required much more than one glamorous restaurant.

Joe Baum, who, while an executive of Restaurant Associates had created several highly regarded, innovative, and successful restaurants, including the Four Seasons (see page 310), was asked by the Port Authority of New York and New Jersey, developers of the World Trade Center, to consult. His mandate was to do a logistical analysis and see what the buildings and the job required, in particular how many people needed to be fed at different price points and styles. Baum, in turn, recruited Michael Whiteman, then the founding editor of *Nation's Restaurant News* to become his partner. Whiteman, in his capacity as the editor-in-chief of what is still the largest circulation restaurant industry publication, was a young man who traveled extensively around the country, and, of course, knew the restaurant business well. Baum felt he needed Whiteman's perspective as an observer of national trends and restaurant systems. Roger Martin, a Restaurant Associates alumnus, introduced the two and the consulting firm of Joseph Baum-Michael Whiteman was born. They would continue to work together, along with another partner, the financial brain, Dennis Sweeney, beyond the World Trade Center project. The trio created, among other projects, five restaurants that would earn three stars from the *New York Times*—a record for any company—including the restored Rainbow Room in Rockefeller Center.

They went to work in 1970, and immediately realized that if all the various food facilities that were needed were operated by separate companies it would be a logistical nightmare and a security problem. Among many other things, each company would need its own loading dock and elevator to get deliveries and dispose of garbage. There weren't enough truck docks to go around. Naturally, having a restaurant on the 107th floor of the building presented special problems.

The answer was to have one company run everything and to build a central kitchen below ground where all the food could be received and prepped, a chef's term for trimming, cleaning, butchering, slicing, dicing, and so on before food is cooked. Here the poultry would be taken out of its crates, off the ice, boned, and trimmed, if necessary. The produce would be separated from its boxes, the vegetables and fruits cleaned and peeled. The shrimp would be cleaned here, the fish scaled and filleted. The idea was to send clean and fresh products to all the facilities, including the 107th floor restaurant, and keep the bulk of the food garbage downstairs, in one place, where it could be disposed of more easily. All the stocks could be made and the sauces started downstairs.

The only exception to this centralized underground prep station was live trout, for which the company had built tanks in the Windows kitchen. Live trout were on the first menu at Windows, but the fish refused to stay alive on the elevator trip to the top of the building. They promptly died of the bends. Trout came off the menu.

Among the big names that were brought in on the project were Jacques Pépin, who con-sulted on the planning and building of the prep station; Alan Lewis, another Restaurant Associates executive, who would become the first general manager of Windows; Albert Kumin, the pastry chef, who ended up leaving Windows to work at the White House; and Barbara Kafka (see page 339), who helped plan the menu for Windows and purchased the table top accoutrements—flatware, glasses, and linens. Milton Glaser, the legendary graphic designer, did the menus and other printed matter. Kevin Zraly, then a wine salesman, and now a top wine educator and consultant, was hired to build the wine cellar and follow through as sommelier. He was so young the press dubbed him "the wine wunderkind." James Beard helped plan menus not only for Windows on the World, but the Market Bar and Dining Room, a restaurant on the concourse level of the complex and one of the other three-star restaurants that the Baum-Whiteman Company created.

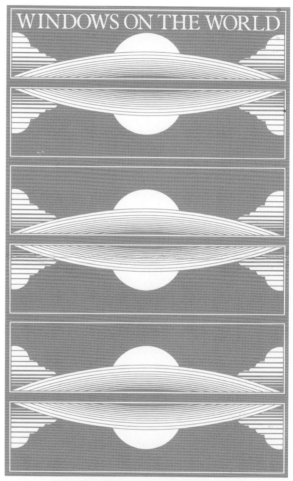

The Baum-Whiteman Company worked for six years on the project, at the beginning merely as consultants, but in the end as the operators of the various food facilities. Dog and pony shows were conducted all over the country to find a company with the capacity and willingness to tackle the proj-ect, but everyone thought it, particularly Windows, was doomed to failure. Finally, Hilton International, which was then owned by TWA, signed a master lease to operate all the restaurants. In turn, they formed a subsidiary called Inhilco and retained Baum-Whiteman to open and operate all the facilities. Inhilco remained the opera-tor until the first terrorist attack in 1993.

Windows, which debuted in 1976, just in time for the city's celebration of the bicentennial, was actually the last of the many food operations to open. The Big Kitchen, on the concourse level, was the first successful food court in this part of the world (there was one in Canada), and it won a Bard Award for urban design, which brought the Baum-Whiteman Company consulting contracts to do the first fast food courts in Japan and Europe.

The Market Bar and Dining Room, which was largely planned by Whiteman himself, was also on the ground level of the towers. It was the first modern restaurant to gear its menu to the daily offerings of the produce market and to name the producers on the menu—before Alice Waters and other California resturants became famous for it. This had a dual purpose, according to Whiteman. Besides ensuring that the menu was seasonal, "it put the suppliers on the line for quality." When you walked into the restaurant, there was a huge display of the day's produce offerings, and at the table diners were visited by a "vegetable sommelier" who would tell them how each vegetable could be prepared. The kitchen would make any individual vegetable or a platter of mixed vegetables. In fact, although the restaurant was meat-centric, the vegetable platters became the best-sellers. To underscore the market theme, as diners left the restaurant they were given double-yolk eggs to take home for breakfast.

Among the other food service operations in the World Trade Center were the Sky Dive restaurant on the forty-fourth floor of Tower One, and the Corner—Good Food on the Square. However, The first restaurant to open in 1972, was Eat and Drink; it was supposed to be temporary but lasted eighteen years. There was also a snack bar on the observation deck, and employee cafeterias for the Commodities Exchange and for the Fiduciary Trust, which was on top of Tower Two, the one that came down first on September 11, 2001.

The press and politicians were skeptical about Windows on the World as soon as the project was announced by the Port Authority. New York City was in a deep recession at the time the towers and the restaurant were being planned, and still when it opened. The city was bankrupt. The West Side Highway had just collapsed. The last thing the city needed, it seemed, was an expensive restaurant on top of the highest building in the world in a neighborhood where no one lived. The only lasting effect all this pressure had on the Port Authority was that it turned the Windows facility into a one-story affair rather than the more efficient (if expensive to start up) and potentially more lucrative two-story restaurant with many more private party and catering rooms.

In the end, the 1976 opening of Windows on the World, in conjunction with Operation Sail and all the hoopla surrounding the bicentennial, turned out to be a tonic for the city. It brought in tourists and said to the country, "Don't count us out!" It was enormously well received by city government, by the press, by the public—it was the only big project in the city at the time. It didn't hurt that the restaurant afforded spectacular views of Op Sail, the harbor crowded with ships from all over the world, and the Statue of Liberty holding her torch over them all. The huge television coverage helped kick off the restaurant, and also gave credit to a highly vilified piece of architecture.

The concept for the food was simple—American with Continental touches. While the towers were being built, Whiteman and James Beard went to the Trattoria da Alfredo, Alfredo Viazzi's restaurant on Hudson Street in Greenwich Village (see page 168), to plan menus. When they wanted to eat something more American (for inspiration) they would go to the Coach House (see page 316). Both were favorite haunts of Beard. Windows was never conceived as one restaurant alone, so there was plenty to plan. Cellar in the Sky was a restaurant within the restaurant, and it was the first in the nation to offer menus with wine pairings. The Hors D'Oeuvrerie, also on the 107th floor of Tower One, was the first international grazing place. Barbara Kafka's had a big influence on that menu. And Windows was a private club at lunchtime. It was ahead of its time in that every club in those days was dark and fusty, with crackling old leather chairs. This club was bright and white.

By the early 1990s, however, the Port Authority became troubled by the restaurant's declining sales and used the terrorist attack in 1993 as an excuse to close the place and terminate Inhilco's lease. Windows was up for grabs, and an international competition was held to find an operator. Companies from thirty-eight countries bid on it. In the end, the contest was between three New York City restaurateurs, Alan Stillman (of Smith and Wollensky fame), Warner LeRoy (the showman restaurateur who created Maxwell's Plum and revived Tavern on the Green), and Baum-Whiteman—again.

Baum at first did not want to compete because he didn't think they'd win. He was already operating the Rainbow Room, which could be construed as Windows' competition. In the end, however, he was convinced that it was a different market and that he liked the idea of running, to use a loose analogy, the two anchor stores in a big shopping center. Because Baum-Whiteman was the original creator of Windows on the World, and the restaurant's operator for three years, the company got the contract. Baum and Whiteman knew the problems of reinventing it, and they could now correct their mistakes. Plus, they were the low bidders.

The new concept was fundamentally the same as the first, but this time they were able to double the size of the facility, increasing the seating in the main restaurant, designing a second floor with more banquet spaces, and putting in a ballroom with a two-thousand-person capacity. And the second time around, they decided to make it more than a destination restaurant attractive to one type of customer—tourists and metro New Yorkers (always tourists in our own town) celebrating special occasions. They were going to attract the local young Wall Streeters after work, and even encourage the "bridge and tunnel" crowd. It was hoped that as they grew older they'd become the customers for the main restaurant. To that end, the Greatest Bar on Earth was conceived. It was twice the size of the old Hors D'Oeuvrerie and jammed every night. It had a sushi station and live Latin music and dancing, among other youthful attractions. Another restaurant, Wild Blue, a fancy meat and potatoes place with limited views, was created for high rollers. When the first terrorist attack came the complex was doing eighteen million in business a year. In 2001 before the second terrorist attack it did thirty-eight million.

The second time around, the menu at Windows, as conceived by Baum-Whiteman's culinary director, Rozanne Gold, was to feature the most spectacular dishes from around the world. But the first chef at the renewed Windows was Phillip Ferret, a young French chef who had been running

ROZANNE GOLD

Rozanne Gold was only twenty-four when she was hired to be the chef at Gracie Mansion for mayor Ed Koch. She went on to revamp the thirty-two Lord & Taylor department store restaurants across the country, then joined the Joseph Baum–Michael Whiteman company as chef-director, developing menus for the Rainbow Room, including its Little Meals bar menu, which became the subject of her first book. She created the concept and menu for the Hudson River Club in the World Financial Center, and among many other projects, she created the menus for the second opening of Windows on the World. She has also been a culinary presence as the entertaining editor of Bon Appetit magazine and the author of the award-winning "1-2-3" series of cookbooks, where all the dishes have only three ingredients.

Restaurant Associates's Café Centro in the Met Life building. Ferret and his brigade would not cook anything they weren't familiar with, which meant anything that wasn't French. So Michael Lomonaco, a Brooklyn-born and -trained chef, moved from the '21' Club to Windows. Lomonaco had a somewhat broader outlook. Again, Milton Glaser did the graphics and designed the china service. The architect Hugh Hardy, who had restored the Rainbow Room with Baum-Whiteman, was brought in to work with architect Warren Platner, who was responsible for the interiors.

Both the first and second Windows broke ground in several ways. It was the first rooftop restaurant with good food, not just a view. It had women managers and captains at a time when clubs and fancy restaurant were being sued because they didn't. And it tipped the balance on wine sales from Europe to California.

The world knows the end to the Windows story. It was open for breakfast when the planes hit the towers.

DANNY MEYER

It was the night before Thanksgiving in 1985 and, as newspaper restaurant critics are never allowed a night off, I made my first visit to the new Union Square Cafe on behalf of the *Daily News*. Something about it reminded me of an old New York restaurant, and I liked it immediately. The owner, Danny Meyer, had apparently given most of his staff the night off. Who was going to go to a brand-new restaurant the night before Thanksgiving? The answer was a bunch of drunken Yuppies and a restaurant critic. The Yuppies were drunk when they came in, so the waitress allowed them only one round before she kindly said that perhaps they should order some food before ordering another round of drinks. They were adamant. They wanted more drink. The waitress took their order but went into the kitchen, not to the bar, and seconds later out walked Danny Meyer in kitchen whites. I understood that he was the owner and host, not the chef, but there was the proof before me that he was going to cook my dinner that night. Meyer introduced himself to the unruly diners, then in the politest manner explained how he would be responsible if something awful happened because of their inebriation and asked if they could please do him the big favor of ordering some food to balance out the booze. When they wouldn't, he asked them to leave; surprisingly, they did. Then, once they were outside, he bolted the door behind them.

They came back only seconds later and, when they couldn't get in to make a disturbance, they kicked in the glass on the doors. Meyer shrugged to me—I was the only one left in the room—and came over and said, "So what would you like to eat?"

It is for warm hospitality, as well as the best contemporary cuisine, for which Meyer's restaurants are known. These include the flagship Union Square Cafe with chef Michael Romano, the Gramercy Tavern with chef Tom Colicchio, 11 Madison Park with chef Kerry Heffernan, Tabla, his Indian-fusion restaurant with chef Floyd Cardoz, and Blue Smoke, his barbecue restaurant. He now has the contract to operate the restaurants in the Museum of Modern Art, and he's even opened a kiosk selling hot dogs, hamburgers, and ice cream in Madison Park.

DREW NIEPORENT

Drew Nieporent knew he wanted to be a restaurateur since his bar mitzvah at Maxwell's Plum—at least, that's what he once told me. The restaurateur who executed that party, Warner LeRoy (see page 318), became his hero, and after Nieporent graduated in 1977 from the esteemed Cornell University School of Hotel Management, he went to work for LeRoy at that very restaurant. Nieporent isn't sentimental or anything, but he bought the famous bar from Maxwell's when it was auctioned off after the restaurant closed. It is now the centerpiece of his Tribeca Grill.

Nieporent also worked for LeRoy at Tavern on the Green, then went to La Réserve, Le Périgord, La Grenouille, and La Régence—all fancy, expensive, very traditional midtown French restaurants. Given that background, it is somewhat surprising that his first personal restaurant venture, in 1985, was to open Montrachet, a decidedly alternative French restaurant in Tribeca, then not at all Hollywood on the Hudson, as it is today, but a sleepy corner of Manhattan that hardly anyone but the real estate brokers knew existed. It was the real estate ads that gave the section its name. Tribeca stands for the "triangle below Canal (Street)." Nieporent says it was the low rent that attracted him to the location.

Nieporent and his dining room staff all wore black and no ties—their shirts were buttoned up to the neck, as was the fashion downtown at the time. His chef was David Bouley. The food was post-nouvelle, although Bouley had yet to hear that New Yorkers like portions bigger than a deck of playing cards. When I dined there during my first weeks as the restaurant critic of the *New York Daily News*, I waited forever for the food and left hungry. Still, Bryan Miller gave the restaurant three stars in the *New York Times*. Nieporent came to regret the kudos, however. Besides the fact that he felt they were yet undeserved—the restaurant was too new, too untried—he realized that Bouley could not deal with the full reservation book that the three-star review created. Nieporent and Bouley quickly parted company. Several talented young chefs have worked in the restaurant over the years, but, as is always the case when a knowledgeable and attentive restaurateur is in charge, Nieporent is the one with whom it is always identified. It is not surprising that Sirio Maccioni of Le Cirque (see page 337) is also a role model for Nieporent.

Montrachet attracted big names in the downtown New York City art world and other celebrated denizens of the gradually gentrifying commercial loft area. Robert DeNiro was a regular and about to buy a nearby warehouse to serve as a production facility for his movie company. He wanted a restaurant downstairs that could be a canteen and a place to entertain. He asked Nieporent to be his managing partner. The Tribeca Grill, decorated with DeNiro's father's paintings, was the result.

In 1993 Nieporent formed a consulting and management company, Myriad Restaurant Group, and the next year opened two new restaurants, Rubicon in San Francisco, again with DeNiro, but also with Francis Ford Coppola and Robin Williams, and, back in New York City, the now internationally famous and much-imitated Nobu, with DeNiro and the innovative Japanese chef Nobuyuki Matsuhisa. There are many other restaurants under the Myriad banner, and almost every one has won honors and awards. Nieporent himself has been honored innumerable times, not only for his accomplishments as a restaurateur but for his humanitarian and charitable work.

ENTRECÔTE WITH GREEN PEPPERCORNS

This was the main course at Le Cirque's opening-night dinner in 1974. It may seem strange now that such a grand restaurant served something as ordinary as steak to an audience of high-roller regulars from the Colony. But saucing the steak with green peppercorns was totally of the gastronomic moment: Green peppercorns were the sun-dried tomatoes of the 1970s, a trendy ingredient that was hard to escape in New York City's top restaurants, and eventually in New York City's home kitchens. Packed in vinegar brine, with an acidic edge as well a peppery tang, they have been forgotten during the last two decades. Too bad! They are still a delicious addition to all kinds of dishes.

Serves 4

This is freely adapted from *A Seasoned Chef,* by Jean Vergnes, who specifies two 10- to 12-ounce steaks. In fact, there is enough sauce here for four steaks that size. I prefer to make two thick 16-ounce steaks, to serve four; I slice them and fan them out on a plate over a small pool of the peppercorn sauce.

2 (1½-inch-thick, 16-ounce) shell steaks (also called sirloin strip, New York strip, or top loin)
Salt to taste
1 tablespoon unsalted butter
1 tablespoon finely chopped shallot

2 tablespoons Cognac
¾ cup heavy cream
1 ½ tablespoons green peppercorns packed in brine, drained
2 tablespoons demi-glace (see Note on page 354)

Take the steaks directly from the refrigerator. Salt them well on both sides.

Over medium-high heat, heat a heavy skillet that is large enough to hold the steaks without touching each other. When the pan is very hot, put the steaks in the pan (no fat is necessary) and cook for 6 minutes on the first side without disturbing them.

Turn the steaks and cook for 5 minutes on the second side—for rare to medium-rare steaks. Remove to a platter and cover the steaks loosely with a piece of tinfoil to keep them warm.

Discard the fat in the pan. Place the pan over low heat and add the butter. Add the shallot and sauté for 30 seconds.

Add the cognac. Let it sizzle for a few seconds, then add the cream and the peppercorns. Stir and scrape the bottom of the pan, deglazing it. Simmer for 1 minute.

Add the demi-glace. Stir well, and simmer gently for another 1 to 2 minutes, increasing the heat if necessary to keep the demi-glace bubbling. The demi-glace should become somewhat thicker than heavy cream. Stir in any juices that have accumulated on the plate with the steaks.

For maximum visual effect, serve the steaks, sliced or not, on top of the demi-glace. Serve immediately.

LE CIRQUE'S CRÈME BRÛLÉE

Crème brûlée is beyond being a contemporary classic dessert. It has become unavoidable. It has become a cliché. The day it was put on Le Cirque's menu in 1982, it captured America's fancy. And, as happens with dishes that are made by everyone, competent cooks and not, it has been tragically degraded. Every flavor known to man has made it into crème brûlée. Whole books, albeit small books, have been written around this simple concept of barely congealed custard topped with a crackling, thin layer of caramel. But no matter how many poorly made ones we've eaten, how many bizarrely flavored, even unrecognizable ones, it always was and always will be a thrill to eat crème brûlée at Le Cirque.

Was it created there? Yes and no. According to Sirio Maccioni, he was on vacation in Spain with his wife, Egidiana, when they took a liking to the classic Spanish dessert *crema catalana*, a rich custard topped with a thick layer of caramelized sugar. Back at Le Cirque, Maccioni asked his pastry chef, Dieter Schorner, to replicate the dessert, but to make it more refined, and, of course, to make it in individual servings for an elegant presentation. It is, one must admit after eating hundreds of crème brûlées that are not as carefully constructed, the ethereal quality of the pure vanilla custard quivering under the thin brittle crust of caramel that makes the original Le Cirque dessert the one to match.

Schoener gets the credit for lightening up the traditional *crema catalana*, but it is pastry chef Francisco Gutierrez who has actually been producing it for the last twenty-odd years.

Serves 8

This recipe is all about technique and equipment. Combining the hot cream and egg yolks is a crucial moment: Do it carefully and quickly. Straining is essential if you want to achieve a flawlessly smooth texture. You will need eight lightly fluted porcelain oval ramekins, each about 3 by 5 inches and 1 inch deep. Because crème brûlée is such a popular dessert today, these are easy to find, as are small gas torches made especially for caramelizing the sugar on top.

Here's a tip from Jacques Torres, who was one of the pastry chefs at Le Cirque: Because the brown sugar needs to be dry so it can be spread evenly (for an even caramel finish), air dry the sugar by spreading it out on a large plate or baking sheet and leaving it, uncovered, occasionally breaking it up, for about 3 hours. When it is ready, it will feel dry and sandy.

1 quart heavy cream	8 egg yolks
¾ cup granulated sugar	1 cup firmly packed light brown sugar,
1 vanilla bean	dried (see headnote)

Preheat the oven to 250 degrees.

In a 1 ½-quart saucepan, combine the cream and granulated sugar. With a sharp knife, split the vanilla bean lengthwise and scrape the seeds into the saucepan. Drop the vanilla pod into the cream too.

Place over medium-low heat and cook, stirring occasionally, until the sugar is dissolved and bubbles are just forming around the edge of the cream.

Meanwhile, in a large mixing bowl, whisk the egg yolks.

When the cream is hot, stir a few tablespoons of it into the yolks to temper them to the heat. Then stir in the remaining heated cream.

Pour the mixture through a fine-mesh sieve or a chinois into a clean bowl, allowing the vanilla seeds to go through but not any stringy or otherwise coagulated egg.

Pour the custard mixture into a measuring cup with a pouring spout.

Place 8 crème brûlée dishes on rimmed baking sheets, or in roasting pans.

Pour the custard mixture into the ramekins, filling them only half full.

Place the pans of ramekins in the oven, then fill the ramekins to the top. Pour hot tap water into the pan, around the ramekins, to come about halfway up the sides of the custard cups.

Bake for 1 hour and 15 minutes, until the custards look firm and just tremble slightly in the middle. (If you are using more than one pan to hold the dishes, be sure to rotate the pans, top to bottom, front to back, for even baking.)

Let cool to room temperature, then refrigerate for at least 3 hours or up to 2 days.

When ready to serve, pass the brown sugar through a sieve to remove any lumps.

Preheat the broiler. Immediately before serving, spread a thin layer of the brown sugar over the tops of the custards. You have spread enough sugar when the custard is no longer visible, about 2 tablespoons for each custard. It is important to spread the sugar evenly; if it is too thick or too thin in places, the caramelization will not be even across the top.

Place the molds on a clean baking sheet. When the broiler is hot, place the baking sheet about 4 inches under the broiler and broil until the sugar is caramelized. Keep a close eye on the crème brûlée during broiling. They are finished when they are light brown.

Alternately, use a small blowtorch to caramelize the sugar: Hold the torch about 1 ½ inches from the surface and keep it moving across the surface until the sugar is evenly browned.

Let cool until the surface crisps, just a few minutes.

Serve immediately.

ILONA TORTE

George Lang, proprietor of Café des Artistes and a longtime power and influence on the city's gastronomic scene, named this gorgeous and seductively delicious Hungarian-style cake after his mother. It is his pride and joy and what instantly comes to his mind if you ask if Café des Artistes has a signature dish. The Ilona torte has always been on his menu, which is why he was so amused when he recently saw it on someone else's menu credited to that chef's grandmother, a Mexican woman. Lang wondered how the chef's mother had come by the Hungarian name Ilona, but he was pleased with the thought that his own mother's namesake cake would live on and on, even if credited to someone else's family.

Makes one 9-inch torte

For the cake:

5 ounces semisweet chocolate, chopped

1 cup sugar

¼ teaspoon salt

¼ cup water

6 tablespoons (¾ stick) unsalted butter, softened

8 eggs, separated

½ teaspoon cream of tartar

8 ounces walnuts, finely ground

2 tablespoons fresh white bread crumbs

10 walnut halves for decoration

For the buttercream:

8 ounces semisweet chocolate, cut into small pieces

2½ teaspoons instant espresso powder

½ pound plus 6 tablespoons (2 ¾ sticks) unsalted butter, softened

4 egg yolks

1 cup confectioners' sugar

George Lang and the Howard Christie Chandler mural at Lang's Café des Artistes.

Preheat the oven to 375 degrees.

To make the cake: Grease a 9-inch springform pan. Line the bottom of the pan with parchment paper, and grease the paper. Sprinkle flour into the pan, shake it around, then knock out any excess.

Put the chocolate, sugar, salt, and water in the top of a double boiler or into a small, heavy saucepan over low heat (or in a small glass or metal mixing bowl placed over a pot of hot water). Do not let the water under the chocolate come to a boil. Stir occasionally until the mixture is smooth. Remove from the heat, and let cool for 15 minutes.

In a medium mixing bowl, or the bowl of a stand mixer, beat the butter until it is light and fluffy. Add the egg yolks one at a time, beating well after each addition. Slowly add the melted chocolate, and beat until well blended.

In a large mixing bowl, beat the egg whites with the cream of tartar until firm peaks form.

Stir half of the whites into the chocolate mixture, to lighten it.

Gently fold in the remaining egg whites, along with the ground walnuts and the bread crumbs.

Pour the batter into the prepared pan, and bake 35 to 40 minutes in the preheated oven, or until the center springs back when lightly pressed.

Let the cake cool on a rack for 15 minutes. Run a knife around the edge of the cake and let it sit 10 minutes more.

Carefully, invert the torte onto a rack, and let cool completely.

Make the buttercream:

Put the chocolate, espresso powder, and ⅓ cup water in the top of a double boiler or into a small, heavy saucepan over low heat. Stir occasionally until the mixture is smooth. Remove from the heat, and let cool for 15 minutes.

Beat the butter in an electric mixer until light and fluffy. Add the egg yolks, one at a time. (If you are concerned about eating raw eggs, leave them out.) Beat well after each addition. Gradually beat in the confectioners' sugar. Stir in the chocolate mixture, and blend thoroughly. Set aside ½ cup of the butter cream for decoration. (The buttercream can be stored in the refrigerator and used later. Make sure to bring the frosting back to room temperature before using.)

Assemble:

Cut the cooled torte into two layers using a serrated knife and a gentle sawing motion. Frost the top layer, cut side up, with about 1 cup of buttercream. Place the bottom layer on top, cut side down. Cover the top and sides of the cake with the remaining buttercream. Put the reserved buttercream into a pastry bag fitted with a small star tip, and decorate the top edges and base of the cake with little rosettes. Garnish the top of the cake with the walnut halves.

TOM VALENTI'S BRAISED LAMB SHANKS

New York City was still in the thralls of the "grill it and garnish it" school of cookery promoted by some restaurateurs and chefs as California cuisine, when Tom Valenti was hired by restaurant consultant Rozanne Gold to open Café Greco on the Upper East Side. This was one of the first attempts at an upscale Greek restaurant in Manhattan. It was owned by a Greek coffee shop operator who wanted to break into the white table-cloth business. Gold suggested to Valenti that he come up with a braised meat dish, as no one was doing braised meat in restaurants in those days. "We were coming off mid-1980s grilled chicken paillards with sun-dried tomatoes over greens. We wanted to do something that was the antithesis of that," says Valenti.

But Tom Valenti's lamb shanks didn't become famous and influential until 1989, when he went to work at a smartly out-of-the-way and small Tribeca restaurant called Allison on Dominick. (This was before Tribeca became Beverly Hills East.) Then the delicious shanks got publicity and caused a wave of braised meat invention that continues to this day. After all, even Daniel Boulud at his most vaunted restaurant, Daniel, serves braised short ribs, once a dish only cooked at home.

Serves 6

In Valenti's words, from his book (with Andrew Friedman), *Welcome to My Kitchen*, "This is without a doubt the most requested recipe I've ever created . . . . Don't omit the step of turning the shanks every half hour; it causes them to caramelize even as they braise." In the unlikely case that the braising liquid seems too reduced at the end of the cooking process, stir additional water into the liquid before straining.

6 lamb foreshanks (foreshanks are meatier than hindshanks)	1 bay leaf
Coarse salt	1 tablespoon black peppercorns
Freshly ground black pepper	3 anchovy fillets
3 tablespoons plus ½ cup olive oil	1 whole head garlic, cut in half
2 ribs celery, roughly chopped	2 cups red wine
1 carrot, roughly chopped	1 cup dry white wine
1 large Spanish onion, roughly chopped	⅓ cup white vinegar
½ cup tomato paste	1 teaspoon sugar
5 sprigs of thyme	2 cups veal broth or 1 cup demi-glace (see Note)
	2 cups chicken broth

Preheat the oven to 325 degrees.

Season the lamb shanks liberally with salt and pepper. With a sharp knife, cut about 1 inch from the bottom (narrow end) of the shank bones and all the way around; this will help expose the bone while cooking. Set aside.

Heat 3 tablespoons of oil in a 2- to 3- quart saucepan over medium-high heat. Add the celery, carrot, and onion to the pot, and cook until very soft, 8 to 10 minutes.

Add the tomato paste, thyme, bay leaf, pepper-corns, anchovies, and garlic. Reduce heat to medium and cook another minute or so, being careful not to burn the tomato paste.

Add the red and white wine, vinegar, and sugar. Stir well. Raise the heat to high and bring to a boil.

Add the veal and chicken broths (or demi-glace). Adjust heat so the sauce simmers gently while you brown the shanks.

In a sauté pan, over medium heat, heat just enough of the remaining ½ cup of oil to cover the bottom of the pan. Brown the shanks well on all sides, about 1 minute for each of the three sides. Use tongs to handle them.

Transfer the shanks to a roasting pan and pour the stock mixture on top. Cover with aluminum foil and cook in the preheated oven for 1 hour.

Remove the foil and cook for another 3 hours, turning the shanks over every half hour until the meat is very soft.

Remove the shanks from the braising liquid and strain the liquid. Skim any fat that rises to the surface and use the liquid as a sauce.

Note: Demi-glace is veal stock that has been reduced by half. High-quality prepared versions, often frozen, are available at specialty food stores.

UNION SQUARE CAFE'S BANANA TART WITH CARAMEL AND MACADAMIA NUTS

This dessert was introduced at the Union Square Cafe in the late 1980s and has since been copied all over the country.

Serves 6 to 8

This recipe, adapted for home cooks, makes one large tart that is cut into wedges for serving. At the restaurant, however, it is baked in individual portions—tarts about 4 inches in diameter (as on page 356).

For the pastry:
8 tablespoons (1 stick) unsalted butter
¼ cup sugar
1 egg yolk
1 teaspoon vanilla extract
1 cup all-purpose flour

For the topping:
4 large ripe bananas
1 tablespoon very soft butter

1 tablespoon superfine sugar

For the glaze:
½ cup sugar
1 tablespoon corn syrup
1 tablespoon butter
1 cup lightly toasted and coarsely chopped macadamia nuts
2 pints vanilla, honey-vanilla, or chocolate ice cream

Make the pastry:

In the bowl of an electric mixer fitted with the paddle attachment, cream the butter and sugar until light.

Add the egg yolk, 2 teaspoons water, and the vanilla. Blend well.

Add the flour and mix until just blended.

With lightly floured hands, gather the dough into a disk and wrap it in plastic. Refrigerate for at least 3 hours, or overnight.

Preheat the oven to 450 degrees. Remove the dough from the refrigerator and let it sit at room temperature for 10 to 15 minutes until pliable.

Remove the bottom from an 8½- or 9-inch springform pan and dust it lightly with flour. Set the ring of the springform pan aside, as it will not be used. Unwrap the dough and place it on the floured pan bottom. With a floured rolling pin, roll the dough out to cover the pan bottom. The dough should be less than ¼ inch thick. Cut off the excess.

Cover a baking sheet with aluminum foil and on it place the pan bottom with the pastry circle. Bake about 15 minutes, until the pastry is light golden.

Remove the crust from the oven and let cool.

Lower the oven temperature to 375 degrees.

Make the banana topping:

Peel the bananas, keeping them whole. Place 1 banana on a cutting surface with the back of the curve toward you. Using a sharp paring knife, slice off the ends of the banana on a sharp diagonal and reserve the ends. Thinly slice the entire banana on the diagonal, keeping the slices together. Repeat with the remaining bananas, reserving the ends.

Carefully transfer 1 of the sliced bananas, intact, onto the baked crust. Position the banana 1 inch from the edge of the circle with the curve of the banana following the curve of the circle. Press your hand gently on the inside curve of the banana, to make the slices lay flat and spread toward the outer edge of the circle. With the tips of your fingers, continue spreading until the banana is fanned over half the circle's edge.

Repeat with the second banana over the other half of the circle's edge, connecting the ends to form an unbroken circle of fanned banana slices. Continue in the same manner to fill the inner part of the tart shell.

Use the reserved end pieces to fill in the center of the tart.

Brush the bananas lightly with the soft butter and sprinkle with the superfine sugar.

Place the tart in the oven for approximately 10 minutes.

Make the glaze:

In a 1-quart saucepan, combine the sugar, corn syrup, and butter. Place the saucepan over medium-high heat and stir to combine.

Bring the mixture to a boil, stirring occasionally, to melt the butter. When the mixture reaches a boil, stop stirring and cook until it has caramelized to a medium amber color. If one area begins to brown faster than the rest, swirl the pan to blend.

Remove from the heat and immediately dip the pan into a cold water bath to slow the cooking. Remove from the water bath while it is still hot and runny. Set aside for a moment.

Remove the tart from the oven. Dip a spoon into the hot caramel and drizzle it back and forth, vertically and horizontally, to create a grid pattern over the surface of the bananas. Allow the tart to sit until the caramel hardens, 1 to 2 minutes.

Leaving it on the pan bottom, transfer the tart to a serving platter. Sprinkle with the macadamia nuts while still warm.

Cut into wedges, topping each serving with a scoop of ice cream.

UNION SQUARE CAFE'S GRILLED FILET MIGNON OF TUNA

Grilled rare tuna may not seem as remarkable now as it did nearly twenty years ago. It is, in fact, ubiquitous in American restaurants. But that's why this recipe is here. When chef Michael Romano introduced it on Union Square Cafe's menu, it was a revelation.

Serves 4

For the marinade:

2 cups teriyaki sauce (there are many good commercial brands)

½ cup dry sherry

4 tablespoons finely chopped fresh ginger

½ cup chopped scallions

2 cloves garlic, thinly sliced

½ teaspoon ground cayenne pepper

2 teaspoons freshly ground black pepper

Juice of 2 lemons

For the tuna:

4 (8- to 10-ounce) yellowfin tuna steaks, trimmed into huge cubes about 3 inches on each side (at the Union Square Cafe, the trimmings are used for the tuna burgers served at lunch)

2 tablespoons olive oil

¼ cup Japanese pickled ginger (available in Asian markets)

Combine all the marinade ingredients in a bowl large enough to hold the tuna. Place the tuna steaks in the marinade and refrigerate for 3 hours, turning every hour.

Thirty minutes before cooking, drain the tuna and let it come to room temperature.

Preheat a griddle, grill pan, or outdoor grill to very hot.

Brush the tuna with the oil. Grill the pieces for 1 to 2 minutes on each of their six sides. The outside of the tuna should be nicely charred, and the center should be barely warm and quite rare. Cooked this way, the tuna will remain moist and flavorful.

Top each piece with pickled ginger and serve.

LINDY'S STRAWBERRY SHORTCAKE

I did that restaurant in Black Rock, you know, in the CBS building. It was supposed to be called the American Deli. And I rode up in an elevator to the executive suite to convince Bill Paley. He had his own elevator, Paley did. Paley didn't admit that he was Jewish but this idea appealed to him, this deli idea. And I made, as part of my presentation . . . basically a knockoff of the old Lindy's Strawberry Shortcake. . . . Now, that's a piece of New York City. It's not a shortcake. It's a sponge cake. Between the layers, it's vhipped cream [she pronounced it with a Yiddish accent]. Sitting in the whipped cream are whole strawberries, then another layer of cake. And the whole thing is iced with whipped cream. And then there are whole strawberries on top, and they brought you a slice, high and wide. I don't know how they got it out to the table, but they brought it to the table with a pitcher of strawberry syrup and a pitcher of heavy cream. It's a great dessert.

Anyway, I arrive in Bill Paley's conference room wheeling in this Lindy's Strawberry Shortcake, and his face lit up. He was sitting at a long table, and there were men sitting on both sides of him and at both ends. And nobody said a word. Only Bill Paley and one guy who would say "yes sir." Anyway, it was supposed to be called the American Deli. It was another one of these fusion American things. But Paley chickened out on that name. So it became the American Charcuterie because that was as close as I could get to American Deli. —BARBARA KAFKA

Makes one 9-inch, 2-layer cake

Gelatin sets quickly, so when you add it to the softly whipped cream, make sure the gelatin is hot. Leave it in its hot water bath until the last moment, then beat it in quickly, and spread the cream on the cake immediately.

A big part of the appeal of this cake is the way it was served at Lindy's—with a pitcher of liquid heavy cream and a boat of strawberry syrup or sauce. The cake sops them up readily, allowing you to make a delicious mess of it as you eat it.

For the sponge cake:
7 eggs, separated and at room temperature
1 cup plus 1 tablespoon sugar (divided)
1 tablespoon boiling water
1 teaspoon vanilla extract
¾ cup cake flour
¼ cup cornstarch

For the filling and topping:
2 pints fresh strawberries, washed and hulled
1 tablespoon plus 1 teaspoon unflavored gelatin
3 cups heavy cream
¼ cup sugar

To serve:
Pitcher of heavy cream
Sauceboat of strawberry syrup (recipe follows)

Make the cake layers:

Preheat the oven to 350 degrees.

Lightly grease and flour two 9-inch cake pans.

In a stand mixer on medium speed, with the whisk attachment, whip the egg yolks for 30 seconds.

Gradually beat in ¾ cup plus 1 tablespoon of the sugar, and continue beating until very thick and pale yellow, about 2 minutes.

At the end of the whipping, with the machine still on, add the boiling water and vanilla.

Sift together the flour and cornstarch.

One third at a time, gently fold the flour and cornstarch into the egg mixture. Transfer to a large, clean mixing bowl. Wash and dry the mixer's bowl and whisk. In the clean bowl, with the clean whisk attachment, whip the egg whites until they turn to a light foam—all white.

With the machine on, add the remaining ¼ cup sugar very gradually in a slow and steady stream. At the end, turn the mixer speed on high for about 30 seconds, until the whites are smooth, silky, and hold soft to medium peaks.

Carefully fold the egg whites into the yolk-starch mixture.

Divide the batter evenly between the two prepared cake pans.

Bake immediately. Place the pans on the middle rack of the preheated oven. Be sure the pans do not touch. Bake for 20 to 30 minutes until the cake springs back to the touch.

Remove from the oven, and allow to cool in the pans on a rack for 10 minutes. However, if the cakes have pulled away from the sides of the pan, unmold them immediately. Otherwise, if necessary, run a spatula or a knife around the sides of the pan before turning the cakes onto the rack to cool thoroughly.

Make the filling and topping:

Choose the largest and most beautiful berries to decorate the top of the cake; it's best if they are about equal size. Plan out the top of the cake before starting to cover it with whipped cream. Place the berries tightly on the un-iced top layer of the cake, then remove them to a plate in the same configuration as they were on the cake. Set aside. Cut the remaining berries in halves or quarters, depending on their size. Set aside.

Put ¼ cup cold water in a small ramekin or custard cup. Sprinkle on the gelatin. Place the ramekin in a skillet with enough water to come up the sides of the ramekin to the level of the gelatin. Heat the water to a simmer. Stir the gelatin until it dissolves. Remove from the heat. Keep it in the hot but no longer simmering water while whipping the cream.

Combine the cream and sugar in the bowl of a stand mixer with the whisk attachment. Whip together on medium speed until the cream holds soft peaks. With the motor running, and holding the hot ramekin of gelatin with a pot holder or oven mitt, pour the gelatin into the cream.

Ice the cake at once—don't wait—as the gelatin starts firming up the cream immediately.

Assemble:

Line a cake platter or stand with 3 overlapping pieces of wax paper—to protect the plate while icing the cake.

Place a layer of cake on the stand. With a spatula, spread a ½-inch layer of whipped cream. Arrange a layer of the cut berries, covering the whipped cream entirely. Spread on a little more cream to totally encase the strawberries.

Place the second layer of cake over the berries and cream. Use the remaining whipped cream to ice the cake entirely.

Cover the top densely with the layer of beautiful strawberries that you have already arranged. Remove the wax paper.

STRAWBERRY SYRUP

2 pints ripe strawberries
½ to 1 cup sugar

Hull and wash the strawberries. Do not dry.

Slice the strawberries, and place in a bowl. Toss with ½ cup of the sugar. Let stand for at least 30 minutes.

Pour the strawberries and the syrup that has accumulated into a small saucepan. Bring the strawberries to a boil and let simmer until the berries are mushy.

Drain the strawberries in a fine mesh sieve, catching the juices in a bowl. Mash the strawberries with a spatula to get as much juice as possible. Discard the strawberries.

Check the sweetness and thickness of the syrup. Add sugar as desired to make it sweeter and thicker, then return the syrup to the heat until the sugar has fully dissolved. The syrup will thicken slightly as it cools. Serve chilled.

GAEL GREENE'S CHOCOLATE WICKEDNESS

Gael Greene is New York City's longest-running restaurant critic, and one of the most influential of the last thirty-something years. Since 1965, when she wrote a feature for the *Herald Tribune* Sunday magazine on French restaurateur Henri Soulé (see page 284), she has been enchanting readers of *New York* magazine, the *Tribune* magazine's successor, with her voluptuous prose, making mouths water when she likes a place, making mouths drop when she dosen't. She founded City Meals on Wheels, which provides two million meals a year to more than seventeen thousand New Yorkers.

Besides her writing on food, some of which was collected in a 1971 volume called *Bite*—she has written two erotic novels and a how-to sex manual called *Delicious Sex*, which featured this recipe. Greene dubbed it chocolate wickedness long before anyone attached such names to chocolate desserts.

Serves about 12

Naturally, the best quality chocolate you can get should be used here. The whole dessert depends on that, and careful beating and folding.

1½ pounds semisweet chocolate
3 egg yolks
½ cup brewed espresso
½ cup crème de cacao (or orange liqueur, such
    as Grand Marnier, or cognac, rum,
    or Scotch)
6 egg whites
Pinch of salt

¼ cup sugar
1 cup heavy cream, whipped

For the sauce:
1 tablespoon vanilla extract
½ to ⅔ cup sour cream
1 cup heavy cream, whipped into gentle peaks

In a heavy saucepan over very low heat, or in the top of a double boiler or a stainless-steel bowl placed over a pot of hot water, melt the chocolate. Remove from the heat.

In a separate bowl, beat the egg yolks until well mixed, then stir them into the melted chocolate.

Stir in the espresso and crème de cacao and stir until smooth. (If the mixture hardens, warm it gently over low heat, stirring, until smooth.)

Transfer the mixture to a very large bowl. Let cool to nearly room temperature.

In a separate large bowl, beat the egg whites together with the salt until they hold stiff peaks.

Add the sugar, a tablespoon at a time, beating after each addition. Continue beating until the whites are very stiff but not dry.

Fold the whipped cream into the egg whites.

Carefully but thoroughly fold the white mixture into the chocolate mixture.

Pour into a large glass bowl or other serving dish. (You can make individual servings by pouring the dessert into goblets or custard cups). Refrigerate for at least 2 hours, and preferably longer, before serving.

Make the sauce: Stir the vanilla into the sour cream, then fold in the whipped cream.

Serve the chocolate with big dollops of sauce.

CHAPTER 21
THE NEW IMMIGRANTS

THE RUSSIANS

RUSSIAN JEWS STARTED ARRIVING IN THE LATE NINETEENTH CENTURY, but it wasn't until after the Bolshevik Revolution of 1917 that non-Jewish Russians found their way to New York City in any number. Mainly, they came from the upper classes—the so-called White Russians. That's why Charles G. Shaw's 1931 guidebook *Nightlife* points out that a waitress at a Russian restaurant may well have been a princess in the old country. Slavic Russians also arrived in greater number after the revolution. They settled in Washington Heights, centering on Broadway and 160th Street.

As happens with every immigrant group that ever comes to New York City, at first the Russians opened restaurants strictly as gathering places for their own community. That's how the Russian Tea Room came to exist "to the left of Carnegie Hall," as its ads used to say. It was opened in 1926 by former members of the Russian Imperial Ballet. It didn't take long for it to catch on with the cultured crowd that worked at or frequented the neighboring concert stage. Only in the 1950s did it start attracting show-business people with well-stuffed wallets. The Russian Tea Room was expensive, or at least it cost a lot, because the best thing to eat there was always the blini and caviar.

By the early 1930s, a few of the Russian restaurants had evolved into places like the Russian Bear, which opened at 139 East Fifty-sixth in 1908, but eventually attracted non-Russians for the colorful show it put on. It called itself "The Meeting Place of the World," providing the "colorful atmosphere of Old Russia," which included red leather banquettes and waiters in billowy red blouses delivering *shashlik* to your table on brass skewers. The Russian Skazka at 227 West Fifty-sixth Street was another one of these colorful places.

In 1931, Charles G. Shaw wrote:

New York is rich in Russian haunts. Especially the Fifties and Lower East Side, where they sprout like so many weeds. The majority are subterranean and feature doormen in Cossack garb. Brilliant lights are strictly taboo and the music is sad and sobby. The floor show, if there is one, will offer an accordionist, and the crazier the décor, the more Russian they would have you believe them.

Most of these sort of Russian restaurants were closed by the early 1960s. Then a new wave of Russians started coming to New York City in the late 1970s, when the Soviet Union allowed those

OPPOSITE:
In Little Odessa, Brooklyn's Brighton Beach, Russian foods fill two floors at M&I International.
BELOW:
The original Russian Tea Room sometime in the 1930s.

363

with Jewish heritage to emigrate. Although technically Jewish, the new population was so out of touch with Jewish customs after nearly seventy years of communism that it didn't, for the most part, observe the Jewish faith.

Most of these Russians settled in the Brighton Beach section of Brooklyn, which became known as Little Odessa—as Odessa is a Russian beach resort. Although Brighton Beach is now almost completely a Russian community—with stores and restaurants catering to the particular

tastes of Russians, and Russian being the primary language—the community, as it has become more affluent, has broadened its area by extending to nearby Sheepshead Bay, and to the upper-middle-class area of Manhattan Beach. Now, mainly catering to Russians, there is an enclave of Turkish restaurants in Sheepshead Bay and in Marine Park, another nearby area. Russians appreciate Turkish food because it is similar to Georgian cuisine.

In fact, none of the many restaurants in Brighton Beach serve Russian food. They have Georgian and Uzbek food, which, during the Soviet years, was more prized in Leningrad and Moscow than any local food. (Those warmer climates of the Caucuses have the agricultural products to form a rich cuisine, whereas frigid Russia under Soviet rule did not.) What traditional fare can't be found in the Brighton restaurants—which, in any case, are really nightclubs with copious food and dangerous amounts of vodka—people buy at stores and eat at home.

Prepared foods at M&I International

Brighton Beach boasts excellent food shopping. The Brighton Beach Russians buy only the best fruits, for instance, and their fruit markets display their produce artistically. There are several bread bakeries, some of which also carry an array of smoked meats, prepared foods, salads, and the various fermented dairy products that Russians love—various kinds of sour cream, yogurt, and kefir—and the most typical drink of the neighborhood, *kvass*, which is a fermented grain beverage. One huge store, sometimes called the Zabar's of Brighton Beach, after the famous food emporium on the Upper West Side of Manhattan, dominates Brighton Beach Avenue shopping. It's called M&I International, and it probably carries more food in one store than was ever available in all of Russia on any one Soviet day—everything a czar's heart could desire.

THE KOREANS

The Hart-Celler Act of 1965 abolished immigration based on national origin and changed New York City's gastronomic fabric immeasurably. Populations from Asia, the Middle East, Latin America, and Africa flooded the city, most of them going to live in Queens. In the 1970s, the foreign-born population in Queens increased by thirty percent and the borough is still the most ethnically diverse. All these groups opened restaurants and groceries, for their own communities and their neighbors', but the ethnic group that made and continues to make the most significant contribution to New Yorkers' everyday lives is the Koreans.

The Koreans entered the produce business immediately because they preferred to run their own businesses rather than work for others. (They are very entrepreneurial, now owning most of the city's dry-cleaning establishments and actually creating a new business for New York City, nail salons.) And they saw that the two other ethnic groups who dominated the produce business—the Italians and Greeks—were leaving it. The older produce sellers were moving up the socioeconomic ladder and even leaving the city for the suburbs.

Koreans changed the produce business. In the early 1970s they were known to buy only the best-looking, largest, and often the scarcest produce in the wholesale market, and they displayed their products with great care in bins that spilled onto the streets, even in winter. I remember spending a day at the Hunt's Point Market in the late 1970s and the produce wholesalers pointing out the merchandise that the supermarkets bought and the better produce that the Koreans bought. They actually purchased higher quality fruit just to supply the Koreans.

Through the same family-and-friends system of sponsorship that other immigrant groups had used before them, the Koreans brought in other Koreans to work for them as they, the entrepreneurs, moved up the social ladder. With this low-salaried, willing, and dependent workforce of people who couldn't yet speak English, the Korean grocers were able to stay open twenty-four hours a day, seven days a week, and pay the high rents in Manhattan that had prevented previous greengrocers from opening small stores.

The only problem with selling gorgeous produce was that when it was several days old and not so gorgeous anymore no one wanted to buy it. The name of the first Korean grocer to cut up and salvage his ripe fruit by selling it at a premium as fruit salad is unknown. But he started a trend that has since snowballed into what has to be considered a later-day replacement for cafeterias—what New Yorkers call the "Korean salad bar." In fact, it is not a salad bar at all, but a self-service buffet of hot and cold dishes, sold by weight to the masses of people who work in Manhattan and can't afford, or don't want to pay, the exorbitant lunch prices charged even at coffee shops. In Midtown, these buffets may display twenty to thirty hot dishes—many of them

Chinese, but also roast turkey, fried chicken, lasagna—plus prepared salads of tuna, chicken, seafood, and vegetables, as well as green salads and vegetables, such as Caesar salad or steamed asparagus. Yet more elaborate Korean-owned buffets in combination with stations for short-order foods, grilled sandwiches, pizza, custom sandwiches, and so on, are opening nearly daily, providing the inexpensive midday food New Yorkers need to survive at work.

THE WEST INDIANS

Brooklyn is home to a vast number of West Indians of every nationality. Jamaicans were the first big wave to arrive from the islands, starting in the late 1960s. Mainly health-care workers, they were attracted to jobs at Downstate Medical Center and Kings County Hospital, a huge complex of research and public-service medical facilities in the Flatbush section of the borough. As that community grew, it supplanted an existing population of mostly Jewish families living in large single family homes, brownstones, and pre–World War II apartment houses. There are now a substantial number of Haitians in Flatbush, as well. And in nearby Crown Heights and Bedford Stuyvesant, there are enclaves of Trinidadians, Bajians, and Guyanese. (Flatbush has a Dominican community, too, but the largest Dominican and Puerto Rican communities are in the Bronx and the north end of Manhattan.) Along Eastern Parkway every summer, one of the world's largest Carnival parades is held. It's a little out of season for this pre-Lenten festival, but Brooklyn rarely does anything the way the rest of the world does.

Nowadays, the smell of Caribbean curry on Flatbush Avenue is as common as the smell of Jewish delicatessen used to be. In the old days, the butchers advertised that they were kosher. Now the signs announce that they carry kid.

Flatbush started out Dutch, became predominantly Jewish in the 1920s—with the usual mix of Italians, Irish, and Germans, too—then became firmly West Indian in the 1970s. I lived in Flatbush through the transition, and I can still conjure up the aroma of pastrami when I walk by the site of the King's Deli, near the Loew's Kings theater, one of the city's grandest movie palaces. I remember that Ebinger's central bakery was on Bedford Avenue, behind where Macy's still stands. I remember Chin's, the Chinese restaurant where Barbra Streisand waited tables while at Erasmus Hall High School. I remember sitting at Sutter's, on the corner of Flatbush and Carton Avenue, enjoying a mocha buttercream roll and other French pastries at a streetside table.

Trinidadian roti at Gloria's, in Brooklyn

I still live off of Flatbush Avenue, but now I can sit in front of the Jamaican bakery around the corner and eat turmeric-colored patties filled with spicy ground meat, shredded chicken, or cabbage. Even though I don't tuck mine into coco bread, as so many people do, I do take home the curried goat, stewed kingfish, and jerk chicken that they sell to go.

Certain Jamaican foods have become assimilated in New York City. Every pizzeria carries those patties. Jerk spicing, fragrant with thyme, allspice, and habanero chilies, has been adopted by young local chefs who aren't Jamaican and who use it on luxury meats in their trendy restaurants. Other Caribbean specialties haven't yet left the neighborhoods. You have to go to Brooklyn for aki and callaloo, roti breads stuffed with Trinidadian curries, and Caribbean drinks such as those flavored with sorrel.

THE GREEKS

"Cheese boorga, cheese boorga," was the punch line of an old John Belushi *Saturday Night Live* routine—"Live from New York!"—that acknowledged the fact that Greeks owned most of New York City's "coffee shops," our urban version of diners. A big question in New York City, and among Greek-Americans themselves, is how the Greeks ever got into the food business. Sure, Greek culture gives high status to the pleasures of the table, but that doesn't explain how Greek immigrants, most of whom didn't arrive until the late 1960s after U.S. immigration laws were relaxed in 1964, came to not only dominate the inexpensive neighborhood luncheonette and coffee shop business, but also compete with the Italians in the produce business.

One explanation is put forth by Katherine R. Boulukos, one of the founders of the Greek Museum: The Center for Greek-American Heritage, which has yet to find a permanent home.

The account goes back to the early 1870s when a former sailor who had visited America, Panagiotis Hatzikiris, returned to New York. He knew the candy-making business from his hometown in Smyrna (now Izmir, in Turkey), so he decided to open a candy factory. He recruited early Greek immigrants and got them to sell his candy in baskets, on the street. His company,

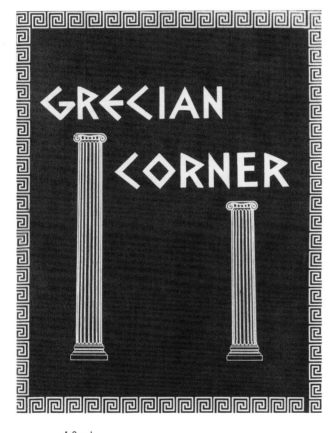

A Greek
diner menu

American Confectioners Company, was started in 1873. First these vendors started off as so-called basket peddlers selling candy. When they made some money, they also sold flowers and fruit. The pay was small, but many preferred this work to other menial factory jobs. They'd rather sell candy on the street than work for someone else. As they expanded their goods, they got pushcarts. After that, many found an outdoor corner to sell their wares, and after that, those who made enough money rented space indoors and set up shops. They continued to expand their lines of goods, some sticking to candy, and making "candy kitchen" shops. Some became greengrocers, while still others added food counters, making sandwiches and other food items. These enterprising, hardworking people managed to expand their ventures so that today, one sees the imprint of these people on the big-time food business occupations.

Until the 1960s, however, Greeks were not much known in the coffee shop business. That phenomenon happened in the way these things always happen, the way that, for instance, Koreans ended up owning most of the non-Hispanic neighborhood groceries in New York City, or that Pakistanis came to dominate the newsstand business: First, one successful Greek sponsored relatives or relatives of friends to work in his business. These workers, once they learned English and had a small degree of economic stability, then opened their own businesses. Dishwashers became short-order cooks who became entrepreneurs. As Boulukos says, Greek men are very independent.

But even before Greek coffee shops proliferated, before New York City's now-iconic takeout coffee cups became blue and white with a Greek key motif, and before Astoria, Queens, changed from an Italian enclave to a Greek enclave—all about forty years ago—Greeks did own restaurants. "When Greek meets Greek, as any vaudeville headliner will tell you, they open a restaurant," wrote Rian James in 1930, in *Dining in New York*. He added, "They open up a French restaurant, or a German restaurant, or a Bavarian restaurant, or a Swiss restaurant—but seldom . . . do they open a Greek restaurant." The big exception was Seafare of the Aegean, one of the city's leading seafood restaurants for nearly forty years. And Leon Lianides of the Coach House (see page 316) is a prime

example of a Greek owning a restaurant that wasn't at all Greek, although mixed in with his supposedly American fare were a few Greek specialties, such as fish dressed with nothing but olive oil, lemon juice, and dill.

Despite Rian James's comment, there were several Greek restaurants in Manhattan before the 1960s boom in coffee shops. Mostly, they were along Eighth Avenue from the West Thirties to Forty-seventh Street, where Molfetas Cafeteria was a popular Theater District restaurant. Perhaps because many of the proprietors of these restaurants hailed from areas of Asia Minor—such as Smyrna—where culture was more oriental than Greek, these restau-

A Greek restaurant in 1904

rants were where you'd go to see belly dancers. I don't remember the food being particularly good, but I do remember vividly the night that, right after my bar mitzvah, my father deemed me old enough to take me to see a performance.

Starting in the late 1980s, upwardly mobile Greek coffee shop owners began to open more upscale restaurants. The first was Café Greco on the Upper East Side. It featured what was then considered groundbreaking "Mediterranean" food, non-nationally specific dishes using ingredients found around the Mediterranean. The consultant was Rozanne Gold and the chef Tom Valenti, neither of whom has a drop of Greek heritage. But together they created a menu that hinted at the Greek owner's heritage. He was still, probably correctly, wary of making the restaurant totally Greek. It took a few more years for truly Greek upscale restaurants to open, but now they are totally accepted in New York City, and there are quite a few, even very expensive places.

THE POLES

Polish food, unless you count Jewish Polish food, didn't make any impact on New York City until the 1970s, when a new flush of immigrants arrived and opened a genre of restaurant that became known as the "Polish coffee shop." These are hybrid restaurants that serve typical American diner/coffee shop fare—sandwiches, salads, and salad platters (tuna, chicken, egg, whitefish), pancakes, eggs any style, hamburgers, meatloaf . . . you get the picture. On the Polish side, they offer hearty soups, blintzes, pierogi, potato pancakes, stuffed cabbage and stuffed peppers, kielbasa in several guises, and, if you can't make up your mind, the "Polish Sampler," a combo plate with a hefty section of kielbasa, a piece of stuffed cabbage and/or pepper, some pierogi—the works.

Of course, these foods are similar, if not identical, to the Eastern European Jewish fare that New Yorkers had enjoyed generations ago. The Polish coffee shops, although they were concentrated in the already heavily Ukrainian East Village, enjoyed such a vogue that they spun off into uptown Manhattan neighborhoods. Curiously, except for Theresa's, which remains on Montague Street in affluent Brooklyn Heights, they didn't fully infiltrate the boroughs.

What's different from the Polish Jewish foods of the past? Kielbasa are pork sausages, forbidden by Jewish dietary laws. Polish pierogi, either boiled or deep-fried, as they were in the Jewish dairy restaurants are not only filled with cheese or potato but also stuffed with Polish wild mushrooms and sauerkraut. And they're topped with sautéed onions, as well as sour cream.

Where the Polish coffee shops have really made their mark, however, is with their marvelous hearty soups—soups so robust you could make a meal of them. For a time in the 1980s and early 1990s, when there were many more Polish coffee shops in the city than there are now, New Yorkers couldn't get enough white borscht, actually a sauerkraut soup. Mushroom barley soup with cream was also immensely popular. And besides wonderful chicken soup with egg noodles (or matzoh balls, a tip of the hat to Jewish New Yorkers), an everyday staple, there are daily special soups, too. In the summer, there's Lithuanian-style cold beet borscht, and some places offer a puree of fruits, heavy on the plums, called fruit soup. The prices are low. The portions are large.

The Greenpoint section of Brooklyn became a Polish enclave about twenty-five years ago with the new influx of Poles. The main shopping streets are Manhattan Avenue, from which pedestrians get a view of midtown Manhattan across the East River, and Nassau Street. Here, there are Polish bakeries and cafes that serve traditional Polish cakes and pastries filled with poppy seeds (*mohn*) and jammy fruit alongside old New York City neighborhood bakery specialties like cheese Danish and babka, and French Continental-style sweets such as éclairs, Napoleons, and all form of buttercream-iced and -filled cakes. The avenues also have bars with neon Polish beer signs hung next to ones advertising Brooklyn Lager, butcher shops that have every type of smoked kielbasa hanging from their ceilings, and fresh kielbasa, plump hams, smoked bacon, and buckwheat-stuffed *kishka* (sausage) in the meat cases. Dumplings and savory pastries are offered for takeout. Polish jarred and canned groceries line the shelves.

The neighborhood used to be Italian and Irish, and as the Polish community assimilates and moves up and out, another group is replacing them, though it's not an ethnic one. Greenpoint is just north of Williamsburg, which has been gentrified by young artists and hipsters in the last decade, and has been feeling the pressure. Young professionals seeking affordable housing near their jobs in Manhattan are moving in. With good subway connections, it's only fifteen minutes to "the city." Rents are rising, and the Polish stores are closing in favor of sushi bars and cool lounges that serve Martinis and Cosmopolitans instead of Polish beer.

OPPOSITE: A Greenpoint meat market

ABOVE: Polish pierogi with sautéed onions and applesauce

THE INDIANS-PAKISTANI-BANGLADESHI

When Julie Sahni, the Indian food expert, arrived in New York City from India in 1968, she says "there were only two kinds of Indian food here. There were many young Indian people because it was Nehru's dream for India to be self-sufficient and many affluent Indian families—Raj people, very English—sent their bright children abroad for an education. Of course, the children were homesick. They wanted Indian food. So there were a few Indian restaurants catering to them—Rajmahal on Fourth Avenue and Kashmir in the Theater District are the two that I remember. Hardly any white people—*goros*, we say—went to them. These restaurants were fairly good considering they had to work with what [was] available—chicken, which would have been very expensive at home, and lamb, which substituted for the goat we ate in India. Shrimp was too expensive. Most of these students came from North India. They were not fish eaters, but they ate *keema*, ground beef curry, and *paratha*, the flaky bread, which was made with all-purpose four here instead of the whole wheat we use in India."

The other Indian food was anything but Indian, however. "Curries" as the dishes were always called, had been a staple of New York City restaurants since the 1920s. These were nothing but béchamel with curry powder, and maybe fried garlic or ginger. "A restaurant would poach shrimp or chicken or have roast meat, and keep it on the side until they got an order, when they would just add whatever the main ingredient was. This curry was a buttery, creamy, lemony-color sauce often with the awful taste of raw turmeric," says Sahni.

It wasn't until the New York World's Fair of 1964 that anyone in New York City who wasn't actually Indian knew anything about genuine Indian cooking. The Indian pavilion had tandoor ovens flown in, which had never been seen in this part of the world. Americans knew nothing about Indian food cooked outside of a saucepan. They didn't know Indians made bread in an oven and they didn't know moghul food at all. "Even the young Indians who frequented the few Indian restaurants ate *paratha* with a fork and knife," says Sahni.

The first tandoori restaurant in the city was Gaylord, which opened in the late 1960s. "American kids ordered whole chickens from the tandoori and ate them like barbecued chicken, licking their fingers," Sahni remembers. Craig Claiborne even ran Gaylord's supposed recipe for tandoori chicken in the *New York Times*—adapted of course for the home oven. He said it was the best way to cook chicken, although if you made the recipe now you'd be sorely disappointed at the anemic seasoning. Other dishes that Gaylord introduced were lamb *pasanda*, a Kashmiri version of *rogan*, and Punjabi red sauce.

Sahni's first cookbook, *Classic Indian Cooking*, was published in 1972. Madhur Jaffrey's *An Invitation to Indian Cooking*, which was equally influential, was published in 1973. Claiborne, who had an abiding interest in Indian food, hailed both books and his columns encouraged more Indian restaurants to open and restaurants to serve Indian food in a more elegant manner. Among the leaders of the pack were Darbar on Fifty-sixth Street and Fifth Avenue, now closed, and Dawat, which still carries on at 210 East Fifty-eighth Street. Madhur Jaffrey created Dawat's menu and continues as its consultant.

Meanwhile, in 1965, the U.S. immigration laws changed, allowing the first large immigration of Indians, Pakistanis, and Bangladeshis, whom Americans then ignorantly lumped together. It didn't take long for the new wave of people to follow the mode of other immigrants before them and open restaurants to serve their own community. And it didn't take long for the Indo-Pak community to climb the ladder toward the American dream. The first big influx of people settled around Columbia University, where many aspired to higher education. They made a claim on New York City's newsstand business, which they still dominate.

Today, there is a very large Indian community in Queens, most noticeably in Jackson Heights, and there is a large Pakistani community in Brooklyn, flanking a stretch of Coney Island Avenue in Flatbush, where there are restaurants, bakeries, butchers, and everything Pakistani including a large mosque. In Flushing and Richmond Hill, Queens, there are large Sikh communities. Many Indians have assimilated, however, and live in the suburbs or outside of specific ethnic enclaves.

The Bangladeshi restaurants on Fifth Street between First and Second Avenues in Manhattan are famous for their cheap fare—and their domination of the street—while the Indian restaurants and stores along Lexington Avenue in the mid-Twenties have given that strip the nickname "Curry Hill," a play on Murray Hill, which is its proper name. Many New Yorkers still view Indian cooking as something that is very inexpensive. After all, a majority of cab drivers are Indian, Pakistani, or Bangladeshi and the cabbie restaurants, like Curry in a Hurry on Lexington Avenue, are pit-stop steam-table restaurants.

In the last five years, however, upscale Indian restaurants have begun to open, and another phenomenom has begun. Almost every neighborhood in the five boroughs, with an Indian population or not, now has an Indian restaurant that makes home deliveries. Is Indian food about to displace Chinese food in the hearts and stomachs of New Yorkers?

THE MEXICANS

Until very recently there hasn't been much good Mexican food in New York City. One reason is that there haven't been many Mexicans. Without a population to prepare the food New York gringos never developed a taste for it. When Texas-born gossip columnist Liz Smith came to town in the early 1950s, El Charro, at 4 Charles Street in Greenwich Village, was about the only place she could find to eat the tacos, enchiladas, and guacamole she craved. She touted the restaurant in her columns for many years. Until the early 1980s there was little else, except for a few other downtown hole-in-the-wall Tex-Mex joints, none of which seem to be recorded in any guidebook. Even El Charro could not survive on serving Tex-Mex combo plates alone. One side of the menu was Mexican fare, the other side Spanish—not that Spanish food was ever popular in New York City.

Zarela Martinez's restaurant was a Mexican breakthrough.

In 1959, El Parador opened at 325 East Thirty-fourth Street. It had more than the usual Tex-Mex combo plates. The atmosphere was nicer. It was a little way uptown from bohemian Greenwich Village.

La Fonda del Sol, which opened in 1960, could be considered the first serious Mexican restaurant, although it wasn't Mexican. It was a glamorous Latin-American restaurant in the Time-Life building. La Fonda del Sol was a Restaurant Associates operation, an idea of the team of Jerome Brody, then president of the company, and Joe Baum, who researched the restaurant by visiting various South American and Central American countries. They also enlisted Elena Zelayeta, a Mexican food writer, and James Beard as food consultants, and Alexander H. Girard as the architect. Girard installed an entire adobe hut in the restaurant to serve as its bar. Niches all around the hut were filled with metal toys from Mexico. Other decorations included Guatemalan, Colombian, and Brazilian dolls, birdcages, and musical instruments. As a centerpiece in the dining room, there was an enormous rotisserie, manned by chefs in toques. For all its show of Latino stuff, the menu, under the supervision of Swiss-born Seppi Renggli, who would later guide the Four Seasons kitchen, was still pretty tame—offering the usual steaks, chops, and seafood, only with some Latin flavor. The most memorable item was the Mexican chocolate cake flavored with a hint of cinnamon..

A pivotal moment for Mexican food came in 1982 when Craig Claiborne and Warner LeRoy staged a mammoth party for a visiting group of five hundred French chefs and their wives at LeRoy's Tavern on the Green. It was apparently Claiborne's idea to fly in chefs from all over the country to prepare their regional foods. (New York City was represented by Abe Lebewohl's Second Avenue Delicatessen.) This would show the French that American food was not just hamburgers. On the recommendation of Paul Prudhomme, who represented Cajun-Creole cuisine, Zarela Martinez, a caterer from El Paso, was asked to prepare the Mexican dishes.

Zarela (she is known mostly by only her first name, like Cher) saw an opportunity in New York City, and moved with her two small twin sons. (One of them is Aaron Sanchez, now a celebrity chef in his own right; Rodrigo Sanchez is a lawyer.) Zarela didn't set up shop on her own right away. She went to work for David Keh, the Chinese restaurateur, who created Café Marimba on Sixty-first Street and Third Avenue to present Zarela's food.

Meanwhile, a Cuban woman, Josefina Howard, moved to town, too. She had lived in Mexico City and worked there as an interior decorator. She was an accomplished home cook as well, with a more middle-class hostess outlook than Zarela, who grew up largely on a ranch and whose food had a more authentic regional Mexican bent. Howard opened Rosa Mexicano on the corner of First Avenue and Fifty-eighth Street, where it still stands. (A second Rosa Mexicano is on Columbus Avenue across from Lincoln Center.)

When Zarela was ready to go out on her own, and had located a place to open a restaurant, she gave her notice to David Keh; he immediately closed Café Marimba. Having two sons to support and a real estate deal that had yet to be closed, Zarela moved into her space, then called Tastings, a wine bar with British attitude and decorations, and took over as "manager" while she waited the months necessary to get a liquor license. Not being able to officially call it Zarela, she didn't put a sign outside. To this day, you just have to know it is there.

There is a growing Mexican population in New York City now, mainly coming from the state of Puebla. They have formed a community in the Sunset Park section of Brooklyn, which is also a new Chinatown. The popular Mexican restaurants in Brooklyn—now spreading to adjoining and gentrified Park Slope—serve mainly tamales, burritos, and rotisserie chickens. In Manhattan, several successful, more ambitious Mexican restaurants have opened. No matter how sophisticated they are, however, Mexican food remains a hard sell in New York City.

CURRIED GOAT

Curry seasoning is a legacy of the indentured servants who were brought from India to the Caribbean islands to work the sugar plantations after African slavery was abolished. Indian people have had a particularly strong culinary influence in Trinadad, Tobago, and Guyana, but curry is also used in Jamaica and Barbados, two islands from which many early West Indian immigrants came.

Serves 4 to 6

West Indian curry powders are formulated differently from regular curry powder, and each island has a favorite blend. You'd have to be West Indian to detect the differences, however, so if you can't find the genuine article, use whatever the supermarket has to offer. You can also make this dish with lamb or beef. And, as goat is actually a very mild meat, veal would be a good choice, too.

2 tablespoons vegetable oil
Salt
2 pounds boneless goat, beef, or lamb, cut into
    1-inch cubes or larger (2 ½ pounds if on
    the bone)
3 cloves garlic, minced
2 medium onions, chopped

¼ cup minced scallion including green top
¼ cup West Indian curry powder (or, super-
    market curry powder)
½ cup diced canned tomatoes
1 Scotch bonnet chile (habanero), seeded and
    minced
½ teaspoon freshly ground black pepper
½ cup coconut milk (optional)

In a 10-inch saute pan or stove-top casserole, heat the oil over medium high heat. Salt half the meat, and brown it in the oil on all sides. Remove to a bowl, and salt and brown the remainder of the meat.

Return all the meat to the pan, and add the garlic, onions, and scallion. Stir well, and continue to cook a few minutes, until the onions exude their juices.

Sprinkle on the curry powder. Stir well, and cook about 2 minutes more.

Add the tomatoes, Scotch bonnet, ½ teaspoon salt, pepper, and 2 cups water. Stir well.

Cover, leaving the lid slightly askew, and bring to a slow, steady simmer. Cook for 1 hour, stirring a few times. Then, uncover and cook another 30 minutes, or until the meat is tender.

For variety or for a milder flavor, when the stew is ready, add the coconut milk, stir well, and simmer another minute. Or, if you want a very hot stew even with coconut milk, double the amount of Scotch bonnet.

Serve hot—even better, reheated—over white rice.

JAMAICAN BEEF PATTIES

Jamaican beef patties have become so thoroughly assimilated in New York City that they are sold in every corner pizzeria. I dare say there are New Yorkers who think they are Italian.

Beef is the most commonly found patty, But they can also be filled with chicken, or "vegetables," which generally means shredded cabbage. Whatever the filling, they are encased in a crisp and flaky pastry that is often colored with golden turmeric. (Golden Krust is, in fact, the name of a chain of Jamaican patty stores in Brooklyn and Queens.) Whatever the filling, they are seasoned with Scotch bonnet chilies, also called habanero, an incendiary pepper that comes in pale green, bright red, yellow, orange, and multicolor. Patty bakeries also sell coco bread, which is a dense, coconut-flavored bread, and New Yorkers, not just Jamaicans, often make a sandwich of coco bread filled with a patty, as heavy as that sounds and is.

Makes 24 patties

Patties are generally a snack food and make great party food. The four-inch size that this recipe produces is a good size to pass around. Although you could make them smaller, four inches is as small as I like to get. Too small a patty and the pastry will overwhelm the filling. Larger patties are good, but can't be eaten neatly out of one hand while the other holds a glass.

Lard or solid white vegetable shortening produces the characteristically flaky pastry. There really is no substitute, but if these fats offend you, margarine is a possible substitute, although it will also add its buttery flavor, which is not a Jamaican feature of this dish.

The recipe can be easily halved, producing 12 patties, but, after they are baked, extras will freeze perfectly.

For the pastry:
4 cups all-purpose flour
½ teaspoon baking powder
1 teaspoon ground turmeric
1 teaspoon salt
1 cup lard or vegetable shortening, at room
    temperature
Approximately 1 cup very cold water

For the filling:
2 slices white bread
1 pound ground beef (preferably chuck)
1 medium onion, finely minced
3 scallions, white and green parts, finely minced
1 clove garlic, minced
2 medium Scotch bonnet chilies
1 teaspoon thyme
2 teaspoons curry powder
1 teaspoon salt
½ teaspoon freshly ground black pepper

Make the pastry:

In a large mixing bowl, sift together the flour, baking powder, turmeric, and salt.

Using a pastry blender or 2 table knives, cut in the shortening until the mixture is the consistency of cornmeal.

Gradually add just enough cold water to hold the dough together, mixing it with your fingers or a fork. Do not overwork the dough. Add water, and mix just until it can be gathered into a ball.

Form the dough into a log, and wrap it in plastic wrap. Refrigerate it until ready to use, up to several days. Let stand at room temperature for 15 to 20 minutes before attempting to roll it out.

Make the filling:

Break the white bread into pieces. Douse them with cold tap water and set aside.

In a large mixing bowl, combine the beef, onion, scallions, garlic, chiles, and thyme. With your hands, knead the ingredients together just until they are well mixed.

Heat a large skillet over high heat until very hot. Add the beef mixture, and fry, breaking up the meat with the side of a wooden spoon, until the meat is brown and all the moisture in the pan has evaporated. This will take about 8 minutes.

Drain excess fat from the meat by tipping the pan and spooning it off.

Add the curry powder, salt, and pepper. Continue cooking over high heat, stirring occasionally but not regularly, allowing a crust to form on the bottom of the pan.

When there is a brown film on the bottom of the pan (the mixture will begin sticking), add the water. Stir, scraping the bottom to incorporate the browned crust.

Squeeze out the bread, and stir the pieces into the meat mixture. Stir well, breaking and mashing the bread into the meat until it disappears.

Cover, reduce the heat to very low, and cook for 15 minutes. Uncover and set aside to cool.

Assemble and bake:

Preheat the oven to 400 degrees.

Cut the dough into 24 equal pieces.

On a lightly floured surface, roll out each piece of dough to a thickness of about ¼ inch and to a little more than 4 inches in diameter. Using a 4-inch diameter saucer as a guide, cut each piece of rolled dough into a circle. Keep the patty dough circles moist by stacking them and covering them with a clean, dry cloth.

After all the circles are cut, take one at a time and spoon about 1 tablespoon of filling on each, covering only half the circle. Fold the other half over, and seal the edges by crimping with a fork.

Bake the patties on ungreased baking sheets in the preheated oven for 30 minutes or slightly longer, until they are lightly browned.

Serve hot when possible, although they are excellent at room temperature.

WHITE BORSCHT

Creamy rich yet briskly tart, this blend of allspice-flavored chicken broth and, of all things, sauerkraut liquid, developed a cult following in New York City in the late 1980s and early 1990s. It continues to be one of the least expensive great meals in the city.

Serves 6

2 pounds sauerkraut (not canned), not drained

2 or 3 chicken legs

3 bay leaves

4 medium ribs celery

2 medium carrots, peeled

2 large leeks, white part only, split and
washed well

2 teaspoons whole allspice

2 teaspoons dried marjoram

4 teaspoons cornstarch

1 cup heavy cream

Salt and freshly ground black pepper to taste

½ to ¾ pound smoked kielbasa, sliced,
at room temperature

1 medium or ½ large boiled potato per person

½ hard-cooked egg per person

In a 2- to 3-quart saucepan, bring 4 cups water to a boil. Add the sauerkraut and simmer, partly covered, for about 30 minutes. Strain the liquid while it is still hot and reserve it; there should be about 5 cups of sauerkraut "stock." Discard the spent sauerkraut.

Meanwhile, make the chicken broth: In a 3- to 5-quart saucepan, combine the chicken, bay leaves, celery, carrots, leeks, allspice, and 2 quarts fresh cold water. Bring to a brisk simmer over high heat, then reduce the heat, partially cover the pan, and simmer for 1 ½ hours.

Strain the broth and set it aside; there should be about 4 cups; if not, add water.

In a 4- to 6-quart pot, combine the 4 cups chicken broth with 4 cups sauerkraut stock. Cover and bring to a boil.

Add the marjoram.

In a small cup or bowl, mix the cornstarch with the remaining 1 cup sauerkraut stock. Whisk the mixture into the briskly boiling soup and cook for 1 minute, stirring slowly. This will not perceptibly thicken the soup, but it will bind it.

Turn off the heat and stir in the cream. Season with salt and pepper.

To serve, in each bowl, place several rounds of kielbasa, a boiled potato (or half), and half of a hard-cooked egg. Ladle on the hot soup.

MADHUR JAFFREY'S TANDOORI CHICKEN

New Yorker Madhur Jaffrey, who is not only one of our leading Indian food writers but an accomplished stage and film actress, helped open New York City's and the country's mind to genuine Indian cooking. She hasn't changed this marinade recipe since her first book in 1973, *An Invitation to Indian Cooking,* but she has reconsidered the cooking method. This high-temperature oven method gives excellent results.

Serves 6 to 8

For the chicken:

1 medium onion, coarsely chopped

6 cloves garlic, coarsely chopped

1 piece of fresh ginger about 2 inches long and 1 inch wide, peeled and coarsely chopped

3 tablespoons lemon juice

1 cup plain yogurt

1 tablespoon ground coriander

1 teaspoon ground cumin

1 teaspoon ground turmeric

1 teaspoon garam masala

¼ teaspoon ground mace

¼ teaspoon ground nutmeg

¼ teaspoon ground cloves

¼ teaspoon ground cinnamon

¼ cup olive or vegetable oil

2 teaspoons salt

¼ teaspoon freshly ground black pepper

¼ to ½ teaspoon cayenne pepper (optional)

½ to 1 teaspoon orange food coloring (use Spanish *bijol*, Indian powdered food coloring, or American liquid kind) (optional)

6 broiler or fryer chicken legs

3 broiler or fryer chicken breasts, halved

For the garnish:

1 medium onion

2 lemons

Extra lemon juice (optional)

Make the marinade:

Put the onion, garlic, ginger, and lemon juice in an electric blender, and blend to a smooth paste, about 1 minute at high speed. Place in a bowl large enough to accommodate the chicken.

Add the yogurt, coriander, cumin, turmeric, garam masala, mace, nutmeg, cloves, cinnamon, oil, salt, black pepper, cayenne, and food coloring. Mix thoroughly. Set aside.

Skin the chicken pieces. With a sharp knife make 3 diagonal slashes on each breast section, going halfway down to the bone. Make 2 diagonal slashes on each thigh, also getting halfway down to the bone. With the point of a sharp knife, make 4 or 5 jabs on each drumstick.

Put the chicken in the marinade, and rub the marinade into the slashes with your fingers. Cover, and refrigerate for 24 hours. Turn 4 or 5 times while the chicken is marinating.

Preheat the oven to its highest baking setting, 500 to 550 degrees, if possible, and move the rack to its highest position.

Make the garnish:

Peel the onion for the garnish, and cut into paper-thin slices. Separate the rings and set in a small bowl of iced water; cover and refrigerate.

Lift the chicken pieces out of the marinade and place on a single layer in a shallow baking or broiling pan.

Bake the chicken for about 40 minutes, turning it once, or until done. Serve immediately.

CHICKEN EL PARADOR

El Parador opened in 1959 and was what passed for the best Mexican restaurant in New York in the 1960s and 1970s. Craig Claiborne said as much in his 1968 restaurant guide, as did *Cue* magazine in its guide of 1971.

The cooks at El Parador were Chinese, and while there is nothing wrong with Chinese chefs cooking Mexican food, what happened to them when El Parador's management changed in 1990 is most interesting. The way I heard the story was that several of them did not care for their new management and left. Knowing a little something about Mexican food, they bought a tortilla machine—you put in a piece of dough and the machine flattens it, and then shoots it out onto a griddle that bakes it—and opened the Fresco Tortilla Grill on Lexington Avenue and Twenty-third Street. They stuffed the tortillas, as a soft taco or quesadilla, with chicken or steak—hacked Chinese style on a wooden block with a Chinese clever—or with cheese, rice and beans, and so forth. It was a huge success: A new cheap, fast food for the city. One Fresco Tortilla led to another and now they are all over town, in every borough, some with the same concept but a slightly different name.

Serves 4

Craig Claiborne not only recommended this dish in his review of El Parador, but included it in *The New York Times International Cookbook*. I've changed his recipe slightly.

1 chicken (about 3 pounds), cut into serving pieces

6 tablespoons peanut oil (divided)

4 cloves garlic, crushed

2 bay leaves, coarsely crumbled

2 teaspoons dried oregano

1 teaspoon paprika

Salt

Freshly ground pepper

1 teaspoon monosodium glutamate

3 tablespoons olive oil

½ teaspoon finely minced garlic

3 tablespoons red wine vinegar

⅛ teaspoon cayenne pepper

½ cup all-purpose flour

1 teaspoon salt

½ cup peanut oil, for frying

1 very large, sweet onion

Place the chicken parts in a large mixing bowl and add 3 tablespoons of the peanut oil, the crushed garlic, bay leaves, oregano, paprika, and monosodium glutamate. Season with salt and pepper. Turn the chicken pieces in the mixture until they are well coated. Cover and refrigerate overnight. Turn the pieces occasionally.

Make the vinaigrette:

Combine the 3 tablespoons of olive oil with the minced garlic, vinegar and cayenne. Season with salt and pepper. Beat with a fork and let stand until ready to serve.

Dredge the chicken, piece by piece, in the flour seasoned with salt and pepper. All the chicken pieces should be well coated with the flour mixture.

In a 10- to 12-inch skillet, heat the remaining 3 tablespoons peanut oil over medium-high heat and add the chicken pieces, skinside down. Do not crowd the pan. Fry in 2 batches, if necessary. Cook the chicken until golden brown on one side, then turn and cook on the other side until golden.

Peel the onion and cut it into 4 thick crosswise slices. Add the whole slices to the skillet, wedging them between the chicken pieces. Brown lightly on one side, then turn. Cook for another 5 minutes.

Arrange the chicken and onion slices on a large platter.

Beat the vinaigrette again to mix it well, then strain it over the chicken.

Cover with a piece of foil and let stand about 2 minutes.

Serve immediately, giving each diner a slice of the onion.

ZARELA'S RED SNAPPER HASH

Zarela introduced this dish on her first menu in 1988. She'd say it was one of her signature dishes in that it is so popular she could never take it off the menu. It has been widely copied or adapted by other chefs, and dishes like it have become standard in contemporary Mexican restaurants. This is a great dish for any kind of party. It can be dressed up as a plated first course, or piled into tacos made either with freshly baked corn tortillas or crisply fried ones. It's great for informal occasions, too, as a dip with chips.

Serves 6 to 8 as a first course, more as a taco filling

8 tablespoons (1 stick) unsalted butter (divided)
6 large garlic cloves, finely minced (divided)
6 to 7 scallions, white and some of green part, minced (about 1 cup)
3 medium ripe, red tomatoes, chopped (about 2 ½ cups)
3 fresh chiles, either jalapeño or serrano, not seeded, finely chopped
¼ cup chopped fresh coriander leaves

1 ½ teaspoons ground true (Ceylon) cinnamon, preferably freshly ground in a spice grinder
½ teaspoon ground cloves
2 teaspoons ground cumin
Salt
2 ½ pounds red snapper fillets, skinned and small bones removed with tweezers

Choose a heavy skillet (preferably nonstick) that will be large enough to hold the fish in one layer. Melt half the butter over medium heat. When the foam subsides, add half the minced garlic, and cook 1 minute, stirring constantly. Add the scallions and cook 1 minute longer, stirring often. Add the tomatoes, chiles, coriander, spices, and a little salt. Stir well to combine. Cook, stirring often, until the sauce is slightly concentrated, about 5 minutes.

Cut the fish fillets into halves or several large pieces, depending on their size. Place them in the pan in one layer. Adjust the heat to maintain a low simmer. Poach the fish, uncovered, just until the flesh begins to turn opaque, about 1 minute. Carefully turn the fillets with a spatula and poach on the other side for about 1 minute more; the flesh should still be slightly undercooked. Allow them to cool in the sauce.

When the fish is cool enough to handle, pull the flesh into shreds with your fingers. Carefully remove any bones that may be left. If the sauce looks watery, drain off a little of the juice.

Heat the remaining butter in a second large skillet over medium heat until hot and bubbling.

Add the remaining garlic and cook for 1 minute, stirring.

Add the shredded fish and sauce; cook just until heated through.

Serve hot, warm, or at room temperature.

AFTERWORD

While researching, writing, and testing recipes for this book, I was asked dozens of times, "What is the most interesting thing you have learned?" The answer is the same now that I am finished as it was while I was working: The most interesting thing—really an amazing thing—is how little the city has fundamentally changed since its founding in the seventeenth century. Of course, New York City is more populous now, the buildings are taller, and the population more diverse, but the essence is the same: It's a business city, and it attracts people from all over the world.

New York City was started as a business. (I believe it is the only city on earth to have that claim.) New Amsterdam was at first nothing but a trading post for the Dutch West India Company. Everything flows from that fact. New York City is about building fortunes and making a name for yourself in the arts, entertainment, and now in food. Real estate has always been the city's middle name. The first Astor started out as a fur trader, but he made his money as a builder and landlord. And while it is true that old family names have always meant something, unless they have money they are powerless. In New York City, you can be nobody one day, but if you earn millions the next day you will be invited to the poshest parties, asked to be on the boards of directors of our cultural institutions, foundations, and hospitals—you will be in demand. The newspapers and magazines will write about you, and every interior decorator will want to do your apartment, then your country house, then your pied-à-terre in Paris.

New York City offers unlimited opportunities to acquire wealth, too. That is why we are so attractive to those others in the world who do not have it—why the city was a magnet for immigrants from the beginning. It's an amazing fact that in 1638, there were 440 people living in New Amsterdam and eighteen languages were spoken. The Dutch may have pitched the first tents, but soon every European had heard how one could better himself here. Today, New York has 8.1 million people within the city limits and an estimated 132 languages are spoken. Now the entire world looks to New York City as the land of opportunity. On top of that, all these different people from all over the world—from Dutch times to now—pretty much get along with each other. Sure, there is still bigotry and hatred in the hearts of some New Yorkers, but the rest of us don't stand for those who express it publicly. We don't accept that as a civilized way to be. New York City is not a melting pot, as it has always been said. In New York City you are allowed, even encouraged, to be who you are and to sustain your original culture's traditions, religion, and foodways. If only the world's terrorists understood this.

ACKNOWLEDGMENTS

If only for having the patience and love to tolerate my nearly daily kvetches about how much work this book turned out to be, I am eternally grateful, as always, to my nearest and dearest, my life-partner Bob Harned; my friends and neighbors Rozanne Gold and Michael Whiteman; my sister and brother-in-law Andrea and Milton Alexander; and my cousin, friend, and fellow food writer-editor, Erica Marcus.

Supreme among the hand-holders was my diligent and ever-reliable personal assistant, Sean Brady, whose help with the kitchen testing, the research, the organization, the bibliography, the permissions and credits—everything but the actual writing—was invaluable.

My regular advisors included Carol Walter and George Greenstein, both of whom contributed not only recipes (most of which never made it into the book), but advice and encouragement on my weakest culinary subject, baking. Food historian Ann Mendelson, who is writing a more scholarly work on the same subject, generously offered guidance and precious information, and had the grace not to feel competitive. New York City historian Barry Lewis put everything in social and political context for me. Susan LaRosa did a masterful job of photo research, digging up stuff I could never hope to find. Professor of pastry Tina Casacelli tested and re-tested the cakes and pastries.

I picked the brains of many a New York savvy friend and colleague, including Ed Schoenfeld on the subject of Chinese food in New York, Julie Sahni and Madhur Jaffrey on Indian food, Joyce White and Jessica Harris on African-American cooking, Michele Scicolone on Italian-American food, and Ed Levine on everything under the sun. Michael Whiteman filled me in on details about many old restaurants, notably the Rainbow Room and Windows on the World, both of which he operated.

Restaurateur George Lang kindly loaned me several old New York City restaurant guidebooks, and Linda Amiel Burns entrusted me with her precious cache of photos from her father's two sports-oriented restaurants, The Turf and Jack Dempsey's. These, unfortunately, will have to wait for this book's sequel. Ditto the materials Myrm Salko loaned to me about her uncle's famous sports restaurant, Al ("Clown Prince" of baseball) Schacht's. Thanks, too, to Patti Dorph. Some of her turn-of-the-century hotel menus are here. Brian Merlis, whose photo collection of old Brooklyn is unsurpassable, loaned me vital shots, and I met Vicki Gold Levy on the internet while we were both gathering material for books—hers is on Times Square. She generously provided some fabulous visual materials. It was through Jonathan Reynolds, the urbane food columnist for the *New York Times Magazine,* that I found Frank and George Shattuck, heirs to the Schrafft's recipe treasure trove. Marie, a listener to my radio show from Oceanside, heard I was looking for Childs' pancake recipe, and sent me an original copy, a carbon on onion skin paper. I don't have a record of all the acts of kindness like that, but I thank everyone in my radio audience that cheered me on or shared a story.

It was a dream working with photographer Chris Callis, and I must thank Jason Vogel of Eric Baker Design Associates for his help.

Beth Huseman of Stewart, Tabori & Chang was the careful and sensitive editor of this book, and, at crucial critical moments she was the one person I could depend on to make me feel all was going a lot better than it actually was. My agent, Jane Dystel, is unbelievably accessible (that's unusual for agents), heroically patient while I vent to her, and very savvy about every aspect of publishing. I pray we have a long relationship. Thank you Leslie Stoker, publisher of Stewart, Tabori & Chang, for acquiring this book, and believing in me.

CONVERSON CHARTS

WEIGHT EQUIVALENTS

The metric weights given in this chart are not exact equivalents, but have been rounded up or down slightly to make measuring easier.

AVOIRDUPOIS	METRIC	AVOIRDUPOIS	METRIC
¼ oz	7 g	11 oz	325 g
½ oz	15 g	12 oz	350 g
1 oz	30 g	13 oz	375 g
2 oz	60 g	14 oz	400 g
3 oz	90 g	15 oz	425 g
4 oz	115 g	16 oz (1 lb)	450 g
5 oz	150 g	1 ½ lb	750 g
6 oz	175 g	2 lb	900 g
7 oz	200 g	2 ¼ lb	1 kg
8 oz (½ lb)	225 g	3 lb	1.4 kg
9 oz	250 g	4 lb	1.8 kg
10 oz	300 g		

OVEN TEMPERATURE EQUIVALENTS

OVEN MARK	F	C	GAS
Very cool	250–275	130–140	½ –1
Cool	300	150	2
Warm	325	170	3
Moderate	350	180	4
Moderately hot	375	190	5
	400	200	6
Hot	425	220	7
	450	230	8
Very hot	475	250	9

VOLUME EQUIVALENTS

These are not exact equivalents for American cups and spoons, but have been rounded up or down slightly to make measuring easier.

AMERICAN	METRIC	IMPERIAL
¼ t	1.2 ml	
½ t	2.5 ml	
1 t	5.0 ml	
½ T (1.5 t)	7.5 ml	
1 T (3 t)	15 ml	
¼ cup (4 T)	60 ml	2 fl oz
⅓ cup (5 T)	75 ml	2 ½ fl oz
½ cup (8 T)	125 ml	4 fl oz
⅔ cup (10 T)	150 ml	5 fl oz
¾ cup (12 T)	175 ml	6 fl oz
1 cup (16 T)	250 ml	8 fl oz
1 ¼ cups	300 ml	10 fl oz (½ pt)
1 ½ cups	350 ml	12 fl oz
2 cups (1 pint)	500 ml	16 fl oz
2 ½ cups	625 ml	20 fl oz (1 pint)
1 quart	1 liter	32 fl oz

BIBLIOGRAPHY

HISTORY

Allen, Oliver E. *New York, New York*. New York: Atheneum, 1990.

Aylesworth, Thomas, and Virginia Aylesworth. *New York: The Glamour Years. (1919–1945)*. New York: Gallery Books, 1987.

Barnes, Donna R., and Peter G. Rose. *Matter of Taste: Food and Drink in Seventeenth-Century Dutch Art & Life*. Syracuse: Syracuse University Press, 2002.

Batterberry, Michael, and Ariane Batterberry. *On the Town in New York*. New York: Routledge, 1999.

Blumenthal, Ralph. *Stork Club*. New York: Little, Brown, 2000.

Brody, Iles. *The Colony*. New York: Greenberg, 1945.

Burke, John. *Duet in Diamonds*. New York: G.P. Putnam's Sons, 1972.

Burrows, Edwin G., and Mike Wallace. *Gotham: A History of New York City to 1898*. New York: Oxford University Press, 1999.

Chatanow, Gerald, and Bernard D. Schwartz. *Another Time Another Place*. Xlibris Corporation, 2000.

Denker, Joel. *The World on a Plate*. Boulder, Colorado: Westview Press, 2003.

Diner, Hasia R. *Hungering For America*. Cambridge, MA: Harvard University Press, 2001.

Earle, Alice Morse. *Colonial Days in Old New York*. New York: Charles Scribner's Sons, 1896.

Freundlich, Lawrence S. *A Time Well Spent*. New York: William Rain, 2000.

Frommer, Myrna Katz, and Harvey Frommer. *It Happened in Brooklyn*. New York: Harcourt Brace, 1993.

Grimes, William. *Straight Up or on the Rocks*. New York: North Point Press, 2001.

Hemp, William H. *New York Enclaves*. New York: Clarkson Potter, 2003.

Kisseloff, Jeff. *You Must Remember This*. New York: Harcourt, Brace, Jovanovich, 1989.

Kriendler, H. Peter, and H. Paul Jeffers. *21*. Dallas: Taylor, 1999.

Levenstein, Harvey. *Revolution At the Table*. New York: Oxford University Press, 1988.

Mariani, John. *America Eats Out*. New York: William Morrow, 1991.

Mariani, John, and Alex Von Bidder. *The Four Seasons*. New York: Crown, 1994.

Mitchell, Joseph. *Up In the Old Hotel*. New York: Vintage Books, 1993.

Morehouse, Ward III. *The Waldorf-Astoria*. New York: M. Evans, 1991.

Morris, Lloyd. *Incredible New York*. Syracuse: Syracuse University Press, 1951.

Murphy, Patricia. *Glow of Candlelight*. Englewood Cliffs, NJ: Prentice Hall, 1961.

Patrick, Ted, and Silias Spitzer. *Great Restaurants of America*. New York: Bramhall House, 1960.

Root, Waverly, and Richard de Rochemont. *Eating in America.* New York: William Morrow, 1976.

Rose, Peter G. *Matter of Taste: Dutch Recipes with an American Connection.* Syracuse: Syracuse University Press, 2002.

Rose, Peter G., ed, trans. *The Sensible Cook.* Syracuse: Syracuse University Press, 1989.

Salinger, Sharon V. *Taverns and Drinking In Early America.* Baltimore: The Johns Hopkins University Press, 2002.

Sante, Luc. *Low Life.* New York: Farrar, Straus and Giroux, 1991.

Sardi, Vincent, and Richard Gehman. *Sardi's.* New York: Henry Holt, 1953

Schoenstein, Ralph, ed. *The Booze Book.* Chicago: Playboy Press, 1974.

Thomas, Lately. *Delmonico's: A Century of Splendor.* Boston: Houghton Mifflin, 1967.

Volk, Patricia. *Stuffed: Adventures of a Restaurant Family.* New York: Alfred A. Knopf, 2001.

Wechsberg, Joseph. *Dining at The Pavillion.* Boston: Little, Brown, 1962.

Witaker, Jan. *Tea at the Blue Lantern Inn.* New York: St. Martin's Press, 2002.

Wolfman, Ira. *Jewish New York.* New York: Universe, 2003.

REFERENCE

Jackson, Kenneth T., ed. *The Encyclopedia of New York City.* New Haven: Yale University Press, 1995.

Rosten, Leo. *The Joys of Yiddish.* New York: Washington Square Press, 1968.

COOKBOOKS

Abrahamson, Mark, ed. *The Grand Central Oyster Bar & Restaurant Complete Seafood Cookbook.* New York: Stewart, Tabori & Chang, 1997.

Anderson, Jean. *The American Century Cookbook.* New York: Clarkson Potter, 1997.

Beard, James. *American Cookery.* Boston: Little, Brown, 1972.

Binns, Brigit Légère. *The Palm Restaurant Cookbook.* Philadelphia: Running Press, 2003.

Brody, Jerome, ed. *The Grand Central Oyster Bar & Restaurant Seafood Cookbook.* New York: Crown, 1977.

Cavallero, Gene, and Ted James. *The Colony Cookbook.* New York: Bobbs-Merrill, 1972.

Clairborne, Craig. *Craig Clairborne's Favorites.* New York: Quadrangle, 1975.

Cornfiel, Robert, and Kathy Gunst. *Lundy's: Reminiscences and Recipes.* New York: HarperCollins, 1998.

Degroff, Dale. *Craft of the Cocktail.* New York: Clarkson Potter, 2002.

Diat, Louis. *Cooking A la Ritz.* New York: J.B. Lippincott, 1941.

Dyer, Ceil, and Rosalind Cole. *All Around the Town.* New York: Bobbs-Merrill, 1972.

Gethers, Judith, and Elisabeth Lefft. *The World Famous Ratner's Meatless Cookbook.* New York: Ballantine Books, 1975.

Glaser, Milton, and Jerome Snyder. *The Underground Gourmet Cookbook.* New York: Simon & Schuster, 1975.

Greenstein, George. *Secrets of a Jewish Baker.* Freedom, CA: The Crossing Press, 1993.

Handwerker, Murray. *Nathan's Hot Dog Cookbook.* New York: Gramercy, 1983.

Kafka, Barbara, ed. *James Beard Celebrations.* New York: William Morrow, 1990.

Kirkland, Alexander. *Rector's Naughty '90's Cookbook.* New York: Doubleday, 1990.

Knoff, Mildred O. *Memoirs of a Cook.* New York: Atheneum, 1986.

Lebewohl, Sharon, and Rena Bulkin. *The 2nd Ave Deli Cookbook.* New York: Harper Collins, 1994.

Levitas, Earlyne S., and Lydia Moss. *Secrets From New York's Best Restaurants.* Atlanta: Secrets, 1975.

Lomonaco, Michael. *The '21' Cookbook.* New York: Doubleday, 1995.

Margittai, Tom, and Paul Kovi. *The Four Seasons.* New York: Simon and Schuster, 1980.

Meyer, Danny, and Michael Romano. *The Union Square Cafe Cookbook.* New York: HarperCollins, 1994.

Mitchell, Jan. *Cooking a la Longchamps.* New York: Doubleday, 1964.

Mitchell, Jan. *Lüchow's German Cookbook.* New York: Doubleday, 1952.

Nathan, Joan. *Jewish Cooking in America.* New York: Alfred A. Knopf, 1994.

O'Neill, Molly. *New York Cookbook.* New York: Workman, 1992.

Pellegrino, Frank. *Rao's Cookbook.* New York: Random House, 1998.

Ranhofer, Charles. *The Epicurean.* New York: Dover Publications, 1971.

Rose, Peter G., ed, trans. *The Sensible Cook.* Syracuse: Syracuse University Press, 1989.

Rosen, Marvin, Walter Rosen, and Beth Allen. *Welcome to Junior's.* New York: William Morrow, 1999.

Sax, Richard. *New York's Master Chefs.* Los Angeles: The Knapp Press, 1985.

Soltner, André. *The Lutèce Cookbook.* New York: Alfred A. Knopf, 1995.

Stallworth, Lyn, and Rod Kennedy, Jr. *The Brooklyn Cookbook.* New York: Alfred A. Knopf, 1991.

Tschirky, Oscar. *'Oscar' of the Waldor's Cookbook.* New York: Dover Publications, 1973.

Van Cleave, Jill. *The Neighborhood Bakeshop.* New York: William Morrow, 1997.

Vergnes, Jean. *A Seasoned Chef*. New York: Donald L. Fine, 1987.

Viazzi, Alfredo. *Alfredo Viazzi's Italian Cooking*. New York: Random House, 1979.

Villas, James. *Villas At Table*. New York: Harper & Row, 1988.

Wondrich, David. *Esquire Drinks*. New York: Hearst Books, 2002.

Zahler, Karen Gantz. *Taste Of New York*. Massachusetts: Addison-Wesley, 1993.

GUIDEBOOKS

Botsford, Harry. *New York's 100 Best Restaurants*. Portland, Maine: Bond Wheelright, 1955.

Chappell, George S. *The Restaurants of New York*. New York: Greenberg, 1925.

Claiborne, Craig. *The New York Times Guide to Dining Out in New York*. New York: Atheneum, 1968.

Cue Guide to Dining in New York. Philadelphia: J.B. Lippincott, 1971.

DeVoe, Thomas F. *The Market Assistant*. Riverside Press, 1967.

Fougner, G. Selmer. *Dining Out in New York*. New York: J.J. Little & Ives, 1939.

Glaser, Milton, and Jerome Snyder. *The All New Underground Gourmet*. New York: Simon & Schuster, 1977.

Hart, Beatrice, ed. *Hart's Guide to New York City*. Hart, 1964.

James, Rian. *Dining in New York*. New York: John Day, 1930.

Manhattan Menus 1983. New York: Restaurant Publishing Corporation, 1983.

Miller, Stan, Arline Miller, Rita Rowan, and James Rowan. *New York's Chinese Restaurants*. New York: Atheneum, 1977.

Shaw, Charles G. *Nightlife*. New York: John Day, 1931.

Street, Julian. *Welcome to Our City*. New York: John Lane, 1912.

INDEX

Recipe Index starts on page 398.

RECIPE INDEX

PHOTO CREDITS